PASSIONS AND EMOTIONS

NOMOS

LIII

NOMOS

Harvard University Press
I   *Authority* 1958, reissued in 1982 by Greenwood Press

The Liberal Arts Press
II   *Community* 1959
III   *Responsibility* 1960

Atherton Press
IV   *Liberty* 1962
V   *The Public Interest* 1962
VI   *Justice* 1963, reissued in 1974
VII   *Rational Decision* 1964
VIII   *Revolution* 1966
IX   *Equality* 1967
X   *Representation* 1968
XI   *Voluntary Associations* 1969
XII   *Political and Legal Obligation* 1970
XIII   *Privacy* 1971

Aldine-Atherton Press
XIV   *Coercion* 1972

Lieber-Atherton Press
XV   *The Limits of Law* 1974
XVI   *Participation in Politics* 1975

New York University Press
XVII   *Human Nature in Politics* 1977
XVIII   *Due Process* 1977
XIX   *Anarchism* 1978
XX   *Constitutionalism* 1979
XXI   *Compromise in Ethics, Law, and Politics* 1979
XXII   *Property* 1980
XXIII   *Human Rights* 1981
XXIV   *Ethics, Economics, and the Law* 1982
XXV   *Liberal Democracy* 1983
XXVI   *Marxism* 1983

NOMOS LIII

Yearbook of the American Society for Political and Legal Philosophy

PASSIONS AND EMOTIONS

Edited by

James E. Fleming

NEW YORK UNIVERSITY PRESS   •   *New York and London*

NEW YORK UNIVERSITY PRESS
New York and London
www.nyupress.org

© 2013 by New York University
All rights reserved

Library of Congress Cataloging-in-Publication Data
Passions and emotions / edited by James E. Fleming.
   p.   cm.
Includes bibliographical references and index.
ISBN 978-0-8147-6014-7 (hardback) — ISBN 978-0-8147-6349-0 (ebook)
ISBN 978-0-8147-6021-5 (ebook)
1. Political psychology. 2. Political participation—Psychological aspects.
3. Emotions.   I. Fleming, James E.
JA74.5.P369 2012
320.01'9—dc23   2012024878

CONTENTS

PREFACE

This volume of NOMOS—the fifty-third in the series—emerged
from papers and commentaries given at the annual meeting of the
American Society for Political and Legal Philosophy (ASPLP) in
Boston on December 29, 2010, held in conjunction with the an-
nual meeting of the American Philosophical Association, Eastern
Division. Our topic, "Passions and Emotions," was selected by the
Society's membership.

The conference consisted of three panels, corresponding to the
three parts of this volume: (1) "Passion and Impartiality: Passions
and Emotions in Moral Judgment"; (2) "Passion and Motivation:
Passions and Emotions in Democratic Politics"; and (3) "Passion
and Dispassion: Passions and Emotions in Legal Interpretation."
The volume includes revised versions of the principal papers delivered at that conference by Jesse J. Prinz, George E. Marcus,
and Robin West. It also includes essays that developed out of the
original commentaries on those papers by Michael L. Frazer, Carol
Sanger, Susan A. Bandes, Cheshire Calhoun, Ken I. Kersch, and
Benjamin C. Zipursky. For the published volume, I invited an additional author for each panel: Charles Griswold, Sharon R. Krause,
and Bernadette Meyler. I am grateful to all of these authors for
their insightful and timely contributions.

Thanks are also due to the editors and production team at New
York University Press, and particularly to Ilene Kalish, Despina Pa-
pazoglou Gimbel, Alexia Traganas, and Aiden Amos. On my own
behalf and on behalf of the Society, I wish to express deep gratitude for the Press's ongoing support for the series and the tradition of interdisciplinary scholarship that it represents.

Finally, thanks to Christine Dieter, Courtney Sartor Gesualdi,
Natalie Logan, and Emily Strauss, my excellent research assistants
at Boston University, and to Danielle Amber Papa, my incredibly

capable, expeditious, and resourceful secretary, for providing invaluable assistance during the editorial and production phases of
the volume.

JAMES E. FLEMING
Boston, October 2011

CONTRIBUTORS

SUSAN A. BANDES
Professor of Law and Dean's Distinguished Scholar,
University of Miami

CHESHIRE CALHOUN
Professor of Philosophy, Arizona State University

MICHAEL L. FRAZER
Assistant Professor of Government, Harvard University

CHARLES L. GRISWOLD
Borden Parker Bowne Professor of Philosophy, Boston University

KEN I. KERSCH
Associate Professor of Political Science, History, and Law,
Boston College

SHARON R. KRAUSE
Professor of Political Science, Brown University

GEORGE E. MARCUS
Professor of Political Science, Williams College

BERNADETTE MEYLER
Professor of Law and English, Cornell University

JESSE J. PRINZ
Distinguished Professor of Philosophy, City University of New York
Graduate Center

CAROL SANGER
Barbara Aronstein Black Professor of Law, Columbia University

ROBIN WEST
Frederick J. Haas Professor of Law and Philosophy,
Georgetown University

BENJAMIN C. ZIPURSKY
James H. Quinn '49 Chair in Legal Ethics, Professor of Law, and
Associate Dean for Research, Fordham University

PART I

PASSION AND IMPARTIALITY: PASSIONS AND EMOTIONS IN MORAL JUDGMENT

1

CONSTRUCTIVE SENTIMENTALISM: LEGAL AND POLITICAL IMPLICATIONS

JESSE J. PRINZ

There is mounting empirical evidence linking emotions to moral judgment. Though open to competing interpretations, this evidence is best interpreted as supporting the kind of sentimentalist theory associated with philosophers of the Scottish Enlightenment. Recent findings also allow us to update sentimentalism by specifying which emotions contribute to moral judgment, and research in history, anthropology, and cross-cultural psychology is providing richer insights into the origins of our emotionally grounded values. If values are emotionally based and culturally diverse, there may be moral conflicts that have no rational resolution. This would have implications for normative ethics, for politics, and for law. Here I review the empirical case for sentimentalism and then draw attention to some of these implications.

1. THE PLACE OF EMOTIONS IN MORAL JUDGMENT

The empirical turn in ethics has been fueled, in part, by the emergence of moral neuroscience. In 2001, Joshua Greene and his collaborators published a paper showing neural activations as people reflected on trolley dilemmas.[1] Since then, scores of other studies have appeared. Brains have been scanned as people make judgments of wrongness, engage in reciprocal exchanges or charitable giving, play morally significant video games, and look at morally meaningful photographs. Throughout the many studies, one common denominator has been emotion. Again and again, areas of the brain associated with emotional response are active when people engage in moral cognition. These areas include the posterior cingulate, temporal pole, insula, ventromedial prefrontal cortex, amygdala, and ventral striatum. Authors of the studies interpret these results in different ways, but one common refrain is that emotions contribute to moral judgment.

The exact nature of that contribution, however, is difficult to assess using neuroimaging, which is a correlational method. We can see this by considering the wide range of models that are compatible with the finding that emotional activations regularly co-occur with moral judgment.

The rationalist model says that some kind of reasoning—either conscious deliberation or unconscious rules—drives our moral judgments, with emotions arising as a consequence.[2] The dual-process model says that emotion drives moral judgments some of the time but that reason can also, depending on the case.[3] The intuitionist model says that emotions constitute intuitions about what is right or wrong and that we use these intuitions to make our judgments; reason then follows to provide post hoc rationalizations.[4] Neo-sentimentalists claim that moral judgments are judgments about whether emotional responses are merited ("I should feel guilty/angry about this"), and we can imagine emotions that typically arise in conditions where we deem them appropriate.[5] The constitution model, which was endorsed by the sentimentalists of the Scottish Enlightenment, says that emotions are components of moral judgments: to think that something is morally wrong is to have a negative emotion toward it.[6] Both the neo-sentimentalists and the old-school sentimentalists agree with intuitionists that reason often plays a post hoc role in the moral domain, but, as we will see in a moment, reason can also make a more substantive contribution.

Given the ambiguity of imaging evidence, how do we decide among these models? I think there are good reasons to be dubious about all but the constitution model. The evidence is behavioral and philosophical. The rationalist model neither explains nor predicts the well-established fact that emotions can influence moral judgments. For example, people assess vignettes as more wrong than they otherwise would if they are hypnotized to feel disgust,[7] exposed to noxious smells,[8] or asked to imbibe bitter beverages.[9] People make more utilitarian judgments when amused[10] and more deontological judgments when feeling elevated.[11] Clearly emotions are not just an effect of moral judgment.

The dual-process model has been supported by appeal to the fact that consequentialist judgments show less activation in emotion centers than deontological judgments in trolley dilemmas, and individuals with ventromedial brain injuries—known for disrupting emotion-based inferences—are more likely than others to make consequentialist judgments. These findings are intriguing, but the fMRI data also clearly show that consequentialist judgments show more emotional activation than nonmoral judgments. Likewise, ventromedial patients do not lack emotions; the very fact that they engage in reward-seeking behavior[12] shows that they are at least capable of experiencing and acting on appetitive emotional states. Their deficit principally involves an inability to curtail reward seeking in light of negative feedback. When confronted with a trolley dilemma, we must normally decide between two moral injunctions: it would be good to help the people in need, and it would be bad to harm someone in the process. These can be regarded as a positive and a negative norm, respectively. VM patients seem to be motivated by the former and indifferent to the latter. They don't lack emotions; they simply lack the ability to regulate positive in light of negative emotions. The dual-process model is undermotivated.

The intuitionist model advanced by Jonathan Haidt is an improvement but remains, in an important way, obscure. Haidt suggests that emotions *precede* moral judgments. That implies that they are not components or parts. What, then, are moral judgments? It can't just be that they are sentences of English, like "Cannibalism is wrong," because one can make a moral judgment without verbalizing it. Also, if moral judgments are the *effects* of emotions, then they should be able to occur without emotions, just because most effects can come about in different ways. But Haidt offers no evidence that we can make moral judgments without emotions, and that would go against the spirit of his approach. A further issue concerns Haidt's very strong skepticism about the role of reason in morality. He gives the impression that reasoning never contributes to moral deliberation. That seems implausible. We often need reason to determine whether something is morally significant. This is especially clear in policy decisions. Is inheritance tax unjust? Is late-term abortion permissible? Should factory farming be regulated? Should we fight to stop vaginal circumcision? Should we assist in foreign wars? Haidt would have us believe that such cases are rare or that the reasoning here always involves some kind of blind social conformity, but there is little reason for such a cynical view.

Let's turn from these psychological theories to an account that has gained currency in philosophy: neo-sentimentalism. This turn covers a range of positions, but they share in common what can be called the meta-move. They say that moral judgments are judgments about the merit, warrant, or appropriateness of an affective response. The meta-move is designed to improve on traditional sentimentalism, which says that thinking something is wrong is a matter of having a negative emotion toward it. Clearly, we sometimes have negative feelings toward things that we would not, on reflection, view as wrong. The wrong is not simply that which causes our disapproval; it is that which warrants it. Or so the story goes. But the view faces some serious worries. First, it seems to mislocate the object of moral judgments; when we say that killing is wrong, we are saying something about killing, not about our feelings.[13] Second, it is hard to define merit without circularity. Depending on circumstances, a murder might merit fear (prudentially speaking) or forgiveness (if we aim for reconciliation). Saying that killing merits anger is to say that it merits it morally, even if these other considerations make different emotions more appropriate overall. But it would be circular to define a moral judgment as a judgment that certain emotions are morally merited, because that is just another moral judgment.[14] There is also an empirical worry: some individuals (children and some people with autism) make moral judgments easily but lack the capacity to form beliefs about emotional states.[15]

This brings us to the constitution model, which says that moral judgments *contain* emotions. To judge that something is wrong, on this view, is to have a negative emotion toward it. This seems to be the kind of view Hume and his contemporaries had in mind, and it overcomes all the difficulties that confront the other models. The most obvious objection to the constitution model is that people often seem to have negative emotions while withholding moral judgments. A person raised in a homophobic community might later in life experience disgust when seeing homosexual affection while insisting that the observed activity is morally acceptable. Doesn't this show that moral judgments are not constituted by emotions? An alternative explanation is that such an individual *does* in fact think homosexuality is wrong at some level but also thinks it's permissible and identifies with the latter conviction. Compare the person who exhibits implicit racism but also believes in racial equality. We should say in both cases that there is an automatic, bigoted appraisal that happens to get outweighed by a considered appraisal. In a questionnaire study, I was able to show that this, in fact, is how ordinary people interpret such cases.

Another worry about the constitution model pushes in the opposite direction, pointing out that we can make moral judgments without emotions. Empirically, this has not been explored, but cases are easy enough to imagine. When we speak in generalities (cruelty is wrong) or about complex policies (sin tax is wrong) or during episodes of numb depression, we might not feel strong moral emotions. But here I caution that we must recognize that there are at least dispositions to emote. Someone who did not shudder at a case of cruelty could not be credited with truly believing the generalization that cruelty is wrong. I like to distinguish emotions, which are occurrent states, from sentiments, which are emotional dispositions. I think moral *judgments* usually contain emotions, but our long-standing moral *values* are sentiments. In some cases, when we say that something is wrong, we are communicating that we have a certain value, not making a judgment based on that value. Compare: I can declare, "Sushi is delicious" at 6:00 A.M., when I have no desire to eat it. But this statement of value would be empty were I not disposed to experience sushi as delicious.

In summary, I think the constitution model can withstand objections and account for the data better than its alternatives. But the model still needs some fleshing out. Moral judgments contain negative feelings, but which ones? Clearly, not every bad feeling is a case of moral judgment.

2. THE NATURE OF EMOTIONS IN MORAL JUDGMENT

To read the literature on sentimentalism, one might think there is
a single emotional state called disapproval. But the empirical literature suggests that moral disapproval is felt differently in different
contexts. We can speak of a family of disapproval emotions.[16]

One important emotion in this family is anger and its variants,
indignation and outrage. Anger arises most typically in cases in
which we learn that someone has intentionally harmed or sought
to harm another. Another form of disapproval is disgust. This
arises when we encounter crimes against nature, such as violations
of sexual taboos, even when no one is harmed (necrophilia, for
example). Corresponding to these other-directed emotions, we
also experience self-directed disapproval when we ourselves misbe-
have. Guilt arises when we harm others, and shame arises when we
violate sexual taboos.

I think all of these emotions originate outside the moral context. Anger is a feeling of the body's preparation to aggress, and
that can occur when we are under threat, even if no norm has
been violated: consider the anger mustered by two boxers in a
bout. Disgust is a feeling of the body's preparation to expel con-
taminants, and it can arise when seeing or tasting rotten foods.
Even shame and guilt may have nonmoral variants. Shame is a
kind of unpleasant embarrassment, manifested as a feeling of the
body as we try to conceal ourselves from others. Guilt may be a
blend of fear and sadness—a feeling in the paradoxical state of
flight preparation even as we reach out dolefully to those we have
harmed. Sadness characteristically arises when we become separated from those we care about, and this is precisely the risk we
incur when we harm someone.

Given that emotions of disapproval can arise in nonmoral contexts, one might wonder what distinguishes the moral cases from
these others. The answer, I think, has to do with the distinction
between self- and other-directed emotions just adduced. If you
see me eating rotten food, you will feel disgusted; but if you eat
rotten food yourself, you will not feel ashamed, you will feel disgusted—an outward emotion for both cases. If you are boxing,
you might feel aggressive irritation when your sparring partner
hits you, but you won't feel guilt when you hit back. The moral

domain is distinguished from the nonmoral by the pairing of disgust and shame on the one hand and anger and guilt on the other. A judgment about an action qualifies as moral if it issues from a sentiment that disposes you to feel other-directed disapproval if someone performs the action.

In summary, to judge that an action is morally bad is to feel an emotion of disapproval issuing from a disposition to feel other-directed disapproval when others perform that action and self-directed disapproval when I do. That disposition is a basic moral value. Of course, there are many actions toward which we have no basic values, such as unfamiliar tax policies, but we can morally assess them by seeing whether they would lead to a basic value violation if instituted. Extensive reasoning is often needed to go from novel cases to basic values.

This explains disapproval, but what about the judgment that something is morally good? Consider the trolley cases, in which the recognition that five people are in danger motivates one to consider helping. In some cases, helping motivation is negative: we judge that it would be bad not to help, and this judgment consists in a feeling of (anticipatory) guilt at the thought of omission. But there might also be a judgment that it would be good to help. This can be understood in terms of a positive valence emotion, perhaps a kind of anticipatory pride. What distinguishes moral pride from other kinds is that actions that make us morally proud would make us feel grateful if we were the beneficiary, rather than the moral agent. Again, moral emotions are ordinary nonmoral emotions that stem from dispositions that have characteristic self- and other-directed manifestations. The disposition to feel pride and gratitude toward some actions can be regarded as a moral value of approval.

Notice that I have neglected the affective construct that is most conspicuous in eighteenth-century sentimentalist theories: sympathy. I said that the desire to help is driven by anticipatory pride, not a sympathetic experience of the suffering of others (what we now call empathy). In making this claim, I do not deny that prosocial motivation is sometimes driven empathetically. But, contra Hume and Smith, I deny that empathy is a component of moral judgments, and I think it is only a precursor on some occasions. We feel empathy when there is a single salient victim, especially if the victim is similar to us. But empathy is less prevalent when we judge that it is good to help a *collection* of people or to join in a political cause (evidence suggests that empathy is not a main contributor to reasoning about justice). Elsewhere I have argued that empathy is not necessary for moral judgment in any way—developmentally, epistemically, motivationally, or normatively.[17] Here I just want to register, more modestly, that, even if empathy sometimes compels us to see that some action is good or bad, other emotional states constitute that resulting moral insight.

3. THE SOURCE OF EMOTIONS IN MORAL JUDGMENT

I have suggested that basic moral values are sentiments (dispositions to feel emotions) and that moral judgments are emotions of disapproval or approval. Reasoning can help us see when basic values are at stake, but basic values themselves do not arise through reasoning. When I recognize that something is a case of calculated killing, rape, or theft, my feelings of disapproval arise immediately without any further inferential steps. Basic values do not arise through reasoning, and they are not acquired that way. Just as we cannot derive an "ought" from an "is," no process of reasoning can entail a value from anything other than another value. Reasoning alone will not suffice.

Where, then, do basic values come from? A popular answer is evolution. I think evolutionary approaches to morality are fundamentally mistaken, but I won't rehearse that case here. For present purposes, I am content to point out that biological evolution does not provide a sufficient explanation of our basic values. There is one simple and decisive reason for this conclusion: basic values differ.

Cross-cultural research suggests that just about every value we cherish is rejected by some other group. We find cultures that practice cannibalism, blood sports, slavery, and bride conquest through kidnapping and rape. Most societies have some norms that protect members of the in-group, but what passes as protection varies greatly. Most state-scale societies have class structures in which some individuals are subjugated by others. Most have restrictions on who can own property, who can have sexual autonomy, who can compete in the labor market, and so on. In the contemporary industrialized world, we find value differences across East and West—with Eastern nations showing a higher degree of collectivist morality, which emphasizes interdependence and self-sacrifice for others. There are also differences between cultures of honor, like the American South or Sicily, and their northern counterparts.[18] Within the many contemporary societies, we also find deep divergence between liberals and conservatives. Haidt[19] has shown that American liberals and conservatives have different basic values, with conservatives showing more concern for purity, hierarchy, and tradition. Lakoff[20] has argued that American liberals have a nurturing ethics, which focuses on the right to self-expression and treats norm violators with understanding, while conservatives have an authoritarian ethics, which focuses on self-reliance and has little tolerance for violations of norms. Liberals don't see how conservatives can oppose abortion and favor capital punishment, but both can be seen as efforts to hold people accountable for norm violation. Likewise, the pro-choice, anti-death-penalty stance of liberals is consistent with the attitude that we should protect those who get into "trouble."

To understand the source of our values, it is not enough to point out that there is variation. We must also investigate why these differences arise. Here I think we should follow Nietzsche in interrogating the genealogy of morals. What we find is that each of our values is a historical artifact. American liberalism emerges from events such as the two major depressions in our history and the civil rights movements. American conservatism issues from frontier libertarianism and the Cold War, among other sources. Genealogical analyses shed light on a wide range of values. Broadening strictures against incest seem to arise with social stratification, to prevent consolidation of wealth.[21] Monogamy norms may have emerged in Christian Europe to reduce family size, increase heirlessness, and line the coffers of the Church.[22] Male-dominant values can be linked to the invention of the plow, which put farming into the hands of men, making them the primary breadwinners. Tolerance of homosexuality seems to go up with economic disincentives to rear children. Slavery disappeared with the industrial revolution, when industrialists wanted to take power from the farming industry. Blood sports are especially common in imperialistic nations that want to encourage military prowess and instill

fear in foreigners. Torture is condoned when there is a perceived
enemy within, as in the case of heretics, revolutionaries, intellectuals, or terrorists. These equations are simplistic, of course, and
more adequate explanations arise when one goes from generalities to specific details: why did Chinese foot binding come and go?
How do American southerners become more violent than northern counterparts? What makes a member of Al Qaeda think it is
okay to kill civilians? What is the genealogical link between capitalism and democracy? Social scientists have developed plausible
answers to these questions.

For the moral psychologist, the main interest of genealogy is
the way in which the moral past sheds light on the moral present.
Trivially, we all believe our values to be right. We also believe that
our basic values derive from some insight into the truth, rather
than from cultural inculcation. We think our moral opponents are
confused or malicious. We bolster our basic values with elaborate
arguments, which are no better than the arguments on the other
side. Pretty much every reason any of us standardly gives for our
basic values is a poor one, meaning that someone cleverer has already considered the argument and debunked it. Moreover, the
arguments we deploy are often acquired long after the acquisi-
tion of the values they allegedly support. To this extent, Haidt is
right about post hocness. There are cases of persuasion through
reason, as I suggested, such as occur for those who come to see
that a basic value extends to a surprising new case—one thinks
of animal rights as an example. But often, I suspect, these cases
of moral persuasion turn on something other than reason: the
cuteness of animals, the allure of joining a liberal cause, the el-
egance of consequentialist theories. Without denying that much
moral discourse turns on rationally decidable questions about
which of our basic values applies in a given case, it is important
to realize that those basic values are not products of personal reasoning, and value change often originates from material pressures
that are outside our awareness and control. This is true even in the
case of causes that we see as moral progress: transatlantic slavery
could not have ended without the industrial revolution; the two
major American women's movements followed on the heels of two
world wars. Did these changes allow *improvement*, or did they just
change the context allowing for a new set of power relations, and,

perhaps, new systems of oppression? These questions are difficult and bound up with historical and empirical facts (Are we better off now? Did slavery hinge on false scientific theories?). Optimists might say moral change is progressive because more people are free and healthy now than in the past. But that is an expression of value. Since many of us share such sentiments, we can celebrate our success, but we should not be stupefied when other cultures view our achievements as retrograde.

4. IMPLICATIONS OF EMOTIONS IN MORAL JUDGMENT

I have claimed that moral values are based on sentiments that dispose us to emotions of approval and disapproval and that these sentiments are shaped by historical processes. I call this "constructive sentimentalism." In this final section, I want to consider some implications, with special emphasis on legal and political domains. I will be sketchy, because there are others in this conversation who are better placed to see what follows. Let me make two main suggestions, corresponding to the sentimentalism and the constructionism, respectively.

First, if morality has a basis in emotions, we should expect moral judgments to be very susceptible to the influence of emotions that are not necessarily relevant to a case at hand. In the context of courtroom deliberation, this means that emotional elicitation through the presentation of disturbing crime photographs, evocative testimony, or emotional expressiveness on the part of plaintiffs or victims is likely to influence jurors' assessments. Empirical evidence supports this conclusion. We should also expect legislators to have such vulnerabilities, and politicians can exploit the emotions of their constituencies. Mustering fear of an enemy within can increase tolerance for judicial torture.

We can guard against some forms of biasing influence, but it is often difficult, in principle, to decide what counts as bias and what counts as evidence. Consider a photo of a murder victim. Emotionally evocative, yes, but the disgust and outrage we experience may help us achieve moral clarity. If badness judgments are composed of such emotions, then this can be viewed as a direct apprehension of the moral badness of the crime. On the other hand, we might think that badness should track actions abstractly characterized (taking a life), not characterized in terms of superficial details (the blood on the victim). But the question of which details matter may be impossible to resolve. By comparison, think of framing effects. Different ways of presenting the same facts can elicit different emotions, even when there is no way to settle which framing is more faithful to reality.

Second, some moral disputes are not rationally resolvable, because participants have different basic values. In the American political context, this is most evident with respect to the liberal/conservative divide. Liberals and conservatives are bewildered by each other, as if we reside in different moral universes. Curiously, public discourse often includes arguments, which are presented as if they provide reasons for adopting liberal or conservative policies. These arguments may influence some undecided voters, but they are largely inert when appealing to the opposition. Liberals stay liberal, and conservatives stay conservative. Personal and economic crises, changes in living situation, material resources, aging, world events, and other factors can shift values, as can powerful rhetoric, but the arguments offered probably don't exert rational influence. Why, then, do we deploy such arguments? I think they are a form of auto-persuasion. For each of us, the veneer of reason boosts confidence, and, for the eloquent leader, a good argument can rally the base. Of course, arguments about arcane bits of policy may do some real work, but only relative to basic values, so these arguments will be less convincing to some than to others.

We can find similar issues of moral division with small-group deliberations in the courtroom. A jury will find itself made up of liberals and conservatives, Jews and gentiles, blacks and whites, men and women. Each of these variables, along with idiosyncrasies of biography, has put us into contact with different sources of moral inculcation. Views about guilt and punishment are sure to vary. For a vivid example, recall the O.J. Simpson trial, in which whites were more inclined than blacks to reject the allegation that the police set Simpson up. Or, to take a literary case, think of the white jurors in *To Kill a Mockingbird*. In such cases, there is a truth about what happened, but value differences influence the interpretation of the evidence and beliefs concerning what should be done when it comes to punishment. Given different inculcated standpoints and incomplete knowledge, there may be no way to settle some disputes rationally.

This may look like a cynical view. It would be nice to think that there is a single true morality, which could be invoked to settle moral disagreements in sociopolitical contexts. Much work in normative ethics aims at such universals, and this is not the place to assess those efforts. I'll settle for the weaker claim that these noble projects have limited bearing on actual moral disputes. Academic insights are usually moot in the courtroom, and the voting public regards our activities with suspicion and contempt. On the optimistic side, one can hope that balanced juries and a balance of political power can ensure that different opinions, equal biases, can weigh in.

These are the kinds of solutions we've devised, but we must remember their limitations. Democracies wage war and even elect dictators. Courtrooms draw juries from specific districts, and women and minorities often capitulate to white men. In any case, it's not clear that deliberation and democracy are adequate answers to sentimental diversity. After all, in the political case, one side wins and then legislates for a diverse populace. An alternative solution would go radically local, scaling legal jurisdictions down to a size that is more commensurate with moral communities. But this strategy brings us into the libertarian situation, in which local groups take care of their own and abuse outliers or neglect distant others in need. Some evidence suggests that the increase in group size and global economic ties has decreased violence dramatically.[23] Small-scale societies killed at rates that exceeded Russian and German mortality during the Second World War.[24]

So constructive sentimentalism leaves us with a practical dilemma. Once we admit that there is moral variation that cannot feasibly be settled by universal reason, we must decide between living in a world where nations and global alliances impose values on populations that are radically heterogeneous and returning to a kind of moral feudalism. Neither option is especially attractive, and the choice looks suspiciously like the irresolvable and value-laden disagreement between liberals and conservatives about centralism and states' rights.

Here there is room for an interesting project. I think we need to think more seriously about what a relativist normative ethics would look like. And we need to think about relativist political theories and legal institutions. To some extent, that's what we have already. However, since it's doubtful that the founders or their followers were convinced of relativism, we are operating within social structures that are shaped under the weight of diversity but not necessarily ideally suited for that end. We might think we've hit on something optimal (or nearly so), but we must think carefully about who the "we" is.

Let me end with two rosier observations. If values are inculcated and unfettered from cool reason, then we may not find a universal basis for morality. On the other hand, we can think of morality as self-expressive in the same way we value other cultural institutions, and we can embrace our morals happily, while recognizing that others' values are not based on confusion or iniquity. Alternatively, we can recognize that our values are historical accidents and pursue programs of moral reform. Reason may not serve as a rudder here, but other nonmoral goals can guide us. We can adopt values that help us live more successful, healthy, and comfortable lives. Politically, this may suggest an agenda of moral reform, rather than poll matching. In terms of legal institutions, we might try to bracket intuitions of justice and focus instead on what nonmoral ends we want those institutions to serve. Of course, reform carries risk. Liberation movements are counterbalanced by catastrophic social experiments. So, optimism must always be tempered by caution.

NOTES

I am extremely grateful to James Fleming for involving me in the NOMOS symposium on passions and emotions, and to Michael Frazer and Carol Sanger for their feedback that has deepened my thinking about these issues. Fleming along with his research assistants Emily Strauss and Courtney Sartor Gesualdi also provided helpful editorial corrections.

1. J. D. Greene, R.B. Sommerville, L. E. Nystrom, J. M. Darley, and J. D. Cohen, "An fMRI Investigation of Emotional Engagement in Moral Judgment," *Science* 293 (2001): 2105–2108.

2. M. Hauser, *Moral Minds: How Nature Designed Our Universal Sense of Right and Wrong* (New York: HarperCollins, 2006).

3. Greene et al., "An fMRI Investigation of Emotional Engagement in Moral Judgment," 2105–2108.

4. J. Haidt, "The Emotional Dog and Its Rational Tail: A Social Intuitionist Approach to Moral Judgment," *Psychological Review* 108 (2001): 814–834.

5. J. McDowell, "Values and Secondary Qualities," in *Morality and Objectivity*, ed. T. Honderich (London: Routledge & Kegan Paul, 1985); A. Gibbard, *Wise Choices, Apt Feelings* (Cambridge, MA: Harvard University Press, 1990); J. D'Arms and D. Jacobson, "Sentiment and Value," *Ethics* 110 (2000): 722–748.

6. F. Hutcheson, "An Inquiry into the Original of Our Ideas of Beauty and Virtue," in *Philosophical Writings*, ed. R. S. Downie (London: J. M. Dent, 1738/1994); David Hume, *A Treatise of Human Nature*, ed. P. H. Nidditch (Oxford: Oxford University Press, 1739/1978); A. Smith, *The Theory of Moral Sentiments* (Amherst, NY: Prometheus Books, 1759/2000); C. L. Stevenson, "The Emotive Meaning of Ethical Terms," *Mind* 46 (1937): 14–31; A. J. Ayer, *Language, Truth, and Logic* (New York: Dover, 1952); J. J. Prinz, *The Emotional Construction of Morals* (Oxford: Oxford University Press, 2007).

7. T. Wheatley and J. Haidt, "Hypnotically Induced Disgust Makes Moral Judgments More Severe," *Psychological Science* 16 (2005): 780–784.

8. S. Schnall, J. Haidt, and G. Clore, "Disgust as Embodied Moral Judgment," *Personality and Social Psychology Bulletin* 34 (2008): 1096–1109.

9. K. J. Eskine, N. A. Kacinik, and J. J. Prinz, "A Bad Taste in the Mouth: Gustatory Disgust Influences Moral Judgment," *Psychological Science* 22 (2011): 295–299.

10. P. Valdesolo and D. DeSteno, "Manipulations of Emotional Context Shape Moral Judgment," *Psychological Science* 17 (2006): 476–477.

11. N. Strohminger, R. L. Lewis, and D. E. Meyer, "The Divergent Effects of Different Positive Emotions on Moral Judgment," *Cognition* 119 (2011): 295–300.

12. A. R. Damasio, *Descartes' Error: Emotion, Reason and the Human Brain* (New York: Gossett/Putnam, 1994).

13. F. Schroeter, "The Limits of Sentimentalism," *Ethics* 116 (2006): 337–361.

14. D'Arms and Jacobson, "Sentiment and Value."

15. S. Nichols, *Sentimental Rules: On the Natural Foundations of Moral Judgment* (New York: Oxford University Press, 2004).

16. P. Rozin, L. Lowery, S. Imada, and J. Haidt, "The CAD Triad Hypothesis: A Mapping between Three Moral Emotions (Contempt, Anger,

Disgust) and Three Moral Codes (Community, Autonomy, Divinity)," *Journal of Personality and Social Psychology* 76 (1999): 574–586.

17. J.J. Prinz, "Is Empathy Necessary for Morality?" in *Empathy: Philosophical and Psychological Perspectives*, ed. P. Goldie and A. Coplan (Oxford: Oxford University Press, 2011).

18. R. E. Nisbett and D. Cohen, *Culture of Honor: The Psychology of Violence in the South* (Boulder, CO: Westview Press, 1996).

19. J. Haidt, "The New Synthesis in Moral Psychology," *Science* 316 (2007): 998–1002.

20. G. Lakoff, *Moral Politics: How Liberals and Conservatives Think* (Chicago: University of Chicago Press, 2d ed. 2002).

21. N. W. Thornhill, "An Evolutionary Analysis of Rules Regulating Human Inbreeding and Marriage," *Behavioral and Brain Sciences* 14 (1991): 247–293.

22. J. Goody, *The Development of the Family and Marriage in Europe* (Cambridge: Cambridge University Press, 1983).

23. S. Pinker, "A History of Violence," *New Republic* 236 (2007): 18–21.

24. R. Wrangham, "Killer Species," *Daedalus* 133 (2004): 25–35.

2

SENTIMENTALISM WITHOUT RELATIVISM

MICHAEL L. FRAZER

We are now in the midst of an exciting multidisciplinary revival of work on the moral sentiments. As recently as 1989, a commentator could reasonably write that he knew "of no living author who has thought to call herself a sentimentalist."[1] The very existence of the present volume is a testament to just how much times have changed. Scholars across philosophy, political science, law, and psychology are now rediscovering that eighteenth-century sentimentalists such as David Hume and Adam Smith were correct to emphasize the centrality of passion and emotion to moral judgment. This work has profound repercussions for how we think about virtually all major questions in ethics, politics, and the law, among other fields. But the sentimentalist theory that moral judgments contain emotions actually has very few important substantive moral implications.

It may sound strange to say that a moral theory may be deeply important without having many important substantive moral implications. By a substantive moral implication of a theory, I mean a concrete, normative conclusion that one must draw from the theory directly on pain of logical contradiction. No further research is necessary, no additional premises need to be posited; anyone who affirms a theory but denies its implications is rationally inconsistent. There are thus many ways that a moral theory can have profound repercussions without having many important substantive moral implications. For one thing, it may have such implications when combined with *other* theories—but these are implications of a conjunction of theories, not of any single theory. Taken by itself, a moral theory may also have methodological rather than substantive implications; it may suggest *how* we should conduct future moral inquiries, rather than *what* we must conclude. More generally, a theory may be a conversation starter, rather than a conversation stopper, suggesting what new questions we should investigate and what new possibilities we should consider, without establishing any new and important conclusions that we must believe. Moral sentimentalism (or just "sentimentalism," as I will call it) is important in all of these ways.

This essay focuses on what Jesse Prinz and many others have taken to be the most important substantive moral implication of sentimentalism. Sentimentalism is thought to imply moral relativism.[2] Prinz defends this common view by arguing that, once the truth of sentimentalism is established, we must face the fact that "there may be moral conflicts that have no rational resolution."[3] I think that Prinz is right here; no one can consistently affirm sentimentalism while denying that there may be moral conflicts that have no rational resolution. But I don't think that anything much further follows from this implication—certainly nothing of particular importance for normative ethics, politics, or law, and most certainly not moral relativism. After all, even if our moral conflicts are not capable of rational resolution, they may nonetheless be resolvable through nonrational means. It is my hope that they can be resolved in this way—and my conviction that they should be— that leads me to oppose relativism as both a philosophical theory and a practical approach to ethics and politics. Yet, both Prinz and I are sentimentalists, and our conceptions of what sentimentalism involves are essentially the same.

So how is it possible for two consistent defenders of sentimentalism to differ on so much else? It might be thought that some of the room for disagreement comes from the ambiguity of sentimentalism itself. While this is not the primary source of the dispute at hand, I do think that there are some ambiguities in the formulation of sentimentalism that need to be addressed.

I accept Prinz's "constitution model" of sentimentalism, which maintains that moral judgments *contain* emotions, rather than simply being judgments *about* emotions as under many so-called neo- (or, really, quasi-) sentimentalist theories today.[4] But, even once one accepts the constitution model, important ambiguities remain. The claim that moral judgments contain emotions can be understood as an empirical generalization, a conceptual necessity, or a normative precept. I actually think sentimentalism is probably true in all three of these ways. But philosophers can feel free to embrace one or two while rejecting the other(s).

First, consider descriptive, empirical sentimentalism: the claim that, as a matter of psychological fact, most of our moral judgments can be observed to contain emotions most of the time. Prinz makes a strong case that this empirical generalization is well supported by recent research in experimental psychology and neuroscience. Yet, this descriptive theory, while undoubtedly preferable to its rivals, is nothing new. To the contrary, it has been widely accepted throughout the Western philosophical tradition. Indeed, it has been accepted even by most philosophers classified as moral rationalists. And any theory embraced by Plato, the Stoics, Spinoza, and Kant, as well as by Hume and Smith, is hardly even deserving of the name "sentimentalism."

One would be hard pressed to find a major, canonical moral rationalist who denied that emotions are a component of most of our moral judgments most of the time. Plato would hardly be surprised to see that most experimental subjects are governed by passion, rather than reason. Most subjects in experimental psychology are undergraduates, after all, and there is nothing more sophomoric than being governed by one's passions. Yet, even if empirical sentimentalism is also true for most of us above the legal drinking age, what allowed Plato to be a rationalist is that he thought that the way most people make most moral judgments most of the time is irrelevant to moral philosophy. He embraced what Prinz, following today's current psychological practice, calls a dual-process model. There are two ways moral judgments can be formed, one of which includes emotion and one of which does not. The former results in moral opinion, while the latter results in moral knowledge. Knowledge is incomparably superior to opinion and wields an authority that opinion lacks.[5] The goal of philosophy is thus to allow us to form judgments on the basis of reason alone. Since only a tiny minority, beneficiaries of either very rare divine gifts or a very particular education (most decidedly not the kind of education available to today's undergraduates), could ever hope to achieve moral knowledge, only they will form moral judgments that do not contain emotion.[6] For those concerned with empirical generalizations, these philosopher-kings (if any exist at any given time) would be mere outliers. Plato's is not the kind of dual-process model subject to empirical falsification.

That said, empirical sentimentalism does imply an empirical version of the claim that not all moral conflicts are capable of rational resolution. As long as the mass of humanity remains stuck in the mire of conflicting passions and, hence, conflicting moral opinions, any disagreement with or among them will not be rationally resolvable. In Plato's view, our only hope is that those who are incapable of moral knowledge may come to possess true moral opinions through nonrational means. The rational few must therefore manipulate the passionate many to comply with reason's demands and must do so through some combination of coercion and deception. This is the ultimate ground of the philosophical elite's right to absolute rule over the nonphilosophical masses.[7]

Of course, one need not be an elitist or anti-egalitarian in order to accept sentimentalism as an empirical generalization while nonetheless remaining a rationalist along roughly Platonic lines. Kant, too, had a dual-process model, one that was just as scientifically untestable as Plato's. Here, the distinction between opinion and knowledge is replaced by a distinction between heteronomous and autonomous moral judgment. While heteronomous judgment is the result of empirically observable causal forces—with what Kant called "*Neigung*" ("inclination") foremost among them—autonomous judgment is the self-legislation of pure, noumenal reason. All rational agents as such are capable of this self-legislation, but even on introspection they can never be sure that they have achieved it. Although an action may clearly be in conformity with duty, we can never be entirely certain it was done from duty and hence possessed genuine moral worth. "In fact," Kant writes, "it is absolutely impossible by means of experience to make out with complete certainty a single case in which an action otherwise in conformity with duty rested simply on moral grounds."[8] And, just as this knowledge is unavailable to agents themselves, it is also unavailable to outside researchers, even those equipped with fMRIs. Kant acknowledges that, because all moral judgments manifest themselves as empirical phenomena, they will certainly appear to be heteronomously determined. As long as humanity remains made of crooked timber, this appearance is accurate for most of us most of the time. But the possibility of rational autonomy remains, and it is incumbent upon all of us to strive to achieve it.[9]

Although rationalists can grant that emotion really is a component of most of our moral judgments most of the time, they maintain that a different kind of moral judgment, one free of emotion, is both possible and normatively superior. Sentimentalism, to be worthy of the name, must rule this out. There are two paths available: either sentimentalists can deny the *possibility* of purely rational moral judgment, or they can deny its *normative superiority*. Either way, sentimentalism cannot simply be an empirical theory.

Let's examine the conceptual path first. Here is hardly the place to rehash the reasons why the impossibility of a phenomenon cannot be established on empirical grounds alone. Even if this claim is not true universally, one is hard pressed to imagine what sort of scientific research could be conducted to rule out the sort of purely rational moral judgment that Plato and Kant describe. Most twentieth-century anti-rationalists therefore sought to rule out this possibility on conceptual grounds. The claim that moral judgment contains emotion is, they claimed, implicit in the very idea of morality itself and can be established using the armchair techniques of conceptual analysis.[10] I think they were probably right, but the literature on the matter has grown so baroque over the past century, and my skills as an analytic philosopher are so limited, that I remain unsure.

Fortunately, the separate path of normative sentimentalism is also available. If conceptual sentimentalism were true, then one of its implications would be normative sentimentalism. Since "ought" implies "can," if purely rational moral judgments are a contradiction in terms, then it cannot be our duty to pursue them. But normative sentimentalism can also be established independently of its conceptual cousin. Even if purely rational moral judgments were possible, there is no reason to believe that they would be superior to judgments containing emotions. Or, more modestly, even if they might be possible for some sort of conceivable rational being, they are not the sort of judgments we should ever attempt. Adam Smith suggests as much when he notes that the kinds of moral judgments that might be appropriate for God to make are not appropriate for creatures such as ourselves.[11] Given the independence of normative from conceptual sentimentalism, twentieth-century analytic metaethicists did sentimentalism a real disservice by focusing almost exclusively on moral concepts and moral language.

It might be easy to confuse my claim that sentimentalism has no important ethical or political implications with the widespread (if nonetheless controversial) view that metaethics is separate from normative ethics.[12] Yet, normative sentimentalism is itself a matter of moral judgments, albeit ones about general psychological processes, rather than specific substantive ethical or political issues. The sharp distinction between conceptual metaethics and normative ethics was unknown to the original sentimentalists of the Enlightenment era and need play no role in the revival of sentimentalism today.

There were, admittedly, rough analogues to the current distinction between metaethics and normative ethics in eighteenth-century philosophy. The seventh and final part of Smith's *Theory of Moral Sentiments*—one of the first modern historical surveys of Western moral philosophy—begins by observing that there are two questions to be considered when examining the principles of morals. "First, wherein does virtue consist? . . . And, secondly, by what power or faculty of the mind is it that this character, whatever it be, is recommended to us?"[13] It might be thought that the first of these is the Enlightenment-era equivalent of normative ethics, while the second is equivalent to metaethics, especially since Smith maintains that the second question, taken in isolation, "though of the greatest importance in speculation, is of none in practice."[14] I will deal at the conclusion of this essay with Smith's insistence that this question is of only speculative importance. For now, though, it is important to note that this is an empirical and psychological question, not a conceptual or linguistic one. Smith divided moral philosophy into descriptive moral psychology on the one hand and a form of virtue-theoretic normative ethics on the other, with little place left for the analysis of moral concepts.

Although Smith has been largely neglected by recent analytic metaethicists, Hume has not been so fortunate. Countless analytic commentators have written under the assumption that Hume must have intended to give something resembling an analysis of moral concepts. Given the superficial absence of such an analysis from his ethical writings, they conclude that it must be lurking somewhere implicitly. Many inconsistent analyses have been proposed. As Michael Slote recounts, Hume has been read as a subjectivist descriptivist ("X is right" means "I approve of x"), an expressivist emotivist ("Hurray for x!"), an ideal-observer theorist ("A precisely specified perfect spectator would approve of x"), a projectivist error theorist ("Our approval of x leads us to assert falsely that it has a property of goodness that it does not actually possess"), and, in Slote's innovation, possibly even a proto-Kripkean reference-fixing theorist (a position too complicated to explain here). Although all these metaethical theories can be categorized as sentimentalist, they are all inconsistent with one another. Slote believes all can be put forward as plausible interpretations of Hume but concludes that, "if one wants to be more consistent than Hume seems to have been, then one has to decide among these theories or advocate some different sentimentalist account."[15]

Yet, there is another option open to sentimentalists: to avoid conceptual sentimentalism entirely and to defend their theory on empirical and normative grounds alone. If this is indeed the path that Hume chose, it should come as no surprise that attempts to wrestle a consistent analysis of moral concepts from the pages of Hume's *Treatise* have led Slote and others to reject Hume as metaethically confused and inconsistent. The same would be true of any author who was simply uninterested in analytic metaethics as it is practiced today.

There are many ways to defend normative sentimentalism without relying on conceptual sentimentalism. First, normative sentimentalists may simply determine that the sort of moral judgments that most of us make most of the time are pretty much fine as they are. Such sentimentalists embrace a single- rather than a dual-process model, claiming that all of us make moral judgments more or less the same way and that no better alternatives are available. One might take this a step further and claim that, when these everyday moral judgments come into conflict with one another—as they undeniably do with remarkable frequency—we should not conclude that one is morally right and the other is morally wrong. All moral sentiments are morally fine for those who feel them; one moral opinion is as morally good as any other.[16]

This universal approval of everyone's moral sentiments is the normative position that I think is most deserving of the label "moral relativism," although the term has also been used to identify a number of other normative views, as well as a variety of theories in conceptual metaethics.[17] As with normative sentimentalism, normative relativism can be defended either via appeal to or independent of its conceptual variant. If moral claims really are claims that are true or false only relative to some feature of the claimant, then it would be wrong to conclude that apparently conflicting claims made by different individuals are actually in conflict. It could then be argued that resolving the apparent conflict between them would be impossible, for there might not actually be any conflict to resolve.[18] Yet, even if it were possible, such resolution might still be normatively undesirable—perhaps because moral conflict ought to be tolerated or even celebrated, rather than resolved away.

As I have already made clear, however, normative relativism is not an implication of sentimentalism. This is because even normative sentimentalism is fully compatible with a kind of dual-process model, one not all that different from the Platonic opinion/ knowledge model or the Kantian heteronomy/autonomy model. Regardless of how most of us make moral judgments most of the time, sentimentalists like Hume and Smith believe that we can do better. In this respect, they are no different from Plato or Kant. But they flesh out this dual-process model in a distinctly sentimentalist way.[19]

As Prinz makes clear, the two main moral sentiments are those of moral approval and disapproval. As he also observes, these sentiments can be self—as well as other—directed. Inherent in feeling a sentiment of self-disapproval is a sense that we are not doing what we ought to be doing, that we can do better. What Prinz fails to mention explicitly is that among the behaviors that can be subject to both self- and other-disapproval are our feelings of approval and disapproval themselves. But I do think this is the best way to make sense of the case he describes of the recovering homophobe, in which a bigoted automatic appraisal that homosexuality is wrong is "outweighed by a considered appraisal" that it is not and in which the agent "identifies with the latter conviction."[20] In other words, the recovering homophobe disapproves of his own disapproval of homosexuality but has only partially completed the process of purging this wayward moral sentiment from his psyche.

Every moral sentiment we feel is a possible candidate for such disapproval, including the higher-order sentiments, which approve or disapprove of our lower-order ones. This raises the possibility of an open-ended process of moral self-scrutiny, in which our moral sentiments are continually turned against themselves.[21] Other mental faculties—reason included—may play a role in this reflective process as well. Despite Hume's famous bit of rhetoric about enslaving reason to the passions,[22] it is clear that this reflection is to be carried out in a nonhierarchical, psychologically holistic way. Although philosophers may rightly distinguish the operations of the mind from one another, Hume consistently maintains that, in reality, they are "uncompounded and inseparable."[23] As a result, reason is neither privileged over nor really enslaved to sentiment, nor are higher-order sentiments privileged over lower-order ones. Our goal is a mind fully in harmony with itself, free from psychic conflict in any form.

Although we can never reach a point when we possess certain, objective moral truths, we can reach a reflective equilibrium in which we can affirm that all our moral sentiments have been thoroughly tested. Such a progress of sentiments genuinely replaces moral opinion with a kind of moral knowledge. Yet, as George Marcus observes in his contribution to this volume, "knowledge takes more than one form."[24] The sort of sentimentalist moral knowledge I want to defend is provisional rather than certain, directed inward into the contingent makeup of the human psyche rather than outward into a noncontingent realm of moral reality—a realm of Platonic forms, or necessary moral laws, or what have you.[25]

The sentimentalist reflective process described by Hume and Smith also involves a proto-Kantian move from heteronomy to autonomy. Only through such a progress of sentiments can we take control of our moral lives. We consciously identify only with those moral sentiments that we can still endorse even after the greatest degree of critical self-reflection. What makes this view sentimentalist, however, is that these autonomous moral judgments contain emotion as surely as do heteronomous judgments.

But the relevant progress of sentiments is not merely a matter of individual reflection, of self-directed approval and disapproval.

It is also a matter of interpersonal evaluation. For better or worse, we approve and disapprove of others' moral sentiments even more readily than we do our own. To be sure, there is nothing in sentimentalism that precludes relativists from approving of moral judgments at odds with their own. But most of us do not share their sentiments. Most of us are inclined to disapprove of judgments we do not share. Will this disapproval survive the process of reflective self-correction that I just described? To some degree, I think it probably will. But it will not emerge at the end of the reflective process unchallenged or unchanged.

The primary challenge to our disapproval of others' moral sentiments comes from sympathy or empathy.[26] Prinz departs from his Enlightenment-era forebears quite strikingly by rejecting their contention that sympathy is central to the psychological etiology of all our moral sentiments. We can bracket this general claim for purposes of this essay, however. Whatever role sympathy may play with regard to our moral sentiments generally, it certainly can play a role in helping improve our judgments of the moral sentiments of others, particularly those from cultural traditions in which moral sentiments very different from our own predominate.

It is not that encountering alien moral views necessarily leads us to empathize with those who advocate them. Far from it; fear and hatred are more common accompaniments to our disapproval of others' moral judgments. If those holding alien worldviews are kept far from us and do not affect our ability to live according to our own sentiments, these negative emotions will likely mellow into cold indifference. None of these attitudes are conducive to sympathy or empathy. But if we must interact on a daily basis with those of whom we disapprove—if we must build a common political life together—then there is a desperate need for some way of accommodating each other.

Here, Herder is a much better eighteenth-century inspiration than Hume or Smith.[27] It was Herder who began the sort of inquiry into the origins of human moral sentiments that Nietzsche would later call "genealogy." But, while Nietzsche sought to debunk our moral commitments by revealing their ignoble origins, Herder sought to affirm most of the diverse moral sentiments he discovered across human cultures. The key, he argued, is to feel your way into the position of those whose histories and cultures

—and, hence, whose judgments—are different from your own. Herder urged his readers to "go into the age, the clime, the whole history. Feel yourself into everything; only now are you on the way toward understanding."[28]

The task is not easy; we must overcome the natural biases of our sympathy, which tend to be strongest for those closest to and most like us and weakest for those who are different, distant, or both. Difficult, yes, but not impossible; Herder maintained that our natural wonder and curiosity at the range of human diversity would be sufficient to motivate the hard emotional work required. Add to this humanistic impetus the practical goal of finding a mode of mutual accommodation in a culturally (and hence also morally) diverse society—a practical goal that Herder did not consider adequately, largely because he was an adamant advocate of culturally uniform nation-states—and there is good reason to believe that many of us will at least attempt to empathize with our fellow citizens when we find ourselves in moral disagreement with them.

Through this imaginative and emotional investigation, you may come to understand that sentiments that once seemed to be strange and unnatural actually speak to human needs and feelings analogous to your own. This, in turn, may change your disapproval into approval. Herder's empathy may therefore look like another path to normative moral relativism. Indeed, many have interpreted Herder precisely that way.[29] But to understand all is not to approve of all. What is more, disapproval that remains after empathetic understanding is achieved seems likely to pass the test of sentimental reflection. The result is not relativism but value pluralism; there is a range of incompatible human values that can all be approved of, but there are also others that cannot be. This, at least, was the lesson Isaiah Berlin took from Herder.[30]

But there is another possibility still. Someone who arrives at value pluralism via a sentimentalist path—as opposed to someone who is convinced that the plurality of values is rationally demonstrable—realizes that, like all moral knowledge, this pluralism can be known only provisionally. There is always the possibility that, with greater sentimental reflection on the part of all parties concerned, all of humanity will gradually converge on a single set of universal moral sentiments. This may seem improbable when it comes to standards of personal virtue, but there is a reasonable hope that it may be achieved when it comes to political justice. While Herder approved of many cultural differences, he also approved of a universal sentiment of justice based on our shared humanity and our love of reciprocity. As is well known, some version of the golden rule is present in all known human cultures, even if it is more honored in the breach than in the observance.[31] Herder believed that, given sufficient intrapersonal reflection and interpersonal deliberation, all would eventually come to embrace this humane ideal more fully, whatever their cultural background. "The law of reciprocity," he insists, "is foreign to no nation."[32]

We will never be able to resolve all our moral disagreements on the basis of a single faculty of reason that all human beings share. But we may be able to resolve many, if perhaps not all, of our moral disagreements on the basis of other features we all share —most notably our susceptibility to emotions, from physical pain to parental love, and our ability to understand and share the emotions of others. It is this Herderian vision of sentimental consensus building that I, for one, would like to see advanced in our moral, political, and legal practices. But the ethics and politics of empathetic universalism are not implied by sentimentalism itself, any more than the ethics and politics of relativism are so implied.

The fact that sentimentalism can consistently be used to defend such different worldviews should come as no surprise. After all, if sentimentalism is true, the ethical and political convictions of rival sentimentalists contain emotions as surely as do all other moral judgments. The differences among their views therefore may not be resolvable through purely rational means. When we speak of the implications of sentimentalism, we are seeking exactly such a rational resolution—a logical deduction, from the shared premise of sentimentalism, that demonstrates why one sentimentalist view is consistent and the other is inconsistent. A more promising approach would be to resolve disputes between sentimentalists in a sentimentalist manner—such as through greater empathetic inquiry into our interlocutors' perspectives and greater reflective scrutiny of our own disapproval of their views. In adopting this approach, however, we must give up the idea that our interlocutors somehow failed to notice the direct normative implications of the premises we have in common. Nothing could be farther from the spirit of sentimentalism than dismissing moral worldviews with which we disagree as necessarily incoherent, let alone condemning those who embrace them as necessarily irrational.

Perhaps this is part of the reason why the debate among the original sentimentalists of the Enlightenment era was such a marvelous model of philosophical civility. Shaftesbury, Hutcheson, Hume, Smith, Herder, and others at the time were united in their conviction that moral judgments contain emotions but divided on most other moral and political questions—from the proper place of religion in public life, to the viability of democracy, to the alleged superiority of European over so-called primitive peoples. But Smith's disagreements with Hume and Herder's disagreements with them both did nothing to lessen their admiration for one another.

Smith was therefore wrong to deny the practical importance of moral psychology. To be sure, sentimentalism has no distinctive position on the question of moral relativism versus moral universalism, let alone on more specific issues such as the proper level of progressivity in our tax system or the proper balance between the claims of individual liberty and those of collective security. But, in its normative form, sentimentalism can offer a distinctive position on how we ought to reflect individually and deliberate collectively on these and all other such difficult moral questions. Sentimentalism need not unleash hateful, unreflective emotions in our public discourse—or even relativist, tolerant indifference. A widespread embrace of specifically Herderian sentimentalism could instead lead to a cultivation of wide-ranging public empathy and might help in the often seemingly fruitless task of rendering our civil life more worthy of the name "civil."

Pointing out the practical importance of sentimentalism does not detract from its importance for what Smith calls "speculation."[33] Sentimentalism may also have profound importance for scholars, for philosophy understood in the eighteenth-century sense to include not only the normative and conceptual work that is today the responsibility of philosophers and political theorists but also the empirical and interpretive scholarship that is now undertaken under the rubrics of the sciences and humanities.

The humanities in particular must not be neglected as a potential resource for enriching sentimentalist thought. Rightly dissatisfied with the arid conceptual analysis that came to dominate

philosophy in the twentieth century, philosophers today have
sought to bring their work in closer contact with empirical reality.
Yet, for too many of them, the turn to reality has taken a detour
through the experimental neuropsychology lab. Many recent empirical sentimentalists have believed this scientific approach to be
in keeping with the spirit of Hume, who famously introduced his
Treatise as "an attempt to introduce the experimental method of
reasoning into moral subjects."[34] Yet, rather than using the term
"experiment" to describe the controlled tests of today's laboratory
science, Hume instead associated "careful and exact experiments"
with the simple "observation of those particular effects which result from . . . different circumstances and situations."[35] If experimentation in general is to be equated with careful observation,
experimentation in the case of "moral subjects" will merely involve
close observation of the operations of the social world around us
and the psychological forces within us. For Hume, who was most
famous in his own time as a historian and an essayist, these observations were to be conducted not in the laboratory under controlled conditions but in the uncontrolled reality of human life,
a reality that can be captured only in history and in literature.
Although controlled experimentation will always be invaluable in
moral psychology—as it is in so many other fields—there is no reason to privilege it over humanistic inquiry when investigating the
nature of human sentiments.

   Although (at least in my preferred version) sentimentalism is
already a normative theory, the need for a humanistic version of
sentimentalism is especially great when we turn from general normative conclusions about the proper place of emotion in moral
judgment to specific ethical or political issues. Since sentimentalism implies that our disagreements on these issues may not always
be resolvable by rational means alone, it might be taken to imply
that rational scholarship has little or nothing to contribute to the
resolution of these disputes. Alternately, however, a sentimentalist
can consistently maintain that scholars can and should continue to
write on particular normative questions. To do so effectively, however, they must not be afraid of employing modes of thought other
than pure reasoning. Here, too, Herder can serve as a model: his
condemnation of European imperialism and his insistence on cultural diversity are not the products of mere logical argument but

rest on an understanding of human difference built from his extensive studies of comparative literature, world history, comparative religion, and all the other fields of humanistic scholarship —fields that require imaginative insight and emotional sensitivity as much as they require sound reasoning and solid empirical evidence.[36] As we emerge from an era in which philosophy was reduced to applied logic—the more formal the better—and into an age in which experimental science stands alongside a priori argumentation as a means of attaining philosophical insight, Herder reminds us that a third, emotionally laden mode of philosophizing is available and is capable of establishing the truth of substantive ethical and political conclusions. In many cases, it may be the only effective means of doing so.

An appreciation that moral philosophy and political theory are emotional as well as intellectual work might lead to profound changes in the practice of these disciplines. The full revolutionary potential of sentimentalism will be apparent, however, only when we realize that the importance of a moral theory can have no correlation whatsoever with the importance of its substantive moral implications.

NOTES

1. Joseph Duke Filonowicz, "Ethical Sentimentalism Revisited," *History of Philosophy Quarterly* 6:2 (April 1989): 189–206, 192. "Most often," Filonowicz continues, "the term is used polemically and tendentiously to brand vague themes thought to be barely worthy of serious consideration." The fact that so many scholars today self-identify as sentimentalists is thus not only a remarkable intellectual development, but also a brazen act of linguistic reappropriation. Unfortunately, however, the term "sentimentalist" still retains its mawkish connotations in everyday usage.

2. See Jesse J. Prinz, "Constructive Sentimentalism: Legal and Political Implications," in this volume, as well as Jesse Prinz, *The Emotional Construction of Morals* (New York: Oxford University Press, 2007).

3. Prinz, "Constructive Sentimentalism," 3.

4. For two prominent examples of such quasi-sentimentalist theories, see Allan Gibbard, *Wise Choices, Apt Feelings: A Theory of Normative Judgment* (Cambridge, MA: Harvard University Press, 1990), and Justin D'Arms and Daniel Jacobson, "Sentiment and Value," *Ethics* 110 (2000):

722–748, the latter of which introduced the idea of calling such views "neo-sentimentalist."

5. For two of the many Platonic discussions of the superiority of moral knowledge to moral opinion, see *Meno* 97a–100b, in *Complete Works of Plato*, ed. John Cooper (Indianapolis: Hackett, 1997), 895–897, and *Republic* 477–480 (1103–1107)).

6. For the claim that only a minority will achieve moral knowledge or understanding, see, among many other passages in the Platonic corpus, *Timaeus* 51e, in Cooper, ed., *Complete Works of Plato*, 1254. The educational plan designed to produce moral knowledge takes up much of the *Republic*; see especially 376–417 (1015–1052), and 503–541 (1123–1155).

7. See, among other defenses of this claim, in the *Republic*, 484b–484d, in Cooper, ed., *Complete Works of Plato*, 1107–1108. There are, of course, many scholars who would dismiss the interpretation in this and the preceding paragraph as a caricature of Plato's actual views, views that are notoriously difficult to pin down on the basis of literary works as complex as the dialogues. My goal here is not so much to interpret Plato accurately (though, for the record, I do believe my interpretation to be correct) as to describe a recognizably Platonic position that can involve the simultaneous embrace of empirical sentimentalism and moral rationalism.

8. Immanuel Kant, *Groundwork of the Metaphysics of Morals*, trans. Mary J. Gregor, in *Practical Philosophy, The Cambridge Edition of the Works of Immanuel Kant*, ed. Mary J. Gregor and Allen Wood (New York: Cambridge University Press, 1996), 4:407, 61.

9. My interpretation of Kant in this paragraph, while not obvious to every reader of the *Groundwork*, is reflective of the current scholarly consensus on the matter. See Allen Wood, *Kant's Ethical Thought* (New York: Cambridge University Press, 1999), 17–49; Paul Guyer, *Kant and the Experience of Freedom: Essays on Aesthetics and Morality* (New York: Cambridge University Press, 1993), 335–393; and Marcia Baron, *Kantian Ethics Almost without Apology* (Ithaca, NY: Cornell University Press, 1995), 146–187. As with my interpretation of Plato, however, my goal here is primarily to outline a recognizably Kantian position that incorporates both empirical sentimentalism and moral rationalism and that does so without the objectionable elitism of the Platonic position described earlier.

10. For the classic statements of metaethical sentimentalism in its "emotivist" variant, see Alfred Jules Ayer, *Language, Truth and Logic* (New York: Dover, 1936/1952), 102–119, and Charles L. Stevenson, *Ethics and Language* (New Haven, CT: Yale University Press, 1944/1960).

11. Adam Smith, *The Theory of Moral Sentiments*, ed. A. L. Macfie and D. D. Raphael (Indianapolis: Liberty Fund, 1759/1790/1984), 166.

12. The first half of the twentieth century was the heyday of the belief

in the moral neutrality of metaethics, a position defended by Stevenson, *Ethics and Language*, and Ayer, *Language, Truth and Logic*, 102–119, among many others. By the 1960s, the dominant view had a number of prominent opponents. See Alan Gewirth, "Meta-Ethics and Normative Ethics," *Mind*, New Series 69:274 (April 1960): 187–205; Gewirth, "Metaethics and Moral Neutrality," *Ethics* 78:3 (April 1968): 214–225; and R. C. Solomon, "Normative and Meta-Ethics," *Philosophy and Phenomenological Research* 31:1 (September 1970): 97–107. In order to appreciate the full importance of this debate, remember that Stevenson, Ayer, and their ilk maintained that only analytic metaethics really qualified as moral *philosophy* and hence that philosophy as such should not be concerned with normative questions. Those who rejected the moral neutrality of metaethics were thus implicitly (and occasionally explicitly) defending the philosophical legitimacy of addressing normative issues. Given the re-emergence of normative moral and political philosophy from the 1970s on, it might be thought that Gewirth and Solomon had decisively won the argument. Yet, a widespread belief in the independence of metaethics and normative ethics remained—albeit now as a defense of a division of labor between two forms of philosophically legitimate enquiry. Indeed, in a reverse of the once-dominant view, some philosophers even began appealing to the moral neutrality of metaethics to argue that only normative ethics was truly worthy of philosophical attention; see Peter Singer, "The Triviality of the Debate over 'Is-Ought' and the Definition of 'Moral,'" *American Philosophical Quarterly* 10:1 (January 1973): 51–56.

13. Smith, *The Theory of Moral Sentiments*, 265.

14. Ibid., 315.

15. Michael Slote, *Moral Sentimentalism* (New York: Oxford University Press, 2010), 47–48.

16. Prinz, *Emotional Construction of Morals*, maintains this view but holds open the possibility that some moral sentiments may be better than others in various nonmoral ways. Some may be more likely to promote the general welfare than others, for example, but this is not grounds for arguing for their moral superiority as such. Since most of us believe that advancing the general welfare is (at least *ceteris paribus*) *morally* desirable, I fail to see how he can distinguish moral approval and disapproval from their nonmoral variants in this way.

17. For an examination of some of the many possible theories that could reasonably go under the name "moral relativism," as well as a defense of most (but not all) of them, see the essays collected in "Part I: Moral Relativism," in *Explaining Value and Other Essays in Moral Philosophy*, ed. Gilbert Harman (New York: Oxford University Press, 2000), 3–99.

18. There are, however, legitimate doubts about the validity of this

argument, as well as all other arguments from conceptual to normative relativism. It is certainly possible that there is a disanalogy here between the relationship between conceptual and normative sentimentalism on the one hand and conceptual and normative relativism on the other. While conceptual sentimentalism implies normative sentimentalism, conceptual relativism may or may not imply normative relativism—and there is no need to determine whether or not it does for purposes of this essay.

19. This sentimentalist account of how we can improve our moral reflection is one of the main subjects addressed in my book *The Enlightenment of Sympathy* (New York: Oxford University Press, 2010). It was not until I was preparing the current essay, however, that I realized Hume and Smith were advocating a dual-process model along roughly Platonic lines.

20. Prinz, "Constructive Sentimentalism," 7.

21. This is the moral component of the "progress of sentiments" described by Hume and made famous by Annette Baier in her book of that title. See Annette C. Baier, *Progress of Sentiments: Reflections on Hume's Treatise* (Cambridge, MA: Harvard University Press, 1991).

22. David Hume, *A Treatise of Human Nature*, in *Oxford Philosophical Texts*, ed. David Fate Norton and Mary J. Norton (New York: Oxford University Press, 2000), 266.

23. Ibid., 317.

24. George E. Marcus, "Reason, Passion, and Democratic Politics: Old Conceptions—New Understandings—New Possibilities," in this volume, 154.

25. For more on the distinction between these two forms of moral knowledge, see Michael B. Gill, "On the Alleged Incompatibility between Sentimentalism and Moral Confidence," *History of Philosophy Quarterly* 15:4 (October 1998): 411–440, especially 428.

26. For purposes of this essay, I can avoid the question of what difference, if any, there is between sympathy and empathy, in part since only the former was available to the eighteenth-century authors who initiated sentimentalism. But do see, among others on the topic, Stephen Darwall, "Empathy, Sympathy, Care," *Philosophical Studies* 89 (1998): 261–282.

27. For a fuller defense of the interpretation of Herder presented in the following paragraphs, see Frazer, *The Enlightenment of Sympathy*,139–167.

28. Johann Gottfried Herder, "This Too a Philosophy of History for the Education of Humanity (1774)," in *Herder: Philosophical Writings*, ed. and trans. Michael N. Forster (New York: Cambridge University Press, 2002), 292.

29. For a few of the many descriptions of Herder as a relativist along roughly these lines, see Robert T. Clark, *Herder: His Life and Thought* (Berkeley: University of California Press, 1955), 320; Frederick C. Beiser,

The Fate of Reason: German Philosophy from Kant to Fichte (Cambridge, MA: Harvard University Press, 1987), 142–143; and Arthur O. Lovejoy, *Essays in the History of Ideas* (Baltimore, MD: The Johns Hopkins University Press, 1948), 172.

30. See Isaiah Berlin, *The Crooked Timber of Humanity*, ed. Henry Hardy (Princeton, NJ: Princeton University Press, 1990), especially 76, as well as Berlin, *Three Critics of the Enlightenment: Vico, Hamann, Herder* (Princeton, NJ: Princeton University Press, 2000).

31. See Jeffrey Wattles, *The Golden Rule* (New York: Oxford University Press, 1996).

32. Herder, "Letters for the Advancement of Humanity" (1793–97), in Forster, ed., *Philosophical Writings*, 417.

33. Smith, *The Theory of Moral Sentiments*, 315.

34. Hume, *A Treatise of Human Nature*, 1. For an experimental philosophy "manifesto" and a collection of essays on the topic, see *Experimental Philosophy*, ed. Joshua Knobe and Shaun Nichols (New York: Oxford University Press, 2008). For a more balanced appraisal of the value of experimental work in the field, see Kwame Anthony Appiah, *Experiments in Ethics* (Cambridge, MA: Harvard University Press, 2008).

35. Hume, *A Treatise of Human Nature*, 5.

36. Herder's utilization and defense of the humanities has important parallels with that put forward more recently by Martha Nussbaum. See Martha C. Nussbaum, *Cultivating Humanity: A Classical Defense of Reform in Liberal Education* (Cambridge, MA: Harvard University Press, 1997), and Nussbaum, *Not for Profit: Why Democracy Needs the Humanities* (Princeton, NJ: Princeton University Press, 2010).

3

LEGISLATING WITH AFFECT: EMOTION AND LEGISLATIVE LAW MAKING

CAROL SANGER

1. Introduction

The field of "law and emotion" takes on the ambitious task of "reckon[ing] with the myriad ways in which the law reflects or furthers conceptions of how humans are, or ought to be, as emotional creatures."[1] In her taxonomy of the field, Terry Maroney states that one way has been the "legal actor approach." On this approach, scholars from our many fields study the people or the categories of people who regularly participate in the activities and arenas of law closely connected to law's affective concerns: the judges and juries, prosecutors and defenders, victims and defendants for whom mercy, compassion, vengeance, forgiveness, empathy, anger, and remorse are served up every day in the criminal justice system.

These same emotions are also the regular stuff of families and therefore of family law. For a preliminary example, consider the predicament of the disastrously married in the days of fault-based divorce and the elaborate perjury-riddled divorce hearings facilitated by bar and bench in order to provide unhappy couples a way out within the law.[2] In time, official reassessment of the emotional lives of families and of law's complicity in the character of those lives led to no-fault divorce reform.[3] Nor is this an isolated example. In recent years, there has been increasingly sophisticated scholarly attention to the affective circumstances of legal actors in family law: parents, children, spouses, would-be spouses, mediators, and so on.[4]

In this essay, I want to expand the idea of Mahoney's "legal actor approach" to consider a "legal *actors* approach." I use the plural not to refer generally to collective categories of legal actors—litigants, judges, and so on—but, rather, to introduce a *particular* category of people acting collectively and for a particular purpose: *making* law. I shall turn our attention to *legislatures* and in this essay begin to consider the complex relations between emotion and legislative law making. At present, there isn't much out there on this more institutional approach. (In this regard, the title of a recent anthology, *The Least Examined Branch: The Role of Legislatures in the Constitutional State,*[5] might easily be adapted to the law and emotion setting.) To be sure, certain institutions or systems—family court, criminal justice, constitutionalism—have been the subjects of law and emotion inquiry.[6] Yet, these are not law-making bodies, and that is my subject here: the role of emotion as it relates to the collective process of law making.

I take up this topic for several reasons. I am responding in part to the call by Jesse Prinz for greater consideration of the political and legal implications (in contrast to the philosophical and psychological origins) of what he has called "constructive sentimentalism." This is the proposition that moral judgments "are based on sentiments that dispose us to emotions of approval and disapproval and that these sentiments are shaped by historical processes."[7] Because law is a regulatory system that, among other functions, structures official approval and disapproval, it makes great sense to think more systematically about the implications of constructive sentimentalism (or any other of the accounts concerning the relationship between moral judgment and sentiments or emotions) for law.[8]

In addition, and independently, for the last several years I have been investigating legislation in an area saturated with sentiment —laws that govern aspects of infant and fetal death.[9] The enthusiastic enactment of new forms of legislation in the areas of abortion, infanticide, and stillbirth tells us a great deal about the historical contingency of what is approved or disapproved, encouraged

or deplored. Returning to Maroney's characterization, it also tells
us a great deal about the ways in which the law commits itself to
certain views about how humans—in this case women—"are or
ought to be as emotional creatures." I am particularly interested in
the explicit use by lawmakers (and, as we shall see, also by constituents) of legislation as a mechanism of emotional influence. My
focus here will be on two recent examples in which regulated persons are meant to *feel* something—better (in one case) and worse
(in another)—by virtue of what specific legislation offers or commands. Indeed, in each case, changing how women feel is the very
point of the legislation.

To get our bearings, I want first to map out a few general points
regarding the role of emotion in law making. Some are historical,
some theoretical, and some phenomenological, but all focus on
the connections between emotion and legislators, legislatures, and
legislation. I recognize that my inventory is not exhaustive; each
topic seems to suggest an essay of its own in which a specific concern is elaborated and refined. Yet I want to get us started thinking about the ways in which sentiment is expressed, transmitted,
and absorbed within a legislative assembly and also about how it
is deployed in the work product of assemblies: law. I shall suggest
that, in recent years, legislatures have been trying out some new
and possibly suspect moves regarding the mobilization of emotion
through law and that it is time to pay more critical attention.

2. EMOTION AND LAW MAKING: A GENERAL RELATIONSHIP

Almost any subject of regulation stirs emotions in those who care
about the issue at hand. Even if one starts small and thinks locally
—I draw from one small city in northern California where I used to
live—examples of emotional investment in law making abound. A
decision whether to cut down particular trees on public land, proposed decibel restraints on the (maddening) jingle of the roving
ice cream truck, the demand for speed bumps on one residential
street and not another—each of these issues produced impas-
sioned protest and debate before eventual resolution by the city
council. Citizens care about all sorts of matters, whether on their
own behalf or on someone else's, and those who care register their
feelings on the subject before and, depending on the outcome,

often *after* a vote has been taken and the matter decided. This is because legislation matters to how people proceed with their lives. Laws not only affect "the freedom and interests of all the members of the community" but do so palpably.[10] Legislation "changes the previously established way of doing things," whether because it "regulates behavior in a new way, or [because it] deregulates behavior and permits individual choice."[11] Any issue that becomes the subject of a legislative determination is therefore likely to produce some degree of passion in those affected as citizens or as subjects.

Legislators and Emotions

Because legislators as citizens are also persons affected by laws, they too are likely to be emotionally invested in this or that piece of legislation. Yet, as elected representatives and professional lawmakers, legislators may also have special and more role-oriented emotional investments in the task before them. Indeed, emotions are on display throughout the legislative process.[12] Legislators may have great pride in passing a particular piece of legislation; we see this in the smiling faces of those who have elbowed out others to stand behind the executive at the now-familiar multipen signing ceremonies. There may also be anguish, as when a legislator feels deeply the personal cost of a particular vote. The historian David Garrow describes Assemblyman George Michaels of New York when he cast the decisive vote for liberalized abortion reform in 1970: with "hands trembling and tears welling in his eyes," Michaels stated, " 'I realize, Mr. Speaker, [that I am] terminating my political career, but I cannot in good conscience sit here and allow my vote to be the one that defeats this bill—I ask that my vote be changed from 'no' to 'yes.' "[13] (Michaels was right about his career.)

Darker emotions—anger, fury, rage—also manifest themselves during legislative deliberations. It has been a while since members of the United States Congress have engaged in serious fisticuffs: the infamous caning of Senator Charles Sumner of Massachusetts on the Senate floor by a member of the South Carolina congressional delegation took place in 1856.[14] Yet, senatorial fistfights have continued into the twentieth century. Following a punchout between the junior and senior senators from South Carolina (again!) in 1902, the Senate added to its rules the provision that "No senator in debate shall, directly or indirectly, by any form of words impute to another Senator or to other Senators any conduct or motive unworthy or unbecoming a Senator."[15] In assemblies in other parts of the world, brawls proceed with some regularity and are now available for viewing on YouTube.[16] In the United States, *verbal* expressions of anger or abuse are more common; a recent example was a Republican congressman who angrily shouted "Baby killer" at pro-life Representative Bart Stupak on the floor of the House during the 2010 health care debate.[17]

Identifying connections between legislative judgments and legislators' emotions in any crisp or clinical way is further complicated by the ordinary demands of politics. It may be difficult to separate out "emotional concerns," by which I mean something like "genuine sentiment," from political *displays* of emotion concerns (a more calculated response).[18]

Deliberation and the Substance of Law

Emotion may be at work even when it is not on display. We are familiar with the idea that a legislator's visceral reaction to a particular event or circumstance may motivate his position on an issue. Much has been written, for example, on the relation between disgust and the formation of moral judgments that inform the prohibitions of the criminal law.[19] There may be disagreement over whether disgust *should* inform moral judgment (say, regarding constraints on same-sex sexual conduct) but not over whether it *does* inform them.[20] These debates are part of the larger project of establishing the continuity between emotion and reason, rather than their imagined incompatibility.

Of course, the exact emotion or its precise connection to a moral judgment may not be readily apparent or knowable. As Prinz has argued, if moral values are based on sentiments that dispose us to emotions of approval and disapproval, it should come as no surprise that moral judgments—including those made by legislators in the course of law making—are likely to be "susceptible to the influence of emotions that are not necessarily relevant to a case at hand."[21] In addition, certain emotions, such as fear, sometimes build upon themselves, producing a frenzied or disproportionate regulatory response. We see this with legislation enacted in response to a "moral panic."[22] The resulting legislation—whether zero-tolerance policies in response to school shootings or the intensified regulation of child-care centers following a report of child abuse—may not be the most considered or efficacious from a policy standpoint, but it may still be emotionally satisfying.[23]

Sometimes, making a statement without concern for efficacy is the *primary* goal of legislation. Here I have in mind legislation that is essentially expressive or symbolic in nature. [24] The legislation is enacted without the intent or expectation that it will actually change anything—prohibitions on flag burning, for example, when flags are infrequently burned or resolutions from the Berkeley City Council declaring Berkeley a nuclear-free zone. The nuclear-free resolution may make the Berkeley City Council members and their constituents *feel* proud, but it is unlikely to make anyone safer during a nuclear war. Legislation may, of course, have an expressive purpose *and* intend to alter behavior. Much abortion regulation might be seen in this light. Prevented by *Roe v. Wade* from criminalizing abortion, a number of states have passed legislation that says, in effect, "Take note that we are not happy about this state of affairs." A good example of this is the regulation of teenage pregnancy and the requirement that a minor must either get permission from her parents or petition a court before she can legally consent to an abortion.[25] Some minors may be deterred, but, even for the many who proceed with their abortion, the law still has significant expressive value. It stands not only as a general statement of opposition to abortion but also in respectful solidarity with parental authority.[26]

Legislators also gesture affectively through enactments that fall slightly short of law. Consider the use of legislative titles and preambles to get a point across. In his study of the use of preambles in Canadian legislation, Kent Roach notes that the Platonic aspirations for preambles as a message to citizens from legislators about "the deliberations and accommodations that preceded enactment" might be profitably revived.[27] Aware of the dangers of "oversell," Roach suggests that preambles may "once again, as Plato imagined, allow legislators to appeal to the heart as well as the mind and to persuade, explain, and inspire as well as command."[28] Congressional resolutions are another example of what

Jacob Gersen and Eric Posner have called "soft law."[29] They note that, because resolutions "do not create binding legal obligations," they are sometimes characterized as "cheap and often happy talk by legislatures, commending military officers for good service or sports teams for winning championships."[30] While Gersen and Posner argue that congressional resolutions may be very serious indeed—"urg[ing] the President to intervene in humanitarian crises . . . , criticiz[ing] allies and enemies, . . . identify[ing] public health threats that need funding, and much more"[31]—it is worth noting that the seriousness is still conveyed expressively, rather than by commanding particular action.

Processes

There is also the interesting and understudied question of how emotional sentiment is transmitted within a deliberative body. One starting point is the use of rhetoric, or the classical art of persuasion. Techniques of argumentation include not only *logos* or logic but also *ethos* and *pathos*, the first intended to build a relation of trust between speaker and listener, the second an appeal to the listener's empathic and imaginative abilities.[32] While few legislators today are likely to have been schooled in formal rhetoric, the features of the classic components have found their way into modern debate, even if "debate" now includes one-minute taped speeches to an empty chamber.[33] While legal scholars—sometimes more associated with "law and literature" than with "law and emotion"— have analyzed the rhetorical structure of judicial arguments, there have also been analyses of rhetoric within legislatures. Megan's Law and "three strikes" legislation are two examples.[34]

There are other, more psychologically rooted theories of transmission. Elizabeth Emens has introduced the psychological theory of "emotional contagion" into the discussion of workplace discrimination to help understand the complex relations between workers and mentally ill coworkers.[35] Emens describes "emotional contagion" as the "automatic absorption of another's affective state, often with no conscious awareness of the process"; unconscious processes of mimicry then lead people to feel like people around them.[36] I am not urging "emotional contagion" as the key to all methodologies for what goes on in Congress. I am saying only that in the workplace that is Congress, affective states and messages relevant to a lawmaker's judgment are transmitted by several means and that, in addition to standard forms of political persuasion, some may be processed subconsciously.

Institutional Constraints on Emotions in Law Making

It is clear that emotion is threaded throughout the process of law making: motivation, planning, deliberation, judgment, negotiation, voting, and its aftermath are all emotionally inflected. We have seen that emotional instincts, insights, and assessments play out in a variety of ways and that most are appropriate, anticipated, and (punching aside) accepted as part of the legislative process. At the same time, passions can heat up and become "unruly" in ways that might disrupt deliberative minimums. With this possibility in mind, precautions intended to modulate the role or at least the force of emotion have been incorporated into the very structure of legislatures and of law making. James Madison diagnosed one possible cause of frenzy as the sheer numbers within a legislative assembly: "In all very numerous assemblies, of whatever characters composed, passion never fails to rest the scepter from reason. Had every Athenian citizen been a Socrates, every Athenian assembly would still have been a mob."[37] In consequence, concerns about emotion in relation to legislative size are often a factor in the organization and architecture of an assembly.

Other structural constraints address the *content* of law. We have, for example, constitutionally capped the quality of retribution that can be enacted in response to fury or vengeance. No matter how much the populace might want to reintroduce thumbscrews (for pedophiles, for example), the Eighth Amendment prohibition against cruel and unusual punishment limits the nature or amount of punishment that may be prescribed.[38] Indeed, we might understand law itself as a structure for channeling emotions. Vengeance is taken out of our individual hands through the criminal law; prejudices are checked by the various requirements of due process.

The content of legislation is further restrained by the general principle that legislation should be enacted for general purposes only. Amy Gutmann summarizes how much can go wrong when legislatures suspend this principle and act more like courts whose province is the singular case before them. Using the much publicized and emotionally charged case of Terri Schiavo, a brain-dead woman whose husband and parents disagreed over whether to continue to keep her on life support, Gutmann explains why legislating for a particular case—Florida enacted "Terri's Law" to enable the reinsertion of Schiavo's feeding tube; the U.S. Congress passed "a unique bill" giving federal courts jurisdiction over this one case—is a bad idea: "Legislatures most often make egregious mistakes when they try to rule on single, high-visibility cases for politically expedient purposes."[39] To be sure, legislation is sometimes *motivated* by and even named for a particular case (for example, a murdered child, as in "Megan's Law"), and, while such laws may raise other problems about the power of emotion, they are at least general in application.[40]

Concerns about the passions of legislatures have also been incorporated into the structure of government. One clear example is bicameralism, a near-universal feature of representative assemblies. While there are many justifications for the second house—multiple bases of representation, the value of redundancy in decision making, and so on—fears about the otherwise unchecked passions of the popularly elected house featured significantly in structuring the U.S. Congress.[41] James Madison described the Senate as a "necessary fence" against the "fickleness and passion" of the lower house.[42] The Senate guarded against "the propensity of all single and numerous assemblies to yield to the impulse of sudden and violent passions, and to be seduced by leaders into intemperate and pernicious resolutions."[43] Not only the presence of cooler (or less fickle) heads but also time itself was understood to help lower the temperature. Washington is said to have told Jefferson that, just as Jefferson poured his coffee into his saucer to cool it down, so, too, "we pour legislation into the senatorial saucer to cool it."[44]

Notwithstanding these structural precautions, legislative bodies are inevitably bound up with emotion. What people care about is the stuff of politics, and certain issues turn the volume up. It is hard, for example, for a legislator to vote against anything that has anything to do with, say, preventing harm to children, as when the law seeks to punish pedophiles or to encourage mothers not to murder their newborns. The latter example explains the wide-

spread passage of "Infant Safe Haven laws" in the 1990s in response to much-publicized discoveries of abandoned newborns in
dumpsters and elsewhere. To discourage this form of neonaticide,
legislation in many states now provides for women to leave their
unwanted newborns anonymously at designated "safe havens"
such as fire stations and to do so with impunity from prosecution
for child abandonment.[45]

Safe Haven laws were passed with astonishing speed nation-
wide. This was despite opposition from child welfare experts who
contended that the laws were a hasty and unproven response to
unwanted pregnancy; from adult adoptees concerned that they
would never find their parents; and from conservative talk show
hosts who characterized the laws as "baby-dumping legislation"
that "help[s] to normalize disgusting behavior."[46] Yet, such critiques rarely found their way into committee hearings, floor debates, or vote tallies. When an Illinois legislator asked about the
legislation's efficacy during the floor debate, he was shut down by
the bill's sponsor, and within minutes the bill passed 56-0.[47] In Massachusetts, Representative Patricia Haddad stated that "I am not
going to nitpick. . . . Let's get it out there rather than hold it up
over foolishness."[48] The claim that quick passage would result in
"one more life saved" was repeatedly invoked. This is all to say that,
despite structural mechanisms designed to slow things down, the
appeal of acting, and especially of *enacting*, works at times to transform deliberation into nitpicking and reflection into foolishness.

3. THE CULTIVATION OF EMOTION

So far, I have offered an overview of some of the involvement of
emotion in law making. Each instance deserves more investigation
than I can provide here. There is, however, one additional category of connection between emotion and the content of law that I
want to consider in some depth. This is the intentional use of legislation to *produce* or *satisfy* a specific emotional state in those who
are subject to the law. At one level, this may sound like a fairly un-
remarkable proposition. Of course people are regularly invested
in legislative outcomes; it is then only a small step for legislators
to mean for them to be. Of course legislators want us in general

8

CAROL SANGER

to feel proud, secure, and self-sufficient. That is why they enacted the 2001 Patriot Act (pardon me, the Uniting and Strengthening America by Providing Appropriate Tools Required to Intercept and Obstruct Terrorism Act of 2001), the Full Employment Act (in 1946 and in 1979), and the Personal Responsibility and Work Opportunity Reconciliation Act of 1996 (ending welfare as we knew it).

These examples are rather showy and may reveal more about the politics of headlines and sound bites than about genuine legislative commitment to what Kathy Abrams and Hila Keren have called "the cultivation of emotion." In their recent project on hope, Abrams and Keren explore and, indeed, endorse the development of positive emotions as "a social good which might be encouraged by the law."[49] In focusing on positive emotions, Abrams and Keren are not naive about law's potential to facilitate negative emotions for the social good: "There may be contexts, for example, where it is socially valuable to cultivate anger or disgust in a population." Yet, they continue, "one can imagine many more settings in which law might serve broader social purposes by cultivating positive emotions such as forgiveness or trust."[50] They focus on hope, "because of its immense importance for individuals or groups who face material disadvantage, inequality, or despair," as a potentially "powerful legal means of fostering social change."[51]

To show how all this might work, Abrams and Keren offer the case of Project Head Start, a federal preschool program started under President Lyndon Johnson in 1965 as part of a larger legislative program of social repair.[52] Project Head Start attempted to cultivate hope in children, in families, and in communities through a variety of structural mechanisms and goals. These included "communicating recognition and vision, introducing activities that allowed for individuation among participants, providing resources, and fostering solidarity."[53] Thus, Project Head Start was not just "feel-good legislation," some cosmetic enactment that only gestured in the direction of betterment; it was an elaborate program with actual resources, strategies, and measurements of success. Hope may have been both an inspiration for and a byproduct of Head Start, but it is important for the integrity of the legal project of emotional cultivation that hope *alone* was not all that was on offer. Abrams and Keren are aware of the risks in cultivating emotion as a strategy for social improvement, and they identified substantive conditions that make success more likely.

Even so, I want to register some concerns about the general project, and I do so not only because of my inherently skeptical feelings about hope as a social goal.[54] Rather, I have less faith than Abrams and Keren in the commitment of legislators to act only in the cause of *positive* emotions or to do so with sufficient attention to the costs that may be involved. I am concerned, as well, about *which* emotions might be cultivated in the service of the social good, as the term itself is often politically contingent. I am further concerned about the deliberate cultivation of emotion aimed at producing not simply a positive affective state but emotion directed at behavioral ends. More specifically, I am concerned about cultivating emotional states for the specific purpose of bringing about behavior that the law cannot otherwise legitimately regulate but that is likely to result once a person has been "emotionally cultivated" to feel a particular way.

To illustrate these concerns and make the case for caution, I present two cases of recent legislation that seeks to mobilize emotion. The first example involves mandatory ultrasound laws, a form of abortion regulation that requires pregnant women to undergo an ultrasound and be offered a look at their "unborn child" before they can legally consent to an abortion.[55] The second example is Missing Angel acts. These are statutes now in effect in some thirty states that authorize the state to issue stillborn birth certificates upon the birth of a stillborn baby.[56]

Each of these statutes regulates a form of pregnancy loss; each is directed primarily at women; and each is saturated with emotional valence and purpose. At the same time, there are interesting differences between the two. One difference concerns the origins of the demand. Mandatory ultrasound is a top-down enterprise; the impetus for the legislation has come from legislators. It therefore illuminates the calculated use of law to *create* or, as supporters contend, to *surface* emotions within the regulated group, rather than to *respond* to an emotional need within the constituency. In contrast, the demand for Missing Angel acts has been entirely grassroots, as organizations of grieving parents demand a particular statutory remedy for their self-identified emotional need. This raises the question of whether emotional needs constitute a sufficient moral basis for a legislative response. Are constituents capable of self-diagnosis, and, more important, are legislatures competent to provide balm in these circumstances?

Before considering these questions, I want to say a word, perhaps unnecessarily, about the susceptibility—the rawness—of particular subjects to emotional appeal and what I shall argue is its misuse by legislatures. Certain subjects—anything to do with families, for example—are emotionally laden even before law gets involved. Where a person stands in a family is often a crucial aspect of identity, fundamental to how people hold themselves out in the world and how they are regarded by others. Laws that concern a person's status or authority within a family—adoption laws, grounds for divorce, parental rights over children, same-sex marriage—are thus often subjects of great passion and debated in the hottest of terms. The same is true for death. A declaration of war, for example, may be presented or considered in terms of patriotism, national exigency, or foreign policy. But it is also about the profound significance of people dying, and sooner or later this is also recognized and discussed. Gun control, the death penalty, and assisted suicide are issues whose regulation is similarly inflicted with the passions that arise when death is on the line. Indeed, politicians sometimes invoke "death" by name precisely to produce a more emotional response in a particular constituency. Consider the dispiriting transformation of "end-of-life care issues" into "death panels" during the 2010 congressional health-care debate.

Issues that combine both issues—death and families—pack a double wallop. That is the case with both Missing Angel acts and mandatory ultrasound statutes. Although stillbirth and abortion are not usually considered together, both concern the potential of family creation and its failure. To be sure, mandatory ultrasounds are associated with voluntary termination of pregnancy, while Missing Angel acts address the involuntary end. We should therefore not be surprised to find that different emotions are recruited in the two cases. At the same time, the distinction does not diminish the heightened emotional potential of either stillbirth or abortion as a subject of legislative regulation. With this in mind, I turn to the details of the two cases.

Mandatory Ultrasound Legislation

As part of the comprehensive bundle of regulation that now governs the legal provision of abortion in the United States, four states—Alabama, Arizona, Mississippi, and Louisiana—provide that, before a woman can consent to an abortion at any stage of pregnancy, she must first undergo an ultrasound scan and be offered a look at the resulting fetal image. Florida mandates the procedure after the first semester; ten other states require that any time a physician performs an ultrasound in connection with an abortion, the patient must be offered the opportunity to view the scan; another eighteen states inform women that they are entitled to an ultrasound and a look at the scan.[57]

The Alabama Women's Right to Know Act illustrates the flavor of these laws. It provides that

> The physician who is to perform the abortion or the referring physician [shall] perform an ultrasound on the unborn child before the abortion. . . . The woman shall complete a required form to acknowledge that she either saw the ultrasound image of her unborn child or that she was offered the opportunity and rejected it.[58]

(Note that the ultrasound is performed not on the woman but on the unborn child). In addition, the signed statement of "rejection" for women who decline to look at the scan is to be kept in the woman's medical files for three years. In the accompanying statement of Findings and Purpose, the Alabama legislature explains why all of this is necessary:

> The medical, emotional, and psychological consequences of an abortion are serious and can be lasting or life threatening. . . . It is [therefore] the purpose of this chapter to ensure that every woman considering an abortion receives complete information on the procedure, risks, and her alternatives and to ensure that every woman who submits to an abortion procedure does so only after giving her voluntary and informed consent to the abortion procedure.[59]

As with other constraints on consent to abortion, such as cooling-off periods, the ultrasound requirement is justified not only in terms of fetal life but also in terms of women's well-being.[60] Looking at the fetal image supplements what a woman thinks she may know about abortion by concretizing just what (or who) is at stake (to the extent there is anything identifiable on the scan to see in early pregnancy). Other states additionally offer women the opportunity to listen to fetal heartbeats.[61] Some simply use words: in South Dakota, abortion patients are read a script informing them that an abortion "will terminate the life of a whole, separate, unique, living human being."[62]

The motivating belief behind these statutes is that a woman who sees her baby's image on a screen will be less likely to abort; only after an ultrasound is she sufficiently informed about what an abortion is or does. Yet, it is hard to accept that women do not understand that abortion ends pregnancy and that, if they have an abortion, they will not have that baby. (They may well have another baby at another time.) Abortion patients know they are pregnant and that abortion terminates pregnancy.[63] Yet, mandatory ultrasound is not so much about what a woman understands as what she is supposed to feel. Mandatory ultrasound is meant to overcome a woman's decision about abortion through the manipulation of sentiment. Pro-life organizations have long recognized what the anthropologist Faye Ginsburg describes as the "conversion power" of fetal imagery.[64] Couched in the language of informed consent, mandatory ultrasound seeks to transform the embryo or fetus from an abstraction to a real baby in the eyes of its potentially murderous mother.

There is a great deal wrong with mandatory ultrasound. As I have discussed elsewhere, there is the problem of coercion, as the woman's own body is commandeered for the purpose of producing evidence to persuade her to change her mind. My focus here, however, is not on the production of evidence but on its use: mandatory ultrasound as a canny and disturbing exercise in the cultivation of emotion—the kindling of maternal sensibilities.

How is this supposed to come about? Many factors contribute to the emotional power of ultrasound. As Susan Sontag observed, the "virtually unlimited authority" of images has replaced experience as the means of knowing something for sure.[65] We see this with regard to pregnancy, where quickening—the physical sensation of movement—as an announcement of arrival now seems pokey and old-fashioned. Of course there's a baby in there; we saw it weeks ago!

Mandatory ultrasound as a mechanism of persuasion does not come out of the blue but draws upon social practices associated with *nonmandatory* obstetric ultrasound. Happily pregnant women in the United States have and anticipate having ultrasounds throughout their pregnancies. The actual screenings, typically conducted by technicians who take pleasure in talking parents through the unfamiliar shapes on the monitor, are part of the whole affirmative experience. The activity that attends the ultrasound gives the procedure even richer meaning: displaying the images, finding out the sex, settling on a name. Everyone now expects to be shown little blurry photos when someone announces a wanted pregnancy. As one woman explained about showing her ultrasound pictures around, "I wouldn't be a good mommy if I didn't."[66]

And here lies the force of cultural practice. Mandatory ultrasound laws require women to participate physically in what has become a rite of full-term pregnancy. Having an ultrasound is now an early step in prenatal care. In a wanted pregnancy, it solidifies the idea of a child so that norms of maternal solicitude begin to take hold. This phenomenological wallop is not lost on those who support mandatory ultrasound. Simply by virtue of having the screening, all pregnant women are scooped into the social category of expectant mother, however brief they may intend that status to be. The social meaning of ultrasound for wanted pregnancies is thereby commandeered for unwanted ones. Requiring ultrasound before an abortion attempts to shift the woman's thoughts, her experience, and her expectations from those of someone who has decided not to remain pregnant into those of an ordinary mother-to-be.

Does looking at the image of the fetus deter women from aborting? Certainly, there is anecdotal evidence that women who have had an ultrasound say that they could never abort thereafter.[67] While much of this data comes from pro-life pregnancy centers, few of us doubt that, in a wanted pregnancy, "meeting one's baby" is typically a joyous and exciting experience. Yet, there are also cases where the information that appears on the monitor is the very thing that decides a woman against the pregnancy. The ultrasound may reveal an unacceptable fetal anomaly, including, in some cultures, a fetus of the wrong sex. Thus, seeing a fetal image is not *always* celebratory.[68] Parents awaiting diagnostic testing sometimes deliberately distance themselves emotionally from the pregnancy as a form of emotional self-protection.[69]

And what is the significance of fetal imagery for women whose pregnancy might have been unwanted from the start? Here we see how pernicious the deployment of emotion in these circumstances really is. I suggest that a two-step process of emotional cultivation may be at work. If mandatory ultrasound works as its supporters mean for it to do, women will be so moved by what they see on the monitor that they will change their minds and not abort. If, on the other hand, they proceed, having produced and then disregarded the image of what the law has identified as their unborn child, there is at least the possibility that they will suffer and that this suffering is part and parcel of what mandatory ultrasound is about.

The idea of compulsory disclosure as punishment was once recognized as such by the Supreme Court. In 1986, in *Thornburgh v. American College of Obstetrics and Gynecology*, the Court considered a Pennsylvania law that required abortion patients to receive medical sketches of fetal development at two-week intervals starting at conception.[70] The Supreme Court struck down the requirement, stating: "The mandated description of fetal characteristics at 2-week intervals, no matter how objective, is plainly . . . not medical information that is always relevant to the woman's decision, and it may serve only to confuse and punish her, and to heighten her anxiety, contrary to accepted medical practice."[71] In 1992, the Court decided in *Planned Parenthood of Pennsylvania v. Casey* that they had gotten it wrong in *Thornburgh*.[72] But what is new is not only the constitutional permissibility of fetal depictions but also their nature. Fetal scans are more than just a high-tech version of medical sketches. From a social perspective, they are more like portraits, and the experience of looking is intended as a forced visual confrontation between a woman and her own son or daughter.

There are several reasons why legislatures might pause before engaging in such tactics. Some have a constitutional flavor: I have argued that, if the right to choose abortion is protected, so, too, must be the deliberative path one takes to reach that protected choice.[73] An analogy with religious freedom may clarify the point. Imagine that before persons could decline to swear on the bible in court, they were required to read a monograph on hellfire or dwell upon Fra Angelico's *Annunciation*. However informative or moving either activity might be, the proposal seems absurd as a precondition to religious exercise. The path to the belief is understood as an integral part of one's faith, not a matter of informed consent. Protecting reproductive choice similarly involves protecting a woman's control over the processes by which her decision is reached.

Here, it may be useful to consider—with great care and cabined applicability—an analogy with the mechanisms by which torture operates. David Sussman has suggested that torture is morally wrong not only because of the pain inflicted but also because of the use of the body to turn the victim against himself: "Torture forces its victim into the position of colluding against himself through his own affects and emotion."[74] Sussman argues that, "[t]hrough the combination of captivity, restraint, and pain, the physical and social bases of rational agency are actively turned against such agency itself."[75] To be sure, mandatory ultrasound does not involve physical pain, captivity, or (a great) degree of restraint. It does, however, seek to turn the bases of rational agency. The fetal image is meant to overwhelm the woman's decision to abort by triggering something like a primitive maternal instinct so that the woman will change her mind.

But "changing her mind" does not quite capture the process by which the ultrasound requirement is intended to work. It is less an appeal to reason than an attempt to overpower it.[76] In other legal settings, the power of fetal imagery has been recognized and its use restricted. Courts have excluded evidence of photos of dead fetuses in criminal and in tort cases as being prejudicial and inflammatory, and not all excluded photos have been gory ones.[77] A Texas appellate court upheld the exclusion of an eight-by-ten-inch color picture of the murder victim and her posthumously extracted unborn child lying together in a casket. The court stated:

> The unborn child in the photograph appears tiny, innocent, and vulnerable. Society's natural inclination is to protect the innocent and the vulnerable. The contents of the photograph ha[ve] an emotional impact that suggests the jury's decision be made on an emotional basis and not on the basis of the other relevant evidence introduced at trial.[78]

This is the very impact that mandatory ultrasound seeks to produce in pregnant women, who, we might remember, are not on trial but are simply citizens exercising a constitutional right.

Missing Angel Acts

I turn now to legislation providing for the issuance of birth certificates for stillborn infants, that is, infants who reach the point of viability in pregnancy but who die in utero or during the birth process and are therefore born dead. Stillborn birth certificates are not issued automatically but only upon a parent's application, and they are issued in addition to a fetal death certificate, which remains compulsory. Since the first Missing Angel act was enacted, in Arizona, in 2001, thirty-one more states have passed similar legislation, and bills are presently pending in two more.[79] The legislation results from the steadfast efforts of grieving parents who, in state after state, have testified with heartfelt passion that a fetal *death* certificate fails to capture the nature of their experience and is an inaccurate, indeed, offensive bureaucratic response to their suffering. As mother after mother has stated, "I just want to acknowledge that Emma [or Cheyanne or Alyssa or Hunter or Brady] existed."[80]

Stillborn birth certificates are a new move in the law of vital statistics. Historically, stillborn deaths were not recorded at all. Because a stillborn infant was not a legal person for purposes of descent, it was of little interest in the official record.[81] Only during the late nineteenth century did public health officials urge the registration of stillborn deaths on the ground that such data were necessary to understand and prevent maternal and infant mortality. Their campaign eventually succeeded, and, by the mid-twentieth century, stillborn death registration had become compulsory.[82]

Missing Angel acts represent a quite different demand on the law's authority. The demand for action here comes directly from constituents who are not concerned with data collection. Rather, they are parents who have lost a *child*. This relational characterization reflects new understandings of prenatal life. Stillbirth in modern societies is no longer "intrauterine demise" or "fetal wastage," as described in the medical literature. The extension of bereavement practices to stillbirth now seems natural: the stillborn baby was already a member of the family; he was known to his relatives who had seen and displayed his ultrasound picture, given him a name, bought him things. The transformation of stillborn infants into accepted subjects of private mourning led to the demand that they also count in the official record, not merely for statistical purposes but as beings worthy of recognition through that traditional marker of arrival—the birth certificate.

The stillborn birth certificate movement developed under the leadership of Joanne Cacciatore, an Arizona mother who started a local support group, Mothers in Sympathy and Support (M.I.S.S.), following the devastating stillbirth of her daughter in 1993.[83] Told that she couldn't get a birth certificate because she "hadn't had a baby; she had had a fetus," Cacciatore organized a successful grassroots campaign to change Arizona law regarding stillbirth documentation.[84] While M.I.S.S. continues to provide emotional support for parents, it has also developed a sophisticated legislative branch to assist parents in other states to lobby for Missing Angel acts. The M.I.S.S. Foundation provides media packs, suggestions for "meeting with your legislators," sample letters and testimony, talking points to use with local legislators, and tips on how to move a bill through to passage.[85]

And, across the nation, Missing Angel legislation has received overwhelming support across party lines. This is not surprising. The essential message is simple and draws upon the elements of classical rhetoric mentioned earlier, though here the persuasion is directed not from one legislator to another but from constituents to their elected representatives. Their argument combines the authority of parental pain (*ethos*), the logic of their claim that the baby was *born*, even if dead (*logos*), and testaments of their suffering (*pathos*). A California state senator, Abel Maldonado, sums up the result: "I wish you could've sat in on some of the meetings we had with these women. When they bring out their albums of pictures, with their hands holding their baby's tiny hand—my Lord. It's just hard."[86] Maldonado stated that the certificate is "a hug from California to grieving mothers."[87]

Should state legislatures be giving their citizens hugs? In raising the question, I am deeply mindful of the fact that Missing Angel acts provide solace to grieving parents. As Elizabeth McCracken explains in her generous memoir of stillbirth, "A still born child is really only ever his death. He didn't live: that's how he's defined. Once he fades from memory, there's little evidence at all, nothing . . . [to] be handed down through the family." [88] Like the few other tangible mementos that might exist—a snippet of hair, an ultrasound scan—the certificate provides parents with evidence of their child's existence.[89] One mother put it simply: "To everyone else it's a piece of paper, but to us it's gold."[90]

No doubt hospitals themselves could make up commemorative certificates for parents, just as they provide memory boxes and help parents arrange for postmortem photographs. But it is not simply the certificate's physicality that makes the paper precious. It is its official nature. In contrast to live births, where the issuance of a birth certificate itself is not particularly celebratory, in a stillbirth the documentation may be the *only* connection between the state and the child that is available to parents. It signifies that the child's existence is a matter not only of familial memory but of the *public* record, and it acknowledges the parents as parents. As Cacciatore stated, it is "dignity and validation. It's the same reason why [people] want things like marriage licenses and baptismal certificates."[91]

Yet, accepting that Missing Angel acts benefit grieving parents may not tell us quite enough. Whatever the merits of the legislation, there is also something unsettling upon first hearing of birth certificates for stillborn children, and it is surely worth investigating the origins of that instinctive unease. Again, I acknowledge that such investigation in the circumstances of stillbirth may sound like cold indifference to suffering. Why not just accept Missing Angel acts as a perhaps peculiar but essentially harmless and possibly beneficial use of law? But it is precisely the use of *law* to soothe parental distress that should concern us. A birth certificate is an official document that carries the imprimatur of the state. Accepting that this may make the certificates especially valuable to parents, it is also important for all of us to understand what is being certified in the name of the larger community and at least to consider what the implications of this empathic use of legislation may be.

The legislation raises a number of concerns. There are questions about demographic integrity and about what I have called "compulsory reproductive mourning," the idea that Missing Angel acts may take on a prescriptive quality about what counts as proper mourning in cases of prenatal death.[92] But I want here to focus on two problems more directly connected to emotion and law making. The first concerns the therapeutic use of law, or what is sometimes called therapeutic jurisprudence; the second questions whether there may be costs to Missing Angel acts, paid by others than stillbirth parents.

The concept of therapeutic jurisprudence first arose in the context of civil commitment hearings in the 1970s, when it was argued that the respectful treatment of the mentally ill not only was a matter of procedural fairness but had therapeutic value, as well.[93] It has since expanded to include the general proposition that "law should value mental health . . . and when consistent with other values, should attempt to bring about healing and wellness."[94] The movement for stillborn birth certificates is similarly premised on the proposition that law has healing potential by providing parents with a form of administrative solace, the "hug from California."

Are there other instances where legislatures have responded to demands that legislation attend to the emotional needs of the polity? One example is victim-impact evidence in capital murder trials, where family members testify in court with anguished specificity about the magnitude of their loss. In 1991, the Supreme Court held that victim-impact evidence, even before sentencing, was not prejudicial but, rather, could help the jury assess the defendant's moral culpability.[95] Victims'-rights groups have argued that addressing the court is necessary for them to achieve "closure."[96] But, as Susan Bandes has explained, the term "closure" is not an accepted psychological concept and means different things to different people.[97] *Some* family members may feel better if they are able to tell the defendant to his face what the personal costs of the crime have been for them. Yet, because of the inherent complexity of the category of "emotional needs," legislators should proceed cautiously when facilitating the resolution of such needs. As Bandes has argued in the case of victim-impact evidence, it is important at least to try to "untangle what one's religion might urge, from what psychiatry might try to achieve, from what politics might dictate, and all of those from what the law can, should, or even attempt to accomplish."[98]

Should similar untangling be considered in the compelling circumstances of stillbirth? That is, should there be constraints on the law's compassionate instincts even when lawmakers are pressed by grieving parents? One issue concerns the *scope* of compassion. At present, stillborn birth certificate legislation is limited only to stillbirths (fetal death *after* twenty weeks). But some women experience grief following a miscarriage (pregnancy loss *before* twenty weeks), and some of them participate in mourning rituals similar to those that accompany stillbirth: naming the child, cherishing its possessions, holding a service. If responses to miscarriage do not differ qualitatively from responses to stillbirth, should birth certificates be issued here, too? Indeed, some couples undergoing in vitro fertilization now conduct "disposal ceremonies" when thawing and discarding unused frozen embryos. Should the law recognize or in some way certify the existence of these earlier forms of embryonic life?

Here we might consider the difference between private and public mourning or the difference between rights and rites. There can be no objection to how parents choose to commemorate the loss of a child, a fetus, or an embryo as a matter of *private* ritual or practice. It is the demand that the *law* participate in these practices that causes uneasiness, in part because at that point an important line has been crossed regarding official complicity with private, often spiritual, desires and needs. We see this in the simple matter of vocabulary: what are angels doing in the title of public legislation? Certainly one understands the comfort that angel imagery may provide to grieving parents: the consolation of heaven and the promise of eventual reunion. Yet, states might pause before inscribing angels in law under a constitutional structure that separates civic from religious sentiment.[99]

There is also the question of the law's competence to provide solace in these circumstances. While Missing Angel acts are characterized as a legislative response to grief, parents may have other emotional responses, such as shame, anger, or guilt that may in part motivate their desire for stillbirth birth certificates.[100] Legislators must take at face value the characterization of need as presented by constituents, but it may be that law is working above its pay grade in this regard. I don't know what effect the issuance of stillborn birth certificates might have on anger or guilt, but I suspect legislators don't either. My point is not to challenge parental diagnoses but only to suggest that providing succor too readily may be a more complicated proposition than it first appears.

A second concern about Missing Angel acts is the use of the law to affirm what to many seems like the existence of life before birth. Supporters of legal abortion have long been concerned that issuing certificates to children who have never lived may serve, however unintentionally, as yet another legal marker equating fetal life with that of born persons and that this will, sooner or later, play its part in the recriminalization of abortion. The concern is that Missing Angel legislation, however compassionately conceived, deepens cultural familiarity with the idea of prenatal death as the loss of a *child*. This may be especially problematic in a country like the United States, where fetuses and embryos have been legally defined as infants, children, persons, and victims as part of a larger political strategy to overturn *Roe v. Wade*. (As I mentioned earlier, South Dakota now requires doctors to inform patients that an abortion "will terminate the life of a whole, separate, unique, living human being.")[101]

In response to such concerns, Missing Angel legislation was redrafted in a number of states to distinguish stillbirth from abortion and to clarify limitations on the use and legal meaning of the certificates. Missouri, for example, specifies that the certificate "shall not constitute proof of a live birth."[102] To prevent the possibility of "outing" abortion patients, the acts provide that only a parent may request a certificate and only in cases of "unintended fetal demise." These negotiations recognize the proviso embedded in the definition of therapeutic jurisprudence presented earlier — that "law should value mental health and *when consistent with other values* should attempt to bring about healing and wellness." While this is not a legal definition, it serves as a reminder that other values—including other *rights*—may be implicated or threatened by legislation that on first glance looks uncomplicatedly beneficent.

The concern is not that Missing Angel acts are part of some pro-life plot but, rather, that the status they confer—here, "holder of a birth certificate" or, perhaps, "born" —may take on a life of its own once it becomes embedded in law. The M.I.S.S. Foundation adamantly distances itself from the abortion debate and recommends that, when lobbying, supporters not "use any language about 'fetal rights' or other vernacular which may stir up [that] discussion."[103] At the same time, legal status is a common, indeed, an important mechanism for the distribution of value and goods in a society, and over time more substantive benefits may attach to that status. There has already been a gesture toward this kind of expansion in the context of stillbirth. Four Missing Angel states —Arizona, Alaska, Indiana, and Missouri—have gone beyond issuing birth certificates and now provide parents with a dependent tax deduction in the year of the stillborn infant's birth.[104]

4. DISCUSSION

With the examples of mandatory ultrasound and Missing Angel acts hovering over the discussion, I want to conclude with a few observations about the cultivation of emotion as a legislative project. The first poses a general question: how is it that cultivating emotion has come to be so readily accepted as an appropriate end of law making? Why is the prospect of intrusion or the risk of harmful, if unintended, consequences not regarded with greater caution, humility, or concern by lawmakers?

One explanation is that, from the perspective of politics, emotional cultivation is often an easy choice for legislators. When initiated by constituents, it is a crowd pleaser; when uncoupled from costly programmatic apparatus, it is a cheap crowd pleaser. Making people *feel* better, for example, by providing them a birth certificate costs almost nothing (making them feel worse may be somewhat more expensive but in many cases is thought to be worth it). Acknowledging constituent needs also helps politicians to appear responsive and respectful. If voters say they need solace and have found the means to achieve it, why second-guess their determination? The costs of second-guessing may be dear, as Governor Bill Richardson of New Mexico found out a few years back. In 2007, Richardson, then a Democratic candidate for president, vetoed that state's Missing Angel bill on the ground that having two documents for a single event might lead to "confusion and potential fraud" and was "not sound policy."[105] The reaction within the Missing Angel community was immediate. "Veto Stuns Tens of Thousands of Bereaved Parents" announced one online headline.[106] Cacciatore stated that Richardson "had flippantly driven a stake through the heart of the legislation" and would lose the votes of "grieving parents across the country."[107] Richardson's subsequent political decline may not have been the direct result of his veto, but it is clear that there are electoral costs to acting against the declared emotional desires of a well-organized and deeply sympathetic interest group.

Another explanation of why emotion is catching on legislatively may be more atmospheric than political. The United States has become a culture that bathes in emotional outpourings—on confrontational talk shows, on reality television, in statements (teary or dry) from wayward congressmen, senators, and presidents. We have become a confessional culture where feeling things and spilling one's guts are commonplace. It is not only acceptable but expected—almost virtuous—to wear one's heart where it can be seen. (This has not always been the case, as Senator Edmund Muskie's apparently disqualifying "crying speech" in the 1972 Democratic primary reminds us.) In light of our current socialization to high (if not salacious) degrees of emotional display, a legislative imprimatur on the production of emotion is perhaps to be expected.

These expectations already extend into certain areas of law. There is an existing familiarity with emotional display in the context of criminal law. We want wrongdoers to feel shame, and we use public shaming punishments to bring that about.[108] We want convicted criminals to express remorse, and therefore sentencing judges and parole boards listen for the right words to be spoken and the right attitude to be struck.[109] Because the demand for these emotional displays is accepted within the criminal justice system, it may seem natural, or at least nothing out of the ordinary, when emotion is called for in other legal contexts.

One problem with this kind of spillover effect is that it works from the criminal law out. In consequence, punishments (shaming) or procedures (remorse at allocution) that may be acceptable when someone has committed a crime become normalized for cases where no crime has been committed, as when a pregnant woman decides to terminate a pregnancy. And there are challenges to the production of emotion even within the criminal system. The philosopher Jeffrie Murphy has characterized shaming punishments as "coercive exercise[s] in humiliation and degradation

—a kind of smug and mean-spirited vengeance with tendencies to lap into arbitrary cruelty."[110] My concern is that, in the context of mandatory ultrasound, the intentional cultivation of guilt encourages a similar mean-spiritedness to proceed unchecked and largely unrecognized as being punitive (though it is hard not to see it as cruel). While this may not matter to pro-life legislators who don't care what price is paid by women who fail to heed the state's message about the value of fetal life, the rest of us must pay attention. Imposing an emotional tax on lawful behavior (terminating pregnancy) operates as an end run around constitutional constraints on the legislature's authority to punish the behavior as a crime. And the surcharge works because of the ineffable quality of emotion. Mandatory ultrasound statutes are, of course, silent on the subject of guilt or maternal instinct—they purport to be about "information," not affect. But this does not mean that we must pretend that emotions have nothing to do with what is going on. They are the mechanism by which the law is meant to work.

There *are* cases where legislators have put their collective foot down and established limits on law's relation to emotion. Consider an example from the highly regulated realm of marriage, where altruism and kindly feelings are understood to do lots of heavy lifting. Yet, even here, the law does not insist that spouses *love* each other. They may owe each other a legal duty of fidelity or a duty of support, but there is no duty of affection. This is not just an evidentiary problem but recognition of the law's lack of competence to regulate how people feel.

Indeed, on occasion, legislators have taken sentiments entirely off the table. I have in mind the legislative abolition of causes of action for wounded feelings that sometimes accompany the breakup of a romantic relationship. By the mid-twentieth century, once-prolific suits for breach of promise to marry, alienation of affection, and criminal conversation were largely abolished through the enactment of "anti-heartbalm statutes."[111] Concerns about the ability of jurors to assess the wounded feelings of a woman plaintiff (victim or golddigger?) and worries about coercive settlements and excessive verdicts cast permanent doubt on a compensatory regime in the tricky realm of affections.[112]

My argument is not that attention to emotions should be thrown out altogether as a legislative project. We might consider a very different example where compensation for *monumental* wrongs has been taken off the table for a grand social purpose: restoring civil society following apartheid in South Africa. In setting up the Truth and Reconciliation Commission, enormous time and thought went into the consequences for the people as a whole, as well as for individuals, of identifying those who had murdered and tortured on behalf of the state and of then letting them go.[113] As the Constitutional Court stated:

> The result at all levels is a difficult, sensitive, perhaps even agonizing balancing act between the need for justice to victims of past abuse and the need for reconciliation and rapid transition to a new future. . . . [I]t is an exercise of immense difficulty interacting in a vast network of political, emotional, ethical, and logistical concentrations.[114]

It was understood that, as a consequence of the Commission's work, individual victims and their families would have to stifle or absorb profound feelings relating to specific injuries and injustices. Moreover, the country as a whole would have to live with a degree of disquietude: "Every decent human being must feel grave discomfort in living with a consequence which might allow the perpetrators of evil acts to walk the streets of this land with impunity."[115] The point I want to emphasize is that none of this was done speedily, or blithely, or easily. There was massive investigation of what emotions were at stake, which might be forsaken, and how to reckon the emotional costs of doing so against the social gain.

There may well be differences between the legislative cultivation of emotion when the "emotions" of a nation are at stake—we talk of South African reconciliation and of German guilt; Drew Faust characterized the postbellum United States as "The Republic of Suffering"[116]—and when the focus is on individual forgiveness, guilt, or sorrow. In this essay, I have addressed only the latter, and I have suggested that, in such circumstances, legislators should proceed with greater deliberation when putting emotion to use in law. I also recognize that the problems I have described may well apply not only to cases of legislating emotion but also to law making in general: legislators enacting law without doing enough research, without thinking about the real-world costs and consequences, and without considering the interaction between the legislation and other laws or rights. Yet, our interest here has been the particular relation between legislation and emotional cultivation. My argument is that in this realm, when deliberately tinkering with how people feel, there should be some greater accounting and imaginative thought as to what might be put in the balance against the attractions of solace or hope or even what some consider well-deserved retribution.

NOTES

Many thanks to Susan Bandes, Richard Briffault, Abbe Gluck, Robert Ferguson, Jim Fleming, Jane Norton, Peter Strauss and Jeremy Waldron.

1. Terry A. Maroney, "Law and Emotion: A Proposed Taxonomy of an Emerging Field," *Law and Human Behavior* 30 (2006): 119, 131. The other approaches under Maroney's schema include emotion theory, legal doctrines that incorporate emotion (such as the heat of passion defense), theories of law (such as law and economics) and its explicit treatment of emotion, emotional phenomena (such as affective forecasting), and the normative question of how emotions *should* be reflected in law.

2. See Walter Wadlington, "Divorce without Fault without Perjury," *Virginia Law Review* 52 (1966): 32, 33–34; Lawrence M. Friedman, "A Dead Language: Divorce Law and Practice before No-Fault," *Virginia Law Review* 86 (2000): 1497, 1507.

3. See *Governor's Comm'n on the Family, 1966 Report of the California Governor's Commission on the Family* (1966); Herbert Jacob, *Silent Revolution: The Transformation of Divorce Law in the United States* (Chicago: University of Chicago Press, 1988).

4. See, e.g., "Symposium: Family Law and Emotion," *Virginia Journal of Social Policy and Law* 16 (2009): 301. In criminal law, see, e.g., "The New Culpability: Motive, Character, and Emotion in Criminal Law," *Buffalo Criminal Law Review* 6 (2002): 1 (Special Issue).

5. *The Least Examined Branch: The Role of Legislatures in the Constitutional State*, ed. Richard W. Bauman and Tsvi Kahana (Cambridge: Cambridge University Press, 2006).

6. See sources cited in note 4. See also András Sajó, "Emotions in Constitutional Design," *International Journal of Constitutional Law* 8 (2010): 354; Martha Minow, "Institutions and Emotions: Redressing Mass Violence," in *The Passions of Law*, ed. Susan Bandes (New York: New York University Press, 1999), 265. Sajo observes that the social interaction of emotions "become

patterns, and the relatively stable social clusters of these emotional patterns become the facts of social life, taking the form of public sentiments. Moral judgments and moral sentiments lend to public sentiment the emotional power that enables these sentiments to shape constitutions."

7. Jesse J. Prinz, "Constructive Sentimentalism: Legal and Political Implications," in this volume, 3, 13.

8. See, e.g., the entire Scottish Enlightenment.

9. Carol Sanger, "Infant Safe Haven Laws: Legislating in the Culture of Life," *Columbia Law Review* 106 (2006): 753; Carol Sanger, "Seeing and Believing: Mandatory Ultrasound and the Path to a Protected Choice," *UCLA Law Review* 56 (2008): 351; Carol Sanger, "Decisional Dignity: Teenage Abortion, Bypass Hearings, and the Misuse Of Law," *Columbia Journal of Gender and Law* 18 (2009): 409; Carol Sanger, " 'The Birth of Death': Stillborn Birth Certificates and the Problem for Law," *California Law Review* 100 (2012): 269.

10. See generally Jeremy Waldron, *Principles of Legislation*, in Bauman and Kahana, eds., *The Least Examined Branch*, 1.

11. George Tsebelis and Jeannette Money, *Bicameralism* (Cambridge: Cambridge University Press, 1997), 15–16.

12. We are also used to seeing legislators display emotion outside their law-making duties, as when they cheer, hoot, and scowl during the president's annual State of the Union Address.

13. David Garrow, *Liberty and Sexuality: The Right to Privacy and the Making of Roe v. Wade* (Berkeley: University of California Press, 1994), 546.

14. See http://www.senate.gov/artandhistory/history/minute/The_Caning_of_Senator_Charles_Sumner.htm. As noted on another website, "The caning of Senator Sumner signaled the end of an era of compromise . . . in the Senate," http://www.senate.gov/vtour/sumner.htm.

15. See http://www.senate.gov/artandhistory/history/minute/Senate_Fistfight.htm. For a more complete history, see Warren Brennan, "Ready to Rumble: Greatest Fistfights of the U.S. Congress," http://www.associatedcontent.com/article/1161398/ready_to_rumble_greatest_fistfights.html.

16. See, for example, "Brawl in the Nigerian House of Representatives," http://www.youtube.com/watch?v=y1x8e_47hWI&feature=related (2010); "Fight in Russian Duma," http://www.youtube.com/watch?v=mZGaaqH2o6I&feature=related (2007).

17. The shouter, Representative Randy Neugebauer, later explained that "In the heat and emotion of the debate, I exclaimed the phrase 'it's a baby killer' in reference to the agreement reached by the Democratic leadership. I deeply regret that my actions were mistakenly interpreted as a direct reference to Congressman Stupak himself." Michael Sheridan, "Rep. Randy Neugebauer: I Yelled 'Baby Killer' during Rep. Bart

68   CAROL SANGER

Stupak's Speech," *Daily News*, March 22, 2010, http://articles.nydailynews
.com/2010-03-22/news/27059779_1_baby-killer-nrlc-health-care-bill.
    18. Michael Teter, "Acts of Emotion: Analyzing Congressional Involve-
ment in the Federal Rules of Evidence," *Catholic University Law Review* 58
(2008–2009): 153.
    19. See Patrick Devlin, *The Enforcement of Morals* (Oxford: Oxford Uni-
versity Press, 1970), 17; William Ian Miller, *The Anatomy of Disgust* (Cambridge, MA: Harvard University Press, 1998).
    20. Compare, for example, Dan M. Kahan, "The Anatomy of Disgust
in Criminal Law," *Michigan Law Review* 96 (1998): 1621, with Martha Nussbaum, "'Secret Sewers of Vice': Disgust, Bodies, and the Law," in Bandes,
ed., *The Passions of Law*, 19.
    21. Prinz, "Constructive Sentimentalism," 13.
    22. Cohen observed that "[s]ocieties appear to be subject, every now
and then, to periods of moral panic" during which "[a] condition, episode,
person or group of persons [a "folk devil"] emerges to become defined as
a threat to societal values and interests; its nature is presented in a styl-
ized and stereotypical fashion by the mass media; the moral barricades are
manned by editors, bishops, politicians and other right-thinking people;
socially accredited experts pronounce their diagnoses and solutions; ways
of coping are evolved or . . . resorted to; the condition then disappears,
submerges or deteriorates and becomes more visible." Stanley Cohen, *Folk
Devils and Moral Panics* (London: Rutledge, 3d ed. 2002), 1.
    23. On child abuse, see Kristen M. Zgoba, "Spin Doctors and Moral
Crusaders: The Moral Panic behind Child Safety Legislation," *Criminal
Justice Studies* 17 (2004): 385–404; Susan Bandes, "The Lessons of Captur-
ing the Friedmans: Moral Panic, Institutional Denial and Due Process,"
Journal of Law, Culture and Humanities 3 (2007): 293. On zero-tolerance
legislation, see Ronald Burns and Charles Crawford, "School Shootings,
the Media, and Public Fear: Ingredients for a Moral Panic," *Crime, Law and
Social Change* 32 (1999): 147, 162–163; see also Gun-Free School Zones Act
of 1990, 18 U.S.C. § 922 (requiring schools in states receiving federal education funding to expel for at least one year students who carry weapons)
(declared unconstitutional in *United States v. Lopez*, 514 U.S. 549 (1995)).
    24. See Cass Sunstein, "On the Expressive Function of Law," *University
of Pennsylvania Law Review* 144 (1996): 2021, 2205.
    25. See Sanger, "Decisional Dignity."
    26. As one Florida judge told a pregnant petitioner after denying her
petition, "Miss, I know this seems like the most terrible thing in the world.
And, I will tell you, as I indicated, a father of two daughters. . . . And, I have
always told my daughters, whatever it is, you can discuss it with me. I'm not
telling you that you can or cannot terminate that pregnancy. I just think,

in your best interest, where you are going to have to go through with it with your parents, it would be best for you to notify your parents. And, I am sure they love you." *In re Doe*, 973 So. 2d 548, 565 (Fla. Ct. App. 2008). The denial of the petition was upheld on appeal. Ibid.

27. Kent Roach, "The Uses and Audiences of Preambles in Legislation," *McGill Law Journal* 47 (2001): 129, 140–141 (discussing the purpose of preambles as a form of persuasion in Plato's *The Laws*). See also Tadas Klimas and Jurate Vaiciukaite, "The Law of Recitals in European Community Legislation," *ILSA Journal of International and Comparative Law* 15 (2008): 61.

28. Roach, "The Uses and Audiences of Preambles in Legislation," 133.

29. Jacob E. Gersen and Eric A. Posner, "Soft Law: Lessons from Congressional Practice," *Stanford Law Review* 61 (2008): 573, 579. The authors define "soft law" as rules "issued by a lawmaking authority that [do] not comply with constitutional and other formalities or understandings that are necessary for the rule to be legally binding."

30. Ibid., 578.

31. Ibid.

32. Kenneth Burke, *The Rhetoric of Motives* (Berkeley: University of California Press, 1969); see also Gerald Wetlaufer, "Rhetoric and Its Denial in Legal Discourse," *Virginia Law Review* 76 (1990): 1545.

33. See Jonathan S. Morris, "Reexamining the Politics of Talk: Partisan Rhetoric in the 104th House," *Legislative Studies Quarterly* 26 (2001): 101.

34. See Daniel M. Filler, "Making the Case for Megan's Law: A Study in Legislative Rhetoric," *Indiana Law Journal* 76 (2001): 315; Samuel H. Pillsbury, "A Problem in Emotive Due Process: California's Three Strikes Law," *Buffalo Criminal Law Review* 6 (2002): 483; see also Chai R. Feldblum, "The Moral Rhetoric of Legislation," *New York University Law Review* 72 (1997): 992 (on anti-gay employment discrimination laws). Political scientists have also paid theoretical attention to the relation between rhetoric and deliberative democracy. See Bernard Yack, "Rhetoric and Public Reasoning: An Aristotelian Understanding of Political Deliberation," *Political Theory* 34 (2006): 417.

35. Elizabeth F. Emens, "The Sympathetic Discriminator: Mental Illness, Hedonic Costs, and the ADA," *Georgetown Law Journal* 93 (2006): 399 (considering the consequences of emotional contagion for the application of employment discrimination law).

36. Ibid., 431–435. My summary is of course greatly simplified.

37. James Madison, Alexander Hamilton, and John Jay, *The Federalist*, No. 55, at 342 (James Madison), in *The Federalist*, ed. Clinton Rossiter (New York: New American Library, 1961).

38. Of course, legislators often find creative ways around such limita-

tions. In response to public outcry following school shootings like Columbine, state legislators responded to calls for harsher punishments by introducing laws that allow minors to stand trial as adults so that they may receive sentences formerly thought suitable only for actual adults. Gregory A. Loken and David Rosettenstein, "The Juvenile Justice Counter-Reformation: Children and Adolescents as Adult Criminals," *Quinnipiac Law Review* 18 (1999): 351.

39. Amy Gutmann, "Foreword: Legislatures in the Constitutional State," in Bauman and Kahana, eds., *The Least Examined Branch*, x. Not only is private legislation likely to get things wrong on the merits—the focus is no longer on the general welfare but on a particular case—but legislation that defies general jurisdictions also "strains institutional legitimacy" and, Gutmann argues, should properly be understood as "a form of institutional corruption." Ibid., xiii. See also D. Don Welch, "Ruling with the Heart: Emotion-Based Public Policy," *Southern California Interdisciplinary Law Journal* 6 (1997): 55.

40. The problems are explored in Jonathan Simon, "Megan's Law: Crime and Democracy in Late Modern America," *Law and Social Inquiry* 25 (2000): 1111, 1139–1142.

41. See generally Samuel C. Patterson and Anthony Mughan, "Senates and the Theory of Bicameralism," in *Senates: Bicameralism in the Contemporary World*, ed. Samuel C. Patterson and Anthony Mughan (Columbus: Ohio State University Press, 1999), 1–3.

42. James Madison, *The Debates in the Federal Convention of 1787 Which Framed the Constitution of the United of America*, ed. Gaillard Hunt and James Brown Scott (New York: Oxford University Press, 1920), 167.

43. Alexander Hamilton, James Madison, and John Jay, *The Federalist*, No. 62, at 379 (James Madison).

44. Patterson and Mughan, "Senates and the Theory of Bicameralism," 15 (quoting James Sundquist, *Constitutional Reform and Effective Government* [Washington, D.C.: Brookings Institution Press, 1992]).

45. See Sanger, "Infant Safe Haven Laws," 753.

46. *Scarborough Country* (MSNBC television broadcast August 25, 2003), LEXIS Transcript No. 082500cb.471, at *5–*6.

47. Illinois Senate, Senate Transcript, S. 92-23, Reg. Sess., 46–48 (2001), http://www.ilga.gov/senate/transcripts/strans92/pdf/ST040401.pdf.

48. Mark Reynolds, "Mother's Crisis Renews Call for Legislation," *Providence Journal*, November 5, 2003.

49. Kathy Abrams and Hila Keren, "Law in the Cultivation of Hope," *California Law Review* 95 (2007): 319, 321. The authors identify their project as falling within "a second generation of scholarship on law and emotion" because it looks not at the use of law to affect *behaviour* but its use to

facilitate the subject's emotional state, particularly with regard to positive emotions. Ibid., 320.

50. Ibid., 321. On forgiveness, see Solangel Maldonado, "Cultivating Forgiveness: Reducing Hostility and Conflict after Divorce," *Wake Forest Law Review* 43 (2008): 441.

51. Abrams and Keren, "Law in the Cultivation of Hope," 321. See generally Valerie Braithwaite, *Annals of the American Academy of Political and Social Science* 592 (2004): 152–165 (Special Issue: "Hope, Power, and Governance").

52. Abrams and Keren, "Law in the Cultivation of Hope," 362. A current example might be the "Dream Act" ("The Development, Relief and Education for Alien Minors"), which but for its defeat in the Senate in 2010 would have granted eventual legal immigration status to undocumented aliens of proven good character who came to the United States as children.

53. Abrams and Keren, "Law in the Cultivation of Hope," 361.

54. My concern is that hope alone (or happiness or confidence or some other positive emotion) may become the *point* of legislation without the substantive measures that would justify the production of a hopeful feeling in those who have actually, not aspirationally, benefited. Hope alone is the danger. As the beleaguered headmaster played by John Cleese in the movie *Clockwise* said, when near the end of his rope: "It's not the despair. . . . I can take the despair. It's the hope I can't stand."

55. See, for example, Alabama's Woman's Right to Know Act, Ala. Code § 26-23A-4 (LexisNexis Supp. 2007).

56. The acts are also sometimes named for the baby whose parents lobbied for passage, such as Florida's "Katherine's Law." See "Katherine's Law" at http://www.doh.state.fl.us/planning_eval/vital_statistics/Birth_Stillbirth.html.

57. See Guttmacher Institute, *State Policies in Brief: Requirements for Ultrasound* (as of June 1, 2011), http://www.guttmacher.org/statecenter/spibs/spib_RFU.pdf. Ten other states require that if a physician performs an ultrasound on a patient in connection with an abortion for purely medical reasons, the patient must be offered the opportunity to view the scan. Ibid.

58. Woman's Right to Know Act, Ala. Code §26-23A-4 (LexisNexis Supp. 2007).

59. Ibid., § 26-23A-2.

60. See Reva B. Siegel, "The Right's Reasons: Constitutional Conflict and the Spread of the Woman-Protective Antiabortion Argument," *Duke Law Journal* 57 (2008): 1641.

61. See Wis. Stat. Ann. § 253.10(3) (g) (West Supp. 2007).

62. *S.D.C.L.* §32-23A-10.1, Section 7, 2005. See Zita Lazzarini, "South Dakota's Abortion Script—Threatening the Physician-Patient Relationship," *New England Journal of Medicine* 359 (2008): 2189. For two constitutional analyses, see Caroline Mala Corbin, "The First Amendment Right against Compelled Listening," *Boston University Law Review* 89 (2009): 939 (focusing on the patient's obligation to listen), and Robert Post, "Informed Consent to Abortion: A First Amendment Analysis of Compelled Physician Speech," *University of Illinois Law Review* 2007 (2007): 939 (focusing on the physician's obligation to speak).

63. *Acuna v. Turkish,* 930 A.2d 416, 418 (N.J. 2007). In that case, a mother of two sued her abortion doctor for malpractice on the grounds that he had failed to tell her "the scientific and medical fact" that her six- to eight-week-old embryo was a complete, separate, unique and irreplaceable human being, that an abortion would result in "killing an existing human being," and that the abortion procedure was "intended to kill [a] family member." The New Jersey Supreme Court found there was "no consensus in the medical community or society" that these statements were "medical information that a reasonably prudent patient would find material." Ibid., 425–427.

64. Faye D. Ginsburg, *Contested Lives: The Abortion Debate in an American Community* (Berkeley: University of California Press, 1989), 104.

65. Susan Sontag, *On Photography* (New York: Farrar, Straus and Giroux, 1977), 153–154.

66. Sallie Han, "Seeing Like a Family: Fetal Ultrasound Images and Imaginings of Kin," in *Imagining the Fetus: The Unborn in Myth, Religion and Culture,* ed. Vanessa R. Sasson and Jane Marie Law (Oxford: Oxford University Press, 2009).

67. See Neela Banerjee, "Church Groups Turn to Sonogram to Turn Women from Abortions," *New York Times,* February 2, 2005, A1. See also Barbara Duden, *Disembodying Women: Perspectives on Pregnancy and the Unborn* (Cambridge, MA: Harvard University Press, 1991).

68. See Margarete Sandelowski and Linda Corson Jones, "'Healing Fictions': Stories of Choosing in the Aftermath of the Detection of Fetal Anomalies," *Social Science Medicine* 42 (1996): 353, 356.

69. See generally Barbara Katz Rothman, *The Tentative Pregnancy* (New York: W. W. Norton, 1987).

70. 476 U.S. 747 (1986).

71. Ibid., 762.

72. *Planned Parenthood Se. Pa. v. Casey,* 505 U.S. 833, 882 (1992) (overruling *Thornburgh*).

73. The discussion here draws from Sanger, "Seeing and Believing," 387–391.

74. David Sussman, "What's Wrong with Torture," *Philosophy and Public Affairs* 33 (2005): 1, 4.

75. Ibid., 33.

76. Jeremy Blumenthal has suggested that this process has a constitutional dimension and may itself create an undue burden under *Casey*. See Jeremy A. Blumenthal, "Abortion, Persuasion, and Emotion: Implications of Social Science Research on Emotion for Reading *Casey*," *Washington Law Review* 83 (2008): 1.

77. See *Steele v. Atlanta Maternal-Fetal Med.*, P.C., 610 S.E.2d 546, 553 (Ga. Ct. App. 2005) (upholding the trial court's exclusion of photographs of dead fetuses because their probative value was "substantially outweighed by the danger of unfair prejudice"); *Erazo v. State*, 167 S.W.3d 889 (Tex. Ct. App. 2005) (holding that admission of a fetal photograph was likely to appeal to the jury's emotions and was therefore harmful error).

78. *Reese v. State*, 33 S.W.3d 238, 240–241 (Tex. Crim. App. 2000).

79. For a complete list, visit http://www.missingangelsbill.org/index.php?option=com_content&view=article&id=76&Itemid=61.

80. Chana Joffe-Walt, "Parents of Stillborn Babies Push for Recognition," http://www.npr.org/templates/story/story.php?storyId=7407248.

81. See generally Edward Higgs, "A Cuckoo in the Nest? The Origins of Civil Registration and State Medical Statistics in England and Wales," *Continuity and Change* 11 (1996): 115–134. The primary exception to law's disinterest was in criminal prosecutions for infanticide where mothers would argue the child has been stillborn, not murdered. See, for example, Elna C. Green, "Infanticide and Infant Abandonment in the New South: Richmond, Virginia, 1865–1915," *Journal of Family History* 24 (1999): 187–210.

82. S. Shapiro, "Development of Birth Registration and Birth Statistics in the United States," *Population Studies* 4 (1950): 86.

83. See *M.I.S.S. Foundation*, http://www.missingangelsbill.org/.

84. Tamar Lewin, "Out of Grief Grows Desire for Birth Certificates for Stillborn Babies," *New York Times*, May 22, 2007, at A16, http://query.nytimes.com/gst/fullpage.html?res=9E07E0DC1F31F931A15756C0A9619C8B63. In addition to being the chief executive officer of the M.I.S.S. Foundation, Cacciatore (now Cacciatore-Gerard) is now an assistant professor of social work at Arizona State University. Her personal bereavement blog is found at http://drjoanne.blogspot.com/.

85. Anita Creamer, "Honoring a Life and Loss," *Sacramento Bee*, April 4, 2007, http://babylossdirectory.blogspot.com/2007_04_01_archive.html.

86. Michael Gardner, "Legislation on Stillbirths Entangled in Abortion Fight," June 4, 2007, http://www.missingangelsbill.org/index.php?option=com_content&view=article&id=65%3Alegislation-on-stillbirths-entangled-in-abortion-fight&catid=1&Itemid=60.

87. See also "M.I.S.S. Foundation, Meeting with Legislators," http://
www.missingangelsbill.org/index.php?option=com_content&view=article
&id=50&Itemid=55 ("We are the voices of the children who cannot speak
for themselves. . . . We will not stop until justice is done.") (quoting Joanne
Cacciatore).

88. Elizabeth McCracken, *An Exact Replica of a Figment of My Imagination*
(New York: Little, Brown, 2008).

89. See Linda Layne, "He Was a Real Baby with Baby Things," *Journal of
Material Culture* 5 (2000): 321, 322.

90. Anya Sosteck, "A Precious Piece of Paper," *Pittsburgh Post-Gazette*,
March 2, 2010.

91. Lewin, "Out of Grief Grows Desire for Birth Certificates for Stillborn Babies."

92. See generally, Sanger, " 'The Birth of Death.' "

93. See generally David B. Wexler and Bruce J. Winnick, *Essays in Therapeutic Jurisprudence* (Durham, NC: Carolina Academic Press, 1991).

94. David Wexler, "International Network on Therapeutic Jurisprudence," at http://www.law.arizona.edu/depts/upr-intj/.

95. *Payne v. Tennessee*, 501 U.S. 808 (1991).

96. Nancy Berns, "Contesting the Victim Card: Closure Discourse
and Emotion in Death Penalty Rhetoric," *Sociological Quarterly* 50 (2009):
383–406.

97. Susan Bandes, "Victims, 'Closure,' and the Sociology of Emotion,"
Law and Contemporary Problems 72 (2009): 1.

98. Susan Bandes, "When Victims Seek Closure: Forgiveness, Vengeance and the Role of Government," *Fordham Urban Law Journal* 27
(2000): 1599, 1601–1602.

99. This is not to say that Missing Angel acts are necessarily unconstitutional. Courts might decide that their primary purpose is not to advance
religion but to provide solace. Angels might also be looked at as convey-
ing an essentially secular message. See, e.g., *Van Orden v. Perry*, 545 U.S.
677 (2005) (Ten Commandments merely acknowledge the role of religion
in nation's heritage). For excellent discussion, see Caroline Mala Corbin,
"Ceremonial Deism and the Reasonable Religious Outsider," *UCLA Law
Review* 57 (2010): 1545.

100. See Linda Layne, " 'True Gifts from God': Paradoxes of Motherhood, Sacrifice, and Enrichment," in Layne, *Motherhood Lost: A Feminist
Account of Pregnancy Loss in America* (New York: Routledge, 2003), 146 (discussing guilt and self-blame by stillbirth mothers).

101. S.D.C.L. §32-23A-10.1, Section 7, 2005; see also *Planned Parenthood
v. Rounds*, 530 F.3d 724 (8th Cir. 2008).

102. MO SB 799 §193.255, 2004.

103. See http://www.missingangelsbill.org/index.php?option=com_content&view=article&id=46&Itemid=53.

104. Missing Angels Bill (MAB) Legislation, State Chart, http://www.missingangelsbill.org/index.php?option=com_content&view=article&id=76&Itemid=61. In addition, the City Council of Wasilla, Alaska, recently passed a resolution approving a one-time tax deduction for a state stillborn.

105. New Mexico Senate Executive Message No. 80, 2007.

106. M.I.S.S. Foundation Press Release, 2007.

107. "New Mexico Governor Bill Richardson Stuns Tens of Thousands of Bereaved Parents and Vetoes the Missing Angels Bill," http://www.danielsstar.org/040707%20NM%20press%20release.html. The failure of officials to acknowledge grief may be particularly upsetting to mourners, as the British royal family learned following the death of Princess Diana; recall the famous *Sun* headline: "WHERE IS OUR QUEEN? WHERE IS HER FLAG?" Michael Streeter, "The Queen Bows to Her Subjects," *The Independent*, September 5, 1997, http://www.independent.co.uk/news/the-queen-bows-to-her-subjects-1237450.html.

108. Toni M. Massaro, "Shame, Culture, and American Criminal Law," *Michigan Law Review* 89 (1990): 1880, 1943.

109. See generally Theodore Eisenberg, Steven P. Garvey, and Martin T. Wells, "But Was He Sorry? The Role of Remorse in Capital Sentencing," *Cornell Law Review* 83 (1997–1998): 1599. The requirement of remorse is, of course, extraordinarily problematic when the defendant is not guilty or when, perhaps for developmental reasons, he is not good at expressing emotion. See Lisa F. Orenstein, "Sentencing Leniency May Be Denied to Criminal Offenders Who Fail to Express Remorse at Allocution," *Maryland Law Review* 56 (1997): 780; Martha Grace Duncan, "'So Young and So Untender': Remorseless Children and the Expectation of Law," *Columbia Law Review* 102 (2002): 1469.

110. Jeffrie G. Murphy, "Shame Creeps through Guilt and Feels like Retribution," *Law and Philosophy* 18 (1999): 327, 338.

111. See Nathan P. Feinsinger, "Legislative Attack on 'Heart Balm,'" *Michigan Law Review* 33 (1935): 979, 986–996; see also Michael Grossberg, *Governing the Hearth: Law and the Family in Nineteenth-Century America* (Chapel Hill: University of North Carolina Press, 1985), 33–38; and Saskia Lettamaier, *Broken Promises: The Action for Breach of Promise of Marriage and the Feminine Ideal, 1800–1940* (Oxford: Oxford University Press, 2010).

112. Feinsinger, "Legislative Attack on 'Heart Balm,'" 998.

113. See Alex Boraine, *A Country Unmasked: Inside South Africa's Truth and Reconciliation Commission* (Oxford: Oxford University Press, 2001).

114. *Azanian Peoples Organization (AZAPO) v. President of the Republic of South Africa* (CCT17/96) [1996] ZACC 16; 1996 (8) BCLR 1015 [CC]; 1996 (4) SA 672 [CC] (25 July 1996).

115. Ibid.

116. See Drew Gilpin Faust, *This Republic of Suffering: Death and the American Civil War* (New York: Knopf, 2008).

4

THE NATURE AND ETHICS OF VENGEFUL ANGER

CHARLES L. GRISWOLD

> For this is your truth: you are too *pure* for the filth of the words: revenge, punishment, reward, retribution.
>
> —Nietzsche, *Thus Spoke Zarathustra*[1]

Vengeful anger is the stuff of countless works of literature and art both great and small. Homer's *Iliad*, one of the founding works of Western literature, begins with a particular word for anger (*mênis*) and is in some sense about anger and its epic consequences.[2] Myriad representations of vengefulness also pervade contemporary film, as we see in movies such as Quentin Tarantino's *Kill Bill* series and in numerous Westerns. It is remarkable how often we encounter the phenomenon in life as well. Reading the news reports of Bernard Madoff's thievery, for example, one is struck by the character and intensity of the anger among those he wronged. Elie Wiesel, whose life savings—along with the resources of his philanthropic foundation—were devastated by Madoff's fraud, is quoted as stating that the punishment he wishes for Madoff is that he spend at least five years in a solitary cell that is furnished with a screen on which pictures of his victims are shown one after the other, day and night, while a voice forces his attention to the injury he did to each individual. He is also reported as saying that he cannot forgive Madoff. The judicial sentence imposed on Madoff —150 years of incarceration—might itself express a form of retributive anger.[3] We are also familiar with the phenomenon and its consequences in relatively petty and unimportant situations —academic politics, for example—as well as in graver contexts, such as broken partnerships where the welfare of children and the division of property are at stake. Famously and lamentably, fury is writ large in war and violent conflict. Such examples capture something of the emotion that I shall be discussing here and suggest that vengeful anger broadly conceived is as universal as any emotion is capable of being. It would certainly be hard to find an adult who is not well acquainted with it from personal experience.

Our intuitions about the virtues and vices of vengeful anger are conflicted. Vengefulness is felt to be vindicating on the one hand and vindictive on the other. A long tradition holds that vengeful anger is not an emotion that a virtuous person would feel, in part because pleasure in the pain of another is one of its elements.[4] That vengeful anger and possibly the taking of revenge are accompanied by pleasure is well established, though there is room for debate about what the pleasure is pleasure in, an issue to which I shall return. Others have argued along consequentialist lines that the desire for revenge is destructive of justice and so is a discreditable motive from which to act. It easily grows into blood feuds, vigilantism, and an unprincipled license to violence. The famous propensity of such anger to consume the soul of its owner and to grow out of all proportion to its causes also supports the intuition that we are better off without it. Vengeful anger does not seem to answer well or at all to the demands of impartiality, proportionality, or norms of fairness. In this light, it is not surprising that the proleptically and comprehensively forgiving attitude of the Amish has been widely praised; their almost heroic stilling of vengeful anger and certainly of revenge in response to the coldblooded murder of a number of their children several years ago commands admiration.[5]

On the other hand, we readily sympathize with, say, the fury of Madoff's victims. Indeed, we are tempted to judge that a failure to feel that fury signals some defect of character—something like a failure in one's ability to stand up for oneself, a failure of self-esteem. Aristotle seems to be expressing just this intuition when, in the *Nicomachean Ethics*, he characterizes as "slavish" (*andrapodôdes*)—a socially loaded term, to be sure—the disposition not to react with anger when one is treated contemptuously and as of no account (literally, as "bespattered with mud," *propêlakizomenon*; 1126a7–8).[6] From his standpoint, the reaction of the Amish to the murder of their children very likely qualifies as "slavish." The reaction of the Amish did generate critical commentary. Your children are murdered; ought you not experience anger in consequence?[7] Then there are consequentialist arguments, as well, that can be adduced in favor of vengeful anger, as suggested by Bishop Joseph Butler.[8] And, of course, in some cultures, the failure to feel anger in response to being wronged and especially the failure to express and act on it are heavily penalized.[9]

Is it ethical to feel such a sentiment or emotion? This is one question I would like to pursue here. I propose to reflect on whether this sentiment or emotion is *ever* justified, by which I shall mean, such as a virtuous person would feel or such as it is virtuous to feel.[10] I am asking not whether it is *always* justified (clearly, it is not) but whether the emotion is ever worth our endorsement and, if so, under what conditions. Of course, the answer is tied to an understanding of the character of this particular emotion, and that is the second question on which I shall focus. As the description of the emotion must precede reflection on its justifiability, I begin with the descriptive or phenomenological issue in section 1.

In section 2, I explore the relation between self-esteem and anger, since this serves as a bridge between the descriptive and definitional issues on the one hand and the normative ones on the other. I further develop the debate about the virtues and vices of vengeful anger in section 3 by examining, briefly and selectively, arguments presented by Aristotle (in the *Nicomachean Ethics* and the *Rhetoric*) and by Seneca (in *De Ira*). My goal in this section of the essay is to articulate several of the key issues involved in the debate about the praiseworthiness of vengeful anger, and the discussion of passages in Aristotle and Seneca is constrained by that purpose. In section 4, I set out conditions that must be met if vengeful anger is to be appropriate and sketch some of the broader considerations that, I believe, would need to be worked out to ground a view about the virtues and vices of vengeful anger. To that end, I develop a distinction (already discussed in section 3) among three senses of "fittingness" and say a bit more about their interconnection as well as their relation to an ethics of vengefulness. I do not attempt to work out these considerations in detail here, let alone which systematic moral theory would best accommodate my arguments about the ethics of vengeful anger. By way of conclusion (section 5), I suggest that the taking of revenge may be appropriate if certain conditions are met but that it is not justified simply because the emotion from which it springs is justified (if indeed it is justified). As I briefly discuss, this leaves us with a surprising distinction, and possibly divergence, between the merits of the emotion of vengeful anger and those of the action that may (and perhaps normally does) follow from it.

My theme is individual rather than group vengefulness. On the present view, individual vengefulness has three characteristics: first, it is what one might call private vengeance (in which revenge is to be taken by oneself); second, it involves the desire for personal revenge in response to wrongs done to oneself rather than to someone else (my primary focus is not indignation or sympathetic resentment); and third, it is directed at a person or persons. The form of vengeful anger on which I focus here assumes all three of these characteristics. For the sake of brevity, I shall speak simply of vengeful (or moral or retributive) anger but will mean, unless otherwise noted, personal vengeful anger in the sense just sketched. Consequently, I am talking about the desire to *take revenge*, not the desire to *avenge* wrongs. I am not exploring the relation between personal revenge and judicial punishment, let alone setting out a theory of punishment. A separate essay would be required to explore issues of collective anger and vengeance. Further, I am not primarily asking about the social utility of norms that sanction the taking of revenge (utility relative to the goal of deterrence, the equalization of power, and so forth).[11] There are many shades or shapes of anger; I am not claiming that the well-known phenomenon I am isolating and evaluating here is the essence or paradigm case of anger and am not committed to any view about anger as a "natural kind."

As to the definition of "emotion," for present purposes I am accepting that offered by Peter Goldie. He writes:

> An emotion, I have argued, is a relatively complex state, involving past and present episodes of thoughts, feelings, and bodily changes, dynamically related in a narrative of part of a person's life, together with dispositions to experience further emotional episodes, and to

act out of the emotion and to express that emotion. Your expression of emotion and the actions which spring from the emotion, whilst not part of the emotion itself, are none the less part of the narrative which runs through—and beyond—the emotion, mutually affecting and resonating in that emotion, and in further emotions, moods, and traits, and in further actions.[12]

This sense of "emotion" informs my reflections here on vengeful anger. I shall be assuming that vengeful anger is also a feeling, that is, that it possesses an affective quality for its owner; the feeling in question may be "hot" or "cold" (these labels are themselves slippery). But, as it is in some way about something in the world, it is also an emotion. I am not going to distinguish here between "emotion" and "sentiment" (I will generally avoid the word "passion" when speaking in my own voice, though in its eighteenth-century usage—for example, in Adam Smith—it seems synonymous with emotion and sentiment).[13] I will speak of vengeful anger, vengefulness, and the desire for revenge, meaning the same by all these phrases.

There are numerous empirical issues involved here, and I am aware of the dangers of armchair psychology passed off as considered convictions, intuitions, and such.[14] While I cite some of the relevant psychological literature and no doubt make assumptions of an empirical nature, this chapter does not attempt to assess systematically the relation between empirical and philosophical analyses of the topic.

1. THE PHENOMENOLOGY OF VENGEFUL ANGER

No, it was not to be that you should scorn my love,
And pleasantly live your life through, laughing at me;
Nor would the princess, nor he who offered the match,
Creon, drive me away without paying for it.
So now you may call me a monster, if you wish,
A Scylla housed in the caves of the Tuscan sea.
I too, as I had to, have taken hold of your heart.
                              —Euripides, *Medea* 1354–1360[15]

Anger is a highly complex, polymorphous phenomenon. Our language reflects some but not all of its forms: we speak of wrath, indignation, fury, ill temper, ill humor, bitterness, irritation, irascibility, resentment, exasperation, pouting, annoyance, and, of course, vengefulness (which can be "hot" or "cold"). These terms are not synonymous or stable in their meanings. Some of these terms are more behavioral or descriptive; others are more physiological (such as talk of ill humor or of something making your blood boil). We predicate anger of nonhuman animals, as well as of infants and young children. Moreover, the meanings of anger-terms vary over time.[16]

By way of isolating the particular shape of anger whose merits I want to assess here, let me start with the relation of hatred and vengeful anger (abbreviated "v-anger" in the rest of the essay): I may hate without being angry and vice versa. For example, I may hate National Socialism or the fact of a significant disparity of economic wealth between peoples or the effects of global warming on my favorite glaciers in Switzerland, but in themselves these are not instances of vengeful anger. In one of its modulations, hatred seems less personal than v-anger, in that it can arise on account of things that don't affect me personally (or even on account of anybody I know personally) and may be directed at entities that lack intentions or at least that are not responsible for their actions.[17] Further, I could describe myself as hating X without ever actually feeling hatred or anger. The phrase "moral hatred" brings hatred closer to v-anger, though again I can certainly ascribe it to myself, even feel it, without its being vengeful. Finally, as Aristotle remarks (*Rhetoric* 2.4, 1382a12–13), hatred need not be accompanied by pain, whereas, in some sense, the emotion of v-anger is thus accompanied (though it is also, as already noted, pleasurable).

Personal v-anger responds to perceived harm done to oneself. There are, of course, many ways in which this harm can be expressed, among them physical harm, harm to those near and dear, and harm to one's property. Further, this harm must also be perceived as a moral wrong. Soldiers in combat are out to harm one another but could in principle see the enemy's attempt to harm them not so much as morally wrong as what soldiers qua soldiers just do. And so it would be possible to respond to being harmed by another—harm one thinks is bad and to be evaded—angrily but not vengefully. V-anger, at least in the form that is the topic of this essay, is elicited by the perception that the harm is somehow wrong morally and hence is bad in a way that goes beyond its painfulness.[18]

Consequently, the anger felt in response to one's desire being frustrated is not necessarily v-anger. Aristotle remarks in the *Rhetoric* that people "become angry whenever they are distressed; for the person who is distressed desires something" (2.2, 1379a11–12).[19] But even if the cause of the frustration consists in someone blocking one's desire (say, in the example just mentioned, one's desire to continue to live), much depends on how or why the blocking is undertaken.

Let me pause for a moment. I have spoken of "perceived" harm or wrong, leaving open the possibility that one's perception is mistaken. One typically experiences personal v-anger in consequence of what one perceives to be a wrong done to oneself, not in response to what one perceives to be a good done to oneself, however painful. I don't want to take revenge on the dentist who quite rightly and expertly performed a root canal, excruciating and hateful though that experience may have been. Further, if a wrong is done to me but I don't know of it, I do not react with v-anger.

As a consequence, v-anger has a cognitive component. No doubt it is also accompanied by a state of bodily excitement or perturbation of some sort. As Aristotle notes in *De Anima* (403a29–403b1), the natural philosopher will describe anger as the boiling of the blood around the heart—a description to be updated but one whose spirit is surely correct. But a necessary condition of v-anger is the perception of wrong, and this may be described, for present purposes, in terms of belief, judgment, recognition, or—in some sense of this ill-defined term—cognition. That cognition is typically described or describable discursively; indeed, a remarkable feature of v-anger is the extent to which it *is* described discursively by its owners, sometimes generating narratives that reach epic length.

Vengeful anger is, then, *moral* anger in the sense I have sketched. Consequently, it takes itself to be *justified*, and quite consciously so; narratives of v-anger are replete with such justification, fueled by and fueling it. Such anger perceives itself as defended by reasons of a noncausal sort. The emotion is thus intrinsically evaluative and highly moralized. V-anger is experienced as righteous.

Part of what makes the relevant harm a *wrong* is that it is *intentionally* inflicted or at least that the offender bears responsibility

for the wrong; this too is essential to explaining the reactive sentiment that is v-anger.[20] V-anger is properly directed at an agent capable of intention and of responsibility for its actions. Though you
angrily curse the cement step on which you stub your toe, or angrily hit the dog that bites you, or angrily rebuke the person who
accidentally steps on your foot in a crowded bus, none of these
responses expresses v-anger. We no more wish to take revenge for
an unintentional wrong than for an intentional right that inflicts
pain. This point may seem obvious, but as we will see, Seneca argues against the propriety of anger in part on grounds that wrong
is never intentionally inflicted.

As my use of the Strawsonian phrase "reactive sentiment" indicates, v-anger also has the characteristic just mentioned; it is reactive, a response to wrong.[21] However, a sentiment might be fitting
or appropriate to something taken to be in the world but might
not respond to—in the sense of address itself to—that feature in
such a way as to seek to affect it. Or to be more precise, a sentiment may or may not seek to affect the agent responsible for that
feature. While not all instances of reactive sentiment may have this
agent-affecting aim, v-anger does, and revenge is its chosen means
to that goal. As should be clear by now, v-anger is other-directed; it
has an intentional structure, as it is "about" some value; it targets
some agent; and, if it is acted upon, results are deliberately aimed
for. There can be no unintentional revenge, for the very meaning
of the idea is closely tied to the aim of the angry person.[22]

And, because it is reactive in its particular way (seeking revenge
in response to a wrong), this emotion also motivates. One can well
understand why, in the *Rhetoric* (2.2, 1378a30–32), Aristotle associates anger so closely with desire (this association is, I add, another
reason that anger is not simply a feeling). This is an emotion that
prompts its owner to *do* something, and it is typically accompanied
by deliberation or, more sinisterly, plotting; hence, Bishop Butler
characterizes it as "deliberate."[23] In this sense too, v-anger is cognitive; it undertakes means-end reasoning, inter alia, and that requires intention on the part of the angry person. Revenge, then, is
plotted so as to inflict harm in response to wrong received.[24]

V-anger therefore possesses an interesting combination of ret-
rospectivity, to borrow a thought from a relevant passage in Anscombe,[25] as well as prospectivity—indeed, one is tempted to say,

the latter because of the former. This again distinguishes v-anger from hatred, as the latter may not be retrospective and perhaps, on occasion, may not be prospective either. V-anger is tied to agency diachronically understood, a point to which I shall return in the next section when discussing its connection to self-esteem.

The target of the emotion and, thus, of the revenge is not so much the wrong action or even intention but its author or owner —the wrongdoer, in other words.[26] I note in passing that this aspect helps to explain why forgiveness "works" on the victim's emotion of v-anger by moderating or alleviating it, if forgiveness is understood as a response to changes in the offender's attitudes or dispositions (changes signaled by, inter alia, contrition). Both v-anger and forgiveness are deeply interpersonal and bilateral and in that sense social; to that extent, they mirror each other. Correspondingly, the notion of v-anger directed against oneself is difficult to make sense of (the mirror notion of self-forgiveness is similarly complex). Further, both are tied to *memory*. One can no more forgive by forgetting than one can be vengeful by forgetting; both vengefulness and forgiving insist that the offender remember. Indeed, the thirster for revenge not only is energetically committed to remembering but has a much-lamented tendency to hang on to the memory in all its vividness.

Unlike ordinary perceptions, v-anger tends not only to linger beyond—often far beyond—the wrong to which it responds but also to augment its intensity.[27] Adam Smith wrote, citing Malebranche, that the passions "all justify themselves, and seem reasonable and proportioned to their objects, as long as we continue to feel them." Smith also remarks in the same paragraph that often "every thing appears magnified and misrepresented by self-love," as when the "violent emotions" (of which v-anger is surely an example) consume us.[28] Ordinary language reflects this aspect of v-anger, as when we speak of enflamed anger consuming everything in its path. Consequently, the object of this emotion is not simply "payback" but payback and then some; it is not just about "getting even" but about getting more than even. Of course, one could certainly get even without counting that as revenge, as when one evens the score in a tennis match.

The currency in which this abundant payback is supposed to be transmitted is, let us underline, pain or suffering. V-anger aims to inflict pain for pain, or suffering for suffering, or death for death.[29] There is no question but that it involves wishing ill for another.

Next, I must make explicit what is perhaps already clear, namely that v-anger typically understands itself to be *retributive* (I am not denying that there may exist other retributive emotions). By this I mean, first, that it is focused on what is taken to be the wrong-doer's desert. In response to a question about why the offender should be made to suffer, the revenge-taker will frequently say something like "Because he [or she] *deserves* it." This is different from a consequentialist rationale (though, of course, one could seek retribution for consequentialist reasons instead or as well), and that seems to me to be important. The primary purpose of personal v-anger is not deterrence, or the achievement of social utility, or some other such goal. The air of moral purity and even sanctity that can surround vengefulness and revenge-taking de-rives from their seemingly high-minded devotion to retributivist moral principle.[30]

However, vengefulness may not be retributively "pure" in that, as I shall also argue, it may aim at consequences of a sort. For exam-ple, it may seek to force the offender to acknowledge some moral principle (hence, revenge is sometimes referred to as "teaching the wrongdoer a lesson," though if revenge is not to reduce to re-taliation or deterrence, this will have to be construed in a manner that does not absolve the wrongdoer of responsibility for having failed to learn the lesson already) or it may seek to restore the vic-tim's self-esteem or both. The very notion that "payback" is to be repayment (with interest!) suggests that something more than des-ert alone is at stake here or at least that desert is being understood in an unusually complex way (not that the notion is straightfor-ward in any case!). Payback seems conceptually and perhaps also, at a deep level, psychologically intrinsic to v-anger (there doesn't seem to be nonretributive agent-directed personal moral anger).[31]

There is one further crucial aspect of this remarkable emo-tion that should be mentioned. As other commentators have noted, vengeful anger would have its target—the wrongdoer—un-derstand the payback not just as painful but as intended by that wrongdoer's victim as payback. This has been referred to as "dou-ble intentionality."[32] In what one might call the paradigm case, the returned harm loses much of its point if the intended recipient doesn't know not just that it is a harm (as would be the case if, say, you stole something whose absence its owner—the offender —never discovered) but that it is meant by this particular victim to be payback for this particular wrong. This observation highlights the fact that the exchange is highly personal: it involves a kind of reciprocity at its core and so mutual awareness on the part of both parties in the manner indicated. In that sense, it is fundamentally *interpersonal.*

Consequently, one is robbed of one's revenge if, say, the wrongdoer is indifferent to the harm the vengeful victim inflicts on him, or is dead, or never knows who inflicted the harm, or doesn't know why the harm was inflicted. Vengefulness is also not fulfilled and, indeed, may be usurped if the wrongdoer is punished by a third party (including by a court of law) instead of by the victim.

It seems to follow that v-anger has a communicative purpose that is intrinsic to it. As the wrongdoer is to understand who is taking the revenge and on account of what, he is also to be made to understand that his deed is (held to be) wrong. This message too seems implicit in the structure of v-anger: what you did to me was wrong, I protest it, and you must recognize that.[33] Indeed, is not the chosen method of protest—inflicting pain of some sort— meant at least in part to compel the wrongdoer to recognize and acknowledge all this? If the answer is affirmative, as I take it to be, we have reason to differentiate between the victim's vengeful wish to inflict pain and that of a sadist or cruel person.

How vengefulness is understood by both parties is therefore essential to its meaning and achievement. The victim is not seeking just to inflict harm or just to see the offender suffer; whatever pleasure may accompany vengefulness need (and ought) not lie just in the suffering or pain of another (else revenge would collapse into sadism or cruelty and lose whatever moral character it may possess). To be sure, wrong must have taken place (or at least be believed to have taken place), so what one might call an "objective" dimension must be present and perceived to be so; but also, both parties to the exchange must understand each other's state of mind in a suitable way—what one might call a "subjective" dimension must be present as well.

Vengefulness cannot be the same, then, as the desire for retaliation, though both have a tit-for-tat structure and are part of the

same family of notions. I can retaliate on behalf of someone else
—call it third-party retaliation—and could do so without experiencing any particular emotion. Further, I can also retaliate without
caring a whit about your recognizing who the retaliator is or why
retaliation has occurred. Retaliation does not require my being
present to witness your suffering as a result of the retaliation. I can
retaliate without thinking that what you did to me is wrong; it may
simply have caused me pain.[34]

Let us take this a step further. I have noted that the desire for
revenge seeks, inter alia, what is commonly referred to as "getting
even." In some sense, the aim seems to be to balance the scales or
to reverse or correct the inequality brought about by the wrongdoing. Reciprocity of a sort seems to be fundamental here. Some
elemental sense of fairness is at work—an intuition that revenge
would be fair insofar as it restores things to how they were before
or at least creates the equivalent thereof. Now, given what I have
also just said about the other aims of v-anger—including that of
forcing the wrongdoer to recognize the source and purpose of the
revenge—it appears that there's a connection between rebalancing (getting even) and the wrongdoer's painful recognition of his
misdeeds. I have also said that v-anger is retributive in holding that
the wrongdoer deserves the given punishment and in wanting to
punish the wrongdoer. And I have pointed to a communicative dimension of v-anger as well.

It is difficult to bring these features together into a coherent account, and one possible conclusion is simply that v-anger is not itself coherent.[35] Let us see if we can avoid that conclusion by reflecting further on the various aspects of the phenomenology. Now,
one temptation is to hold that the rebalancing consists in creating
equal amounts of pain on both sides. On this view, vengefulness
seeks to rebalance by reestablishing a semblance of the previous
balance, but in a peculiar way—by creating an analogous parity
of condition between the parties involved. You took my eye, and
now you shall lose yours, so we are once again even—though my
sight is not thereby restored. Hence there seems to be something
tragic in revenge as a response to loss, in that the simulacrum of
the earlier balance is rarely more than that. People frequently seek
to dissuade revenge-takers for precisely this sort of reason; taking

the offender's eye won't give you yours back, won't make it not be the case that yours was taken. What of the natural desire to take two eyes for one, in spite of *Lex Talionis?* And what of the importance of forcing the wrongdoer into awareness of the cause and rationale of the revenge? The account of rebalancing just sketched not only fails to take into consideration the wrongdoer's consciousness and interpretation of his pain or the victim's wish both to be and to be known as the instrument of revenge but also ignores the fact that vengefulness often seeks to inflict *more* pain than was received. So, reestablishing balance or equality of condition cannot be the whole story, even granting that the status quo ante cannot literally be regained in many cases (I cannot get my eye back by depriving you of yours).

Perhaps the core idea is, instead, something more like this: v-anger seeks to restore equality of regard, not of pain or condition, and it sometimes uses means—say, the taking of an eye (or two) for an eye—that *compel* recognition of that equality. Perhaps what vengefulness hopes to regain is a kind of parity, with suffering employed in part because of its capacity to symbolize and communicate equality and in part to compel the wrongdoer to acknowledge that parity.

Now, in some cultural contexts especially, vengefulness may seek to command regard or recognition by a third party—one's peers, say—of the equality of the two parties primarily concerned. Aristotle perceptively but perhaps too narrowly defined anger (*orgê*) this way: "Let anger be [defined as] desire, accompanied by [mental and physical] distress, for conspicuous retaliation because of a conspicuous slight [*oligôria*] that was directed, without justification, against oneself or those near to one" (*Rhetoric* 2.1, 1378a30–32; the word translated here by "retaliation" may also be translated as "vengeance" or "revenge"). A "slight" presumably diminishes or belittles one (a connotation implicit in the word Aristotle here uses), at least in the eyes of others. One's standing—or, as one might say in some contexts, one's honor or the esteem in which one is held—is diminished. V-anger might then be understood as seeking to restore that standing in the eyes of third parties by forcibly asserting that one is not to be treated as inferior (hence Aristotle's *NE* use of the term "slavish," earlier mentioned

—as though not to feel the appropriate anger confirms one's lowered standing). Empirical studies evidently support Aristotle's definition.[36] So natural is this thought that Elster states: "I believe the
phenomenon of honor to be the key to understanding revenge.
Asserting one's honor, like enjoying other people's envy of one's
assets, is an aspect of a deep-rooted urge to show oneself to be
superior to others."[37] This would, then, seem to be key to the emotion that typically prompts revenge.

If social standing as determined by a third party is the core issue,
however, then forcing the wrongdoer to understand and admit his
wrongdoing seems besides the point. The more important object
would be to show the third party, rather than the offender, that
one is not "slavish." By contrast, it also seems possible to want revenge even though no third party is aware of the transaction or
even though social standing is not at issue. Interpreting personal
vengefulness in terms of its social usefulness, then, seems not to
get to the core of the emotion.

And yet there is some truth to the notion that vengeful anger
may counter the perception of lowered standing, as seen from the
vantage point of the victim. That is, it initially seems plausible that
vengefulness is somehow meant to reassure *the victim* of his or her
equal standing and worthiness of equal regard, in that way restoring the earlier balance. Aristotle's definition would limit the cause
of v-anger to one or another form of belittling (he mentions three
in the chapter of the *Rhetoric* from which I just quoted: contempt,
spite, and arrogant insult [*hubris*]); and if what we have in mind
here is something like a sense of one's own proper worth in one's
own eyes, we arrive at the question of the connection between self-
esteem and v-anger. Let us see if further sense may be given to the
idea of restoring equality of regard.

2. SELF-ESTEEM AND VENGEFULNESS

Let me reformulate one key thought implicit in Aristotle's account
of anger. V-anger is the emotion one feels in response to an affront
that both belittles or dishonors or disrespects one in some way and
that communicates that one is not and ought not to be accorded
due regard or esteem. I said earlier that v-anger assumes that the
wrongdoer acts willingly and intentionally, as well as wrongly. Now,

one could imagine responding just as one would to wrong done to another person: with indignation, even calm reasoned indignation and a demand for justice, or with studied indifference, depending on the circumstances (including the kind of wrong done, as well as the status of the wrongdoer). One could also imagine retaliating for, say, purposes of deterrence. But reacting with *v-anger* signals that one takes the wrong *personally* in some sense that goes beyond simply being the target of the wrong.

One intuitive way to make sense of that is as follows: v-anger expresses its owner's suspicion or, perhaps, anxiety about the possibility that he or she deserves the affront, that the negative judgment about oneself implicit in the wrongdoing is true. Someone comments publicly on the inferior status of your scholarly work, and you respond not by laughing it off or by calm refutation but with v-anger; does this not suggest that perhaps you are in fact worried that the accusation may carry a kernel of truth? If it never crossed your mind to imagine that the affront might somehow be true of you, why should you respond specifically with *vengeful* anger, as I have defined it? Responding with v-anger suggests that your self-esteem is called into question.[38]

There exists clinical literature pointing to interesting ways in which fantasies of revenge can help restore a sense of agency, empowerment, and control over one's life.[39] That a wrong might have this effect of requiring restoration of self-esteem is perfectly understandable, of course, but implies that vengefulness is rooted in weakened self-esteem.[40] Insofar as it is, the term "resentment" —though more narrowly defined here than in Butler (where it comes to what I'm calling v-anger, irrespective of the angry person's level of self-esteem)—seems to capture its meaning. And, insofar as resentment is combined with a feeling of powerlessness, "*ressentiment*"—the French for "resentment," which Nietzsche endowed with this special sense—seems to be the right term.[41] Vengeful resentment may have transient value for its owner, as I have just indicated.

Vengefulness as a response to feeling belittled does make some initial sense of revenge as "getting even" or "payback," for what is to be restored—or so the victim believes—is the victim's own self-regard. V-anger might be thought of as restoring the victim's internal sense of equilibrium by providing "proof" to oneself—in the form of one's power to inflict harm on the offender—that the implicit or even explicit charge contained in the wrongdoing is false.[42] A sort of internal rebalancing is achieved that feels like restoration, like an equalizing. Specifically, vengefulness and perhaps the taking of revenge might feel, to one whose self-esteem is in question, like a restoration of a strong sense of self, a sense of one's own agency. This might also feel like a "reversal" of the state of affairs brought about by the wrong that one has suffered. Moreover, understanding v-anger as an effort to restore self-esteem sheds light on the "and then some" character of the "repayment," especially in cases of (what is felt to be) grave injury, for the nature of the task, self-reassurance, naturally seems to call for reiteration and reinforcement. Let me briefly expand on this point.

Vengeful anger is a structurally flawed strategy if the goal is the restoration of lowered self-esteem. Inflicting pain on those who have wrongly harmed you can never really address the causes of a weak sense of self, for those very probably preexisted the event in question. Lowering another person to a level beneath you does not actually raise you in the decisive sense, though it may have the instrumental and passing value of showing you that you have the ability to lower the offender (and may permit you to rank yourself above the offender, without, however, actually making you more estimable). Further, if your self-esteem hinges on forcing the wrongdoer to acknowledge that you ought not to be treated thus, then your sense of self depends in part on the esteem extracted from another. In the nature of the case, such esteem is always going to be contingent, variable, temporary, and suspect in any reassurance it offers. The strategy is unsuccessful, and perhaps that helps to explain the "and then some" character of the "payback" so often associated with v-anger: the disproportion of the returned harm that v-anger often generates expresses the lack of suitability of means (revenge-taking) to the end (restoration of self-esteem). As there is no proportional "getting even" that will work, one is forced to ever greater measures. It would certainly be difficult to formulate a defense of the ethical value of v-anger if v-anger expresses and seeks to counter lowered self-esteem, especially if proper self-esteem is conceived of as an appropriate disposition to be cultivated, rather than thought of simply in terms of its instrumental psychological utility (with regard to, say, restoring a sense of agency).

Putting ethical considerations aside for a bit longer, though, and staying within a phenomenological frame, let us ask: must v-anger stem from or at least be accompanied by lowered self-esteem? The answer strikes me as negative. I can feel v-anger precisely because my self-esteem is *not* harmed. My conviction that I ought not be treated in a certain way may be affectively expressed as protest, as objection, as standing up for myself—all premised on the firm conviction that I am worth defending, worth my own defense. You may treat me in a way that is demeaning and humiliating or belittling; it does not follow that I am demeaned or humiliated or belittled if I do not regard myself as such. I am interested here in describing and evaluating a form of v-anger that does not stem from and is not a response to low self-esteem.

Yet this leads to another puzzle: if one has been wronged and one's self-regard has not thereby been damaged, would not the appropriate response to a wrong to oneself be a bloodless, affect-less rectification of the wrong? The victim would, it seems, respond impersonally, as though the injustice had been done to someone else. Indeed, why not respond in the manner Nietzsche praises in the passage quoted at the start of this chapter—by rising above any thought of revenge? What warrant for personal v-anger could remain if self-esteem were *not* at stake?

In order to pursue this normative question and, more broadly, the ethics of v-anger, let me turn to the debate between Aristotle and Seneca on the virtues and vices of anger.

3. Aristotle and Seneca

[L]et us cultivate our humanity. Let us not bring fear or danger upon any one. Let us look down on damages and wrongs, insults and carping criticisms. Let us bear with greatness of mind our short-lived troubles. As they say, we have only to look back, only to turn round—quick now, here comes death!

—Seneca, *De Ira* 3.43.5[43]

My purpose in this section is not, as already noted, to offer a scholarly assessment of the debate between Aristotelians and Stoics about the nature of the emotions or of Aristotle's and Seneca's views as such. Rather, I shall pick out several of their arguments as a way of furthering, within the confines of this brief discussion, the normative question about the place of v-anger in the good life. In the relevant passages of the *Rhetoric* and the *Nicomachean Ethics*, Aristotle's focus seems pretty clearly to be on the angry desire for revenge. Seneca's subject in *De Ira* certainly includes v-anger and arguably is principally v-anger; indeed, he says that his definition is not far from those of some unnamed others, and Aristotle appears to be among them (1.3.3; see the editors' n. 8, p. 20, in the edition of *De Ira* that I'm using). His analysis at 1.2–3 focuses on vengefulness and distinguishes it from such things as the "anger" of a wild animal or that of a child who falls down and is in pain. I am not claiming, however, that both of their analyses isolate every feature of v-anger in precisely the way that I have. I do believe that what they say about anger sufficiently overlaps with the phenomenology I've offered to permit use of their views to illuminate fundamental features of the debate about the ethics of anger. Further, as will soon become clear, I am not endorsing either of their positions. Let me turn, then, to a brief examination of several relevant aspects of their views.

Aristotle

In Book II of the *NE*, Aristotle writes:

> By feelings [*pathê*] I mean appetite, anger [*orgê*], fear, confidence, envy, joy, love, hate, longing, jealousy, pity, and in general whatever implies pleasure or pain. By capacities I mean what we have when we are said to be capable of these feelings—capable of being angry, for instance, or of being afraid or of feeling pity. By states [*hexeis*] I mean what we have when we are well or badly off in relation to feelings. If, for instance, our feeling is too intense or slack, we are badly off in relation to anger, but if it is intermediate, we are well off; the same is true in the other cases. (1105b21–28)

Aristotle argues that virtues are "states." That there is such a thing as being well or badly off with respect to anger is established in Book IV, when Aristotle discusses the virtue of "mildness" (*praotês*), which he declares to be the mean concerned with anger. Aristotle terms the excess of anger "irascibility," and although the defect of anger is nameless, its possessor, as already noted, is termed "slavish" (1125b26–29, 1126a8). Aristotle remarks: "The person who is angry at the right things and toward the right people, and also in the right way, at the right time, and for the right length of time, is praised." Such a person is "mild" and thus "undisturbed (*atarochos*), not led by feeling, but irritated wherever reason prescribes, and for the length of time it prescribes" (for both quotations, see 1125b31–1126a1). So Aristotle seems to think that the virtuous person will feel anger as appropriate. Anger is part of the emotional makeup of the virtuous person. Why does Aristotle think this?

It cannot be because *every* emotion has a "mean"; the description of envy in the *Rhetoric* 2.10 (where it is defined as "a certain kind of distress at apparent success on the part of one's peers in attaining the good things that have been mentioned, not that a person may get anything for himself but because of those who have it"; 1387b23–25) does not make it sound like the sort of thing one could have toward the right thing at the right time and so forth. This inference is validated by *Rhetoric* 1386b16–1387a5 and especially 1388a35–36 ("envy is bad [*phaulon*] and characteristic of the bad [*phauloi*]"). Indeed, at *NE* II.6, Aristotle tells us that "not every action or feeling admits of the mean," and he cites envy inter alia (1107a8–11). For such feelings are inherently base (*phaulon*; 1107a13); presumably one is to extirpate them from one's soul. Why isn't vengeful anger, an emotion reputed to be ugly and dangerous, inherently base and also to be extirpated?

Aristotle's answer is surprisingly hard to flesh out.[44] Certainly, the definitions of anger in the *NE* and the *Rhetoric* make it sound as though the emotion can be *fitting* in multiple senses. To begin with, it might be fitting or appropriate to the fact of an affront, to the magnitude of the affront, to the fact that it was an intentional affront, and so forth.[45] Now, one could perhaps construct a case that envy, too, is "fitting" in this sense, even while holding with Aristotle that one ought not feel envy. Fittingness in this first sense may be a necessary condition of ethical praiseworthiness but cannot be a sufficient condition.

Aristotle's biting comment about the deficiency of anger takes us further. He says:

The deficiency—a sort of inirascibility [*aorgêsia*] or whatever it is
—is blamed. For people who are not angered by the right things,
or in the right way, or at the right times, or toward the right people,
all seem to be foolish. For such a person seems to be insensible and
to feel no pain, and since he is not angered, he does not seem to
be the sort to defend himself. Such willingness to accept insults to
oneself and to overlook insults to one's family and friends is slavish.
(*NE* 1126a3–8)

This passage suggests a mix of rationales favoring v-anger as commendable (under the right circumstances and so on). One is consequentialist, having to do with the requirements of self-defense.
But another, suggested as much by the tone of the passage as by
the term "slavish," holds an appeal to honor as well as to the requirements of pride and to self-esteem. It "is blamed"—the relevant public blames you—if you don't stand up for yourself and
yours. You come across as submissive, as deserving humiliation, as
not just unable but—far worse—as unwilling to protest affronts.
By contrast, anger signals to others that you protest. The context is
ineluctably social, and the judgment Aristotle articulates is that of
a moral—indeed, moralizing—community.

As the readers of Aristotle's report about how a failure to feel
anger appropriately will be interpreted, we are meant to buy in.
The way the account is phrased implicitly invites a connection between our self-regard and how others regard us.[46] This may turn
out to be a matter of relative social position; more subtly, it may
also evince the view that our nature is fundamentally "political"
(in Aristotle's sense). But that sort of approach does not give us a
particularly impressive ethical justification for v-anger, and in any
case it appeals to considerations that are secondary on the analysis
I am offering (since it has to do with social status).

There seem to be two other sorts of fittingness at work here,
however. One has to do with what is fitting if one is to be a noble
person rather than a base (*phaulos*) or slavish person. This sense
of the fitting is relative to a picture of the ideal person or life. The
other has to do with what is fitting to us as composite (made of
body and soul, matter and form), dependent, and vulnerable creatures. Let me say something about these second and third senses
of the fitting.

Aristotle's most detailed picture of the noble person is that of the *megalopsuchos*, offered almost immediately before his discussion of virtuous anger. In the *Posterior Analytics* (97b14–26) Aristotle cites *megalopsuchia* as an example of an equivocal term. It may mean, he says, either the sort of thing that Alcibiades, Achilles, and Ajax had in common, that is, an "intolerance of insults," or the sort of thing that Lysander and Socrates had in common, an indifference to good and bad fortune, indifference (*apatheia*) instead of "not brooking dishonour."[47] Clearly, Aristotle lauds the first meaning and Seneca the second.

Since the *megalopsuchos* is "worthy of the greatest things, he is the best person [*aristos*]" (*NE* 1123b26–27). One might argue that he's best because he possesses all the virtues (1124a1–2; there it is clear that the *megalopsuchos* does have all the virtues), but that is unhelpful since we are trying to understand why there should be a virtuous state with respect to the feeling of anger. Aristotle doesn't explicitly say that the magnanimous man (for Aristotle, this character does seem to be male, hence my gendered expression) will experience such anger and does say that he is not prone to remember evils (1125a4–5), though he will speak evil of his enemies when it is a matter of their *hubris* (which Irwin translates as "wanton aggression"; 1125a8–9). The magnanimous man does have "hatreds" (1124b26)—presumably of persons who have dishonored him—which surely includes retributive anger. And, since he has all the virtues, he must also have that of "mildness." The idea seems to be that this noble character will in general not react to wrongs with anger, except when the wrongs are great and are delivered by those worthy of his vengefulness. His opinion of himself is (justifiably, by his lights) extremely high. In not needing the approval of others in any routine way, he is self-sufficient and will "determine his life" (1124b31–1125a1; his friends may help, however). The alternative, Aristotle says, "would be slavish" (*doulikon*; 1125a1). So, self-sufficiency seems to be one mark of noble character but also a kind of self-possession, a self-respect grounded in the perception—which he lives up to without inner conflict—that he is "worthy" or honorable. The *megalopsuchos* is in those ways proud of himself.[48]

At the same time—and arguably this is at odds with his self-sufficiency—he is also concerned not just with being honorable but with being honored, though only by the greatest honors (*NE*

1123b20–24; 1124a4–12). That is supposed to be another mark of
his greatness. While there is much to say about this complicated
sketch of the noble soul, it initially seems that when the magnanimous man does rise to anger, it is not because his self-esteem is
damaged. Otherwise, magnanimity would be corrupted by low
self-esteem, which Aristotle assigns to the vice of pusillanimity
(1125a17–27). Magnanimous anger is not the self-doubting resentment I discussed in section 2, and it is certainly not *ressentiment*. Presumably the magnanimous man's appreciation of and
desire for honor demands that, when it is denied to him, he react
with anger and that those dishonoring him know of his displea-
sure. It does seem to matter to him that they do know—why else
does he care whether or not they honor him (and that he know
that they know that he both knows of and appreciates the honor)?
Why else would it not suffice that he alone honors himself appropriately? The communicative or signaling function of anger seems
crucial here.

At this deep level, he is not self-sufficient but dependent. By im-
plying that the magnanimous man will respond angrily when it is
fitting to do so, Aristotle makes it clear that his paragon of ethical
virtue is vulnerable: the magnanimous man can be wronged and
angered if great honors are inappropriately withheld. Deserved social regard (offered by those of exceptional virtue) is a chief object
of concern for him. The corresponding vulnerability is consistent
with Aristotle's view that ethical virtue can be frayed and, in extreme cases (such as that of Priam), badly frayed (*NE* 1101a6–13;
note the use of *megalopsuchos* at 1100b32–33).

Why the magnanimous man should be vulnerable in regard to
honor remains unclear. Aristotle doesn't say enough to help us
understand exactly why or how the magnanimous man is dependent in this regard (is it an epistemic question, for example, such
that he cannot know he is honorable unless honored by the right
people?). He does not explain why being honored *matters* to the
magnanimous man, and this corresponds to his silence about why
feeling the right degree of anger is a virtue. Suppose that other
great souls fail to honor you, a great soul: so what? Why not just
brush it off? Why does not the great man's magnanimity flow into
the second sense of *megalopsuchia* that Aristotle mentions in the

Posterior Analytics (97b14–26), the one that Lysander and Socrates are credited with?

The opacity of Aristotle's analysis on this issue opens up space for the suggestion that the magnanimous man embodies an unstable combination of self-sufficiency and dependence. It is not that the two *must* form an unstable combination but that, because *honor* matters so greatly to the *megalopsuchos*, the demands of self-sufficiency and of dependence seem destined to collide. Another conception of *megalopsuchia* is required, a Stoic critic might maintain, in order to avoid just this collision.

But perhaps it is possible to help Aristotle out by examining another thought that seems to underlie his picture of virtuous anger, though it is largely unarticulated in the description of the magnanimous man. The thought concerns the importance of assessing what is fitting to us as composite (made of body and soul, matter and form), dependent, and vulnerable creatures. This is the third sense of "fittingness" mentioned earlier, and it stands out by way of contrast when Aristotle sketches the life of theoretical virtue in Book X. The paradigm of theoretical virtue is god, and on Aristotle's account, that noncomposite being lacks emotions to habituate and therefore has no need for the moral virtues. (Aristotle refers in different places to "god" as well as "the gods," but that does not affect the point I am making here.) As a reactive emotion, v-anger concedes that we are vulnerable to other intentional agents and thus that we exist in some sort of community with them, but the divine shares none of these traits (*NE* 1178b10–19). For Aristotle the emotions are in some sense somatic, as we saw with reference to *De Anima* 403a29–403b1, and this may be another reason why Aristotle takes it as a given that we humans cannot be without anger. By contrast, as noncomposite, as pure mind, god has no body. Aristotle's god feels no v-anger and hence cannot stand in a praiseworthy relation with respect to it; god has no interest in honor and is truly "self-sufficient" (see *NE* 1177a27 and context; also 1177b21–22). Insofar as we achieve the godlike life, then, our understanding of which—if any—moral virtues and emotions are appropriate to the noble soul is bound to change profoundly. Aristotle's case for virtuous anger is offered in the context of reflection on what is fitting to embodied, nongodly, political (in his sense) agents.

This line of thought about a third sense of fittingness points to what D'Arms and Jacobson helpfully term "anthropocentric constraints on human value." These come to light through a cluster of reflections on what sorts of emotions and virtues are appropriate to creatures like us, and their weight can be assessed in part by asking what of ourselves we would have to give up if we changed the constraints.[49] The considerations in question concern what D'Arms and Jacobson call "suitable standards of fittingness for humans."[50] These determine what I am calling the third sense of fittingness. The second sense of fittingness I sketched has to do with the virtues that are intrinsic to a picture of the ideal person —in the Aristotelian case, a picture of (limited) self-sufficiency and high honor. In combination with Aristotle's view that anger is fitting in the first sense mentioned (as tracking features of the world), we have the core of his defense of the idea that anger can be ethically praiseworthy.

By way of sharpening the issues at stake, let me turn briefly to Seneca.

Seneca

De Ira is a sort of grab-bag of arguments about and against anger. There is no question about the main thesis: anger should be extirpated from the virtuous soul. My present purpose is narrow: I simply aim to articulate elements of Seneca's disagreement with Aristotle that help focus my discussion about the ethics of v-anger.

The first argument is that anger misinterprets the *import* of the (moral) facts about the world to which it takes itself to be responding, and hence it is a species of cognitive error, an example of bad reasoning. As I read Seneca, his point is neither that there does not exist such a thing as wrongful or unjust treatment of a person nor that v-anger necessarily errs in taking itself as responding to injustice. Rather, the idea is that, as the victim, I should not take myself to be harmed thereby and that furthermore I have positive reasons—regard for my own psychic health, for example—not to interpret the wrong as harming me. Consequently, I should not feel angry. I can grant that you did me wrong and insist on the appropriate punishment (1.15.1); yet, at the same time, I may refuse to see myself as having been harmed, degraded, demeaned, or diminished.[51] The ancestor of this view is undoubtedly Socrates' proud proclamation—delivered, interestingly, to the jurors in the *Apology* (41d1–2)—that no harm can come to a good man. Not surprisingly, Socrates also said that he is not angry with his accusers as they find him guilty (*Apol.* 35e1–36a1), even though what they are doing is unjust (*Apol.* 39b1–6).

Seneca's emphasis on the possibility of choice about whether or not to feel anger (once one is past the pre-anger phase, the initial stirrings caused by the "impression" of the wrong; 2.1–4) helps him to create some space for cognitive readjustment: I was wronged but need not internalize it and need not take myself as harmed. The assumption seems to be that if I had been harmed, then anger *might* be fitting, but as I am not harmed (since I am a Socratic or Stoic), then it is irrational to respond angrily. The important conclusion from this line of reasoning is that anger may be fitting in my first sense of the term but still not warranted or appropriate. Seneca's position is analogous to one that holds that a joke is funny but not morally appropriate to laugh at.[52]

To turn to a second argument: in response to the question "is it virtuous to be angry at wickedness?," Seneca insists on a negative answer (2.6–10). He notes in support of his answer that people do not do wrong knowingly and thus are not responsible for their wrongdoing. Hence, something like excuse or pardon is the appropriate response: "To avoid anger with individuals, you must forgive the whole group, you must pardon the human race" (2.10.2). It makes no sense to be (vengefully) angry with a child or with nature, and you are able not to be so: "But being human is more of an excuse, and a juster excuse, than being a child" (2.10.2). Instead of responding with anger, look upon the wrongdoers "with the kindly gaze of a doctor viewing the sick" (2.10.7). If Seneca is right about this, then v-anger does look to be based on a mistake. By contrast, I held, with Aristotle, that v-anger assumes that the wrongdoer is responsible for his or her action. Obviously, to settle the matter would require an entirely different discussion. For present purposes, I will stipulate that our commonsense notion that wrongdoers are at least sometimes responsible for their deeds is correct. At least sometimes, they are not to be understood as though they were children, or natural events, or ill. This does not prevent us from recognizing that Seneca's views about comprehensive excusability go hand in hand with his quite moving appeals to our common fallibility (3.26.4: "All of us are *bad*"; cf. 1.14.2, 3) and humanity (3.43.5).

And this brings me to a third argument of *De Ira*. As the sentences I have quoted suggest, Seneca has a picture of the noble soul to set against Aristotle's. The difference between the two turns on the competing interpretations of *megalopsuchia* or highmindedness already mentioned. Why is it nobler to rise above all insults and belittlement and expressions of dishonor or disrespect than to respond with anger as the occasion demands? A cluster of considerations directs Seneca to his interpretation of highmindedness. For example, he says that anger is a sign of a mind aware of its own weakness (1.20.3), that is, lacking self-esteem; but "A mighty mind with its true self-awareness will not avenge, since it has not noticed the wrong done to it" (3.5.7; I take Seneca to mean that a "mighty mind" does not feel harmed). To subscribe to some such view requires that our virtue be invulnerable to external pressure, that it be the case that we are not harmed unless we think ourselves so, and, of course, that it is psychologically possible to prevent ourselves from becoming angry. Seneca insists that we can indeed be rid of anger completely (2.12, 13): "Anything that the mind commands itself it can do" (2.12.4).[53] The highest end is happiness understood as tranquility (see 1.21.4), and it is in our power to achieve it. Tranquility and, hence, proper self-care are incompatible with any degree of anger (3.4.4), as anger is toxic to its possessor—especially given the Stoic theory of emotion.[54] And, with this, the Aristotelian link—Seneca would say, the unstable link—between self-sufficiency and dependence through sensibility to honor is severed.

The debate between these positions is obviously multilayered and complex, and, in the debate about the merits of v-anger, a great deal will hinge on one's conception of the ideal human type, as the disagreement about the desirable sense of *megalopsuchia* shows. That is one upshot of this discussion. In the next section, I shall offer a list of conditions that a defense of v-anger would have to satisfy. Doing so will lead me back to consideration of our third sense of fittingness.

4. The Conditions of Ethical Vengeful Anger

It seems to me that a number of considerations must be brought to bear on the question of whether it is ever virtuous to feel vengeful anger as I have described that emotion. Whether and how to assign differing weights to these considerations would require a separate essay. However that is worked out, the particular features of v-anger should be preserved in its vindication. It would not be persuasive to vindicate it simply by arguing for the merits of a sense of justice or of righteous indignation. That is too impersonal for present purposes and is a defense of related but distinct dispositions. Vengefulness is, I have argued, personal and requires that the agent (the victim) intentionally wish to inflict harm on the wrongdoer in return for wrong and also that the wrongdoer be able to identify the agent and his or her reason for wanting revenge.

First, for v-anger to be justifiable, it must correctly represent its target. Since v-anger is a response to wrong, the wrong must in fact be just that, and must in fact have been enacted by the person against whom the anger is directed. In those ways, the anger must be fitting in our first sense of the term: the beliefs that it implies or assumes must be true.[55] Further, it must be proportionate or exhibit what Adam Smith calls "propriety" (*TMS* I.i.3.6). No doubt a separate essay could be written about how proportionality is to be assessed, but we do recognize the notion of over- (and less frequently, under-) reaction. I have also stipulated that the offender is, in some sense, responsible for his or her wrongdoing and that justifiable v-anger assumes that the offender acted intentionally (in whatever sense accompanies responsibility) and is capable of understanding that he or she committed a wrong, specifically against this victim.

Second, it would make no sense to desire vengeance against an offender who is contrite and has expressed contrition, taken responsibility, made amends, and taken every other conciliatory and emendatory step one could reasonably wish for.[56] This, in turn, means that one ought not be resistant to forgiveness, or become hard-hearted, or succumb to the ongoing pleasures of fury. V-anger should be forsworn and hence be forswearable, so to speak, when faced with the appropriate forgiveness or excuse conditions.

Third, I suggest that v-anger that stems from and is meant to compensate for low self-esteem is not an emotion the virtuous person would endorse. To begin with, raising one's self-esteem by wishing to inflict pain on the wrongdoer is an unsuccessful strategy, as already mentioned. It is true that I can get angry because of my poor self-esteem but refrain from acting on it in recognition of the fact that such anger is self-defeating in practice. But the sort of abiding low self-esteem that is one source of v-anger is itself a sign of a deficiency of character (whether because one actually deserves higher self-esteem or because in fact one deserves low esteem). I do not see how a defense of v-anger can be successful if it hinges on defending low self-esteem. And while v-anger can be instrumentally useful for increasing one's deserved self-esteem, that vindication is not of the sort sought here. So a justification of v-anger has somehow to be compatible with and perhaps the expression of warranted self-esteem.

Fourth, however one is to understand the pleasures of vengefulness, they must not collapse into enjoying cruelty or sadism. In the best case, the pleasure of vengefulness seems to come to pleasure both in what is right and in righting a wrong.

Fifth, v-anger must be such (in its intensity and duration) as not to damage its owner ethically (by making him or her incapable of other virtues). This is necessary in order to answer Seneca's point about the toxicity of anger to its owner.[57] V-anger that met the conditions just enumerated would seem largely immune to the toxicity he describes. It seems to me that v-anger can, in principle, meet these conditions.

Satisfying the conditions just mentioned would help ensure that v-anger is (on the relevant occasion) not unjustifiable. But a further step is needed if it is to be positively commendable.[58] As noted at the end of section 3, an upshot of the present inquiry is the suggestion that one cannot resolve the problem of the praiseworthiness of v-anger without also working out which ideal of the good life is to be affirmed and so without working out the second sense of fittingness, as well as the first.

Obviously, I cannot undertake that project here, but as prolegomenon to that effort, I mention two points pertinent to the Aristotle-Seneca debate about archetypes of praiseworthy character that lead back to the third sense of fittingness. The first point is that Aristotle's paragon of ethical virtue is a social or political being in a way that Seneca's is not. Seneca insists on one's being a part of the community of human beings, as his concluding sentences (quoted at the start of section 3) indicate, and his vision is cosmopolitan rather than political. Aristotle has something much more local in mind, it seems: this virtuous person's standing in and ties to this or that community. The relations of honor are not cosmopolitan. From a noncosmopolitan perspective, sensitivity to this or that belittlement by this or that person is harder to brush off. V-anger is fundamentally social in character: it expresses and assumes one's connectedness to other particular agents. For Aristotle, we care about these individuals but not about all individuals as such; for Seneca, we care about humanity but about no individual (much) more than another. The second point is that while Aristotle is certainly assuming that the virtuous person is self-directed, in the sense of governed by reason in view of the noble (*to kalon*), his paradigm of the virtuous agent is not autonomous in the way that Seneca's is, as is particularly evident in Seneca's notion that one can be wronged but not harmed if the agent judges him- or herself unharmed. Perhaps another rough and ready way to put the point is that Aristotle assumes (I once again bracket *NE* X) that we are embodied and affective rational animals and hence that our character is not immune to the corresponding pressures. On Seneca's picture, that inference need not follow, if only we follow our reason implicitly.

Can we follow our reason in that way? This brings us to the third sense of fittingness mentioned earlier—fittingness to our situation as human beings. Both Aristotle's and Seneca's competing versions of the ideal of high-mindedness are revisionist (imagine what it would mean to take seriously Aristotle's *megalopsuchos* as your role model). One way to assess which revisionist scheme is preferable is to ask what would have to be given up in order to achieve the ideal in question. As already noted, D'Arms and Jacobson have furnished us with a helpful distinction between "wide" and "deep" concerns, and it should be brought to bear here.[59] That adopting Seneca's view about anger would require wide and deep changes to ordinary human psychology does not seem terribly controversial. Even Seneca seems aware of that, as when he offers the provocative view, already quoted, to the effect that if your father is murdered and your mother raped, you ought not respond with anger. What would have to be true of you in order that you *not* react with anger to such wrongs? What changes in yourself would you have to make in order to become a Senecan Stoic with respect to anger? If any emotion satisfies the "deep concerns" criterion, it is vengeful anger. To be sure, that is an empirical point, and another upshot of this discussion is that the question of the ethics of vengeful anger cannot be settled absent reliance on empirical propositions of that sort.

The defense of v-anger also seems to satisfy the "wide concerns" criterion, as D'Arms and Jacobson's comments about anger suggest.[60] Aristotle does not require us to eliminate anger, and that alone may make his view seem more congenial because it is responsive to wide and deep concerns. While in the *Nicomachean Ethics* he is remarkably silent about such concerns when discussing anger, in *Politics* 7.7 there is a suggestive passage about the connection between "spiritedness"—itself generative of anger—and love as well as friendship. Aristotle writes: "For as to what some assert should be present in guardians, to be affectionate toward familiar persons but savage toward those who are unknown, it is spiritedness [*thumos*] that creates affectionateness; for this is the capacity of soul by which we feel affection. An indication of this is that spiritedness is more aroused against intimates and friends than against unknown persons when it considers itself slighted [*oligôreisthai*]" (1327b38–1328a3).[61] As Fisher suggests, anger seems to be a necessary consequence of others *mattering* to us profoundly; if that is true, then its elimination would require tearing out the emotions of love and friendship, as well—a very high cost to pay.[62] The combination of these deep and wide concerns, if buttressed by the empirical data, helps explain why the appropriate response to the relevant sort of wrong to oneself ought not be a bloodless, affect-less avenging or simply a calm turn to judicial redress.

But this third sense of fittingness is not sufficient, only necessary for the justification of v-anger. For there may be emotions or dispositions that are undesirable and yet may also, for all we know, satisfy the wide-and-deep-concerns criteria. Indeed, *un*warranted v-anger (anger that does not fulfill the requirements of the first sense of fittingness, say) may be fitting in this sense. The concerns, that is, must be the right ones. And this suggests that what is needed in order to build the ethical case for v-anger is the conjunction of all three senses of fittingness I have mentioned. That is a further upshot of this essay. Let me offer a few more words, then, about the connection between the second and third senses of fittingness (i.e., about fit relative to a moral ideal that is not outside the bounds of the wide-and-deep-concerns criteria). Much more remains to be said, to be sure, about the conceptual relations among the three senses of fittingness I have sketched.

Aristotle's candidate for the ethical paradigm—the *megalopsuchos*—suffers from its own difficulties relevant to the present discussion. I refer not just to the lack of argumentative support with regard to the place of anger in the virtuous life but also to the unstable combination of self-sufficiency and dependence on the appropriate honors granted by (suitably qualified) others. It is, at the end of the day, difficult to tell whether the *megalopsuchos* responds with anger to what he regards as the unjustified denial of honor because his self-esteem is *not* called into question or because it *is* called into question along with his social standing.

If vengeful anger is to have a defensible place in the emotional repertoire of the virtuous person, we shall have to accept not only the importance of respecting wide and deep concerns but also some sort of dependence of self on other that often is more particularized, less cosmopolitan, than anything Seneca would allow or, at least, "thicker" in its human and moral ties. The picture of the ideal life will in that respect be more Aristotelian than Stoic. However, the instability I have ascribed to Aristotle's picture would need to be overcome and thus the role of self-esteem stabilized. This would require, I suggest, jettisoning the central importance that Aristotle's magnanimous man places on being honored for noteworthy achievements and deeds. Reliance on being honored ties one's sense of self-worth too tightly to public perception of one's worth. What is needed is a certain dependence on the moral regard of others who matter, one that does *not* call into question self-esteem and yet is not only admirable but also consistent with the wide-and-deep-concerns criteria. The task would be to explain the possibility of v-anger, and thus of being harmed, among people of solid self-esteem who are dependent as well as ethically admirable.[63] It seems to be a part of that picture that the offender be granted the standing to be worthy, so to speak, of one's v-anger;

this comes to a kind of esteem of or respect for the offender.[64] Some such view about the offender belonging to the same moral community does not fit well with either the Aristotelian or the Stoic picture, albeit for different reasons in each case, though of the two, the Aristotelian is the more congenial. In sum, one would need to make sense of the idea of responsive agency, of the ability to direct one's life on the basis of a firm sense of who one is, while having—and exhibiting—dependency on others (for example, by desiring their esteem).

That is obviously a large task, and I shall move to conclude this much more limited effort by attempting to be a bit more precise about how this task might unfold in the present case. V-anger's insistence that the offender be made to know both the reason for and the agent of the revenge testifies to our interdependence, to our character as social beings, and to the fact that others *matter* to us. How is that dependency compatible with strong self-esteem and lack of concern about social standing? This is one of the deepest issues raised by this analysis, and I do not pretend to have resolved it here. The challenge is to explain how the wrong can be taken personally such that the victim may wish to be the instrument of revenge and wish that the offender know who is taking revenge and why, without the victim's self-esteem or concern for social standing or honor being at stake. At the same time, v-anger does not simply consist in the wish that justice be done (by someone). Perhaps an example will help move the discussion forward.

Imagine the case of a betrayal by a partner you had thought of as committed to you (and vice versa) for life. Given the large amount of time, the effort, trust, intimacy, and importance with which you have endowed the relationship (perhaps expressed through the allocation not just of love but of economic resources as well), the betrayal certainly matters greatly to you and likely elicits your v-anger, but not necessarily because of any weak self-esteem on your part. You do not react angrily because some great honor has been denied you or because your self-esteem or sense of social standing is damaged. Rather, something essential of who you are, your identity over time, is contained in this long-term relationship, and its brutal disruption through betrayal is a harm to you. V-anger acknowledges the importance of the relationship by wanting to force—through the imposition of pain and suffering—the other to acknowledge and respect you, as well as the role each of you has played in the other's life. It is also the expression of self-respect, not an attempt to maintain one's standing to claim it, let alone to maintain social standing. Something analogous could be said in cases in which one is assaulted by a complete stranger, for relations of mutual respect as fellow citizens or as fellow human beings are also profound and "thick" in their own ways.[65]

The list of human attachments that are enmeshed with our identities is long. To extirpate vengeful anger surely violates the wide- as well as the deep-concerns criteria, as it suggests that we would have to transform our identities such that others don't matter to us very much (which is the implication of what Seneca is saying). It would also violate what I would argue is a defensible, non-Senecan ethical ideal built on stable self-esteem but committed to ethical excellence in our relations—affectively felt and expressed as appropriate—to others and to ourselves. Fittingness in our second sense should, it seems, be regulated by fittingness in the third sense (I leave open the possibility that, in turn, the third should in some way be conditioned by the second). All this suggests, just as many have said, that the Stoic ideal—and with it, the condemnation of anger—is not acceptable. At the same time, as I have argued, the unstable role of self-esteem in Aristotle's ethical version of the *megalopsuchos* requires revision of Aristotle's view, even though that view has the merit of preserving a place for anger in the virtuous life.

5. Taking Revenge

Two vices are opposed to vengeance: one by way of excess, namely, the sin of cruelty or brutality, which exceeds the measure in punishing: while the other is a vice by way of deficiency and consists in being remiss in punishing. . . . But the virtue of vengeance consists in observing the due measure of vengeance with regard to all the circumstances.

—St. Thomas Aquinas, *Summa Theologica*[66]

The justifiability of taking revenge does not follow simply from the justifiability of vengeful anger. Let us limit ourselves here to cases in which the wrong would normally be subject to the state's authority, while acknowledging that there exists a spectrum of vengeful actions that do not normally fall under jurisprudential or police purview (as when one takes revenge in an interpersonal context by withholding love). To take personal revenge in the sorts of cases at issue here is to take the law into one's own hands. If that is to be done justifiably, a number of considerations must be brought to bear. To begin with, if justified revenge-taking expresses v-anger, such that its merits reflect those of the anger from which it springs, then the latter, too, must be justifiable in the ways already described. Further, taking personal revenge is justifiable only if considerations that to considerable extent parallel those mentioned in section 4 with respect to v-anger are satisfied: the alleged wrong must really be such, the target of revenge must in fact be the offender, the revenge must be proportional to the offense, the offender must deserve punishment, and the revenge must not be the instrument of sadism or cruelty.[67] And one would have to carefully consider the psychological costs to oneself quite possibly involved in actually making another human being suffer or in taking a human life (this roughly parallels the fifth condition enumerated toward the start of section 4).

However, taking revenge is also answerable to a host of other considerations that are not pertinent when evaluating the merits of vengeful anger. One certainly has to justify not deferring to the given judicial system. If the system is working reasonably well and fairly, what could warrant one's taking revenge as one sees fit? That question must be answered impartially before revenge is taken. If it is the case that the system is corrupt or simply does not exist, then one first has to assess the feasibility of alternate routes of action, such as taking steps to get a judicial system up and running. I would argue that those routes would have to be shown to be out of reach or not timely given the circumstances to justify one's taking revenge. One also has to satisfy legitimate demands for impartiality and proportionality across cases, so that the law one has taken into one's own hands preserves relevant features of *law*. Such considerations are motivated not only by the demands of fairness but also by the famous problem of spiraling tit-for-tat violence that revenge-taking can instigate. And, of course, one has to assess the physical dangers to oneself involved in taking revenge. I venture the suggestion that in view of the problems of social coordination (to which a judicial system should respond), the chaos that results when people take the law into their own hands, and the other considerations just mentioned, the case against taking revenge is overwhelming even if defeasible, though much depends on the empirical circumstances at the relevant time.

In sum, the virtuous person will feel vengeful anger as appropriate but will take revenge only after careful deliberation and in view of the additional considerations and conditions just sketched. This leaves us with what I referred to at the start of this essay as a surprising distinction—in some cases, collision—between justifications for vengefulness and justifications for taking revenge. For if my vengeful anger is justified, then it seems that the wrongdoer deserves to be punished at my hands (and to know that that is the case and why)—this is his or her just desert that only my acting can provide—and yet good reasons of a different order may proscribe my acting, such that the offender must be deprived of this just desert. When reason forbids the revenge to which I am entitled, regret and even angry disappointment may well follow. The potential here for tragic moral conflict is undeniable.[68]

NOTES

I am grateful to Julia Annas, Jeffrey Blustein, Richard Carrington, Roger Crisp, Remy Debes, Zina Giannopoulou, Peter Goldie, Trudy Govier, Stephen Griswold, Jeffrey Henderson, P. J. Ivanhoe, Simon Keller, Erin Kelly, David Konstan, Annice Kra, Josh Landy, Mitchell Miller (to whom I am especially indebted for discussion about my last paragraph, as well as some of the phrasing thereof), David Roochnik, Amelie Rorty, Steve Scully, Jeffrey Seidman, Nick Smith, Daniel Star, and John Tomasi for discussion about and comments on this essay. I also thank Kelsie Krueger for her work in assembling secondary sources and David Jennings for his careful proofreading. Drafts of this chapter were presented at the American Philosophical Association (2009 Eastern Division Meeting), as part of an invited panel on "Transitional Justice, Reconciliation, Identity, and Memory," and at Boston College (as an A. J. Fitzgibbons Lecture), Brown University, Davidson College, the University of Memphis, the University of New Hampshire, and Vassar College. I am indebted to these various audiences for their questions and comments. I gratefully acknowledge fellowships from the American Council of Learned Societies and the Boston University Humanities

Foundation that supported my research during the 2009–10 academic
year, and a Fellowship Research Grant from the Earhart Foundation that
supported my work during the summer of 2010. I dedicate this essay to the
late Peter Goldie with deep gratitude for his friendship.

1. Nietzsche, "On the Virtuous," in part II of *Thus Spoke Zarathustra*,
in *The Portable Nietzsche*, ed. and trans. W. Kaufmann (New York: Penguin,
1976), 206.

2. The *mênis* referred to at the start of the *Iliad* is, of course, that of
Achilles. Homer's vocabulary for "anger" is complex, and "mênis" (also
translatable as "wrath") is but one term that he uses. There may be sev-
eral types or shapes of anger described in the *Iliad*. For discussion, see D.
Konstan, *The Emotions of the Ancient Greeks* (Toronto: University of Toronto
Press, 2006), 48–56.

3. I am relying on the reports published by CNN, February 27, 2009,
http://www.cnn.com/2009/CRIME/02/27/wiesel.madoff/index.html,
and by the *New York Times*, February 26, 2009, http://www.nytimes.com/
2009/02/27/business/27madoff.html (the latter states that Wiesel and his
wife "lost their life savings" as a result of Madoff). On the judicial sentence
imposed on Madoff, see the *New York Times* report of June 29, 2009, http://
www.nytimes.com/2009/06/30/business/30madoff.html?pagewanted
=1&ref=bernardlmadoff. That report contains quotations from other of
Madoff's victims.

4. For example, C. S. Lewis remarks: "The least indulgence of the passion for revenge is very deadly sin. Christian charity counsels us to make
every effort for the conversion of such a man: to prefer his conversion, at
the peril of our own lives, perhaps of our own souls, to his punishment;
to prefer it infinitely." *The Problem of Pain* (New York: Macmillan, 1967),
109. See also T. Govier, *Forgiveness and Revenge* (London: Routledge, 2002),
11–13; and in a historical vein, D. H. Frank, "Anger as a Vice: A Maimoni-
dean Critique of Aristotle's Ethics," *History of Philosophy Quarterly* 7 (1990):
269–281.

5. For an account of the events referred to, see D. B. Kraybill, S. M.
Nolt, and D. L. Weaver-Zercher, *Amish Grace: How Forgiveness Transcended
Tragedy* (San Francisco: John Wiley, 2007). For a popular case (billed as
a "National Bestseller") against anger, see T. N. Hanh's *Anger: Wisdom for
Cooling the Flames* (New York: Riverhead Books, 2002).

6. I am using T. Irwin's translation throughout: *Aristotle: Nicomachean
Ethics* (hereinafter *NE*), 2nd ed. (Indianapolis: Hackett, 1999).

7. On criticisms of the Amish's response to the murder of their children, see Kraybill et al., *Amish Grace*, 57.

8. See *The Works of Joseph Butler, D.C. L.*, ed. W. E. Gladstone, 2 vols.

(Oxford: Clarendon Press, 1896); vol. II, Sermon VIII ("Upon Resentment"), 136–149, and Sermon IX ("Upon Forgiveness of Injuries"), 150–167. My citations and quotations from Butler are from this edition of these sermons. The consequentialist argument just referred to is to be found in "Upon Resentment," 139–143 (the idea is basically that God gave us that emotion for the purpose of the prevention or remedy of injury). I note that Butler uses the term "resentment" as synonymous with "deliberate anger" (e.g., 140), the meaning of which overlaps closely with what I am calling vengeful anger. A similar appeal to the utility of anger or resentment is found in Shaftesbury's *An Inquiry Concerning Virtue or Merit*, in *Characteristicks of Men, Manners, Opinions, Times,* introduction by D. Den Uyl (Indianapolis: Liberty Fund, 2001), 2:83–85. However, Shaftesbury also offers stringent criticisms of anger in those pages. I offer commentary on Butler's two sermons, and some discussion of resentment more generally, in my *Forgiveness: A Philosophical Exploration* (Cambridge: Cambridge University Press, 2007). The present essay builds on—and, I hope, complements—*Forgiveness.*

   9. On cultural norms favoring or even requiring revenge, see J. Elster, "Norms of Revenge," in *Ethics and Personality: Essays on Moral Psychology,* ed. J. Deigh (Chicago: University of Chicago Press, 1992), 163–165.

   10. For an analogous effort, see K. Kristjánsson, *Justifying Emotions: Pride and Jealousy* (New York: Routledge, 2002). However, he grounds his views about the morality of these emotions in what he calls "a sophisticated form of utilitarianism" (5). For an argument in defense of envy, see J. D'Arms and D. Jacobson, "Anthropocentric Constraints on Human Value," *Oxford Studies in Metaethics* 1 (2006): 119–125. See also J. Murphy's instructive "Two Cheers for Vindictiveness," ch. 2 of his *Getting Even: Forgiveness and Its Limits* (Oxford: Oxford University Press, 2003), 17–26.

   11. My focus is thus substantially different from that of C. K. B. Barton, *Getting Even: Revenge as a Form of Justice* (Chicago: Open Court, 1999). He writes: "The central claim [of his book] is that victim justice, to be worthy of that name, requires the substantial empowerment of victims by law, giving them the legal right to become involved in the relevant legal processes, some of which may culminate in impositions of punishment on their wrongdoers." He is out to vindicate "revenge's undeservedly poor image" (see xiv for both quotations), whereas I am primarily out to consider the ethical merits of vengeful anger.

   12. P. Goldie, *The Emotions: A Philosophical Exploration* (Oxford: Oxford University Press, 2002), 144. This definition seems broad enough to handle the case of someone who undertakes vengeful plotting over time, only sometimes experiencing the "hot' " emotion. For further discussion of the cognitive nature of the emotions, see R. Debes, "Neither Here nor There:

The Cognitive Nature of Emotion," *Philosophical Studies* 146 (2009): 1–27.
I shall not be talking about vengeful anger as a "mood," both because that
seems out of keeping with common parlance and so as to sidestep the complicated question as to the relation between moods and emotions (about
which see Goldie, *The Emotions*, 143–151).

13. Some theorists distinguish between sentiments and emotions. For
example, see A. Ben-Ze'ev, *The Subtlety of Emotions* (Cambridge, MA: MIT
Press, 2000), 83, as well as J. Prinz, "Constructive Sentimentalism: Legal
and Political Implications," in this volume, 10 (he there glosses sentiments
as "dispositions to feel emotions").

14. J. Prinz remarks in *Gut Reactions: A Perceptual Theory of Emotion* (Oxford: Oxford University Press, 2004), 29: "Intuitions derive from reflecting
on our concepts (hence 'conceptual analysis'), and concepts may contain
information that is false or misleading." After enumerating other dangers,
he continues: "These concerns threaten traditional philosophical methods quite broadly. Anyone who hopes to make progress by reflection alone
should be wary. Reflection may reveal more about the person reflecting
than about the phenomenon on which she is reflecting. If one wants to
explain something other than one's own personal beliefs, one should exploit more objective methods" (ibid., 29). I have perhaps not exploited
those methods sufficiently but have nonetheless tried to cultivate the requisite wariness.

15. Trans. R. Warner, in *Euripides I* (Chicago: University of Chicago
Press, 1975), 105. This is a volume in *The Complete Greek Tragedies*, ed. D.
Grene and R. Lattimore, and includes an Introduction by R. Lattimore.

16. See *Ancient Anger: Perspectives from Homer to Galen*, ed. S. Braund and
G. Most (Cambridge: Cambridge University Press, 2003); R. A. Kaster, *Emo-
tion, Restraint, and Community in Ancient Rome* (Oxford: Oxford University
Press, 2005); W. V. Harris, *Restraining Rage: The Ideology of Anger Control in
Classical Antiquity* (Cambridge, MA: Harvard University Press, 2001); S.
Knuuttila, *Emotions in Ancient and Medieval Philosophy* (Oxford: Oxford
University Press, 2004); and especially Konstan, *The Emotions of the Ancient
Greeks*, ch. 2 (on anger).

17. Ben-Ze'ev notes: "Hate may be characterized as involving a global
negative attitude toward someone considered to possess fundamentally
evil traits. . . . Anger is similar to hate and disgust in involving a negative
evaluation, but it is the evaluation of a specific action rather than a global
attitude." He also remarks: "Hate is a long-term attitude whose generation
is frequently not triggered by a personal offense. Hate requires an evaluation of the object as possessing inherently dangerous traits; the object
of anger is guilty of merely instrumental negative actions." *The Subtlety of
Emotions*, 380 and 381, respectively. At *Rhetoric* 2.4 (1382a2–7), Aristotle

too notes that anger is directed at individuals, whereas hatred may also be concerned with classes thereof (say, all thieves). He adds that anger but not hatred is curable in time and that, while anger wants revenge, hatred aims for the extirpation of its object.

18. My approach differs from that of S. Uniacke, who claims that, unlike vengeance, "Revenge can be taken for an injury that is not an offence nor regarded as such by the person taking revenge. We can believe ourselves to have been injured, and resent the injury, without regarding ourselves as wronged." Her examples include resenting "someone's beating me in what I accept was fair competition." Further: "The emotion that gives rise to the desire for revenge is resentment: bitter feelings about an injury sustained. The emotion appropriate to vengeance is moral indignation: anger excited by perceived meanness, injustice, wickedness, or misconduct." S. Uniacke, "Why Is Revenge Wrong?," *Journal of Value Inquiry* 34 (2000): 62–63. That seems implausible. We might jokingly call beating our tennis partner next time around "revenge," but, if it were really such or if the effort really were accompanied by resentment, we would judge it (and the accompanying emotion) inappropriate precisely because no moral wrong is being responded to. So I am also disagreeing with G. Wallace, who urges that we distinguish "between vindictive and non-vindictive revenge. Shylock exemplifies the pursuit of the former, our squash victor achieves the latter. It must be stressed that in both cases it is correct to talk of revenge; it is neither flowery nor metaphorical to suggest that the squash player gains his revenge." "Wild Justice," *Philosophy* 70 (1995): 372. This leads Wallace to such counterintuitive statements as: "Revenge can be sought without malice and without endangering friendship" (373). (I am grateful to Roger Crisp for discussion of the possibility of nonmoralized vengeful anger.)

19. *Aristotle, On Rhetoric: A Theory of Civic Discourse*, trans. with Introduction, Notes, and Appendices by G. A. Kennedy (Oxford: Oxford University Press, 1991), 127. I am using this translation of the *Rhetoric* throughout.

20. The relation between intention and responsibility (not to mention the related idea of "taking responsibility") is, of course, complex. There may be a spectrum of cases in which one has warranted v-anger at someone who has not intentionally done wrong but is responsible (or culpable) for the wrong.

21. See P. F. Strawson, "Freedom and Resentment," in *Freedom and Resentment and Other Essays* (New York: Methuen, 1980), 1–25. Strawson speaks of "*reactive* attitudes and feelings" (6) rather than sentiments, but in the present instance this seems to be a semantic point, especially given his concluding comment: "It is a pity that talk of the moral sentiments has fallen out of favour" (24). Strawson also refers to reactive attitudes such as

resentment and forgiveness as "essentially reactions to the quality of others' wills towards us, as manifested in their behaviour: to their good or ill will or indifference or lack of concern. Thus resentment, or what I have called resentment, is a reaction to injury or indifference" (14). This is in line with my argument.

22. In this I am in agreement with R. J. Stainton, "Revenge," *Critica* 38 (2006): 15. He there adds to the condition that an agent taking revenge must intend to do so and have reasons, that the "agent must also have the concept REVENGE."

23. Butler, "Upon Resentment," 139.

24. What Prinz says of Aristotle's theory of the emotions generally fits v-anger nicely: "Emotions are, thus, felt, action-directed, cognitive states of the body." *Gut Reactions*, 11. In characterizing Aristotle's theory, Prinz notes that it is a hybrid—a behavioral, a cognitive, as well as a feeling theory. Ibid., 10–11. This much seems to be consistent with the characterization of "emotion" by Goldie quoted at the start of this essay.

25. G. E. M. Anscombe, *Intention* (Ithaca: Cornell University Press, 1969), 20: "I will call revenge and gratitude and remorse and pity backward-looking motives, and contrast them with motive-in-general," for they give "something that *has happened* (or is at present happening) . . . as the ground of an action or abstention that is good or bad for the person (it may be oneself, as with remorse) at whom it is aimed." Further on, she remarks: "I call a motive forward-looking if it is an intention" (21). Anscombe refers in these pages to revenge, not vengeful anger, but her point applies to both.

26. I agree with Prinz's observation that anger tends to focus on the person who, say, uttered the offensive words, rather than on the words: "Insults instigate anger, but anger latches onto the insulter." *Gut Reactions*, 227.

27. On the debate about whether emotions are perceptions, see Prinz, *Gut Reactions*, ch. 10. He there concludes that "emotion is a form of perception" (240).

28. Adam Smith, *The Theory of Moral Sentiments* (hereinafter *TMS*), ed. D. D. Raphael and A. L. Macfie (Indianapolis: Liberty Press, 1982), III.4.3. I am using this edition of *TMS* throughout. Interestingly, the famous *Lex Talionis* (*Exodus* 21:24) may be interpreted as an effort to *restrain* the otherwise spiraling ambitions of revenge-taking, as is suggested by N. H. Frijda in "The Lex Talionis: On Vengeance," in *Emotions: Essays on Emotion Theory*, ed. S. van Goozen, N. Van de Poll, and J. Sergeant (Hillsdale, NJ: Lawrence Erlbaum, 1994), 264.

29. As Aristotle notes in *De Anima*, 403a30–31.

30. Does the legitimacy of v-anger therefore depend on a retributivist

theory of punishment? The answer may well be affirmative, though the line from a theory of the moral emotions to the theory of punishment is not direct and, in any event, is not my topic here.

31. Of course, not all retribution is revenge or vengeful; judicially administered punishment might be thought of as retributive in some sense but not necessarily as revenge or vengeful. Retribution may thus be impersonal, whereas revenge is personal, as R. Nozick argues in *Philosophical Explanations* (Cambridge, MA: Harvard University Press, 1981), 367.

32. I refer to the fine article by G. Bar-Elli and D. Heyd, "Can Revenge Be Just or Otherwise Justified?," *Theoria* 52 (1986): 71–72. As they put it: "Furthermore, for the act of revenge to be fully successful, it must be understood by its recipient as intentional. This feature of 'double intentionality' is very significant for the understanding of the nature of revenge. It highlights the *personal* dimension which is its most important, though theoretically disturbing, trait" (71). Several of the points I am making in this paragraph are elegantly stated by Adam Smith (*TMS* II.i.1.6): "if the person who had done us some great injury, who had murdered our father or our brother, for example, should soon afterwards die of a fever, or even be brought to the scaffold upon account of some other crime, though it might sooth our hatred, it would not fully gratify our resentment. Resentment would prompt us to desire, not only that he should be punished, but that he should be punished by our means, and upon account of that particular injury which he had done to us. Resentment cannot be fully gratified, unless the offender is not only made to grieve in his turn, but to grieve for that particular wrong which we have suffered from him." For a brilliant argument to the effect that Smith is ambivalent about the emotion of resentment (vacillating between a view tied to an ethic of honor and retaliation and one tied to an ethic of equal dignity and mutual accountability), see S. Darwall, "Smith's Ambivalence about Honour," *Adam Smith Review* 5 (2010): 106–123. I am indebted to Darwall's discussion of Smith and of resentment in that article as well as in his *The Second-Person Standpoint: Morality, Respect, and Accountability* (Cambridge, MA: Harvard University Press, 2006). See esp. pp. 67–68 and 80–86 of *The Second-Person Standpoint* on resentment, indignation, and retaliation.

33. Nozick too sees revenge (and in a different way, retribution, which is his main focus in this respect) as having a communicative function. *Philosophical Explanations*, 370. P. J. Ivanhoe has suggested to me that perhaps the communicative character of revenge should be stated more broadly: it informs others that it is wrong to treat *anybody* in the way that I was treated and so is a protest registered on behalf of other victims (even potential ones). Moreover, revenge can also publicly mark the offender as untrustworthy. I have not foregrounded these possible functions of revenge-taking

because I am avoiding reference to social utility as the basis for explaining and defending v-anger. A more Socratic line would emphasize that punishment aims to *cure* the wrongdoer (see *Gorgias* 478e2–4, 480a6–b5).

34. Nozick notes: "Revenge involves a particular emotional tone, pleasure in the suffering of another, while retribution either need involve no emotional tone, or involves another one, namely, pleasure at justice being done. Therefore, the thirster after revenge often will want to experience (see, be present at) the situation in which the revengee is suffering, whereas with retribution there is no special point in witnessing its infliction." *Philosophical Explanations*, 367. I add that interpreters tend to assume that the pleasures of imagining and plotting revenge carry over to the act of taking revenge itself; but different hedonic, as well as moral, valences may attach to each.

35. Indeed, Bar-Elli and Heyd conclude that "the metaphors of balancing, restoration, and equality are misleading when used in this context [of revenge]. They are already hard enough to apply on the 'material' level of penal justice. However, they seem totally paradoxical when extended to the 'mental' level of personal attitudes, which are not controllable by penal intervention and are partly a matter of the individual's free choice." "Can Revenge Be Just or Otherwise Justified?," 84.

36. See J. Haidt, "The Moral Emotions," in *Handbook of Affective Sciences*, ed. R. J. Davidson, K. R. Scherer, and H. H. Goldsmith (Oxford: Oxford University Press, 2003), 856. With respect to Aristotle's point in the *Rhetoric* 2.2 (1378b1–2) that anger is accompanied by the (pleasurable) expectation of revenge, Haidt remarks: "More recent studies confirm that anger generally involves a motivation to attack, humiliate, or otherwise get back at the person who is perceived as acting unfairly or immorally . . . . The fact that anger often involves a motivation for revenge has been noted in a great many cultures." Ibid., 856.

37. Elster, "Norms of Revenge," 176.

38. Uniacke comments: "While the desire for revenge seems principally grounded in notions of self-esteem and reputation, there are significant exceptions." "Why Is Revenge Wrong?," 66. The sorts of exceptions she cites, however, are about (in my terminology) retaliation or even, as she notes, a desire to make sense of a tragedy that has befallen a loved one by "blaming someone, however unreasonably." Ibid., 67. J. Hampton usefully distinguishes an action that has the effect of diminishing one's value and rank from one that has "*revealed* a rank that is lower" than one had thought. See J. G. Murphy and J. Hampton, *Forgiveness and Mercy* (Cambridge: Cambridge University Press, 1988), 50. In describing the resentment a victim feels in response to wrongdoing, she credits it with the "fear" that one's worth can be lowered or has been revealed to be lower than one

thought. Ibid., 57. Hence resentment is "a personally defensive protest," meaning among things that it is "a defense against the action's attack on one's self–esteem" (ibid., 56, phrase in the second quotation italicized in the original). Hampton also notes: "resentment is nonetheless an emotion which betrays weakness. Resenters mount a defense against a challenge to their value and rank to which they are in danger of succumbing" (ibid., 148). As I understand the argument, this protest or defense is retributive in character (e.g., see ibid., 142–143). In the terms I am adopting, Hampton roots resentment, that is, vengeful anger, at least in part in low (or lowered) self–esteem and thus brings it close to Nietzschean *ressentiment*, as Murphy implies (ibid., 93).

   39. See M. J. Horowitz, "Understanding and Ameliorating Revenge Fantasies in Psychotherapy," *The American Journal of Psychiatry* 164 (2007): 25; Frijda, "The Lex Talionis," 276–277; and J. R. Averill, *Anger and Aggression: An Essay on Emotion* (New York: Springer-Verlag, 1982), 173–174. As Averill notes, the relationship between low self-esteem and anger is complex, since "persons with very low self-esteem may perceive a threat as justified (e.g., as congruent with their own self-image)" and *not* respond with anger. Ibid., 174. He there continues: "At the other extreme, persons with high self-esteem are less likely than others to perceive as threatening minor slights or rebuffs." R. S. Lazarus writes that anger has several "*primary appraisal* components, the third of which is introduced as follows: "The basic motive to preserve or enhance self-esteem against assault, which is one *type of ego-involvement*, must also be activated for anger to occur." *Emotion and Adaptation* (Oxford: Oxford University Press, 1991), 222. The close tie between vengeful anger and self-esteem is also drawn by P. Fisher, *The Vehement Passions* (Princeton, NJ: Princeton University Press, 2002), 176–177: "The excitations of anger mark out the places where self-worth or honor has been transgressed"; and "A measure of self-esteem, or of endangered self-regard, is defended with the energies of anger that locate and announce that injustice has been felt and must be revenged." See also Fisher, ibid., 184–194.

   40. I agree with the definition of self-esteem in J. Deigh's "Shame and Self–Esteem: A Critique," *Ethics* 93 (1983): 229: "So while we would have said, loosely speaking, that self-esteem came from one's having a good opinion of oneself, we may now say more strictly that it comes from a good opinion of oneself as the author of one's actions, more generally, one's life. Accordingly, this opinion comprises a favorable regard for one's aims and ideals in life and a favorable assessment of one's suitability for pursuing them." I am not here concerned with the interesting problem of the relation between self-esteem and self-respect, about which see S. Darwall, "Two Kinds of Respect," *Ethics* 88 (1977): 48; and D. Sachs, "How to

120   CHARLES L. GRISWOLD

Distinguish Self-Respect from Self-Esteem," *Philosophy and Public Affairs* 10 (1981): 346–360.

41. See F. Nietzsche, *On the Genealogy of Morality*, trans. M. Clark and A. J. Swensen (Indianapolis: Hackett, 1998), First Treatise, Section 10, p. 19: "The slave revolt in morality begins when *ressentiment* itself becomes creative and gives birth to values: the *ressentiment* of beings denied the true reaction, that of the deed, who recover their losses only through an imaginary revenge. Whereas all noble morality grows out of a triumphant yes–saying to oneself, from the outset slave morality says 'no' to an 'outside', to a 'different', to a 'not-self': and *this* 'no' is its creative deed." Nietzsche's "noble human being" (ibid., 21) bears an interesting family resemblance to Aristotle's *megalopsuchos*, though the latter does permit himself vengeful anger (but not *ressentiment*). There can be no hitting of the Aristotelian mean with respect to *ressentiment*, and I will not be making the case that *ressentiment* could be justifiable.

42. Once again, consider Frijda, who comments on the propensity to cruelty, including that associated with revenge: "Need for proof of power or self-efficacy at this level has a ring of need for proof of a sense of self —again, as the counterpoint of being a victim." "The Lex Talionis," 281.

43. In *Seneca: Moral and Political Essays*, ed. and trans. J. M. Cooper and J. F. Procopé (Cambridge: Cambridge University Press, 2003), 116. I am using this edition and translation of *De Ira* throughout and have incorporated the page references directly into the text. I am not drawing here on any other of Seneca's writings.

44. R. Kraut notes: "Unfortunately, he [Aristotle] finds it so obvious that anger should sometimes be felt and expressed that he does not argue against a hypothetical opponent who advocates its elimination. The latter view was adopted by the Stoics; see esp. Seneca, *De Ira*." *Aristotle: Political Philosophy* (Oxford: Oxford University Press, 2002), 334 n. 23.

45. D'Arms and Jacobson remark in "Anthropocentric Constraints on Human Value": "Reasons of fit are those reasons that speak directly to what one takes the emotion to be concerned with, as opposed to reasons that speak to the advisability or propriety of having that emotion. So reasons of fit for fear are roughly those that speak to whether or not something is a *threat*." Ibid., 108. This seems tolerably close to the first conception of "the fitting" I am sketching here.

46. D. Konstan comments: "Anger for Aristotle, then, is anything but a reflex to pain or harm, even when the cause is intentional. Aristotle envisages a world in which self-esteem depends on social interaction: the moment someone's negative opinion of your worth is actualized publicly in the form of a slight, you have lost credit, and the only recourse is a compensatory act that restores your social position. Anger is precisely the

desire to adjust the record in this way." *The Emotions of the Ancient Greeks*, 74–75.

47. See *The Complete Works of Aristotle* (Revised Oxford Translation), ed. and trans. J. Barnes (Princeton, NJ: Princeton University Press, 1995), I:161.

48. For some helpful discussion of pride, self-respect, and self-esteem with reference to the *megalopsuchos*, see Kristjánsson's *Justifying Emotions*, 95–97, 104–108. With regard to the relation between gender and (the acceptability of) v-anger, an issue that has much to do with the perceived "standing" to be angry, see M. Frye's "A Note on Anger," in *The Politics of Reality: Essays in Feminist Theory* (Freedom, CA: Crossing Press, 1983), 84–94; E. V. Spelman, "Anger and Insubordination," in *Women, Knowledge, and Reality: Explorations in Feminist Philosophy*, ed. A. Garry and M. Pearsall (Boston: Unwin Hyman, 1989), 263–273; and A. Lorde, "The Uses of Anger: Women Responding to Racism," in *Sister Outsider: Essays and Speeches* (New York: Crossing Press, 1984), 124–133.

49. D'Arms and Jacobson helpfully distinguish between two sorts of considerations bearing on the question of the cost of a revisionist moral view. The first has to do with our "deep concerns," ones that "are firmly entrenched in their possessors, such that it would be either impossible or extremely costly to excise them." The second has to do with our "wide concerns." These "play a broad psychological role in the mental economy of their possessor. When the object of a concern prompts a variety of evaluative attitudes, not just a single emotion or desire; when desire for it (or aversion to it) arises in many different situations; when it is implicated in the ability to get or avoid many other things people care about; when its pursuit or avoidance grounds disparate actions and plans; when, in short, it is firmly enmeshed in our web of psychological responses, this is evidence of the width of a concern." "Anthropocentric Constraints on Human Value," 116. As an example of a wide concern they cite anger, and in disagreement with the "stoic and Christian foes of anger" they note: "Yet anger is not just a passion for vengeance. It also manifests concern for social regulation, which focuses on personal slights and social transgressions." Ibid., 117. They immediately concede that one could have concern for respectful treatment independently of anger, however, which is a bit confusing (and provides Seneca with an opening). The more general claim is "that psychological facts constrain the tenability of norms of fittingness. . . . Rationalists can point to a sublime Socratic ideal of a person so self-sufficient in his virtue that he does [*sic*] care about honor, wealth, or even life; or to an impartial observer whose only concern is to maximize net happiness. If nothing matters but the state of one's soul, and no harm can befall the virtuous person, then there is truly nothing to fear." Ibid., 118. They also remark: "But why should the fact that the stoic has been

able to describe a logically possible human being who can embrace these consequences be thought to show that they are suitable standards of fittingness for humans?" Ibid., 118. I am in sympathy with both these more general points, as will become clearer in section 4.

50. Ibid., 118.

51. Seneca takes this all the way at 1.12.1: " 'Tell me then, is the good man not angry if he sees his father slain and his mother ravished?' No, he will not be angry. He will punish and protect." Consider also 1.12.5: "Anger for one's friends is the mark of a weak mind, not a devoted one." So we are not to rise to indignant anger or sympathetic resentment, either. This seems quite close to the conclusion drawn by the Amish (though no doubt they do so on somewhat different grounds).

52. He thus would not seem to succumb to what D'Arms and Jacobson call the "moralistic fallacy." See their "The Moralistic Fallacy: On the 'Appropriateness' of Emotions," *Philosophy and Phenomenological Research* 61 (2000): 66 (they there use the example of the joke). They remark: "Put most simply, to commit the moralistic fallacy is to infer, from the claim that it would be wrong or vicious to feel an emotion, that it is therefore unfitting. We shall contend, to the contrary, that an emotion can be fitting despite being wrong (or inexpedient) to feel." Ibid., 68–69. Their definition here of "fitting" as a match-up between emotion and features in the world it takes itself to be responding to (ibid., 72) captures my first sense of "fitting."

53. For an interesting discussion of the Epicurean condemnation of anger, see J. Annas, *The Morality of Happiness* (Oxford: Oxford University Press, 1993), 194–200. Her remarks on 218–219 about the importance of the conception of our final end to the assessment of the propriety of anger mesh perfectly with my argument.

54. As Seneca indicates in *De Ira* 2.3.4, the emotion of anger (as distinct from the "impression" that sets it going) has already enlisted (faulty) reason on its side. So, once we are angry, reason cannot stand *against* the anger; it is already working on behalf of the anger (e.g., by rationalizing revenge-taking or exaggerating the harm done to the victim). And that underlines the danger of anger—its toxicity—and the impossibility of moderating it to the point that it expresses moral excellence. (My thanks to Julia Annas for pressing this point on me.) The mitigated defense of anger I am working toward in this essay would require rejecting this Stoic theory of the emotions.

55. This may be contested on the grounds that it suffices for the agent to have good reasons for believing that his or her v-anger tracks what is in fact the case (so that the agent's course of action is subjectively right, even if it is objectively wrong). While this is too large an issue to be further

explored here, my broadly Aristotelian approach (for Aristotle, the virtues depend on *phronesis*, and reason or judgment tracks truth; e.g., *NE* 1140b5, 21) avoids the counterintuitive result that it would be virtuous to feel v-anger that is mistakenly directed at the innocent, for example. A full assessment of the matter would have to take into account whether or not the mistake is culpable. (I am grateful to Daniel Star for pressing me to confront this point.)

56. The steps I would argue for are to be found in my *Forgiveness*, ch. 2.

57. One question to be addressed in working out this point is whether a "unity of the virtues" thesis is being assumed.

58. For a similar point, see G. Taylor, "Justifying the Emotions," *Mind* 84 (1975): 397–402. My list is compatible with—and to some extent overlaps with—hers (see 394–397). As she rightly notes: "Justifying one's anger on any particular occasion is, then, a complicated procedure" (397).

59. See note 49.

60. See the passages cited in note 49 from D'Arms and Jacobson, "Anthropocentric Constraints on Human Value." I read their comments about anger as applying to vengefulness.

61. *Aristotle: The Politics*, trans. C. Lord (Chicago: University of Chicago Press, 1985), 208. Aristotle continues at 1328a8–12: "But it is not right to say that they are harsh toward those who are unknown. One ought not to be of this sort toward anyone, nor are magnanimous persons [*megalopsuchoi*] savage in their nature, except toward those behaving unjustly. And, further, they will feel this rather toward their intimates, as was said earlier, if they consider themselves treated unjustly" (ibid.).

62. I refer to Fisher's gloss on these *Politics* passages: "Aristotle's seemingly odd claim can be restated as an argument that the sudden anger we feel driving us to retaliate also informs us of two things: first, that we have been held in contempt; second, that the person who has slighted us matters to us. The flaring up of anger informs us about how much we care for this person's regard, and how injured we are by any sign of contempt on his or her part." *The Vehement Passions*, 192.

63. One of the greatest modern reflections on the problem of reconciling interdependence, anger, and strong self-esteem is to be found in Rousseau's *Emile* (the epigraph to which is taken from *De Ira*). The present essay will be developed further in conjunction with a study of Rousseau and Adam Smith.

64. Correspondingly, one would have to grant that the offense does not dehumanize the offender or make him or her into a "moral monster." Aristotle's view seems to be that many offenders are simply not worth one's anger—they don't have the standing to warrant it. And while Seneca emphasizes our common humanity, in comparing the offender to a natural

event, child, or illness—with the result that the wrongdoer is not worthy of one's anger—his view risks dehumanizing the offender. By contrast, the view I am pointing to holds that the wrongs to which v-anger responds are the work of agents who *qua* agents have the standing to be addressed by this emotion, as it were. That helps to explain why equality of regard (and therefore the offender's regard of the victim) matters. The idea of second-personal address is worked out systematically in S. Darwall's *The Second-Person Standpoint.*

65. V-anger holds the wrongdoer accountable and thus is also mobilized for the sake of that other, as it seeks to get him or her to see what it means both for you to have been wronged and that you are not to be wronged. In holding the offender accountable, one stands in for his or her better self (this is not incompatible with desert, even when the offender deserves death). This thread of the justification for v-anger preserves its communicative function and might be all the more relevant if the other has mattered greatly to you.

66. Aquinas, *Summa Theologica*, trans. Fathers of the English Dominican Province (New York: Benziger Brothers, 1947), 2:1658 (Q. 108 Art. 2, reply to Objection 3).

67. This list overlaps to some extent with that of P. French, who posits four conditions for defensible revenge-taking. See his *The Virtues of Vengeance* (Lawrence: University Press of Kansas, 2001), 115. But French's analysis is not only focused on revenge-taking rather than on the emotion of vengefulness; on his view, revenge may justly be taken on behalf of another (hence he speaks throughout of avenging; see, e.g., ibid., 172).

68. This is not to say, however, that the virtuous person's v-anger is therefore turned into Nietzschean *ressentiment* (such that v-anger is *repressed*) when revenge ought not be taken. Self-command and repression, the reasoned decision not to act on a sentiment and the inability to act on it, are quite different things. The view being sketched here would have to be joined to an appropriate conception of agency such that *not* acting on warranted v-anger does not compromise agency. John Tomasi suggests to me that a conception of political agency (which reflects one's status as citizen) might help to resolve the tension here.

PART II

PASSION AND MOTIVATION: PASSIONS AND EMOTIONS IN DEMOCRATIC POLITICS

5

REASON, PASSION, AND
DEMOCRATIC POLITICS:
OLD CONCEPTIONS—
NEW UNDERSTANDINGS—
NEW POSSIBILITIES

GEORGE E. MARCUS

1. ENDURING BUT STATIC DEBATES

Humans are social creatures reliant on both emotionality and reasoning. As a consequence, these qualities and how we understand them are central to the empirical question of how democracy works and to the normative questions of how well it works. The differing assessments of the empirical and normative features of democracy by its friends and critics have sustained ongoing debate extending over the millennia since Athens's creation sprang into life.[1]

But, even among democracy's friends, difficulties arise. As Jim Fishkin points out in a recent fine book, democracy often rests on conflicting principles.[2] And, because these principles conflict, no one version of democracy can secure each and every one. Fishkin focuses on three principles. As he notes, democracy flourishes when lots of people participate. That is so because maximizing participation ensures that more interests will be brought forth; however they are resolved, the larger the public involvement, the greater the likelihood that, all things being equal, the outcome will be widely accepted as legitimate. It is also the case that democracy offers a sovereign arena within which the public can examine and address claims of injustices that often arise within the many hierarchies that we also inhabit.[3] Most societies, those with democratic regimes no less than those with other forms of governance, rely on many institutions that employ integrated patterns of superordination and subordination to assign authority to the few along with the expectation and imposition of deference by the many.[4] The nominal equality of "one person, one vote" available within democracy, however qualified and undermined in practice, offers at least a modicum of equal station so that those high and low, those of ancient lineage and those newest to the community, stand on equal footing.[5]

Finally, Fishkin points out that deliberation is also an essential feature of any politics that seeks both to formulate the public interest and to secure legitimacy.[6] But, as Fishkin argues, achieving these three, participation, equality, and deliberation, generates what he describes as a "trilemma."[7] Fishkin holds that one democratic regime variant, mass democracy, enables the principles of equality and participation but at the cost of deliberation. A second variant, mobilized deliberation, devotes considerable effort to reach and engages many, though hardly all, in the service of civic education, thereby securing participation and a modicum of deliberation but at the cost of equality. A final variant that Fishkin considers, microcosmic deliberation, uses a variety of devices—deliberative juries, panels, and other small-scale settings—to offer a depth and continuity of engagement so as to enhance deliberation and equality, at least for those participating, but at the cost of broad participation.

These three variants of democracy hardly exhaust the array of institutional settings or the historical variants.[8] I begin with Fishkin's taxonomy to make one important observation that is central to the analysis that follows. In such considerations as Fishkin's, the underlying presumption is that democratic principles or values are universally applicable. Hence, for example, participation should always and everywhere be high. I do not intend to begin an argument on this point at this juncture; that awaits a later and fuller exposition elsewhere in this essay. I want here to point out that the trilemma arises because of the unstated presumption that any political decision ought to be the result of a politics in which all three of these principles—wide spread participation, political equality, and fulsome deliberation—are realized. If and only if the three principles are each universal in their applicability is there a trilemma.

Let's turn to another feature evident in democratic regimes. We can easily locate democratic regimes along a spectrum, with those regimes that seek to shield political representatives from public attention and pressure at one end and those regimes that seek to give the public every opportunity to fully participate in the formulation of and choice among policy options at the other end.[9] The latter presumes a competent and active electorate, what we might call, in the evocative phrasing of Benjamin Barber, "Strong Democracy."[10] Those calling for weak democracy do so because they find the public largely so deficient in competency and engagement that their role must be reduced to that of a passive audience, while the active judgmental role is given principally, if not totally, to political elites.[11] Intermediate are those who argue that the public has sufficient discernment such that it can offer rational judgment, at least under favorable conditions.[12]

How much public involvement is warranted expressly turns on the empirical assessment of the electorate's competence for judgment and engagement.[13] The importance of this empirical assessment grew when, in the mid-twentieth century, survey data gave scholars greater access to the thoughts and considerations evident within the electorate. It is worth noting that, while democratic participation for the many is held dependent on their demonstrated competence, there is little in the way of a companion conditional consideration of elite competence as a prerequisite for elite involvement in governance.[14]

The initial formative analyses, principally but hardly limited to those by the American Voter team,[15] claimed to find the public largely bereft of coherent political beliefs, indeed, so much so that the prospect of leaving the direction of public affairs to the public seemed implausible.[16] More specifically, the "Normal Vote" portrait of the American electorate revealed an electorate composed of two categories of voters.[17] The largest segment, the partisan portion, is knowledgeable but obdurate in its steadfast reliance

on partisan convictions. The other segment, the so-called swing or
independent vote, is largely devoid of political knowledge, largely
inattentive to politics, but, when made the focus of dueling campaigns, "persuadable," at least in the sense that they were moved
by the general "tenor of the times" and evocative messages to mo-
mentarily take sides.

In this view, then, the American electorate is thought to be
constituted of voters obstinately disinterested in thoughtful and
fair consideration of contemporary affairs so wedded are they to
their partisan convictions and of voters who actually decide outcomes for all of us but do so without the application of critical
judgment or sufficient knowledge to make a rational judgment.[18]
Walter Lippmann,[19] relying on his experience in the Woodrow
Wilson administration as it sought and secured public support for
U.S. participation in World War I and importantly, on Plato, found
the public gullible and ignorant of public affairs and, hence, easily moved this way or that by government propaganda.[20] Rigorous
investigations of the public's political knowledge continue to show
an apparent void of content.[21]

One primary defense of democracy, in the American context,
is that advanced by Sam Popkin.[22] He argues that people by relying on their convictions achieve a measure of rationality. Popkin
bases his argument on research in psychology that suggests that reliance on habituated convictions, heuristics, often achieves favorable outcomes.[23] Hence, Popkin concludes that the public, though
inarticulate and ignorant of much of the grist of politics, achieves
a sufficient standard of judgment, if not exactly the more fulsome
variant advanced by many democratic theorists.[24]

Another defense advanced by some is that we can and should
pay less attention to deliberation. Some argue that, inasmuch as
politics is about conflicting claims, we should just get on with it
and gear up for political combat.[25] One weakness of this view is
that it generates blind obedience to convictions even in the face of
discrediting evidence.[26]

At the core of these empirical assessments is the foundational
consensus that the public is neither sufficiently knowledgeable nor
sufficiently capable of reasoning, at least not in the classic sense
of these terms. Hence, the principle of deliberation thought to be
an essential part of democratic politics is sacrificed because of the

apparent limitations of the electorate. But giving up on delibera-tion is a serious withdrawal from a fully realized democratic vision. Deliberation is mandated by the need to move from self-interest to the public good so as to prevent a politics of the many against the few.[27] A focus on deliberation is also mandated by the need to secure legitimacy for policy outcomes. And, finally, a focus on de-liberation is mandated because it compels a venue for the public's critical and public examination of policy offerings as an essential preliminary stage before enacting public judgment.

The conventional accounts agree on the essentials of the em-pirical literature on the American electorate. First, as noted, it is widely believed that the public is largely ignorant of political af-fairs. Second, because of that ignorance, the public makes political choices by relying on either submissive acceptance of elite rhetoric or truculent reliance on extant convictions, neither of which quali-fies as thoughtful assessment of policy alternatives. To some, for example, Mueller,[28] this is the best one can do. Those who aspire to a more full-throated democracy are often driven to abandon de-liberation.[29] But, no matter the response, the foundational status of this empirical portrait is largely taken as axiomatic.

In all, the various conceptions of democracy, no matter how much they argue for a fuller or a lesser role for the public in gov-erning, share a number of foundational views of the normative standards and empirical grounding of democratic rule. The vari-ants arise from different claims as to which principles are under-stood as the most precious and from what are perceived to be nec-essary compromises with the perceived failure of the electorate to meet these essential standards.[30]

No matter the differences in the democratic arrangements, emotion and reason and how they have been understood remain deeply implicated. For example, it has long been held that reason is weak but nonetheless the only normatively sound basis for po-litical and moral judgment because only reason achieves universal rather than partial application of principle. Additionally, only rea-son offers explicit grounds for judgment, which satisfies the need to make the grounds for agreement and opposition visible and thereby available for public disputation and agreement.

On the other hand, it has been widely held that emotion—ex-cept for some "good" emotions, most typically empathy[31]—is not an acceptable foundation for judgment because, though potent, emotion is held to be at best arational, though more often irrational. Further, emotion is mysterious in its foundations. That is, we cannot be confident that we grasp our own emotions' sources, let alone the causes of emotion observed and hidden in others. This has the unfortunate consequence of leaving affective states largely inaccessible for introspection or shared inquiry.

And, as judgment requires explicit reasoning—the fulsome engagement with reflective deliberation[32]—the possibility of a helpful role for emotion is largely ignored because, in the main, it is imagined to be detrimental. No matter the specifics of different democratic regimes, much rests on the question of who can reason properly, for reason and its product, knowledge, are the sole bases for sovereign decisions. Those dubious of the public's capacity for rational judgment turn, with reluctance or enthusiasm, to elite dominance. Those more optimistic about the public's capacity for reasonableness, if not rationality, favor greater public participation.[33]

To this point, I have argued that knowledge and a particular form of judgment, the explicit use of reasoning, are two foundational premises of democracy, no matter the particulars thereof. Let me add a third foundational premise: autonomy. It is a given that citizens who sell their votes for payment or for a drink of whisky undermine the premise that the vote reflects that person's autonomous assessment of interests, self and public. Similarly, a citizen who acts to accommodate the parochial claims of the powerful or too easily submits to the call of the many, as de Tocqueville feared, is also subverting democracy.

A citizen is expected to be able to discern his or her interests, through introspection and deliberation with others, and to act reliant on autonomous judgment, though with and for others, to secure those interests. But more problematic than the inability of people to "stand up" for their own interests is the now common observation that people too often thoughtlessly set aside any consideration of their moral obligations when confronting injustice or immorality.[34] This conclusion is now a standard lesson in the disciplines of both social psychology and history.[35] The proclivity to do nothing in the face of injustice or evil has been a recurring theme of the twentieth and, now, the twenty-first centuries.

In sum, four principles—reliance on reason, reliance on sound

knowledge, willingness and capacity to sustain individual autonomy, and willingness to engage moral considerations—are the preconditions for governance that is just—securing the rights of all
—and that reaches for the public good. The apparent failure of
the public to manifest each of these principles leaves democracy
suspect even to its friends.

Not all the proclaimed failures and fallibilities of democracy rest
on the capacity of the public to accumulate political knowledge, to
engage in reason, to demonstrate individual autonomy of thought
and action, and to apply moral considerations when appropriate.
Suffice it to say that democracy becomes dystopic unless it can rely
upon the public to exemplify some modest application of these
foundational principles.[36] To these normative assertions let me
add a fifth. We need to find in the public the capacity not only
for autonomous thought but also for autonomous action. Thought
that leads to inaction, to nowhere, however enjoyable the mental
exercise, leaves a void for other factors to fill. The presumption
that mindful intention leads to guided action is then a necessary
normative presumption for the viability of democratic regimes.
Thus, five basic ideas, while not exhaustive of the topic of emotion
and democracy, are central to understanding democratic politics.

2. The Empirical Premises of the Four Normative Standards

The various conceptions of democratic governance all rest, to some
degree, on these presumptions about how human beings function:

Autonomy of thought as a condition of citizenship: Expressed thoughts,
beliefs, and values are the necessary grist for democratic politics.
Thoughts expressed in words make visible our preferences, our
knowledge, and our reasoning. And, via speech, we also gain the
means to share preferences, knowledge, and reasoning with others
(at least for those who truthfully reveal them).

Moreover, our expressed thoughts ought to be "ours" even if
widely shared with our partisan colleagues, not the passive retransmission of the thoughts of others.[37] The suspicion that this premise is not viable is central to the explicit or implicit critiques of democracy offered by Erich Fromm,[38] Leon Festinger,[39] and Milton
Rokeach,[40] among many others. The concern with the gullibility

of the masses, as forcefully articulated by Plato, Hobbes, Walter Lippmann, and others, could as easily be broadened to include the gullibility of elites in general[41] and political leaders in particular.[42]

Self-generated action as a condition of citizenship: This presumption follows from the first. The actions we undertake must be driven by the thoughts that motivate them. If our actions are thoughtless, they might be excused as acts of frailty or folly, but such will not serve as justification for the actions themselves. We expect that citizens will have reasons for their actions and that those reasons will be connected in a meaningful way to the actions that they generate (citizens and leaders often lie, but that is another issue). It is the plausibility of such a linkage that Gustave Le Bon[43] and Hannah Arendt,[44] in different ways, attack.

The claim that knowledge as truth, rather than opinion, ought to be the basis for judgment: This presumption goes back at least to Plato.[45] Plato argues that access to knowledge is the essential requirement for sovereign rule. To the extent that the people live in a realm of shared opinions, delusions, they ought to be excluded from participating in collective rule. The common practice of defending beliefs even (indeed, especially) when the beliefs are implausible is a condition described by psychologists as "motivated reasoning,"[46] wherein some valued opinion is protected against any contrary option or evidence. This is actually a common pattern that we can all readily observe easily when displayed by others but are less likely to acknowledge when we so indulge. Plato, having introduced the distinction between knowledge as truth, that is, access to the real state of the world (or, more precisely, his theory of forms), in contrast to the local beliefs that are merely vague and distorted representations of the immediate circumstances, offers the most popular and enduring ground for delegitimizing democracy. Knowledge is presumed to require a particular skilled stance, that of the objective—even distrusting—observer. Moreover, knowledge is held to be difficult, requiring explicit general explanations that identify causal relationships to account for observed recurring patterns. For many scholars, until and unless the many approach the world as scientists, the many are best left resting in the easy comfort of delusion while others better suited do the hard task of governing.[47]

Finally, *all collective judgments, but most especially those that impact on justice, are to be achieved by the application of universal principles.*

Though often political preferences arise as expressions of self-interest, the collective actions reached by citizen endorsement ought to be based on principles that are expressible in and derived from universalizing reason. It is widely understood that a politics based on self-serving preferences leads to injustice.[48] Judgments made out of emotion (e.g., the Furies),[49] or out of prejudice,[50] or out of casual, thoughtless obedience[51] are inherently suspect.

In sum, democracy and widely spread and fully engaged citizenship rests on the presumptions that:

- Autonomy is the principal and universal stance from which citizens engage others.
- Self-generated self-conscious action is the primary legitimate expression of the democratic citizen.
- Truth is the definitive criterion for knowledge and action. Moreover, truth is universal (i.e., stable across time and space) and expressed in semantic terms.[52]
- Justice, meaning our moral judgments as well as political issues that touch upon equality, is a matter of explicit judgment of applied laws, principles (governing evidence, witnesses, and so forth), and juries of our peers.

The ancients were deeply interested in theories of personality (who has the capacity to rule), socialization (what can be done to train those who can rule), institutions (what arrangements can strengthen public judgment), and decision making. They, and we, believe that justifications for who should rule depend primarily on the rulers' demonstrated ability to make sound decisions. For Plato, the answer is found in aristocratic rule, rule by the best. For Aristotle, the answer is found in collective judgment of the many, rule by democracy, though he notes that this entails the risk of folly, a risk no less plausible when authority is vested in the hands of a few.

Among the ancients, reason and passion were understood as unalterable aspects of our nature. With the Enlightenment came a new view that it was hoped would yield a new world, more cosmopolitan, more beneficent, and more rational.[53] A major intention of the Enlightenment project's many contributors was to replace religious authority with secular authority as the basis of morality for two reasons.

First, the religious wars were seen by Enlightenment scholars as inherently destructive. The unrelenting efforts to secure a specific religious doctrine seemed always to bring forth war and inquisition.[54] Second, the location of religious doctrine in divine authority meant that there would be an inevitable conflict between science and the expected gifts that derived therefrom on one hand and the static claims of religious conviction and faith on the other. Additionally, they expected a continuation of conflict between progress in cultural production (music, the arts in general, and literature) and the obligation to remain obedient within the traditions of moral certainty articulated by a designated clerical authority.

But destroying religious authority does not thereby produce a new secular authority, as Edmund Burke made clear in his commentary on the French Revolution.[55] Hence, there remained the task of locating authority elsewhere than in tradition or the divine. The principal solution was to opt for the Kantian route of generating a secular moral foundation that could encompass an ever-changing populace (which was expected to be ever enlarging and ever more cosmopolitan). But the effort to identify secular moral foundations led to a continuing intellectual and political combat between those animated by a view of moral sentiments located in habits of heart and those who located morality in thoughtful reason.[56]

To achieve those ends, Enlightenment scholars introduced a modification of the long-established two-fold taxonomy, reason and emotion. The full story is well told by Albert Hirschman.[57] In the modern taxonomy, a third category was invented and inserted between reason and passion: interest. Interest was understood as a calculating emotion and remains current, as reflected in our usage of such terms as "self-interest" and "public interest." Interest has the action-enabling feature of emotion, meaning that interest has the ability to move us to action, something that reason famously lacks. Though, like emotion, not resident in the conscious mind and therefore remaining similarly hidden and mysterious, interest, nonetheless, is rational. Because interest is linked to some end —say, safeguarding one's farm or protecting some activity, such as one's profession, or one's nation—it is goal-protecting and goal-seeking. Interest is thus rational because it links means with ends.

Adam Smith, with the help of others, developed the notion of interests as he formulated his views on the market economy.[58]

Human action would shift to rational guidance through reliance on the potent but inarticulate force of interest. Markets would enable interest-bearing individuals to interact to their mutual exchange and felicitous benefit. Hence, interest and markets would produce an auspicious future, the ever-expansive commonwealth. This new taxonomy envisioned the emergence of a new world with ever-expanding free exchange that yields an ever more inclusive and beneficent society.

The taxonomy of mental states was enlarged to incorporate this vital third mental category, interest. Table 5.1 shows the old and new taxonomies, along with shared but unstated presumptions.

The language of interest permeates the modern discussion of politics.[59] We have "special" interests (economic sectors, such as mineral extraction corporations; organized groups, such as unions; regions; age cohorts; and economic classes are all often seen as having "interests"). We have the "public" interest (the enduring array of just requirements of some polity). We have warring interests, as when we speak of our "economic interests" as adverse to our "social interests." It is common to proclaim that "interest groups" are the core of democratic politics.[60]

Because interests are presumed to reside outside the self-aware mental region wherein conscious reason resides, we may surmise that we do not even know what our true "interests" are. This presumption then gives birth to the notion of "false consciousness," the idea that we have interests but misconstrue them. And, since individuals may not know their interests, we as scholars, or as pundits, or as casual observers can ascribe to others what we hold their "real" interests to be.[61] We can say someone has a "vested" interest in some affairs (as when we might consider a politician, judge, or bureaucrat to be corrupted by virtue of some "interest" that, we assert, alters the appropriate decision-making process). Hence, interests provide a potent and highly useful concept to explain political judgment and behavior, with the added advantage (or disadvantage) of being somewhat elusive.

Table 5.1 outlines the major comparisons and commonalities in pre-modern and modern conceptions. There is one implicit presumption that this particular modern conception shares with the premodern, and that has to do with the focus on the spatial locations of reason and emotions as an essential point of demarcation.

TABLE 5.1. ANCIENT AND NEW TAXONOMIES OF MENTAL STATES

MENTAL STATES

Pre-Modern		Post-Enlightenment		
Reason	Emotion	Reason	Interest	Emotion
Located in the mind with weak control over the body; too easily pushed aside by passion, but able to assess and make explicit reasoned decisions.	Located in the body; very powerful, direct control over the body; turbulent, and often irrational.	Located in the mind with weak control over the body; too easily pushed aside by passion, but able to assess and make explicit reasoned decisions.	Neither mind nor body; but a distinct combination of calculating emotion, enduring, powerful, and rational (in serving self-interest).	Located in the body; very powerful, direct control over the body; turbulent, and often irrational.

OFTEN UNSTATED PRESUMPTIONS

• These mental states (Reason, Emotion, and Interest) are concurrent;
• Apart from interest, the relationship between reason and emotion is largely antagonistic;
• Reason (resident in consciousness) has full access to knowledge while emotion does not;
• Because the mental states co-occur but are discrete one to the others, it is held that the primary relationship between the components is spatial (body and mind; heart and mind; central versus peripheral in the language of dual-process models in psychology; consciousness and subconsciousness in the language of psychodynamic analysis).
• To which we can add, because we reside in consciousness, there are the visible and the hidden in our mental states. Only reason resides within the visible realm of consciousness leaving interest and passion "outside" pressing in (raising the risk of passion overwhelming reason's otherwise capable guidance).

It has long been believed that emotion and reason have different qualities, especially with respect to their different relationships to action and rationality. But, as we shall see, these conceptions of mental states, their qualities, and their relationships one to another have been largely shown to be false.

Many of our normative and empirical expectations for democratic rule rest, to a large extent, on the validity of these presumptions. Given that the troubled empirical record suggests the implausibility of these foundations, it would be useful to find sounder ground, a new foundation that might offer new possibilities.

3. A NEUROSCIENCE PRIMER ON EMOTION AND REASON

There are three basic findings from neuroscience that fundamentally alter our conventionally held views of mental states. First, the fundamental relationship between cogitation (thinking) and affect (feeling) is temporal, not spatial. Second, we have not one genre of knowledge but two. And, third, we have two routes to judgment and action, not one. Each is largely reliant on its own class of knowledge.[62] As I noted earlier, the dominant tradition of understanding emotion and reason organizes them into spatial locations and characterizes them, in the main, as antagonistic to each other. Feeling and thinking have long been viewed as discrete states, each with its own qualities, even if they often interact. This view combines with another conventional view holding that conscious, calm reason ought to be protected against the turbulent irrationality of the Furies.[63] From the Stoics to the present, our belief has been that maturity, dignity, and civility require the gentling of our turbulent and mysterious emotions (giving rise to the terms "gentleman" and "gentlewoman"). As John Locke makes clear,[64] the fundamental goal of education is precisely this task, as it was for Freud.[65] In all of these, Freud's language of description is spatial: superego, consciousness, and subconscious (above, the middle realm wherein we live, and below).[66]

The work of Benjamin Libet[67] established that, because of the neurological processes that are required to generate it, the mental state of consciousness, though subjectively experienced as instantaneous, is a delayed representation. He established that it takes five hundred milliseconds, one-half second, for the brain, upon the arrival of various external sensory streams and somatosensory streams, to generate consciousness. What is very impressive is how well the brain masks this delay. Only in brief instances can we observe that this delay exists.

Also important, the subjective state of consciousness is a "best guess" in that the brain does not passively record the external world. Rather, the brain is actively formulating consciousness by

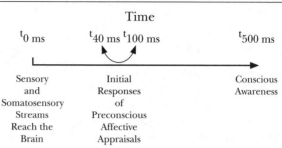

FIG. 5.1. TIME, AFFECT, AND COGNITION

interposing expectations so that what we see, hear, and so forth is generated from a combination of internal and external signals that rely on prior knowledge of how these fit together. Visual illusions are one broad class of instances of the brain's guesswork. I shall offer one interesting example later.

This revelation creates a new challenge. Given that there is a substantial lag between conscious representation and dynamic events as we act in the world, how do we act in the world? The principal answer is shown in Figure 5.1. The brain does not wait for the full construction of consciousness to be completed before it generates an understanding and acts on that understanding.

The brain begins identifying salient characteristics well before conscious representation is completed. For example, we identify the gender of a person within one hundred milliseconds of the arrival of the sensory stream in the brain. Our brains "know" the gender of a newcomer four hundred milliseconds or more before we consciously observe the individual. We also "know" that an object is heading toward us before we "know" that an object is moving side to side or that the object has color.[68] We "know" these things before we are conscious of these features. A key feature of this preconscious realm is that the fundamental languages of these processes are affective appraisals.[69] That we have no consciousness of these dynamics makes it hard for us to grasp that we even have a preconscious realm. Yet it is in this preconscious temporal realm that many, though not all, of the decisions that powerfully affect our lives are made.[70]

Let's begin with the sensory streams that flow into the brain.

What is the volume of information that reaches the brain from the five senses?[71] Neuroscientists have measured the capacity of the brain and of the conscious mind to display each of these data streams (i.e., sight, sound, touch, taste, and smell). Table 5.2 displays these capacities for each of the five senses, that of the brain and that of the conscious mind.

Before I comment on the contents of Table 5.2, I want to advance two more points about the topic of knowledge. First, the somatosensory stream, which conveys to the brain the complex array of information from various sensors in the body about where and what is going on, is linked primarily to the preconscious systems. On the other hand, the somatosensory stream is only broadly and vaguely depicted in conscious representation.[72] We know we can do such mundane tasks as write a letter or type a message, but we don't actually know the messy details of how the brain coordinates external and internal representations and the sequencing of muscular tightening and loosening so as to manage deft movement.[73] Second, to manage the processing of preconscious sensory and somatosensory data properly, the brain has a memory system to sustain the tasks that fall within the domain of the preconscious realm. This system of memory, most often called procedural but sometime labeled associative, is tasked with learning the deft movements of our sundry habits, both their execution and the details of the external realms in which these actions unfold.[74] We are aware that we have memory, but we actually have multiple memory

TABLE 5.2. PROCESSING CAPACITIES —
PRECONSCIOUS AND CONSCIOUS STATES

Sensory system	Brain bandwidth (bits/sec)	Conscious awareness (bits/sec)
Visual	10,000,000	40
Auditory	100,000	30
Touch	1,000,000	5
Taste	1,000	1
Olfactory	100,000	1

Source: Manfred Zimmermann, "The Nervous System in the Context of Information Theory," in *Human Physiology*, ed. R. F. Schmidt and G. Thews (Berlin: Springer Verlag, 1989).

systems.[75] What is challenging is that our conscious stream does not have access to procedural memory. We observe ourselves acting in the world, but the detailed manner by which this is accomplished is stored in procedural memory and executed by preconscious processes. And of that we have little conscious awareness.

Now let's return to Table 5.2. The preconscious neural processes have access to a vastly richer array of data about the external world than does consciousness. The ratios vary from taste, with a ratio favoring the preconscious data of 1000 to 1, to vision, with a ratio of 250,000 to 1. All taken together, the preconscious realm has access to its data far sooner and processes that data so as to arrive at conclusions far faster than is possible for consciousness.

Finally, the preconscious processes are far more deft in controlling our actions than the cruder and slower processes available to consciousness. An example might help make clear some of these important differences between brain and mind.

In Figure 5.2 I display two circles drawn to the exact same dimensions. They should appear exactly the same because, in fact, I did not draw two circles. Rather, I created the first and duplicated it. In Figure 5.3, are shown again two circles, each the same size as the other, but with added information. What you see is the Titchener illusion. The circle on the left appears larger, while the identically sized circle, on the right, appears smaller.

FIG. 5.2. Two Identical Circles

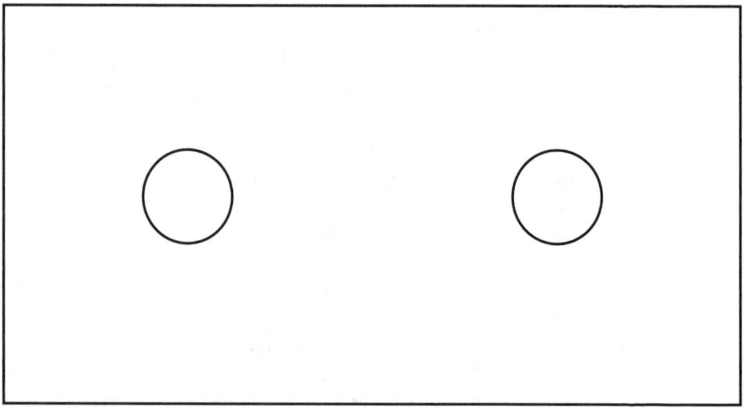

You should easily deduce why this illusion takes place. Our visual system takes into account the size of the circles that surround each circle. The smaller circles around the left circle make that circle appear to be larger than the the circle on the right, which has the far larger circles around it. The surrounding circles give us a sense of the size of each central circle, and we give less weight to their direct comparison.

It is easy to manipulate the magnitude of the illusion by changing the sizes of the surrounding circles. So, for example, if I drew the surrounding circles for each left and right center circle to be the same dimension, there would be no distortion at all.

Now let's consider what would happen if we put a poker chip on top of a paper on which these two center circles were printed. We would use chips sized so that they exactly fit the inner circles. A group of neuroscientists[76] did precisely that as they investigated whether a person reaching to pick each poker chip would use a narrower grip for the right circle than for the left circle.[77] If conscious vision controlled our actions, we would expect the subject to use a narrower grip to reach out and pick up the right hand chip than when he or she reached out for the left chip because of a conscious perception of a difference in their respective sizes. The subjects in the experiment saw, as I hope was apparent to you, that the left circle appeared larger than the right circle.

FIG. 5.3. THE TITCHENER CIRCLE ILLUSION

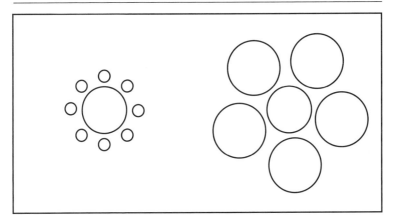

But, that's not what actually happened.[78] Though the subjects consistently reported that they observed that the two chips appear to be of different sizes, they consistently extended their forefinger and thumb to the same width for each chip. The conscious mind was fooled by the illusion, but the preconscious brain, the neural processes tasked with executing behaviors, was not.[79]

This example brings us to the final important foundational insight of neuroscience. We have two ways of understanding the world, preconscious appraisal and consciousness, each with a separate kind of knowledge and each sustained by its own dedicated memory system. We also have two ways of acting. The first has come to be called "automaticity."[80] From the perspective of consciousness, that term is apt. But, with respect to the execution of tasks, the term "automaticity" is not apt because the brain is integrating historical knowledge, stored in procedural memory, with contemporary somatosensory and sensory data so as to make dexterous and fluid adjustments in the service of achieving intended goals.[81] The brain is not docile in these tasks. It is making many subtle "upstream" and "downstream" adjustments as actions unfold.

The second route is to initiate actions that rely on our familiar conscious subjective state, the "theater of consciousness," as some have labeled it.[82] This dual capacity has come to be known as "dual process."[83] This third foundational claim indicates we have two, not one, mechanisms for knowing, judging, and action. Our familiar realm of consciousness is laggardly and slower in its capacities as well as less deft in its control of action. The hidden realm of the preconscious can obtain and act on its knowledge earlier and faster and is more deft in its capacity to execute precise movements. One final point: Roy Baumeister's work suggests that reliance on consciousness is both highly energy consuming, thus depending on a resource often readily depleted, and most often reliant on nonconscious processes in ways not evident to the conscious mind.[84] Hence, consciousness is not capable, for all these reasons, of acting alone as the sole executor of our actions.

This raises a most interesting question: if consciousness is so crude, clumsy, and slow, why do we have it? The fuller answer awaits later in this essay. But, in general, preconscious processes presume a close match between past experience and present requirements. Reliance on previously mastered and automated preconscious mechanisms does not have great likelihood of success in novel or uncertain conditions. For such situations, the clumsy, slow, but usefully deliberative processes of consciousness bring a distinct ability to represent and reflect without taking immediate action that proves most useful. In other words, consciousness is a useful space for "error correction."[85]

Finally, though I have depicted these dual neural routes in stark terms—the intuitive reliance on automaticity of preconsciousness and the deliberative reliance on thoughtful, explicit reasoning in consciousness—you should not take these two states as mutually exclusive. Even when we are in a deliberative mode, we are still relying on numerous preconscious processes. Some of those act without regard to the shift from one dual route to the other (e.g., pupil dilation and contraction), and some of these are essential even as we rely on deliberation to animate our judgments and actions (as, for example, the autonomic and vestibular systems). And, even when we are in the deliberative mode, we are still influenced by affective states too swift and too slight to be subjectively experienced in consciousness, as well as those affective appraisals that are robust enough to be described as "feelings."[86] And, by consciously intervening, we can modify our preconscious routines.[87]

It is the goal of the theory of affective intelligence to provide a unified account of how preconscious and conscious neural processes serve democratic politics.

4. AFFECTIVE INTELLIGENCE: APPLYING NEUROSCIENCE TO DEMOCRATIC POLITICS

Since preconscious processes are hidden from us, existing ahead of rather than below consciousness and operating in a nonsemantic fashion, describing them in language is a challenge.[88] But taking up that challenge is well worthwhile because, as I hope to show, it leads to new understandings that allow us to escape the recurring and frustrating conflict between our conceptions of the necessary ideals that animate democracy and realities that have bound[89] and blinded[90] us for so long.

There is one more foundational feature that needs mention. Consciousness has a single integrated coherence. Though object identification, object movement side to side or forward to back, and color attribution are each separately determined in the brain, they are, in the final stages of processing, integrated into the seamless sensation of consciousness. Indeed, each of the senses contributing to consciousness is processed separately before then being combined into the seamless representation that arises in consciousness.[91]

On the one hand, preconscious processes are largely concurrent processes, some tightly integrated but others more distinct. An example of a distinct process is the dilation and contraction of the muscles that control the size of the pupil to allow less or more light to fall on the inner surface of the retina. This process is pretty well isolated from other preconscious neural processes. On the other hand, the vestibular system, which manages balance, is more deeply integrated with other systems insofar as balance and movement need to be deftly, swiftly, and precisely integrated to prevent clumsy movements and to avoid the danger of falling. In sum, while the conscious state is experienced as a singular integrated whole, the preconscious state has simultaneous, multiple, ongoing, concurrent neural processes as its norm.

The goal of the theory of affective intelligence is to depict the nature and function of two of the most important of these neural systems.[92] I begin with the first of the two, the disposition system, as depicted in Figure 5.4. The disposition system, capable of millisecond timing, integrates three streams of information.

First, in the top box on the left, is the vast inventory of learned behaviors, which encompasses muscular movements and skeletal and muscular linkages, as well as goals these behaviors are intended to achieve. It also encompasses language comprehension, speech production, and the derivation of semantic meaning from spoken or read words.[93] Hence, for those of us with a strong political interest, our identification as liberal, progressive, conservative, or libertarian is itself a vast repertoire of habits of understanding, action, and expression. Someone who is a "conservative" has learned what topics are important, which positions are offensive, which sources are to be trusted, which to be disregarded, and much more. All this resides within the habituated realm of procedural memory.

The intermediate box represents the somatosensory stream. Any human movement relies on swift and accurate information

FIG. 5.4. THE DISPOSITION SYSTEM RESIDENT IN THE PRECONSCIOUS

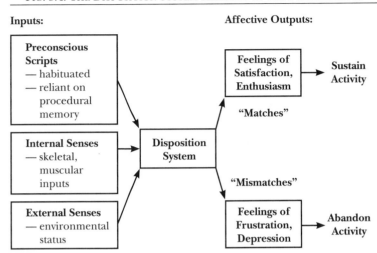

on the position and movements of the body. If I were to extend my hand to shake the extended hand of an old friend, the sensory stream, depicted in the bottom box, and the somatosensory stream must convey data on many aspects of the body so as to enable the disposition system to produce an integrated solution so that my right hand moves from a position alongside my body upward while also turning to the proper position and taking the proper shape, so as to link up at the proper location in space, so as to meet with the moving hand of my compatriot, fingers open and arm extended forward. The same deft fluidity applies to conversation no less than it does to physical movement.[94]

The disposition system continuously assesses the success of these solitary actions and of those coordinated with the actions of others, generating a continuous assessment expressed in affective outputs. This assessment is best described as variations along a dimension of increasing enthusiasm, as things go well, or decreasing enthusiasm, as actions fail or prove unexpectedly difficult or frustrating.[95] The disposition system must marshal neural and physical resources to enact previously learned goals by integrating the how, stored in procedural memory, and the now, what is going in both the external immediate realm and in the self, to achieve deft speech and action. The disposition system can swiftly adjust so as to best accomplish the immediate goal by speeding up or slowing down an action or by making other adjustments as necessary. But, to do this, it needs an ongoing appraisal of success or failure. It needs a swift means for self-appraisal. Similarly, if actions are failing (perhaps because the task is more difficult in this instance than is the norm, perhaps because the person is coming down with the flu or didn't get enough sleep), then, here again, a means of appraisal is needed to suggest stopping the program, at least for now. In each case, fluctuating levels of enthusiasm serve to provide swift assessments of programmed action as it unfolds. Feelings such as elation, excitement, or satisfaction provide ongoing appraisals of success. Feelings such as frustration, glumness, or even depression signal failure and often foretell abandonment of the ongoing action. All of this works quite well, without any requirement of conscious intervention, so long as the current field in which action is undertaken is much like that which has gone before.

But, as depicted in Figure 5.5, the present is not always compliant. Sometimes we confront an environment that to some extent

FIG. 5.5. THE RISK OF THE UNPREDICTABLE

FIG. 5.6. THE SURVEILLANCE SYSTEM RESIDENT IN THE PRECONSCIOUS

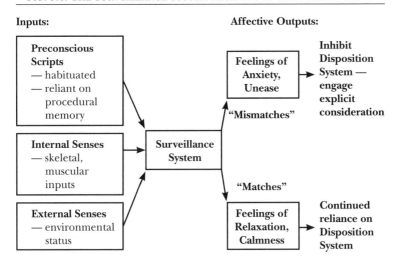

is unlike anything that we have previously experienced. The unusual makes it less likely that any habituated action will unfold successfully. Familiar departures from the norm can be managed by familiar practices we have long ago mastered as habits. Having learned how to ride a specific type of bike, say an on-road bike, we quickly feel comfortable on a bike designed for off-road riding. But, in general, novelty and uncertainty are not well suited to "automaticity."

Conveniently, we have a preconscious system, the surveillance system, to swiftly identify such circumstances. But this system does more than just identify the presence of novelty. It also makes a series of critical changes in how we go about managing such circumstances. Figure 5.6 depicts the operations of the surveillance system.

As you can observe in Figure 5.6, the input side is simpler than that of the disposition system. The task of the surveillance system is to surveil the immediate circumstances and to identify when we confront unusual circumstances. It conveys its continuous analysis by elevating or diminishing the subjective experience, best described as varying one's level of anxiety. The more familiar the circumstance, the lower the level of anxiety. And, because most of the time we inhabit familiar contexts of home, work, and public spaces designed to be recurring and familiar, most of the time this system does little. When we confront a less familiar situation, the surveillance system generates a higher level of anxiety. But that is only one aspect of its output.

The output side of the surveillance system is more complex than that of the disposition system. If novelty becomes apparent, the surveillance system initiates three important processes.

First, it inhibits continued reliance on habituated routines then in play. If anxiety rises, then we stop what we are doing. Automaticity is interrupted.

Second, it shifts our attention away from whatever tasks are then being undertaken and directs it toward the novelty. Hence, as the surveillance system activates, it stops ongoing action, directs our attention to the novel, and directs us to gather new information on and about the novel intrusion (i.e., stop what you're doing and look around).

Third, and most important, the surveillance system, having already inhibited automaticity, then activates deliberative processes. We shift from easy reliance on our preconscious processes to effortful reliance on conscious abilities to assess, evaluate, contemplate, and act.

Among those aspects of the contemporary environment we are likely to consider are our affective states; we inquire as to what we feel and why. We are also as likely to expressly examine whatever has unexpectedly arisen and consider what options avail themselves. If the issues of the moment are ones of collective action, we are also likely to consider whether invigorating old or constructing new alliances will better serve us. Additionally, we may seek out who can best articulate which options are most appealing, as well as which party, program, or leader we wish to trust to guide us.[96]

But we have to return to the disposition system, for it has one more capacity that is of grave significance for politics. Figure 5.7 displays images of political gatherings that are also often managed by the disposition system. These are all photos of recent conservative rallies. We could add similar images of liberal rallies.

We also learn how to manage familiar but punishing circumstances, just as we acquire habituated routines that achieve famil-

FIG. 5.7. CONFRONTING FAMILIAR THREATS

iar rewarding outcomes. In both instances, we acquire habits that "automatically" manage these recurring tasks. However, there is one important difference in the operation of the disposition system in such circumstances. The characteristic affective appraisal, the appraisal that identifies how substantial the offense is and how well we are marshaling our resources to meet the challenge, is aversion.[97]

In the English lexicon, there are many words that depict the various forms of aversion. Among them are contempt, hatred, bitterness, distaste, and loathing. In particular, disgust offers the best literal insight into the meaning and practice of aversion. To find something aversive leads one to avert one's eyes, to turn away. And we often describe our opponents as disgusting, meaning we wish to disgorge or expel that which is distasteful.[98] We have such mechanisms to save us from familiar insults (here I use that term in the medical meaning of something that has caused harm).[99] Thus, the disposition system, as depicted in Figure 5.4, needs only a slight change in the affective output that is attached to success in

FIG. 5.8. THE DISPOSITION SYSTEM AS IT OPERATES WITH
AVERSIVE STIMULI

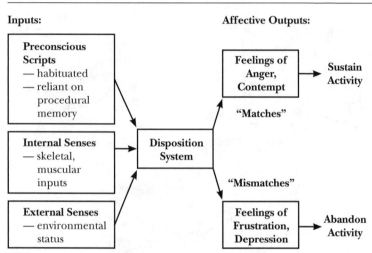

mastering the robust familiar threats we often confront in life and in politics to produce rage, hatred, and the like, rather than the affective terms we use to describe the upper reaches of enthusiasm, as shown in Figure 5.8. And frustration in meeting the challenge of familiar insults leads to affective states and descriptive terms, such as bitterness, or, at a slightly higher level of success, contempt, that plumb the lower, lesser reaches of aversion.

One reason why consciousness is a delayed representation is that constructing consciousness requires a lot of prior neural processing. Recall that, apart from smell, the brain is receiving external data in the form of electrical signals. From the eyes, electrical signals generating the rod and cone cells in the retinas arrive via the two optic nerves. Similarly, electrical signals arrive from the ears, from the tongue, and from skin surfaces. As these various electrical pulses reach the various cortical sites, a number of distinct assessments take place.[100] Downstream processing integrates these separate modalities (sight, sound, and so forth) into the unified representation that is consciousness. Additionally, having the capacity of language provides a powerful way to describe what is before us, what was in the past, and what we might imagine not only to ourselves but also to others.

The primary function of the preconscious realm is not to generate a unified representation of the external world. Rather, these processes are primarily action oriented, rather than representationally oriented. Furthermore, the depictions of the external and internal states that are critical to preconscious processes are not representational so much as they are action linkages that are rapidly appraised in affective, that is, nonrepresentational, terms. Affective appraisals assess the effectiveness of our actions as they play out in the variety of conditions that are habituated. They do not represent the things in and of themselves.

This action focus of the preconscious and the representational focus of consciousness highlight one of the qualitative differences between preconscious knowledge and its memory system on the one hand and conscious knowledge and its memory system on the other. The former is admirably suited to its "automaticity" orientation, the tight, deft linkage of goal, action, and result. The latter is admirably suited to the task of problem recognition and error correction. Insofar as novelty finds us in a situation of varied elements (some known and familiar, and some not), the universal representational capacity of consciousness, together with its delinking of goal to action, is well crafted to a world of uncertainty.

It is the principal purpose of the surveillance system to preconsciously determine whether, at any given moment, executive function should remain within the preconscious realm (the default condition) or be shifted to conscious considerations. Thus, we have a system, reliant on a preconscious appraisal, that initiates and empowers deliberation. Consciousness, if given executive control, offers advantages in managing novel circumstances that preconscious processes cannot match.

Some will object that knowledge should remain defined, as it has long been, as that which can be expressly described in language. To many, truth claims should be posed in scientific or ethical language—that is, in universal terms that can be tested scientifically or justified morally because such claims are made explicit and expressible by semantic, neo-Kantian terms. The capacity to express something in language is often taken to be a mark of "knowing" that is distinctly human (for, of course, all animal species also "know" how to manage their lives).

But this constricted and restrictive view of knowledge, however useful in arguing for the distinctive features of our species, is more useful in an effort to remove the many from a role, however modest, in collective decisions, as was the intention of both Plato and Hobbes. Knowledge takes more than one form. Each form has its uses and its vulnerabilities, a point I will return to in the section that follows.

This brief primer is quite apolitical. I chose to make it so in part because these processes apply across the full range of human actions, political and nonpolitical. Also, I chose nonpolitical examples because you may grasp the basic ideas more easily when they are presented in the more tranquil realm of mundane activities. But these processes are very consequential to politics in general and to democratic politics in particular. The next section examines how.

5. READDRESSING FOUR NORMATIVE STANDARDS IN LIGHT OF AFFECTIVE INTELLIGENCE

In this section, I show how the four normative standards stand in conflict with the understandings of our natures that are generated by neuroscience. I begin with knowing.

The Error of Treating Semantic Knowledge as Comprehensive and Our Basis for Knowing

Though it may surprise many, the corpus of knowledge available as observed or recalled in consciousness is but a small and biased sampling of what we know. Much of that "hidden" knowledge is not semantic and is not stored in declarative memory. Rather, it is retained in procedural memory and is vital in execution of the various preconscious processes. That form of knowledge is largely unavailable to us when we restrict our self-definition to our conscious realm. Knowledge of the sort that is stored in procedural memory is "unknown" because it is largely inaccessible to "us."

But the knowledge we do have before us, the knowledge of the sort that resides in encyclopedias, textbooks, and scholarly tomes,

is—contrary to conventional wisdom—too often blind. It is unaware of neural systems that sustain many of our choices and actions. Indeed, a large body of research conducted by the psychologist Timothy Wilson shows that, because many of our choices are
made preconsciously, if we are asked to state our preferences, we
often get them wrong. This is so precisely because we do not have
access to the procedural memory wherein our preferences are retained; hence, guessing is the best we can do. And, when we guess,
we often guess wrong.[101]

Let me offer two examples, one of a mundane task and the
other more political. First, the mundane. Consider a fairly easy
and common task: lifting a cup to mouth to take a drink. As noted,
we have no conscious access to the specific cortical regions that in-
tegrate somatosensory inputs (where our body is in all its components, both still and moving), sensory inputs (how far away, what is
the type of cup, and so forth), and the procedural sequences mastered in the execution of what has become habituated as a simple
skill/task. Consider all the variations that this simple task encompasses. What are the critical features of the object to be grasped? Is
the cup paper, plastic, metal, or ceramic? These introduce differences in fragility, weight, and capacity to insulate (important when
the liquid is very hot or cold). Is the cup empty, partially filled, or
filled to the brim (important as to weight and balance and the risk
of spillage). Are you in the dark, or is the immediate area clearly
lit? Is the cup in a saucer? Is the cup large, extra-large, or small? Is
the cup on the edge of a shelf, or in the middle of a table, or high
or low, relative to yourself, and are you sitting, standing, moving,
or still? Is the cup near enough for you to just reach for it, or must
you lean, as well, or must you walk toward its location? Is your hand
gloved, and, if so, with a fine leather fingered glove or a woolen
mitten? Is your other hand free to provide aid or balance? Is the
cup surface slippery or rough? Does the cup have a handle? All of
these features intersect to form hundreds of variations. Yet, they
each demand subtle differences in execution. And, to reiterate,
in the conscious realm, all of these many variations are mastered
to varying degrees of accomplishment and are subsumed under
the broad and simplistic phrase "I know how to pick up a cup,"
though the many details that are required to realize and actualize
that claim are not available or known to our conscious minds.[102]

Let's now turn to a political example. If asked about our political identities, some of us may describe ourselves as Democrat or
as Republican, or as liberal, progressive, conservative, an advocate
of the Tea Party or the Green Party, or libertarian. These are summary labels. They function as general labels and, of late, have been
taken to be evidence of one's core identity.[103] And, while they do
serve well to identify us, they are also far more than that. Consider
the various tasks that fall under these broad domains of partisan or
ideological identity.

Let me cover just a small portion of the tasks that are covered
within the domain of actions that are the repertoire of being a partisan or an ideologue.[104] Partisanship encapsulates the sundry tasks
of partisanship: the ready and quick use of phrases to solidify common cause with a likeminded individual or group, the marshaling
of the light jibe to those suspected of wavering, the hard jibe designed to disarm someone of the other camp, the grimace offered
when a jibe is directed against us, inclinations about whom to pick
on a ballot listing dozens, whom to watch with trust and whom to
reject with disfavor, and the ready-to-hand use of sustained argument bolstered by an array of authoritative claims—talking points,
if you will—to defend or attack as the situation warrants. This covers but a small array of the many actions that fall within the domain of ideological and partisan habits.

Those who are less partisan and less ideological but nonetheless to some degree politically engaged also have an array of skills,
habits, and so on that enable them to engage in the various tasks
that their more modest engagement demands.[105] Even as we use
the simple phrase "here I am lifting a cup," the actual task is complex, and the learned repertoire covers a wide array of variations
deployed in many different ways and in many different circumstances, all mastered in their complexities and crudely summarized by the semantic phrase. Similarly, describing oneself as an
FDR Democrat, or a progressive, or a conservative, or a Constitutional Originalist says much more than that we have a specific political identity. And, just as we have no access to the precise details,
let alone the execution of the sundry habits in daily life, we have
no greater access—apart from after-the-fact observation and speculation—as to the fullness and range of our political habits.[106]

In sum, most people have at hand many political skills and

know quite a lot about politics. Indeed, they know far more than they are often given credit for, in part because the standard knowledge quiz is not especially useful in probing this reservoir of hidden knowledge. The general commandment to be knowledgeable and to know thyself is considerably more complicated because we know far more than we think we do. The challenge is that much of what we "know" is largely inaccessible to "ourselves." We consciously know one kind of knowledge. But we also have another kind of knowledge, more vast than semantic information but differently constructed. Having two systems of knowledge, even if they are mutually disengaged, is a powerful adaptive benefit, as each is suited to the contextually dependent tasks that fall within its focus.

The Error of Universal Excellence

Thoughtful consideration, alone or with other methods, is a useful way of addressing novel circumstances or even, and perhaps especially, old tried and true circumstances thrown into confusion by challenges to the normative status of the tradition under examination. But achieving a result often turns not on the ability to rely on deliberation but also on the strength of the convictions that fuel the collective movements. Such convictions require the steadfast certainty of causes that sustain solidarity. Deliberation is not well suited to sustaining social and political movements because deliberation is blind to the many features of the self, including preferences and the actions we have learned to realize our preferences. And, deliberation cannot easily execute actions that require deft coordination of the self or self-other interactions necessary to most actions, political and nonpolitical. Indeed, deliberation is far more likely to raise questions, to raise doubts, to undermine resolve. And, while those might be admirable evidence of even-handedness, they are qualities not much valued in the midst of battles that depend on sustaining common cause and sustained devotion.

That we are often reliant on unthinking execution of our political actions might suggest to some that our autonomy is at risk. That observation is a natural response, given the long history in the Western tradition of seeing explicit reason, cogitating, as the only proper basis for rational action. But, as Isaiah Berlin recognized, we are not fully free simply when external barriers are removed (a variant of freedom he labels "negative" freedom).[107] To be fully free, we need the capacity for action, and that in turn rests on talent, imagination, and craft, which together give rise to fluid and deft action. Berlin categorizes the mental faculties that sustain free action as "positive" freedom. It is this latter form of freedom that serves our autonomy by enabling competent sustained action, individual and collective. But we are not always well advised to rely on partisan solidarity to determine our political actions. When our goals are safely secure from doubt, that is one situation, but when our goals merit reflection and when our circumstances are novel, that is another. The former is well served by the "automatic" route of reliance on learned habits executed swiftly and deftly by our preconscious neural routines. The latter is better given over to the representational and deliberative capacities served by consciousness.

Conveniently, we have two neural mechanisms, each of which offers the necessary support for its designated route to decision and action. Setting forth universal standards of thinking, feeling, and acting about citizenship misunderstands the relevance of context and the benefits that come from having two appropriate neural strategies, each designed to function within a context. Having the flexibility to shift from partisan steadfast resolve to explicit reconsideration of what to do, whom to do it with, and how best to accomplish whatever goals seem best suited to the moment advances our capacities to act as effective citizens.[108]

Though this duality has only recently become apparent, it nonetheless leads to the conclusion that the conventional requirements of democratic politics should no longer be presented as a singular coherent set of universal standards. Rather, democratic politics requires very different and often conflicting capabilities. Hence, the expectations and standards we ought to use to assess citizenship competence must begin with the conflicting requirements that flow from conditions of familiarity as against conditions of novelty.

As it happens, single-minded devotion resides in and relies on preconscious habits of expression and action. That capacity is well suited to achieving success in familiar and recurring actions. On the other hand, this capacity, if applied in conditions of novelty and uncertainty, would be far less satisfactory. Happily, we also have the capacity for thoughtful consideration of our options, freed from the grip of our convictions. And that capacity rests on consciousness's capacity to represent an external world in a less normatively dedicated fashion. This capacity comes with a number of limitations. As the principal foci of this nonnormative state are reflection, introspection, and reconsideration, this capacity has very limited access to the action-goal linkages that animate the preconscious.

These two neural pathways provide alternative ways of understanding and acting. Each is well suited to its particular but limited array of challenges. And, if each is efficacious, it is so in one context while inapt in the other. The application of competing lists of competence standards for citizenship is currently on display between those who tout deliberation as the primary framework for democratic politics[109] and those who tout solidarity's capacity to achieve justice and public purposes.[110] However, as vital as deliberation is to conditions of contestation when one is debating perspectives on justice[111] and as vital as partisan resolve is to achieving political ends, each has a critical vulnerability.

Figure 5.9 clarifies a frequent confusion evident in the academy but also found among the chattering classes. We often find

FIG. 5.9. THE VARIABLE NORMATIVE STATUS OF
TWO DIFFERENT "NEGATIVE" EMOTIONS

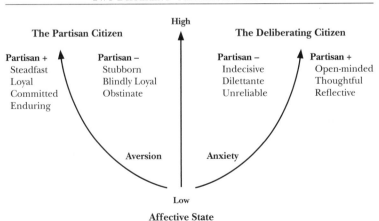

ourselves decrying "negativity" in politics, and it is easy to see why. We often wish for tranquility and the comfort of rewarding familiarity, but politics often places us in contentious and uncertain circumstances. We often depict such circumstances as "negative," meaning both intensely confrontational and uncomfortably uncertain, but these are quite different in their respective antecedents and also in their respective "downstream" consequences (as noted in Figures 5.6 and 5.8). Though I focus here on two negative affects, anxiety and aversion, the partisan route is also animated by emotion and enthusiasm. We are often "happy warriors," to use the felicitous phrase associated with Hubert Humphrey.

Figure 5.9 advances three points. First, without robust affective appraisals, there is no citizenship of any kind. Second, which form of citizenship is made manifest depends on which of two appraisals is dominant. Third, the citizenship variant's normative suitability depends on the match between the affective assessment and the actual contemporary circumstances.

The normative status of each citizenship orientation depends on the accuracy of the affective appraisal. If we are in a state of heightened aversion while in uncertain conditions, then it is quite appropriate to describe us as stubborn, blindly loyal, and obstinate. But, if we face a determined but familiar foe, then we often find ourselves best girded for action with like-minded partisans, all steadfastly reliant on shared and proven protocols. Similarly, deliberation is apt in conditions of novelty and inapt in conditions of familiarity. What is appropriate due diligence in novel conditions can become dithering in familiar circumstances.

We are better off having two mental states, each better suited to its contextual niche than either would be across the full range of circumstances.[112] And the weight of the evidence is that people can adopt either status (the deliberative citizen or the partisan citizen) as they become politically engaged.[113] William James, some 120 years ago, summarized the matter quite well:

> The great thing, then, in all education, is to make our nervous system our ally instead of our enemy. It is to fund and capitalize our acquisitions, and live at ease upon the interest of the fund. For this we must make automatic and habitual, as early as possible, as many useful actions as we can, and guard against the growing into ways that are likely to be disadvantageous to us, as we should guard against

the plague. The more of the details of our daily life we can hand over to the effortless custody of automatism, the more our higher powers of mind will be set free for their own proper work. There is no more miserable human being than one in whom nothing is habitual but indecision, and for whom the lighting of every cigar, the drinking of every cup, the time of rising and going to bed every day, and the beginning of every bit of work, are subjects of express volitional deliberation. Full half the time of such a man goes to the deciding, or regretting, of matters which ought to be so ingrained in him as practically not to exist for his consciousness at all. If there be such daily duties not yet ingrained in any one of my readers, let him begin this very hour to set the matter right.[114]

Kill All the Poets

I begin this brief section on moral judgment by recalling Plato's advice for the founding philosopher king. He encouraged the philosopher king to hire a poet to craft the founding myth for the demos but then to kill all poets because, as Hobbes well understood, those who have a great gift for imagination would soon bring challenge to the moral certainties that Plato hoped to protect as enduring guides to proper behavior.

By its structure, democracy invites and protects the fuller use of imagination.[115] The concepts of liberty and equality, however much they may be in mutual tension, nonetheless invite the free use of that faculty. And, as an institution, the practice of democracy accepts the normality of disorder and the likelihood of surprises that await. For why otherwise would elections be mandated at regular intervals if not for the expectation that time brings new challenges?

Much of late has also been made of the role of neuroscience in exploring the neural foundations for moral judgment.[116] In this broad stream, the research finds moral judgments located, as with other familiar tasks, within the realm of the preconscious. This argument has been most associated with Jonathan Haidt.[117] But, in this, as with many other "new" perspectives, we can find its precursors in Aristotle,[118] Edmund Burke,[119] the Scottish Enlightenment school, and, more recently, Michael Oakeshott,[120] among many others of like mind. Of course, this view has long been in contention with the Kantian alternative, which suggests that justice flows from the product of collective deliberation.[121] Each perspective has its proponents, and each views the other as, at best, misguided.

As the events of the nineteenth and twentieth centuries demonstrated, the Enlightenment project remains largely unfinished business. The task of replacing religious moral authority with secular moral authority remains a work in progress, with science and religion in frequent and contentious rivalry for our affections.

The norms of proper behavior solely based on the habits of self-interest, sustained by an ideology of determined libertarianism (think Rand Paul) or overstated claims of the virtues of deregulation (the "perfect market") have lead to rapacious norms in institutions large and small, public and private. Asking humans to leave one moral foundation for another seems likely to be a project fraught with failure. But, having two means of generating moral judgments gives us purchase to attend to morality anchored in "automaticity" by applying reasoning on explicit principles of justice.

Understanding how the dual-model approach, in general, and the theory of affective intelligence, in particular, can be applied to moral judgment remains largely a task awaiting further exploration. One of those tasks is to better understand how the brain defines a task as "moral." Applying the dual-process approach here suggests that there are two routes to moral judgment. It is easy to reflect on the evident evil in the world. But goodness in response to evil seems to rely on preconscious processes.[122] And it is also clearly the case that we can be brought to rethink what we otherwise might be inclined to ignore.[123]

We need research to better identify and understand the neural pathways by which both "hidden" and explicit judgments arises.[124] While some of the citations I point to are promising, much of the research to date has focused on identifying "the" locale of moral judgment on the premise that there is but one. But, the fact that our most frequent moral dilemmas are managed by "automatic" preconscious processes, as Haidt argues,[125] does not establish that this route is the exclusive feature of our neural mechanisms for making moral judgments. Haidt lays out two modes of reaching moral judgment, each served by one of the two dual-process routes. That served by preconscious processes he calls the intuitive system, and that served by conscious processes—that is, explicit deliberation—he calls the reasoning system.[126]

FIG. 5.10. HAIDT'S TWO MORAL SYSTEMS

The intuitive system	*The reasoning system*
Fast and (with respect to consciousness) effortless	Slow and consciously effortful
Process runs "automatically"	Process is represented consciously
Process is inaccessible: only results enter awareness	Process is consciously accessible
Does not demand attentional resources	Demands attentional resources, which are limited
Parallel distributed processing	Serial processing
Common among mammalian species	Unique to humans over age 2 and perhaps some language-trained apes
Context dependent	Supports context invariance
Platform dependent (depends on the brain and body that houses it)	Platform independent (the process can he transported to any rule following organism or machine)
Expresses moral judgments in action and emotional expression	Expresses moral judgments in semantic form (i.e., "reasons" and "reasoning")

And, just as Haidt argues for the intuitive system, Hannah Arendt[127] advanced the view that locating sound moral judgments within the realm of habits risked the banality of evil, that is to say, thoughtless willingness to do whatever one's betters demand.[128] This view has been further entrenched with the work of Stanley Milgram[129] and the industrious Philip Zimbardo.[130] This suggests that a Kantian approach, demanding or requiring that citizens engage reason and thereby enable themselves to stand fast against evil, is the primary defense for ensuring "never again." But, reason has its own record of generating evil, whether scientific Marxism in Russia or variants in China or Cambodia, as in many other instances.[131]

Figure 5.10 displays a slightly modified version of Haidt's account. While he argues that we rely on the first, we can rely on the second. In fact, not all moral dilemmas are processed via the preconscious route.[132] Hence, the challenge here, as with other forms of political contestation, is often between those guided by one mental state and those guided by the other. The question is thus not "Burke or Kant?" but, rather, "when and where Burke, and when and where Kant?" Those who seek to secure old normative practices "know in their bones" the rightness of their views, while those seeking (new) justice must cause trouble to "awake" bystanders from their too-confident comfort in current practices.[133] We observe ourselves. We may do that less than might be recommended. That judgment is most likely to be forthcoming from those who seek to awaken us from our comfortable slumber because they need our energetic efforts on their behalf. We can give ample time and energy to consider the rightness or wrongness of anything within our ken. We are not limited by the preconscious mechanisms; indeed, these mechanisms enable and elicit our deliberative capacities. But, then, we can also turn to and rely on our deliberative capacities via conscious mechanisms.[134]

Yet, the capacity to imagine new realities, especially when driven by moral imperatives, has its dangers. Reason unhinged from strict adherence to precise description allows us to imagine new and possibly better worlds. But, as Leon Festinger's important work shows, our imaginative capacity, a valued feature of the reasoning system, brings with it the risk of delusion.[135] Given the choice between discomforting evidence and the rightness of their beliefs, people more often than not opt to protect their beliefs.[136]

In sum, neither route guarantees a good result. Each has the capacity to generate good; each has capacity to generate evil.[137] Our biology gives us some capacity for perspective taking, though the one perspective is often quite resistant to being jarred loose.[138] Still, for all that, we do have some capacity to reflect and reconsider, however ill used that capacity might be. To make better use thereof, we depend on the willingness of the weak and ill treated to make a public forceful case, to disrupt the comfort of the familiar.[139] But, comfort can also be the foundation of the good life, and so disruptions, whether driven by intention or by crises unbidden, come with costs and bring unknown results.[140]

The dual-model character of the theory of affective intelligence argues that the foundational concepts of autonomy of thought, autonomy of action, knowledge, and moral judgment anchored in explicit consideration of and reliance on universal principles tell an important part of the story of the psychology of democracy. But, it is only a part, a part that distorts by failing to consider the role of "automaticity," anchored in preconscious processes that enable and thereby empower citizens to grasp the essential features of the world they inhabit and to act. It is only a part because conventional views of knowledge fail to acknowledge the essential knowledge that the brain uses to manage the recurring mundane tasks in all their many variations, including the political.[141]

6. Democracy Re-imagined

We now understand that the conventional formulations, formulations that rest on misunderstandings of our neural apparatus, generate a dystopic conflict between ideals and empirical realities. I argue that it is largely a waste of our intellectual efforts to continue relying on what are now implausible formulations that rest on a seriously distorted and incomplete grasp of human nature.

The new groundings I have sketched herein provide the basis for inviting new questions and imagining new possibilities. Among these are the following.

First, most considerations of politics, both as to leadership and as to followership, entertain personality as an important component.[142] But the batteries that make up the derived scales of personality, the "big five" currently being the received and favored model, arise from self-description. People are presented with lots of items generated by those who generate these items, and people are asked how well these items describe them: "I am a cautious person" and the like.[143] But, if we have access primarily to what we consciously know of ourselves and very limited and remote access to the actual processes of much of our behavior, verbal and social no less than physical, then how comprehensive are the conceptions and measures? For example, Feldman argues that the personality trait of social conformity, which arrays people according to the importance of sustaining and defending social norms, is largely quiescent in safe conditions.[144] Those high on this trait do not manifest authoritarian defenses unless they confront some evident threat. Hence, many such people, as they observe themselves, might not recognize this authoritarian capacity that lies within. Asking people what they are like may well elicit, even when honesty prevails, only a partial portrait. The missing elements reflect our inability to know what our preconscious inclinations hold. Much work awaits before we will have a sound conceptual grasp of these preconscious neural processes, how we differ one from another, and how we differ in response to different circumstances and challenges.

Second, we have the protean capacity to shift from preconscious reliance to deliberative processes and back. As such, we misunderstand politics if it is reduced to a domesticated form of combat (using votes rather than weapons of war to achieve victory of "us" over "them"). And we also misunderstand politics if we require that it be limited to thoughtful deliberation over what the circumstances require, freed from the grip of convictions and established loyalties. Democratic politics is both of these. That leads to a critical research task to explore. Do we manifest the proper mental resources in the right circumstances? And to what extent, and why, do we misconstrue circumstances as familiar when they are novel (and the reverse)? And how often and why do we act decisively with steadfast certainty when we should be flexible and open minded (and the reverse)?

Third, the role of rhetoric, that too-often despised craft,[145] needs to be re-imagined, as Bryan Garsten has recently argued.[146] The role of language is quite different when it is used in the service of the preconscious articulation of convictions[147] and when it is used in the service of deliberation.[148] Here, again, applying some universal criteria, a good rhetoric perhaps juxtaposed against a rhetoric that is demagogic, ignores these dual roles. If rhetoric takes two forms, one that articulates the various defenses suited to solidarity and one suited to engaging deliberation, much as citizenship in general takes two forms, then we have different practices to explore, not one.[149]

Those seeking to apply a singular array of citizenship standards, and here I mean not only those applicable to citizens but also those applicable to the leaders and institutional design all expected to interact to realize those standards, will continue to confront a recalcitrant reality. I have sketched a new psychology, a new human nature, one more complex than that which has preceded. The dominant citizenship standards—the capacity to make full use of our deliberative faculties to identify interests, self and public; to consider which is the most promising of an array of options; to consider the appropriate principles of justice and their application in diverse conditions—all merit respect and praise.

But, while we have the neural capacities to animate these standards, we also have neural capacities to animate other approaches to politics. What we have learned to date is sufficient to conclude that much of the enduring back-and-forth between those critical of and those defending democracy can largely be set aside as insufficiently complete with respect to their grasp of human nature's ability to reach a sound conclusion. I trust this essay will encourage a new discussion, one that sits on firmer foundations than those of the past.

This conclusion might be taken as an overly optimistic assessment. It is not. Rather, my primary purpose is to argue that the current aspirations for a fully deliberative politics will prove to be a dead end. And, if that expectation remains the normative premise of democracy, then democracy cannot succeed on those terms. Democracy rests on more than human nature. Democracy depends on institutions, such as the rule of law (and all that encompasses), a free energetic and critical press, and competent political leaders who have the capacity to lead by thoughtful and rousing articulations of the policy choices they favor, rather than seeking market appeal of simplistic catch phrases.[150]

Aeschylus, in the *Oresteia Trilogy*,[151] celebrated the invention of a new system of justice wherein the Furies were displaced from the public realm in favor of reliance on juries who would render the verdict innocent of direct experience of the underlying plaint.[152] But, in doing so, the Athenians, guided by Athena's wisdom, sought not to eradicate the Furies but, rather, to restrict their compass to the hearth wherein love resides and where the crude and blind features of reasoned justice cannot reach. The Furies became the Eumenides (the kindly ones), relieved, the Athenians hoped, of the burden of securing justice. We are better off for the institution of law and the ordered means of justice we thereby obtain. Our natures may incline us to intuitive moral judgments, but our natures also lead to the creation of and a reliance on codes of justice and the institutions of judges, juries, and law courts. And, having done this, we can rely on each, though we may each feel more inclined toward the older moral foundation, especially for those cases that elicit the Furies once again.[153] We can construct institutions to change the balance. We can revitalize institutions, such as a vigorous and free press, to generate, probe, and prod consideration. We can institutionalize a diverse and open suffrage. These, and more, can help ensure that our inclination for quiet comfort is open to challenge.

Whether a given array of institutions is sufficient also has a lot to do with how much and how well democracy serves. But, notwithstanding that democracy requires traditions, institutions, and leaders, it also needs a psychology that is both sound and aspirational. If we abandon the ancient and Enlightenment visions of reason and emotion, we have new possibilities available. Whether those new possibilities will produce new conclusions that are more satisfying than those that precede them remains to be seen. But, if we continue to be embrace those visions, there will be little basis for optimism.

NOTES

This chapter is a revision of an essay presented at the Annual Meeting of the American Society for Political and Legal Philosophy, in conjunction with that of the American Philosophical Association, Eastern Division, December 29, 2010, in Boston. A number of colleagues offered thoughtful queries that yielded a fuller and, I hope, sounder presentation. Among these are Peter Steinberger, Susan Bandes, Cheshire Calhoun, Ben Pauli, and several colleagues at Rutgers University, where an earlier version of this chapter was presented.

1. Plato, *The Republic* (New York: Penguin, 1974); Stephen L. Elkin and Karol E. Soltan, *Citizen Competence and Democratic Institutions* (University Park: Pennsylvania State University Press, 1999); George E. Marcus and Russell L. Hanson, *Reconsidering the Democratic Public* (University Park: Pennsylvania State University Press, 1993); Giovanni Sartori, *The Theory of Democracy Revisited* (Chatham, NJ: Chatham House, 1987); Joseph A. Schumpeter, *Capitalism, Socialism and Democracy* (London: George Allen and Unwin, 1943); Dennis Thompson, *The Democratic Citizen: Social Science and Democratic Theory in the Twentieth Century* (New York: Cambridge University Press, 1970). The Founding Fathers, in shaping the Constitution, gave Americans a republican form of government, rather than a democracy, because they read the history of democracy as fundamentally flawed by the instability of popular judgment and by the public's inherent self-bias. As Madison succinctly put it: "As long as the reason of man continues fallible, and he is at liberty to exercise it, different opinions will be formed. As long as the connection subsists between his reason and his self-love, his

opinions and his passions will have a reciprocal influence on each other; and the former will be objects to which the latter will attach themselves." James Madison, Alexander Hamilton, and John Jay, *The Federalist* No. 10, at 58 (James Madison), in *The Federalist*, ed. Jacob E. Cooke (Middletown, OH: World, 1961).

2. James S. Fishkin, *When the People Speak: Deliberative Democracy and Public Consultation* (New York: Oxford University Press, 2009).

3. Jürgen Habermas, *The Theory of Communicative Action* (Boston: Beacon Press, 1984).

4. Felicia Pratto, Jim Sidanius, Lisa M. Stallworth, and Bertram F. Malle, "Social Dominance Orientation: A Personality Variable Predicting Social and Political Attitudes," *Journal of Personality and Social Psychology* 67 (1994): 741–763. Economic enterprises, social organizations such as country clubs, families, and religious organizations of most, if not all, denominations are both hierarchical and bounded (controlling who is eligible for membership, who is in and who is out). Their boundedness limits who can raise issues of injustice in these arrangements. Those inside most likely to do so are subordinated and hence often have limited means for effective resistance, though see James C. Scott, *Weapons of the Weak: Everyday Forms of Peasant Resistance* (New Haven, CT: Yale University Press, 1985). Moreover, various doctrines, such as "private property," "states rights," and privacy generally are often asserted to preclude the intervention of the state or of "outsiders." Small and traditional villages often generate and defend norms that diminish the rights of newcomers or visitors, "outsiders," to weigh in on local disputes.

5. John R. Hibbing and Elizabeth Theiss-Morse, *Stealth Democracy: Americans' Beliefs About How Government Should Work* (Cambridge: Cambridge University Press, 2002), and Jane J. Mansbridge, *Beyond Adversary Democracy* (New York: Basic Books, 1980). There is considerable evidence that the formal status of citizen is often undermined, sometimes by the citizens themselves and sometimes by the fervent efforts of partisan forces to exclude or at least intimidate those opposing.

6. Tom R. Tyler, *Why People Obey the Law* (New Haven, CT: Yale University Press, 1990); Tom R. Tyler, "The Psychology of Legitimacy: A Relational Perspective on Voluntary Deference to Authorities," *Personality and Social Psychology Review* 1 (1997): 323–345.

7. Fishkin, *When the People Speak*.

8. David Held, *Models of Democracy* (Cambridge: Polity, 2006); John Keane, *The Life and Death of Democracy* (New York: W. W. Norton, 2009).

9. As Madison makes clear in his *Federalist* papers, the proposal the founders sought to advance was a republic, not a democracy. This is because the former makes use of the principle of representation to enable

the public good and justice to be more properly central to political outcomes, a result they believed would not result from democracy.

10. Benjamin Barber, *Strong Democracy: Participatory Politics for a New Age*
(Berkeley: University of California Press, 1984).

11. The language of elites and masses flows naturally to this variant's
presumptions as they, wittingly or not, draw an analogy from Newtonian
physics: mass is inert and rests unmoved because it does not have self-
actualizing resources to move without the essential external application
of energy. Elites provide that energy, leading the public to follow along,
providing endorsement when competing elites align and offering some
influence beyond legitimizing elite consensus only when elites publicly
debate, thereby offering the limited possibility for public influence. This
conception of the passive mass public and active energetic elites is central to such otherwise varied scholars as Schumpeter, *Capitalism, Socialism
and Democracy*; Sartori, *The Theory of Democracy Revisited*; Walter Lippmann,
Public Opinion (New York: Macmillan, 1922); John Zaller, *The Nature and
Origins of Mass Opinion* (New York: Cambridge University Press, 1992); and
John Mueller, *Capitalism, Democracy and Ralph's Pretty Good Grocery* (Princeton, NJ: Princeton University Press, 1999), among many others.

12. V. O. Key Jr. and M. C. Cummings, *The Responsible Electorate: Rationality in Presidential Voting 1936–1960* (New York: Vintage Books, 1966);
Benjamin Page and Robert Y. Shapiro, *The Rational Public* (Chicago: University of Chicago Press, 1992).

13. Thompson, *The Democratic Citizen*; Robert Dahl, "The Problem of
Civic Competence," *Journal of Democracy* 3 (1992): 45–59; Elkin and Soltan,
Citizen Competence and Democratic Institutions; Marion Smiley, "Democratic
Citizenship: A Question of Competence?" in Elkin and Soltan, *Citizen Com-
petence and Democratic Institutions*, 371–383.

14. There is a rich array of historical instances of elite failure (Barbara
W. Tuchman, *The Guns of August* [New York: Macmillan, 1962]), as well
as social science examination of elite failures (Irving L. Janis, *Groupthink*
[Boston: Houghton Mifflin, 1982]). I cite just two examples here from
among a wealth of candidates. In light of the recent failures of economic
elites in all venues—political, financial, and academic—to prevent the
preventable (e.g., 9/11, Katrina, Ponzi schemes, and more; a fuller list
would be quite long), it is interesting that few presume that relying on
elites merits contempt rather than admiration, as has been the fashion
among many pundits and scholars with respect to public involvement in
collective decisions. When the public follows elite opinion, too often that
has led to disastrous consequences.

15. Angus Campbell, Philip E. Converse, Warren E. Miller, and Donald

E. Stokes, *The American Voter* (New York: John Wiley, 1960); Angus Campbell, Philip E. Converse, Warren E. Miller, and Donald E. Stokes, *Elections and the Political Order* (New York: John Wiley, 1966).

16. Philip E. Converse, "The Nature of Belief Systems in Mass Publics," in *Ideology and Discontent,* ed. David Apter (New York: Free Press, 1964), 206–261; Philip E. Converse, "Democratic Theory and Electoral Reality," *Critical Review* 18 (2006): 297–329.

17. Philip E. Converse, "The Concept of the Normal Vote," in Campbell et al., *Elections and the Political Order,* 9–39.

18. If one thinks this is too harsh, then read Phil Converse's recent reflections on the competence of the American electorate (Converse, "Democratic Theory and Electoral Reality"). Or Don Kinder: "By any reasonable standard, Americans are affluent, well educated, and virtually swimming in news of politics. And yet despite these advantages, most Americans glance at the political world mystified by its abstractions and ignorant of its particulars. So it was, according to Converse, nearly a half century ago, and so, by and large, it remains today." Donald R. Kinder, "Belief Systems Today," *Critical Review* 18 (2006): 216.

19. Lippmann, *Public Opinion.*

20. The public's gullibility to rhetoric was, of course, also Hobbes's principal argument for monarchy, though it had to be, in his view, secured by public endorsement. Thomas Hobbes, *Leviathan* (London: Penguin Books, 1968).

21. Michael X. Delli Carpini and Scott Keeter, *What Americans Know About Politics and Why It Matters* (New Haven, CT: Yale University Press, 1996).

22. Samuel L. Popkin, *The Reasoning Voter: Communication and Persuasion in Presidential Campaigns* (Chicago: University of Chicago Press, 1991).

23. Gerd Gigerenzer, Peter M. Todd, and ABC Research Group, *Simple Heuristics That Make Us Smart* (New York: Oxford University Press, 1999).

24. Seyla Benhabib, "Toward a Deliberative Model of Democratic Legitimacy," in *Democracy and Difference: Contesting the Boundaries of the Political,* ed. Seyla Benhabib (Princeton, NJ: Princeton University Press, 1996); Joseph M. Bessette, *The Mild Voice of Reason: Deliberative Democracy and American National Government* (Chicago: University of Chicago Press, 1994); James Bohman and William Rehg, *Deliberative Democracy: Essays in Reason and Politics* (Cambridge, MA: MIT Press, 1997); John S. Dryzek, *Deliberative Democracy and Beyond: Liberals, Critics, Contestations* (New York: Oxford University Press, 2000); Jon Elster and Adam Przeworski, *Deliberative Democracy* (New York: Cambridge University Press, 1998); James Fishkin, *Democracy and Deliberation* (New Haven, CT: Yale University Press, 1991); Jürgen

Habermas, "Three Normative Models of Democracy," in Benhabib, ed., *Democracy and Difference*, 21–30; Mark E. Warren, "Deliberative Democracy and Authority," *American Political Science Review* 90 (1996): 46–60.

25. Nancy L. Rosenblum, *On the Side of the Angels: An Appreciation of Parties and Partisanship* (Princeton, NJ: Princeton University Press, 2008); Lynn M. Sanders, "Against Deliberation," *Political Theory* 25 (1997): 347–377; Ian Shapiro, "Enough of Deliberation: Politics Is about Interests and Power," in *Deliberative Politics: Essays on Democracy and Disagreement*, ed. Stephen Macedo (New York: Oxford University Press, 1999): 28–38; Iris Marion Young, *Inclusion and Democracy* (New York: Oxford University Press, 2000).

26. For example, liberals and Democrats are often ready to cite the Republican opposition to President Bill Clinton's tax increases and budget in 1993 as blind obedience to a flawed set of economic principles, principles that seemed undermined by the financial boom that resulted. But liberals and Democrats have not been so willing to cite their own opposition to Clinton's later endorsement of welfare reform, certain as they were that their continued support for generous and unending welfare financial support was warranted even as the legislation signed by Clinton proved liberal and Democratic fears to be misguided.

27. Amy Gutmann and Dennis Thompson, *Democracy and Disagreement* (Cambridge, MA: Harvard University Press, 1996); John Rawls, *A Theory of Justice* (Cambridge, MA: Harvard University Press, 1971).

28. Mueller, *Capitalism, Democracy and Ralph's Pretty Good Grocery*.

29. Barber, *Strong Democracy*; Sanders, "Against Deliberation"; Shapiro, "Enough of Deliberation."

30. By focusing on the American instance, we get, of course, a narrow view of democracy. Over the same period, Spain, Portugal, Brazil, Argentina, Chile, and Greece, to name but these, transitioned from military and autocratic rule to stable and seemingly enduring democracies. Moreover, even the autocratic rulers in Iran and China, to name but two, seem to find it necessary to claim they have the support of their people. And there are few exalting any form of governance other than democratic forms (with some theocratic variants importantly being the exception).

31. Michael E. Morrell, *Empathy and Democracy: Feeling, Thinking, and Deliberation* (University Park: Pennsylvania State University Press, 2010).

32. Peter J. Steinberger, *The Concept of Political Judgment* (Chicago: University of Chicago Press, 1993).

33. Key and Cummings, *The Responsible Electorate*; Page and Shapiro, *The Rational Public*; George E. Marcus, *The Sentimental Citizen: Emotion in Democratic Politics* (University Park: Pennsylvania State University Press, 2002).

34. Nancy L. Rosenblum, "Navigating Pluralism: The Democracy of Ev-

eryday Life (and Where It Is Learned)," in Elkin and Soltan, eds., *Citizen Competence and Democratic Institutions*, 67–88.

35. Christopher R. Browning, *Ordinary Men: Reserve Police Battalion 101 and the Final Solution in Poland* (New York: HarperCollins, 1992); Erich Fromm, *Escape from Freedom* (New York: Avon, 1965); Solomon E. Asch, "Effects of Group Pressure upon the Modification and Distortion of Judgment," in *Groups, Leadership and Men: Research in Human Relations*, ed. Harold Guetzkow (Pittsburgh: Carnegie Press, 1951); Craig Haney, Curtis Banks, and Philip Zimbardo, "Interpersonal Dynamics in a Simulated Prison," *International Journal of Criminology and Penology* 1 (1983): 69–97; Stanley Milgram, *Obedience to Authority* (New York: Harper and Row, 1974); Muzafer Sherif, *Group Conflict and Competition* (London: Routledge and Kegan Paul, 1966); Philip G. Zimbardo, *The Lucifer Effect: Understanding How Good People Turn Evil* (New York: Random House Trade Paperbacks, 2008).

36. Among the other important issues that can eviscerate or strengthen democracy is the broad topic of the architecture of democratic institutions. Such issues as the width or narrowness of suffrage, the frequency of elections, the role of recall and referendum, and similar concerns are vital but not within my brief for this essay.

37. As when we describe a lawyer who acts as our "mouthpiece." While he can, and while we expect that our lawyer will add expertise to the claims he pronounces, he is honor bound by both legal doctrine and court oversight to state our claims as we would have them asserted. Only when a lawyer is authorized to act as a trustee can a lawyer advance a claim not articulated by his or her client. A client too young, too old, or judged unsound will have his or her interests given over to another, a trustee, to adjudicate on his or her behalf.

38. Fromm, *Escape from Freedom*.

39. Leon Festinger, *When Prophecy Fails* (Minneapolis: University of Minnesota Press, 1956).

40. Milton Rokeach, *The Three Christs of Ypsilanti: A Psychological Study* (New York: Knopf, 1964).

41. Raymond Aron, *The Opium of the Intellectuals* (Garden City, NY: Doubleday, 1957); Arthur Koestler, *Darkness at Noon* (New York: Macmillan, 1941); Czeslaw Milosz, *The Captive Mind* (New York: Knopf, 1953).

42. Janis, *Groupthink*; Robert Jervis, *Perception and Misperception in International Politics* (Princeton, NJ: Princeton University Press, 1976).

43. Gustave Le Bon, *The Crowd: A Study of the Popular Mind* (London: Unwin, 1986).

44. Hannah Arendt, *Eichmann in Jerusalem: A Report on the Banality of Evil* (New York: Viking, 1963).

45. Plato, *The Republic*.

46. Ziva Kunda, "The Case for Motivated Reason," *Psychological Bulletin* 108 (1990): 480–498.

47. Lippmann, *Public Opinion*; Hobbes, *Leviathan*; Karl Marx and Friedrich Engels, *The Communist Manifesto* (Penguin Classics, 2002). Hobbes, Lippmann, and Marx are in agreement on this point even as they subscribe to, respectively, monarchial, liberal, and communist regimes. The critique of this view is that given by Aristotle, *The Politics* (New York: Penguin Books, 1983) and taken up in a somewhat different fashion by the pragmatists (John Dewey, *How We Think* [Boston: D. C. Health, 1910]; John Dewey, *Experience and Nature* [Chicago, London: Open Court Publishing Company, 1925]; John Dewey and Arthur F. Bentley, *Knowing and the Known* [Boston: Beacon Press, 1949]). I shall come back to this point later in this chapter.

48. Immanuel Kant, *Groundwork of the Metaphysics of Morals* (New York: Harper and Row, 1964); Immanuel Kant, *The Doctrine of Virtue*, Part II of the *Metaphysic of Morals* (Philadelphia: University of Pennsylvania Press, 1971); Madison et al., *The Federalist*.

49. Aeschylus, *The Oresteia* (New York: Viking Press, 1975).

50. Patricia G. Devine, "Stereotypes and Prejudice: Their Automatic and Controlled Components," *Journal of Personality and Social Psychology* 56 (1989): 5–18; Patricia G. Devine, Margo J. Monteith, Julia R. Zuwerink, and Andrew J. Elliot, "Prejudice with and without Compunction," *Journal of Personality and Social Psychology* 60 (1991): 817–830.

51. Arendt, *Eichmann in Jerusalem*; Milgram, *Obedience to Authority*; Browning, *Ordinary Men*.

52. The claim that sovereignty rests on truth unites Plato with others who seek to protect hierarchic authority, such as the Catholic Church, though they differ on the manner by which truth is obtained (divine revelation in the instance of the Church, philosophic inquiry in the case of Plato).

53. Immanuel Kant, "Idea for a Universal History with a Cosmopolitan Purpose," in *Kant's Political Writings*, ed. Hans Reiss (Cambridge: Cambridge University Press, 1970): 41–53.

54. Religious wars had a long history in the West, including the Catholic Church's first effort to secure religious orthodoxy in authoring its first crusade against the Cathars in southern France.

55. Edmund Burke, *Reflections on the Revolution in France* (Garden City, NY: Anchor Books, 1973).

56. Sentiment was often recruited on the side of the Enlightenment vision by some, principally romantics, but Smith (Adam Smith, *The Theory of Moral Sentiments* [Indianapolis, IN: Liberty Fund, 1959]) and Hume (David Hume, *A Treatise of Human Nature* [London: Penguin Books, 1984]) also

did not find a purely rational vision of mankind to be attractive or plausible. Michael Frazer, *The Enlightenment of Sympathy* (New York: Oxford University Press, 2010).

57. Albert O. Hirschman, *The Passions and the Interests: Political Arguments for Capitalism before Its Triumph* (Princeton, NJ: Princeton University Press, 1977).

58. Adam Smith, *The Wealth of Nations* (New York: Viking, 1986), Books I–III.

59. Interest in the passions did not, of course, disappear with the appearance of this new taxonomy. Jennifer Montagu, *The Expression of the Passions: The Origin and Influence of Charles Le Brun's "Conference sur L'Expression Generale et Particulière"* (New Haven, CT: Yale University Press, 1994).

60. David B. Truman, *The Governmental Process: Political Interests and Public Opinion* (New York: Knopf, 1951).

61. We should not see this observation as one specific to Marxist thought. The notion of voting one's interests, whether or not one accurately comprehends them, has been applied as a criterion of rationality in standard voting analyses. Richard R. Lau and David P. Redlawsk, "Voting Correctly," *American Political Science Review* 91 (1997): 585–598.

62. A fuller exposition is available in Marcus, *The Sentimental Citizen.*

63. Aeschylus, *The Oresteia*; Martha C. Nussbaum, *The Therapy of Desire: Theory and Practice in Hellenistic Ethics* (Princeton, NJ: Princeton University Press, 1994).

64. John Locke, *Some Thoughts Concerning Education* (Indianapolis, IN: Hackett, 1996).

65. Sigmund Freud, *Civilization and Its Discontents* (New York: W. W. Norton, 1961); Sigmund Freud, *Totem and Taboo: Some Points of Agreement between the Mental Lives of Savages and Neurotics* (New York: W. W. Norton, 1962); Sigmund Freud and Leon Pierce Clark, *Inhibition, Symptoms, and Anxiety* (Stamford, CT: The Psychoanalytic Institute, 1927); Sigmund Freud, Alix Strachey, and James Strachey, *Inhibitions, Symptoms, and Anxiety* (New York: Norton, 1989).

66. Academic psychology has long adopted the same spatial depiction. Work on "subliminal" effects makes the same spatial presumption as do the early formulations of the "dual-process" model, which held that people could rely on "central" or "peripheral" processes to arrive at judgments. More on that later.

67. Benjamin Libet, Elwood W. Wright, Bertram Feinstein, and Dennis K. Pearl, "Subjective Referral of the Timing for a Conscious Sensory Experience," *Brain* 102 (1979): 1597–1600; Benjamin Libet, Curtis A. Gleason, Elwood W. Wright, and Dennis K. Pearl, "Time of Conscious Intention to Act in Relation to Onset of Cerebral Activity (Readiness-Potential),"

Brain 106 (1983): 623–642; Benjamin Libet, "Unconscious Cerebral Initiative and the Role of Conscious Will in Voluntary Action," *Behavioral and Brain Sciences* 8 (1985): 529–566; Benjamin Libet, Dennis K. Pearl, David Morledge, Curtis A. Gleason, Yoshio Morledge, and Nicholas Barbaro, "Control of the Transition from Sensory Detection to Sensory Awareness in Man by the Duration of a Thalamic Stimulus," *Brain* 114 (1991): 1731–1757; Benjamin Libet, *Mind Time: The Temporal Factor in Consciousness* (Cambridge, MA: Harvard University Press, 2004).

68. Actually, color is not an inherent feature of objects but, rather, an interpretation of the electrical signals sent by the cone cells in the retina to the brain. Semir Zeki, *Vision of the Brain* (Oxford: Blackwell Scientific Publications, 1993).

69. An often used definition of "cognition" is not thinking (in the sense of cogitation) but, rather, more expansively, "information processing." That's fine, but it is vital to point out that this expansion of the term obliterates the distinction between affect and cognition inasmuch as affect is information processing. And, more important still, the manner and features of each—as information processing systems—are quite distinct in their capacities. I shall turn to that later.

70. When I presented this work in 1983 to the political science department faculty upon returning from a sabbatical leave that was the beginning of my work on emotion, the response, especially from the political philosophers, was explosive rejection. Of course, to most, but especially philosophers, the centrality of "free will" to our sense of self is deeply held (much as were the beliefs of the cave dwellers in Plato's cave). Taking away that core foundation left them adrift. This essay is a much delayed act of repair insofar as I was less adept then than now in offering an alternative conception that had some positive promise.

71. This information arrives as electrical signals. Electricity is what enters the brain from four of the five senses, all but smell. The olfactory bulb, a piece of the brain, extends into the sinuses, enabling the brain to actually touch the molecules that float "out there." The brain interprets what it touches as the sensation of smell. Gordon M. Shepherd, "Perspectives on Olfactory Processing, Conscious Perception, and Orbitofrontal Cortex," *Annals of the New York Academy of Sciences* 1121 (2007): 87–101.

72. Indeed, there are important fabrications. For example, if you touch your nose with the finger of one hand at the same time as you touch a toe with a finger of the other hand, you will sense these two touches as simultaneous because the brain "knows" that they co-occurred. But, in fact, the electrical signal from the toe, having a longer route to traverse from the toe up the leg to the spine and then to the brain, arrives measurably later (i.e., the brain knows, though consciousness does not, that the two signals

arrived with a 1/20th of a second gap. Such a gap is well within the capacity of the brain to distinguish, much as good musicians can discriminate semitones, which requires distinguishing between temporal waves at 1/10th of a millisecond). Similarly, the brain knows, though consciousness does not, that there are two blind spots, one in each eye's visual field. This occurs because, at the back of the retina, where the optic nerve connects to the retina in order to convey the electrical signals to the brain's visual processing regions, there are no cones or rods to record levels of light. The brain "fills in" these blind spots with its best guess as to the likely content, giving consciousness the seamless representation we observe as the world.

73. Marc Jeannerod, *The Cognitive Neuroscience of Action* (Cambridge, MA: Blackwell, 1997).

74. So, for example, how we write depends on knowledge of what we are writing with—chalk, ballpoint, pencil, fountain pen—and on what surface—wood, blackboard, white board, and varieties of paper. All these and their many combinations are subtly different and require different movements and pressures. These details are largely ignored in the conscious realm precisely because the preconscious realm and procedural memory combine to manage these tasks seemingly "effortlessly" (so long as one understands that the "effortless" part refers to the conscious realm; these processes require considerable effort by the preconscious brain).

75. For more on memory systems, the references that follow cover the basics pretty well. Christopher F. Chabris and Daniel J. Simons, *The Invisible Gorilla: Thinking Clearly in a World of Illusions* (New York: Crown, 2010); Jeansok J. Kim and Mark G. Baxter, "Multiple Brain-Memory Systems: The Whole Does Not Equal the Sum of Its Parts," *Trends in Neurosciences* 24 (2001): 324–330; Joseph E. LeDoux, "Emotion, Memory and the Brain," *Scientific American* 270 (1994): 32–39; Mortimer Mishkin and Tim Appenzeller, "The Anatomy of Memory," *Scientific American* 256 (1987): 80–89; Edmund T. Rolls, "Memory Systems in the Brain," *Annual Review of Psychology* 51 (2000): 599–630; Daniel L. Schacter, *The Seven Sins of Memory: How the Mind Forgets and Remembers* (Boston: Houghton Mifflin, 2001); David F. Sherry and Daniel L. Schacter, "The Evolution of Multiple Memory Systems," *Psychological Review* 94 (1987): 439–454; Larry R. Squire, *Memory and Brain* (New York: Oxford University Press, 1987); Mark E. Stanton, "Multiple Memory Systems, Development and Conditioning," *Behavioral Brain Research* 110 (2000): 25–37.

76. Salvatore Aglioti, Joseph F.X. DeSouza, and Melvyn A. Goodale, "Size-Contrast Illusions Deceive the Eye but Not the Hand," *Current Biology* 5 (1995): 679–685.

77. They measured the distance between the thumb and forefinger as the subjects reached out to take each chip. They had a number of

important variations, which, in the interest of space, I shall ignore here. It is a well-crafted study and well worth reading.

78. The visual system of the brain takes electrical signals generated by cones and rods, specific cells that lie along the surface of the retinas. These cells convert light into electricity. Upon arriving in the brain, these signals are processed in two different pathways, a ventral stream that is focused on perceptual information and a dorsal stream that supports action. In addition, different regions of the brain are functionally focused, for example, V5 on motion, V4 on color, and V3 on dynamic form (i.e., how shapes are identified as they move against a background), as well as regions V2 and V1. Though we experience vision as an integrated representation, the brain constructs this representation in pieces and with sequential and parallel analyses. We have no introspective access to these distinct streams or their intermediate analyses and the downstream effects on action they have. Zeki, *A Vision of the Brain*.

79. For an argument that the two streams, dorsal and ventral, are each reliant on a common perceptual representation, see V. H. Franz, F. Scharnowski and K. R. Gegenfurtner, "Illusion Effects on Grasping Are Temporally Constant Not Dynamic," *Journal of Experimental Psychology: Human Perception and Performance* 31 (2005): 1359–1378. For evidence of the differentiation of conscious representation and action systems, see Lawrence Weiskrantz, *Blindsight: A Case Study and Implications* (Oxford: Oxford University Press, 1986); Lawrence Weiskrantz, *Consciousness Lost and Found: A Neuropsychological Investigation* (Oxford: Oxford University Press, 1997).

80. John A. Bargh, Shelly Chaiken, Rajen Govender, and Felicia Pratto, "The Generality of the Automatic Attitude Activation Effect," *Journal of Personality and Social Psychology* 62 (1992): 893–912; John A. Bargh and Tanya L. Chartrand, "The Unbearable Automaticity of Being," *American Psychologist* 54 (1999): 462–479; John A. Bargh and Melissa J. Ferguson, "Beyond Behaviorism: On the Automaticity of Higher Mental Processes," *Psychological Bulletin* 126 (2000): 925–945.

81. A. D. Milner and Melvyn A. Goodale, *The Visual Brain in Action* (New York: Oxford University Press, 1995).

82. Bernard J. Baars, *In the Theater of Consciousness* (New York: Oxford University Press, 1997).

83. Shelly Chaiken and Yaacov Trope, *Dual Process Models in Social Psychology* (New York: Guilford Press, 1999); Eliot R. Smith and Jamie De-Coster, "Dual-Process Models in Social and Cognitive Psychology: Conceptual Integration and Links to Underlying Memory Systems," *Personality and Social Psychology Review* 4 (2000): 108–131; Jonathan St. B. T. Evans, "Dual-Processing Accounts of Reasoning, Judgment, and Social Cognition," *Annual Review of Psychology* 59 (2008): 255–278. Even as insular a discipline as

is economics has belatedly begun to give notice. Daniel Kahneman, *Thinking, Fast and Slow* (New York: Farrar, Straus and Giroux, 2011).

84. Roy F. Baumeister, Ellen Bratslavsky, Mark Muraven, and Dianne M. Tice, "Ego Depletion: Is the Active Self a Limited Resource?," *Journal of Personality and Social Psychology* 74 (1998): 1252–1265; Roy F. Baumeister, E. J. Masicampo, and Kathleen D. Vohs, "Do Conscious Thoughts Cause Behavior?" *Annual Review of Psychology* 62 (2011): 331–361.

85. Jeffrey Alan Gray, *Consciousness: Creeping Up on the Hard Problem* (New York: Oxford University Press, 2004).

86. Psychologists have recognized that inaccessible "attitudes" exist, unavailable for recall, because they do not reside in semantic memory. The Implicit Attitude Test was developed as a means of bypassing the limits of introspection. Boris Egloff and Stefan C. Schmukle, "Predictive Validity of an Implicit Association Test for Assessing Anxiety," *Journal of Personality and Social Psychology* 83 (2002): 1441–1455; Russell H. Fazio, Joni R. Jackson, Bridget C. Dunton, and Carol J. Williams, "Variability in Automatic Activation as an Unobtrusive Measure of Racial Attitudes: A Bona Fide Pipeline?," *Journal of Personality and Social Psychology* 69 (1995): 1013–1027; Anthony G. Greenwald and Mahzarin R. Banaji, "Implicit Social Cognition: Attitudes, Self-Esteem, and Stereotypes," *Psychological Review* 102 (1995): 4–27; Anthony G. Greenwald, Brian A. Nosek, and Mahzarin R. Banaji, "Understanding and Using the Implicit Association Test: I. An Improved Scoring Algorithm," *Journal of Personality and Social Psychology* 85 (2003): 197–216; Anthony G. Greenwald, Andrew Poehlman, Eric L. Uhlmann, and Mahzarin R. Banaji, "Understanding and Using the Implicit Association Test: Iii. Meta-Analysis of Predictive Validity," *Journal of Personality and Social Psychology* 97 (2009): 17–41; Andrew Karpinski and James L. Hilton, "Attitudes and the Implicit Association Test," *Journal of Personality and Social Psychology* 81 (2001): 774–788.

87. Patricia G. Devine, "Stereotypes and Prejudice: Their Automatic and Controlled Components," *Journal of Personality and Social Psychology* 56 (1989): 5–18; Patricia G. Devine, Margo J. Monteith, Julia R. Zuwerink, and Andrew J. Elliot, "Prejudice with and without Compunction," *Journal of Personality and Social Psychology* 60 (1991): 817–830.

88. Consciousness is well suited to semantic depiction as it evolved as an aid to consciousness. But words are too crude to depict the complexities and subtleties of preconscious processes (a strained but apt analogy is that conventional watches that ably handle Newtonian range time—seconds, hours, and days—are too crude to handle time at the level of quantum dynamics, just as words handle description at the fairly broad level).

89. Another example of how conceptions can lock us in is the long period in the mid-twentieth century during which the standard view of

childrearing held that too much physical contact and emotional connection between parents and child stunted a child's development. Harry Harlow's research (Harry F. Harlow, "The Nature of Love," *American Psychologist* 13 [1958]: 673–685; Harry F. Harlow, *Learning to Love* [San Francisco: Albion, 1971]; Jim Ottaviani and Dylan Meconis, *Wire Mothers: Harry Harlow and the Science of Love* [Ann Arbor, MI: G.T. Labs, 2007]) was for a long time rejected by a resistant academy and the childrearing punditry of the time.

He had a long slog in arguing that such advice led to affective attachment disorders and, at the extreme, even death (as was amply demonstrated decades later in the horrific conditions in eastern Europe for abandoned children, especially but not exclusively Romania).

90. It has often been said that emotion is blind (the heart is blind is a common trope), but, as I have already explained, preconscious perception is fuller, faster, and less distorted than is conscious representation. A number of scholars have turned to reexamination of emotion with an eye to recovering earlier scholarship on its beneficial value. Among the more recent publications are Frazer, *The Enlightenment of Sympathy*; Barbara Koziak, *Retrieving Political Emotion: Thumos, Aristotle, and Gender* (University Park: Pennsylvania State University Press, 2000); Sharon R. Krause, *Civil Passions: Moral Sentiment and Democratic Deliberation* (Princeton, NJ: Princeton University Press, 2008); Morrell, *Empathy and Democracy*.

91. It is likely that the processing demands of integrating within and across the senses, along with completion of other tasks, is what contributes to the slowness and crudeness of conscious representation. How all of this is accomplished is, at this point in time, only partially understood. Stanislas Dehaene, *The Cognitive Neuroscience of Consciousness* (Cambridge, MA: MIT Press, 2001); Jeffrey A. Gray, *Consciousness: Creeping Up on the Hard Problem* (Oxford: Oxford University Press, 2004); Weiskrantz, *Consciousness Lost and Found*.

92. For a broader treatment of the many preconscious processes involving emotion, see Jaak Panksepp, *Affective Neuroscience: The Foundations of Human and Animal Emotions* (New York: Oxford University Press, 1998).

93. Stanislas Dehaene, *Reading in the Brain: The Science and Evolution of a Human Invention* (New York: Viking Adult, 2009).

94. Erving Goffman, *Forms of Talk* (Philadelphia: University of Pennsylvania Press, 1981); Erving Goffman, *Frame Analysis: An Essay on the Organization of Experience* (Boston: Northeastern University Press, 1986).

95. I chose the handshake example as the young, in particular, have discovered the joy of converting a mundane act, a simple handshake, into a complex dance. Executing a complex series of movements to make a more sequential and elegant array of movements, instead of a single conventional gesture, generates a higher level of this preconscious marker.

While requiring more practice, a more difficult movement successfully and deftly completed generates a great "hit" of enthusiasm (in the interest of simplicity and clarity I will avoid the specifics of neurochemistry—that is, the neurotransmitters and such that make this system work).

96. Thus, the theory of affective intelligence does not argue that affect plays its role solely in preconscious processes and in, via anxiety, shifting to a rational mode devoid of affect. Rather, affective states in the preconscious realm swiftly undergird the dynamic enaction and variations of actions. In the realm of deliberation, in consciousness when in "error-correcting" mode, affect offers an output in nonrepresentational language of various appraisals that are now subject to conscious consideration. In this, Frazer (*The Enlightenment of Sympathy*) misconstrues the realm of consciousness from the perspective of our work as one we expect to be largely driven by solely rational processes with little regard for affectively encoded information.

97. Marcus, *The Sentimental Citizen*; George E. Marcus, "The Psychology of Emotion and Politics," in *Oxford Handbook of Political Psychology*, ed. David O. Sears, Leonie Huddy, and Robert Jervis (Oxford: Oxford University Press, 2003): 182–221; Michael MacKuen, Jennifer Wolak, Luke Keele, and George E. Marcus, "Civic Engagements: Resolute Partisanship or Reflective Deliberation," *American Journal of Political Science* 54 (2010): 440–458.

98. Mary L. Phillips, Andrew W. Young, C. Senior, Michael J. Brammer, Christopher Andrew, A. J. Calder, Ed T. Bullmore, D. I. Perrettk, D. Rowland, Steven C. R. Williams, Jeffrey A. Gray, and A. S. David, "A Specific Neural Substrate for Perceiving Facial Expressions of Disgust," *Nature* 389 (1997): 495–498; Paul Rozin and April E. Fallon, "A Perspective on Disgust," *Psychological Review* 94 (1987): 23–41; Paul Rozin, Jonathan Haidt, and Clark R. McCauley, "Disgust," in *Handbook of Emotions*, ed. Marc D. Lewis and M. Haviland-Jones (New York: Guilford Press, 2000): 637–653.

99. And schaudenfreude is that subtle combination of pleasure and aversion that occurs when we successfully secure victory over some insult or observe the downfall of some despised opponent.

100. The parallel processing and downstream integration are characteristic. For example, reading is driven by two processes, one devoted to recognizing shapes (letters, letter pairs, and then words) and one devoted to discerning meaning. Problems can arise in either process that degrades the final experience of "reading." Stanislas Dehaene, *Reading in the Brain: The Science and Evolution of a Human Invention* (New York: Viking Adult, 2009).

101. Timothy D. Wilson, Dana S. Dunn, J. A. Bybee, D. B. Hyman, and J. A. Rotondo, "Effects of Analyzing Reasons on Attitude-Behavior

Consistency," *Journal of Personality and Social Psychology* 47 (1984): 5–16; Timothy D. Wilson and Dana S. Dunn, "Effects of Introspection on Attitude-Behavior Consistency: Analyzing Reasons Versus Focusing on Feelings," *Journal of Experimental Psychology* 22 (1986): 249–263; Timothy D. Wilson, Dana S. Dunn, Dolores Kraft, and Douglas J. Lisle, "Introspection, Attitude Change, and Attitude-Behavior Consistency: The Disruptive Effects of Explaining Why We Feel the Way We Do," *Advances in Experimental Social Psychology* 22 (1989): 287–343; Timothy D. Wilson, Dolores Kraft, and Dana S. Dunn, "The Disruptive Effects of Explaining Attitudes: The Moderating Effects of Knowledge about the Attitude Object," *Journal of Experimental Social Psychology* 25 (1989): 379–400; Timothy D. Wilson, Douglas J. Lisle, Dolores Kraft, and C. G. Wetzel, "Preferences as Expectation-Driven Inferences: Effects of Affective Expectations on Affective Experience," *Journal of Personality and Social Psychology* 56 (1989): 519–530; Timothy D. Wilson and Jonathan W. Schooler, "Thinking Too Much: Introspection Can Reduce the Quality of Preferences and Decisions," *Journal of Personality and Social Psychology* 60 (1991): 181–192; Timothy D. Wilson, Sara D. Hodges, and Suzanne J. LaFleur, "Effects of Introspecting About Reasons: Inferring Attitudes from Accessible Thoughts," *Journal of Personality and Social Psychology* 69 (1995): 16–28; Timothy D. Wilson, *Strangers to Ourselves: Discovering the Adaptive Unconscious* (Cambridge, MA: Belknap Press of Harvard University Press, 2002). The work of the neuroscientists Michael Gazzaniga (*The Social Brain: Discovering the Networks of the Mind* [New York: Basic Books, 1985]) and Lawrence Weiskrantz (*Blindsight*) is especially pertinent on this point.

102. If pressed, we will, of course, add details such as "I reached over and picked up the cup by gripping the sides," but that is merely an external observation, not a full account of the sequential muscular tensioning and relaxing or the interim assessments of balance and movement that are executed without conscious knowledge or intervention.

103. Leonie Huddy, "From Social to Political Identity: A Critical Examination of Social Identity Theory," *Political Psychology* 22 (2001): 127–156; Leonie Huddy, "Group Identity and Political Cohesion," in Sears et al., *Oxford Handbook of Political Psychology*, 511–558; Kristen Renwick Monroe, James Hankin, and Renée Bukovchik Van Vechten, "The Psychological Foundations of Identity Politics," *Annual Review of Political Science* 3 (2000): 419–447; Elizabeth Theiss-Morse, *Who Counts as an American?: The Boundaries of National Identity* (Cambridge: Cambridge University Press, 2009).

104. Please recognize that I am not talking primarily or just about extreme partisans or the very ideologically oriented. In fact, just as with cups, being a partisan has many varieties, as is also the case with ideological

identifications, which can be strong or weak, have Northern or Southern variants, be social or economic in focus, and so on. 105. Those alienated will also have an array of habits that enable and defend their views and actions. They employ, for example, such clichés as "they're all out for themselves" or "they're all a bunch of crooks," along with the appropriate gestures and facial displays of disdain when confronting the more politically trusting and engaged and the ready snide remark among the like-minded. 106. Hence, the common presumption that, since we don't know when we began to think of ourselves as "Democrats," "liberals," "Republicans," or "conservatives," it must have been in some distant past, whereas it is far more likely that we acquired the various skills over many years in the many different tasks and repetitions. That process might have begun when we were young, but the embellishment and elaboration of those sundry practices become automated through mimicry and practice extending over many situations and, likely, many years. And further, the array is modified as practices become obsolete or are replaced by others. 107. Isaiah Berlin, "Two Concepts of Liberty," in *Four Essays on Liberty* (Oxford: Oxford University Press, 1969): 118–172. 108. MacKuen et al., "Civic Engagements: Resolute Partisanship or Reflective Deliberation"; Marcus, *The Sentimental Citizen*; George E. Marcus and Michael MacKuen, "Anxiety, Enthusiasm and the Vote: The Emotional Underpinnings of Learning and Involvement during Presidential Campaigns," *American Political Science Review* 87 (1993): 688–701; George E. Marcus, W. Russell Neuman, and Michael B. MacKuen, *Affective Intelligence and Political Judgment* (Chicago: University of Chicago Press, 2000). 109. Benhabib, "Toward a Deliberative Model of Democratic Legitimacy"; Fishkin, *Democracy and Deliberation*; Fishkin, *When the People Speak*; Habermas, *Communication and the Evolution of Society* (Boston: Beacon Press, 1979); Habermas, "Three Normative Models of Democracy"; Warren, "Deliberative Democracy and Authority." 110. Sanders, "Against Deliberation"; Shapiro, "Enough of Deliberation"; Young, *Inclusion and Democracy*. 111. Gutmann and Thompson, *Democracy and Disagreement*; Rawls, *A Theory of Justice*. 112. This should not be taken to mean that these two modalities are equally distributed across situations or across individuals. Deliberation is the less frequent inasmuch as humans have long sought familiar environments. In this, deliberative theorists have good grounds to argue that we too often take too much for granted and that our current and past practices are given far too little critical attention from the vantage of both justice and efficacy. And some of us are far more oriented to risk taking

184   GEORGE E. MARCUS

than others, and some of us are strongly wedded to stable traditions no matter the justness of continued reliance thereon, whereas others are far less tolerant of accepting things to come merely because they have a long history. And, for those who are wedded to their convictions, it is true that it takes a higher level of anxiety to initiate the shift from partisan resolve to deliberation. David P. Redlawsk, Andrew J. Civettini, and Karen M. Emmerson, "The Affective Tipping Point: Do Motivated Reasoners Ever 'Get It'?," *Political Psychology* 31 (2010): 563–593.

113. MacKuen et al., "Civic Engagements"; George E. Marcus, "Different Situations, Different Responses: Threat, Partisanship, Risk, and Deliberation," *Critical Review* 20 (2008): 75–89.

114. William James, *The Principles of Psychology* (Cambridge, MA: Harvard University Press, 1890), 122.

115. Though history is replete with instances of democratic regimes failing to protect freedom, most often in times of threat. Richard Polenberg, *Fighting Faiths: The Abrams Case, the Supreme Court, and Free Speech* (New York: Viking, 1987).

116. Joshua D. Greene and Jonathan Haidt, "How (and Where) Does Moral Judgment Work?," *Trends in Cognitive Sciences* 6 (2002): 517–523; Jana Schaich Borg, Debra Lieberman, and Kent A. Kiehl, "Infection, Incest, and Iniquity: Investigating the Neural Correlates of Disgust and Morality," *Journal of Cognitive Neuroscience* 20 (2008): 367–379; Michael Koenigs, Liane Young, Ralph Adolphs, Daniel Tranel, Fiery Cushman, Marc Hauser, and Antonio Damasio, "Damage to the Prefrontal Cortex Increases Utilitarian Moral Judgements," *Nature* (2007): 1–4; James R. Rest, Darcia Narvaez, Stephen J. Thoma, and Muriel J. Bebeau, "DIT2: Devising and Testing a Revised Instrument of Moral Judgment," *Journal of Educational Psychology* 91 (1999): 644–659; Alexander Todorov and John A. Bargh, "Automatic Sources of Aggression," *Aggression and Violent Behavior* 7 (2002): 53–68; Liane Young, Joan Albert Camprodon, Marc Hauser, Alvaro Pascual-Leone, and Rebecca Saxe, "Disruption of the Right Temporoparietal Junction with Transcranial Magnetic Stimulation Reduces the Role of Beliefs in Moral Judgments," *Proceedings of the National Academy of Sciences* 107 (2010): 6753–6758 ; Jorge Moll and Ricardo de Oliveira-Souza, "Moral Judgments, Emotions and the Utilitarian Brain," *Trends in Cognitive Sciences* 11 (2007): 319–321; Jorge Moll, Ricardo de Oliveira-Souza, Griselda Garrido, Ivanei E. Bramati, Egas M. A. Caparelli-Daquer, Mirella L. M. F. Paiva, Roland Zahn, and Jordan Grafman, "The Self as a Moral Agent: Linking the Neural Bases of Social Agency and Moral Sensitivity," *Social Neuroscience* 2 (2007): 336–352.

117. Jonathan Haidt, "The Emotional Dog Does Learn New Tricks: A Reply to Pizarro and Bloom," *Psychological Review* 110 (2003): 197–98.

118. Aristotle, *Nicomachean Ethics* (New York: Odyssey Press, 1985).

119. Burke, *Reflections on the Revolution in France*.

120. Michael Oakeshott, *On Human Conduct* (Oxford: Oxford University Press, 1975).

121. Immanuel Kant, *Groundwork of the Metaphysics of Morals* (New York: Harper and Row, 1964); Amartya Sen, *The Idea of Justice* (Cambridge, MA: Belknap Press of Harvard University Press, 2009); Rawls, *A Theory of Justice*.

122. Kristen Renwick Monroe, *The Heart of Altruism: Perceptions of a Common Humanity* (Princeton, NJ: Princeton University Press, 1996).

123. Rosenblum, "Navigating Pluralism."

124. Patricia G. Devine, "Stereotypes and Prejudice: Their Automatic and Controlled Components," *Journal of Personality and Social Psychology* 56 (1989): 5–18.

125. Jonathan Haidt, "The Emotional Dog and Its Rational Tail: A Social Intuitionist Approach to Moral Judgment," *Psychological Review* 108 (2001): 814–834.

126. Ibid.

127. Hannah Arendt, *On Revolution* (New York: Viking Press, 1963).

128. It is worth noting that Arendt's claims resulted from watching primarily the defense's portrait of Adolph Eichmann at his trial in Israel. Had she bothered to do more than that, she might have discovered his fanaticism, especially in ensuring, against the will of his betters, the roundup of Hungary's Jews so that they would be killed at Auschwitz. Indeed, the particulars of Eichmann suggest the plasticity of reason to sustain evil, rather than its absence.

129. Milgram, *Obedience to Authority*.

130. Craig Haney, Curtis Banks, and Philip Zimbardo, "Interpersonal Dynamics in a Simulated Prison," *International Journal of Criminology and Penology* 1 (1983): 69–97; Zimbardo, *The Lucifer Effect*.

131. James C. Scott, *Seeing Like a State: How Certain Schemes to Improve the Human Condition Have Failed* (New Haven, CT: Yale University Press, 1998).

132. Joshua D. Greene, R. Brian Sommerville, Leigh E. Nystrom, John M. Darley, and Jonathan D. Cohen, "An fMRI Investigation of Emotional Engagement in Moral Judgment," *Science* 293 (2001): 2105–2108; Joshua D. Greene, Leigh E. Nystrom, Andrew D. Engell, John M. Darley, and Jonathan D. Cohen, "The Neural Bases of Cognitive Conflict and Control in Moral Judgment," *Neuron* 44 (2004): 389–400.

133. E. E. Schattschneider, *The Semi-Sovereign People* (New York: Holt, Rinehart and Winston, 1960). To give but one example among many available, one of the methods by which AIDS activists, members of the group ACT-UP, sought to draw attention to the spread of AIDS was to disrupt a Sunday Catholic Church service, led by Cardinal O'Connor, by throwing

condoms. This "outrageous" act served to draw wide attention, the goal of the action. For some, perhaps most, this event served to reinforce extant convictions of homophobia, enhanced with disgust at the disruption. But, for some, though we have no way of knowing how many, this event stimulated them to think, to ponder, to make (new) sense of what they saw. For at least some of the former, the disease was a just retribution for the sin of homosexuality. For some of the latter, if they came to understand that the disease could spread by "normal" sexual contact, then the disease was a human problem, rather than a homosexual problem.

134. Ilan Goldberg, Shimon Ullman, and Rafael Malach, "Neuronal Correlates of 'Free Will' Are Associated with Regional Specialization in the Human Intrinsic/Default Network," *Consciousness and Cognition* 17 (2008): 587–601. That turn is most easily achieved by those with the talent or an occupation that rewards the deliberative mode.

135. Festinger, *When Prophecy Fails*; Leon Festinger, *A Theory of Cognitive Dissonance* (Stanford, CA: Stanford University Press, 1957).

136. Kunda, "The Case for Motivated Reason"; Plato, *The Republic*; Milton Rokeach, *The Open and Closed Mind* (New York: Basic Books, 1960); Rokeach, *The Three Christs of Ypsilanti*.

137. However we come to define those often contentious terms. Sorely missed is the general faculty of prescience, for if we could foresee the end results of our endeavors, we would at least escape the sad commentary "but if I only had known."

138. Redlawsk et al., "The Affective Tipping Point."

139. Schattschneider, *The Semi-Sovereign People*.

140. The large public demonstrations in Iran after the 2009 elections were met by the regime's thugs, who used bullets and torture to reaffirm the government's control. In Tunisia, the unwillingness of the regime's military to shoot its people—much like what happened with the Hungarian border guards in 1989—was critical in the demise of the regime. A public uprising, whether in Tiananmen Square, Myanmar, or Hungary in the 1950s tells one story. When Martin Luther King Jr. led a march, meant to go from Selma, Alabama, to Montgomery, and was met at the Edmund Pettus Bridge in Selma by police and troopers intending to break up the march, no one could foretell the many reactions, local, statewide, national, and international. Sometimes "disruption" has a good but costly result, but, sometimes, even when a regime totters, the regime resists, and tyranny remains.

141. Those of you who care about baseball might consider the following. The task of calculating the trajectory of pitcher's fastball (or curve, or slider, or other pitch), the moment when and if a swing should begin, and the trajectory at which the bat must travel from its resting point to intersect

the pitch ("squaring up on the ball"), is a calculation that, if undertaken by the conscious mind, setting aside the task of how to command the muscles and movements to achieve the desired end, would require that quadratic equations be solved. You may not have known this, but if you play soccer, tennis, squash, golf, or almost any sport, your preconscious brain has long been solving such dynamic calculations, integrating time, space, and distance to achieve deft and successful movements. You may not have known it, but the solutions have long resided in your procedural memory—no matter how inept you might be at solving quadratic equations.

142. Theodor Adorno, Else Frenkel-Brunswick, Daniel Levinson, and R. Nevitt Sanford, *The Authoritarian Personality* (New York: Harper and Row, 1950); Alan S. Gerber, Gregory A. Huber, David Doherty, Conor M. Dowling, and Shang E. Ha, "Personality and Political Attitudes: Relationships across Issue Domains and Political Contexts," *American Political Science Review* 104 (2010): 111–133; Jeffery J. Mondak, Matthew V. Hibbing, Damarys Canache, Mitchell A. Seligson, and Mary R. Anderson, "Personality and Civic Engagement: An Integrative Framework for the Study of Trait Effects on Political Behavior," *American Political Science Review* 104 (2010): 85–110; Paul M. Sniderman, *Personality and Democratic Politics* (Berkeley: University of California Press, 1975); David G. Winter, "Motivation and Political Leadership," in *Political Leadership for the New Century: Personality and Behavior among American Leaders*, ed. Linda O. Valenty and Ofer Feldman (New York: Praeger, 2002).

143. Raymond B. Cattell, *The Description and Measurement of Personality* (New York: Harcourt Brace Jovanovich, 1946); James J. Conley, "Longitudinal Consistency of Adult Personality: Self-Reported Psychological Characteristics across 45 Years," *Journal of Personality and Social Psychology* 47 (1984): 1325–1333; Oliver P. John, "The 'Big Five' Factor Taxonomy: Dimensions of Personality in the Natural Language and in Questionnaires," in *Handbook of Personality Theory and Research*, ed. Lawrence A. Pervin (New York: Guilford Press, 1990): 66–100; Herbert W. Marsh, Oliver Ludtke, Bengt Muthén, Tihomir Asparouhov, Alexandre J. S. Morin, Ulrich Trautwein, and Benjamin Nagengast, "A New Look at the Big-Five Factor Structure through Exploratory Structural Equation Modeling," *Psychological Assessment* 22 (2010): 471–91; Robert R. McCrae and O. P. John, "An Introduction to the Five-Factor Model and Its Applications," *Journal of Personality* 60 (1992): 175–215.

144. Stanley Feldman, "Enforcing Social Conformity: A Theory of Authoritarianism," *Political Psychology* 24 (2003): 41–74.

145. Hobbes, *Leviathan*.

146. Bryan Garsten, *Saving Persuasion: A Defense of Rhetoric and Judgment* (Cambridge, MA: Harvard University Press, 2006).

147. Ziva Kunda, "The Case for Motivated Reason," *Psychological Bulletin* 108 (1990): 480–98.

148. Fishkin, *When the People Speak.*

149. I have focused on the role of emotion and reason at the individual level. But emotion acts in the social realm to unite and divide us and to sustain or to undermine the bonds between leaders and followers. Aristotle, *The Politics*; Aaron Ben-Ze'ev, *The Subtlety of Emotions* (Cambridge, MA: MIT Press, 2000); Ted Brader, *Campaigning for Hearts and Minds: How Emotional Appeals in Political Ads Work* (Chicago: University of Chicago Press, 2006); Charles Darwin, *The Expression of the Emotions in Man and Animals* (New York: Oxford University Press, 1998); Janaki Gooty, Shane Connelly, Jennifer Griffith, and Alka Gupta, "Leadership, Affect and Emotions: A State of the Science Review," *Leadership Quarterly* 21 (2010): 979–1004; Elaine Hatfield, John T. Cacioppo, and Richard L. Rapson, *Emotional Contagion* (Cambridge: Cambridge University Press, 1994); Roger D. Masters and Baldwin Way, "Experimental Methods and Attitudes toward Leaders: Nonverbal Displays, Emotion, and Cognition," in *Research in Biopolitics*, ed. Steven Peterson and Albert Somit (Greenwich, CT: JAI Press, 1996); Edmund T. Rolls, *Emotion Explained* (New York: Oxford University Press, 2005).

150. Garsten, *Saving Persuasion.*

151. Aeschylus, *The Oresteia.*

152. The play celebrates the replacement of binary vengeance wherein the injured party owns the plaint, as well as the obligation for defining and securing redress even if informed by community norms, for a system that reduced the injured party to a plaintiff—one who brings a plaint before others who have the authority to receive it, to interpret, and to install a just result. Brian Barry, *Justice as Impartiality* (Oxford: Clarendon Press, 1995); Dale T. Miller, "Disrespect and the Experience of Injustice," *Annual Review of Psychology* 52 (2001): 527–553; William I. Miller, *Bloodtaking and Peacemaking: Feud, Law, and Society in Saga Iceland* (Chicago: University of Chicago Press, 1990).

153. Recent events, such as the location of "a mosque" near the "sacred site" of 9/11 or as far from that specific "sacred circle" as the building of a mosque in Tennessee or the resistance of many to "giving" rights to terrorists, suggest just such difficulty in moving from initial repugnance to thoughtful reflection on the relevant principles.

6

EMOTION AND DELIBERATION: THE AUTONOMOUS CITIZEN IN THE SOCIAL WORLD

SUSAN A. BANDES

Emotion theory poses a challenge to several of the central verities of democratic theory. Most centrally, it challenges the dominant assumption that the passions play no beneficial role in the process of deliberative democracy. In challenging that assumption, emotion theory raises subsidiary questions about the valorization of autonomous thought and action, the low regard for rhetoric and persuasion, the dismissal of the role of intuition, and the focus on universalizable principles that permeate much of political discourse. In "Reason, Passion, and Democratic Politics,"[1] George Marcus describes these standard premises, explores the current cognitive psychological and neuroscientific evidence that poses a challenge to them, and closes with some questions about the implications of that evidence for reassessment of the standard verities.

Marcus's ongoing scholarly project on passion and politics has been instrumental in opening up a crucial conversation. It is a pleasure to be able to comment on such a sophisticated account of emotion theory, one that recognizes that emotion is an important component of political thought and action. This comment is largely in sympathy with Marcus's approach. However, I will raise concerns about Marcus's conception of the interplay between emotion and cognition, which sometimes comes too close to the conventional folk notion of a sharp, unidirectional divide between untamable, inaccessible feeling and mature, deliberative knowing. This notion of an opposition influences Marcus's description of political thought, his description of the uses of rhetoric and persuasion, and his description of the dynamics of social change.

I will also argue for shifting and widening the focus on individual decision making that has prevailed both in political discourse and, more generally, across disciplines. Scholarly discussion of the political process commonly takes the individual as its unit and individual autonomy as the unquestioned goal. However, political and moral decision making is best understood not as a solitary activity but as a process that takes shape in a social milieu as part of a complex set of interactions between the individual and the social and institutional structures in which she operates.

The valorization of autonomous thought and action needs to be revisited, not only because it enshrines a descriptively inaccurate goal but also because it enshrines one that is normatively questionable. Indeed, the question of whether autonomous thought and action are the gold standard for democratic participation is not one that ought to be answered in the abstract, irrespective of context. Too often, democratic participation is portrayed as something that happens only at the ballot box. Opportunities for democratic participation and political involvement take many forms, including formalized participation in electoral politics, formalized participation in legislative or administrative law making, and more informal deliberative practices such as community organizing, social networks, and myriad sites for argument, persuasion and mobilization. The optimal tools for effective democratic participation may be as varied as the contexts in which that participation occurs.[2]

The study of emotion's role in politics has been hampered by the tendency to view emotion reductively, mainly as a set of quick, intense, uneducable, and unreflective bursts of feeling. It has been hampered by the failure to distinguish among several different sorts of emotional phenomena, including, as Jeff Goodwin, James Jasper, and Francesca Polleta put it, "immediate reflex emotions, longer-term affective commitments, moods, and emotions based on complex moral and cognitive understandings."[3] Because the concept of "emotion" is viewed reductively, the category has been deployed, mostly in a derogatory fashion, in ways that cloud analysis of a range of phenomena. The use of rhetoric and persuasion to convey political ideas is derogated as an emotional, manipulative set of practices directed at the easily led. The populace is depicted as reaching political conclusions by way of emotion and intuition, elites and experts by way of reasoned deliberation. The reductive understanding of emotion also takes the form of a failure to distinguish the inquiry into individual, internal emotions from a set of macro-level questions about how emotion interacts with social structure. The notion of collective decision making is too often equated with groupthink and herd mentality, contrasted with the presumably thoughtful, deliberative behavior of the autonomous actor. In order to address these assumptions, it becomes crucial to sort out individual from collective dynamics, the question of how reasoning works from the question of what public reasons ought to look like, and the concept of emotion from the concept of intuition.

1. HIGH ROAD, LOW ROAD: SAME ENTRANCE

The debate about the relationship between emotion and reason has raged since ancient times. The notion that the two are antagonistic has always existed in tension with the notion that the two act in concert, but the former notion has long been ascendant, and one of the important goals of "Reason, Passion, and Democratic Politics" is to refute it. The consensus over the past couple of decades in the cognitive sciences is that, at least as a descriptive matter, emotion is and has always been inextricably part of the reasoning process. "There may be no such thing as pure cognition without emotion, or pure emotion without cognition."[4] Although some would argue that emotionless cognition is a worthy goal even if no one has yet attained it, there is mounting evidence that cognition without emotion is often undesirable, as well as unattainable.[5]

Marcus attacks the traditional notion of antagonism between reason and emotion, providing a rich neuroscientific account of the evidence refuting it. He argues that the relationship between the two is temporal, rather than spatial: that the heart and the head do not war for territory. Instead, they share space, but the head corrects for the cognitive errors of the heart. He is quite right that if we can stop thinking about the heart in opposition to the head or emotion in opposition to reason, we are making real progress. The challenge is to find a better way to capture the complexity of political decision making without replicating unhelpful oppositions. Although Marcus begins with a discussion of emotion and politics and a primer on reason, emotion and neuroscience,[6] his discussion of emotion and its role in the democratic process soon shades into something else—a discussion of intuition, or preconscious decisions, or automaticity.[7] Marcus begins to equate emotion with intuitive, preconscious thought and with automatic action and begins to use these terms in opposition to terms describing conscious, effortful deliberation. One of the daunting challenges of writing about emotion theory is the definitional problem. Emotion terms and other terms describing internal processes are notoriously slippery and have no fixed, agreed-upon meanings.[8] Sometimes, the best one can do is to be clear and consistent about working definitions. Marcus's account poses a problem because it shifts terminology midway without explanation. The conflation of emotion and intuition is problematic. Intuitions are not necessarily driven by emotion. Emotions are not necessarily quick, intuitive, automatic, or preconscious. They may require substantial thought and cognitive processing. And deliberation—to the extent it is presented as an alternative way of understanding the world—is not emotion-free. On the contrary, the emotions that help shape preconscious appraisals pervade more conscious, effortful appraisals as well. I will discuss each of these points in turn.

Intuitions Are Not Necessarily Emotions—or Driven by Emotion

In his section on the neuroscience of emotion and reason, Marcus argues that we have "two ways of understanding the world, preconscious appraisal and consciousness, each with a separate kind of knowledge, and each sustained by its own dedicated memory system."[9] Marcus refers to dual-process theory, which posits two systems for appraising, organizing, and prioritizing the sensory and informational data that bombard us. Influential and useful as dual-process theories are, they need to be approached with caution. The categories are very much in flux, and debate continues about the functions of the systems, the overlap between them, and the nature of the distinction between preconscious and conscious processes.[10] Any attempt to divide the workings of the brain or the mind or the self into dual systems risks replicating the very oppositions that emotion theory sets out to debunk.

Marcus frequently equates intuition and emotion or subsumes emotion under the category of intuition. Neither word has a fixed meaning, but each has many assumed meanings, associations, and resonances that can muddy the analytical waters. The term "intuition," for example, is generally used to describe processes that are quick, automatic, outside consciousness, and nondeliberative, and, indeed, Marcus generally seems to use it in precisely this way.[11] The term emotion, as discussed earlier, is too often saddled with this same definition, but this use of the term is reductive and misleading. It is a particularly problematic definition of emotion when the question at hand is what role emotion ought to play in the political process—it reduces the emotional components of political thought and action to quick, preconscious, automatic impulses.

One consequence of the conflation of terms can be seen in Marcus's discussion of the Titchener circle illusion as an illustration of the operation of the preconscious system. This illusion is presented as a failure of the intuitive system. But what has happened to the role of emotion in this explanation? Is the "circle illusion"[12] a product of emotion or passion? It may be proof that our initial instincts and appraisals can fail us, but it is not clear where emotion comes into the picture(s) or what the illusion tells us about emotion.

This is not merely a quibble about semantics. Jerome Kagan, discussing the unruly definitional landscape, noted that, although most emotion researchers insist that "emotion" includes some sort of affect or arousal or feeling, Antonio Damasio defines emotions as "complicated collections of chemical and neural responses . . . with some kind of regulatory role to play."[13] As Kagan observes, Damasio's definition treats brain states as emotions and thereby "permits almost every moment to be an occasion for an emotion."[14] Whether such a broad definition is problematic depends on what work the definition is meant to do. A definition that works when one is discussing the cognitive processes used for mathematical calculation may not work when one is discussing the cognitive preconditions for political participation, and that is where the problem arises.

In the case of the circle illusion, we can confidently say that our intuitions "fail" because we have measured the circles and declared their apparent difference in size an illusion. This illusion tells us something about a particular set of cognitive skills having to do with calculation or visual assessment, but it is not clear it tells us anything at all about the role of emotion (or the role of intuition, for that matter) in deciding normatively complex political issues. As I have written elsewhere, this conflation of the cognitive tools needed for mathematical calculation with those needed for normatively complex problems is a common and problematic move (and not one I believe Marcus intends to make). In fields like behavioral law and economics, heuristics and mental shortcuts are frequently evaluated in situations requiring judgments about quantifiable, measurable phenomena, such as judgments that rely solely on a calculation of probabilities. They are often shown to lead to incorrect results in situations where slower, more effortful deliberation would lead to more accurate results. The next step causes the problem. Heuristics and mental shortcuts are then equated with intuition, with preconscious thought, and with affect and emotion.[15] The deleterious influence of heuristics on mathematical calculation is wrongly assumed to apply to the role of heuristics, intuitions, and emotions on judgments about complex normative issues with no definitive answers.[16] And, thus, emotion or affect comes to be tagged and dismissed as a hindrance, an unreliable shortcut to judgment that adds no value to the equation.

Emotions Are Not Necessarily Quick, Intuitive, Automatic, or Preconscious

Just as the conflation of emotion and intuition may misdescribe the notion of intuition in unhelpful ways, it may also misdescribe emotion. Emotions are not necessarily quick, intuitive, or preconscious. They incorporate appraisals, and these may be effortful, slow, and conscious. This distinction is crucial for the discussion of the role of emotion in the political realm, in which emotion is too often dismissed and marginalized as instinctual and unthinking. As Polleta, Jasper, and Goodwin explain:

The startled fear that one feels when a figure rushes out of the dark is not the same fear that one develops of plans for a hazardous waste dump in the neighborhood or of abuse by a racist police force. . . . Some emotions are more constructed than others, involving more cognitive processing. Little cognitive processing is required to fear a lunging shadow, whereas quite a lot is needed before one fears a garbage dump or the policies of the World Trade Organization. . . . The emotions most relevant to politics, we believe, fall toward the more constructed, cognitive end of this dimension. Moral outrage over feared practices, the same of spoiled collective identities or the pride of refurbished ones, the indignation of perceived encroachment on traditional rights, the joy of imagining a new and better society and participating in a movement toward that end— none of these are automatic responses. They are related to moral intuitions, felt obligations and rights, and information about expected effects.[17]

Marcus does not mean to dismiss either emotion or intuition as a mere hindrance. His project is quite to the contrary. An important insight of Marcus's essay is that intuition is an essential part of the deliberative process. It is not, as the bounded rationality scholars would have it, simply a quick and dirty second-best path to insights that are better reached by slow deliberation.[18] As Marcus quite properly points out, the intuitive system does most of the work of sorting and prioritizing stimuli, and we could not function without it.[19] But, although Marcus rightly rejects the view of intuition as inherently irrational, he still depicts intuition as inaccessible and untamable in a way that sounds too close to the old rejected "emotion as the opposite of reason." My concern is that his equation of the terms "emotion" and "intuition" clouds the question of what role emotion ought to play in either the intuitive or the deliberative realm. The political conditions that Marcus ascribes to his preconscious, intuitive realm[20] include stubborn partisanship and blind loyalty of a sort that, while perhaps useful for certain purposes, lend additional credence to the notion that intuitive faculties are cognition-free, unreachable, and resistant to new information. Moreover, the intuitive realm, in Marcus's account, can shade into the realm of obedience to evil explored by Hannah Arendt and Stanley Milgram. This is a troublingly broad claim about the role of intuition or emotion—and one that can be used to reinforce the view of emotion as unthinking and deleterious to an informed citizenry. There is a rich literature on the causes of blind loyalty, willful blindness, and unquestioning obedience to immoral orders that is beyond the scope of this discussion, but it would be quite off the mark to simply lay these evils at the doorstep of too much emotion and too little cognition.[21]

Deliberative Thinking Does Not Operate Free from Intuition or Emotion

Marcus views deliberation as a separate path to knowledge—one that sounds too close to the old rejected "rationality as the opposite of emotion." I will argue that his account underestimates the influence of both emotion and intuition on deliberation and the fluidity of intuition itself. One problem with describing intuition and deliberation as separate paths to knowledge is that our slower, more deliberative appraisals generally incorporate our quick, preconscious appraisals.[22] It is more likely that intuition is a gateway through which all incoming stimuli enter, rather than one of two alternative paths to knowledge. We subject all information to quick intuitive appraisal and then revisit some of it when the need to do so seems to arise.

A key point for our purposes is that the need to revisit our intuitions doesn't *seem to* arise all that often. In Marcus's temporal metaphor, deliberation follows and corrects intuition—it can free us from the grip of our intuitive convictions. But, if our intuitions are steering us wrong, we have few internal mechanisms for identifying our own blind spots or biases. Even more problematic, we are inclined to ward off information that might trigger reappraisal. Much of the information that bombards us, for example the wisdom of Glenn Beck for liberals or of Rachel Maddow for conservatives, is likely discarded before being considered on the level of cognitive awareness. At that point, all the slow, effortful, individual deliberation in the world will not rehabilitate it.[23]

Moreover, what happens when the deliberative system does get triggered? Does deliberation free us from the grip of intuition? Here is what the cognitive neuroscientist Jonathan Haidt says about the situation in which one's later deliberation conflicts with one's deeply held moral intuitions: "[although] a person could, in principle, simply reason her way to a judgment that contradicts her initial intuition . . . such an ability may be common only among philosophers, who have been extensively trained and socialized to follow reasoning even to very disturbing conclusions."[24] In Haidt's view, people are rarely capable of scrutinizing or even identifying their own intuitive assumptions. Moral reasoning works best through other people.[25] In his view, "moral judgment is not just a single act that occurs in a single person's mind but an ongoing process, often spread out over time and over multiple people."[26]

This becomes a crucial point for participatory democracy— there is no value added from slower deliberation unless we build in ways of reappraising those initial intuitive assessments. To the contrary, unless there is a way to scrutinize those intuitions, deliberation might simply act as a way of dressing up preconscious intuitions with post hoc reasons and allowing attitudes to harden and become more polarized.

As Marcus rightly emphasizes, this caveat is as true of experts as it is about the lay public.[27] Dan Kahan and his coauthors have found in a series of studies:

> Factual disagreement on matters such as the death penalty, environmental protection laws, gun control and the like is highly polarized across distinct social groups—racial, sexual, religious, regional, and ideological. Such divisions persist even after education is controlled for; indeed, they have been shown to characterize differences of opinion even among experts who specialize in the methods necessary for establishing the empirical consequences of public policies.[28]

One dubious advantage of the times we live in is that this point about the human fallibility of experts is so easy to illustrate. Alan Greenspan told the nation he had discovered a small flaw in his economic model—he neglected to figure in the vagaries of human behavior. As it turned out, unregulated self-interest did not necessarily lead to shareholder well-being or a self-regulating market. Greenspan's deliberations rather uncannily kept endorsing his intuitions, because he protected both from countervailing information. Subsequent efforts to determine the causes of the economic crisis that began in 2008 have run into precisely the same problem, with determinations of causation and fault deviating quite markedly depending on the political ideology of the expert in question.[29] Deliberation in an echo chamber simply succeeds in

replicating selective empathy and reinforcing assumptions about
sympathy and blame, causation, responsibility, and victimhood, up
and down the ladder of intuition, belief, attitude, and ideology.[30]
Experts, as well as laypeople, gather and evaluate data in light
of implicit assumptions about how the world works and ought to
work. For experts to add value to the equation, they need more
than just more data. They need a means of identifying their own
background assumptions and recognizing the emotional influences that animate them, as well as a means of splitting off the
influences that interfere with sound judgment. There is some evidence that experts may be particularly bad at identifying their own
fallibilities. Correction is more likely to come from debate with
others and exposure to differing viewpoints than from continued
private deliberation.[31]
Nevertheless, under the right conditions, we are capable of reappraising not only our deliberative thoughts but also our intuitive ones. As Marcus rightly points out, intuitions are not really
automatic; they just don't operate in full consciousness. However,
I would go further. Marcus describes intuitions as part of "procedural memory," a place where our preferences are retained but to
which we have no access.[32] This description comes too close to the
old folk conception of conscious and subconscious minds, which
assumes that the subconscious influences the conscious but not
vice versa and that the conscious has no awareness or control over
what the subconscious is doing. But, as one scholar summarized
the current scientific consensus: "the boundaries between our conscious and unconscious are permeable, dynamic, and interactive,
and there is no valid scientific support for a sharp dichotomy."[33]
Intuitions are fluid rather than static. Simply directing attention to internal states often seems sufficient to reverse or reduce
the effect of certain implicit attitudes, stereotypes, and associations.[34] Moreover, the subconscious can learn from past behavior,
thus improving subsequent subconscious behavior. People can be
trained to improve their empathic capacity, "despite its instantaneous, unconscious operation."[35] In short, despite the fact that
much of our decision making operates automatically, outside our
awareness, and with great speed, this "low-road" decisional capacity is eminently educable.[36]
For example, we have been living through an extraordinary de-

bate about the proper balance between liberty and security. The September 11, 2001, terrorist attacks caused many people to re-evaluate not just their beliefs about issues like racial profiling and torture but also their underlying values about the balance between civil liberty and security. Intuitions and gut feelings about how the world works were, of course, deeply affected by this horrific demonstration of how the world can work. We saw the difference between abstract notions of terrorism and the concrete, salient reality of it. The intuitions themselves do not necessarily steer us wrong. There is a different kind of information up close than at a remove: arguably, our fear and anger and grief gave us informa-tion—that perhaps we'd been in denial that it could happen on American soil; that perhaps we had been too complacent; that it is easy to undervalue safety and security when you don't think they are really at risk. Also, arguably, the immediacy clouded our judg-ment—steered us toward pernicious criteria about whom to fear, made us willing to trade off too much liberty before weighing costs and benefits. There is no answer to those questions that entirely transcends intuitions about liberty and security. To simply ignore or override the intuitions is not a viable solution in a deliberative democracy in which the appropriate balance between liberty and security is a core concern of the citizenry. What has been instruc-tive since September 11th is that intuitive reactions did not remain inert. For one thing, other experiences became salient, including our own experience of putting up with various indignities atten-dant on heightened security, our outrage at notions of tapped phones and airport scans, but also empathy for those in detention or outrage at governmental abuse of prisoners. For another, we have been engaging in a national debate, and in that debate both intuitive and deliberative sentiments have been aired, scrutinized, put to the test, and reappraised.

It is the airing, the scrutiny, and the appraisal that hold the key to participatory democracy. We have many ways of acquiring knowl-edge, many ways of *reasoning*, but not all of them will translate into legitimate *reasons* for public action. As the political scientist Sharon Krause argues, "the norms that obligate us ultimately must be jus-tifiable with respect to the things that matter to us."[37] However, the things that matter to us will not necessarily remain static. "Al-though not infinitely malleable, the content of moral sentiment is

fluid rather than fixed . . . and moral sentiment itself depends on
the practices of democratic deliberation, which generate discussion and contestation about its proper content and scope."[38] And,
ultimately, the arguments that are reflected in policy ought to be
those that "appeal to sentiments and concerns that are generally
shared by citizens, or to publicly accessible reasons."[39]

2. EMOTIONS AND INSTITUTIONAL DESIGN

The conventional view of democratic participation valorizes autonomous thought and autonomous action. It tends to portray positions arrived at through interaction and group deliberation using
unflattering terms like "gullibility," "passive retransmission," "peer
pressure," and "blind loyalty." It tends to portray rhetoric as a "despised craft,"[40] a demagoguery that speaks to the lowest passions
and instincts of the masses. It tends to portray collective action
with pejoratives like "mob action," "groupthink," and "crowd dynamics."[41] In this account, the solitary deliberative individual is the
gold standard. It is an account which is increasingly out of synch
with current understandings of moral reasoning as a process that
unfolds in a social context. [42]

As Marcus properly insists, we need to work from what we know
about human nature, rather than from unrealistic models of how
citizens ought to behave. Otherwise, we construct institutions that
have little chance of either reflecting our best emotions or creating and sustaining conditions that will encourage an engaged, informed, and participatory citizenry. Marcus focuses on the dynamics of individual deliberation. For the remainder of this essay, I will
argue that, as important as that focus is, it is essential to widen it.

It is difficult and, in some respects, counterproductive to cor-
don off a realm of purely individual deliberation. At the very least,
it is essential to separate out various strands that are often left
entangled:

- Individual deliberation rests on assumptions, values, and
  norms that take shape in the social world. These assumptions, values, and norms are inculcated, refined, and challenged in the context of the social institutions that shape
  and define our lives.

- Individual deliberation on matters of political import is not synonymous with deliberation about personal matters. It is not necessarily an expression of personal preference. "On many issues, citizens vote on the basis of principled commitments so that their votes express beliefs about what the correct policies are."[43]

- The dynamics of private, individual deliberation cannot be usefully transposed to the public realm, which has its own complex dynamics. Public deliberation occurs as an interactive, collective process. To draw conclusions about its dynamics or about how to reform them, it is essential to focus on the particular type of deliberation at issue and the goals and constraints of the institution in which it takes place.

The problem with focusing on the autonomous individual is already apparent in a microlevel analysis. Understanding how individual emotions are shaped requires inquiry into social dynamics. The autonomous actor is unavoidably shaped in the social world, in public and private settings that communicate, model,[44] and enforce emotional norms.[45] Units of social organization communicate and reproduce lessons about the feeling and display of emotion, and they inculcate emotions. To help prepare effective citizens of a participatory democracy, it becomes essential to focus on collective institutions, on the academic, moral, emotional, and social environment they create, and on the traits they encourage. One task for a participatory democracy is to determine what sorts of citizens it aims to produce and encourage. We might want schools, for example, that encourage or model certain traits compatible with participatory democracy, such as critical thinking, or persuasiveness, or empathy for others, or tolerance. We might want to avoid schools that inculcate shame or helplessness or blind obedience. More generally, there is much work to be done in the social sciences on the reciprocal interaction between emotion and social structure: how emotion sustains or changes social structural arrangements and how social structure channels and shapes the feeling and display of emotion.[46] For political theorists, there are two pressing questions: what sorts of citizens and what sorts of values should our institutions encourage, and what sorts of institutions are best suited to encouraging the conditions of participatory democracy?

These sorts of questions require a focus on collective, as well as individual, emotional dynamics. Even individual deliberative dynamics must be understood as based on norms and assumptions that take shape in institutional settings, and thus we need to consider how to construct the institutions that guide us and reflect our values. Even individual political deliberation must be understood not as an aggregation of individual preference but as a process by which we determine the values we choose to live and be governed by as a polity. And, when the discussion turns to group dynamics, for example, to questions of how deliberation works in a group setting or questions about group dynamics and the engines of social change, it is essential not to extrapolate from assumptions about individual decision making. A group is "not simply an aggregate of single persons, but *sui generis*, an entity with its own characteristics."[47]

Groups have their own emotional climates and emotional dynamics that arise through mechanisms like contagion and synchronization and through the creation and enforcement of emotion norms.[48] So, for example, in Marcus's account of the dynamics of individual deliberation, he argues that intuitions help us navigate efficiently through the habitual, familiar world, whereas deliberation is needed when we face the novel. In this account, intuitions are linked to automaticity of action, whereas deliberation impedes action. A description of the emotional dynamics of group settings would look quite different. Consider social changes such as the Montgomery bus boycott[49]—or the more recent example of changing attitudes toward Don't Ask Don't Tell and same-sex marriage or the reaction in France to the sexual assault arrest of Dominique Strauss-Kahn, which has caused new awareness of the prevalence and toleration of sexual coercion in that country.[50] Here, novelty is linked to intuition: a moral shock, an imaginative intuitive leap across an empathic divide. The deliberative component is needed to sustain the commitment to concerted action once the novelty wears off.[51]

There is a growing literature arguing for what the business journalist James Surowiecki calls "the wisdom of crowds"[52]—the notion that groups may make more informed and better decisions than individuals. The journalist Tina Rosenberg argues in her recent book that peer pressure is a far more potent force for social change than information and that it can be harnessed to "persuade people to take action that is crucial to their long-term well-being but appears unpleasant, dangerous, or psychologically difficult today."[53] Whether or not groups make "better" decisions depends on the context, but there is increasing evidence that institutions can be structured to promote a range of values and attributes and that we ought to pay careful attention to the question of which values and attributes are worth promoting in particular contexts. For example, institutions can be structured to increase participation, to increase awareness of or empathy for diverse viewpoints,[54] to encourage more thorough and informed deliberation, and to work toward other goals that are consistent with participatory democracy.[55]

Important empirical research is being conducted on a variety of questions related to the conditions conducive to informed deliberation and the relationship between informed deliberation and the heterogeneity of the decision making body. The psychologist Sam Sommers, for example, is engaged in a series of fascinating experiments on the effects of racially diverse juries on the cognitive processes of jurors, both individually and as a group. He reports that:

> The relationship between group composition and performance in general is clearly complicated, but from a strictly decision-making perspective, both sides of the debate regarding diversity effects are compatible with the hypothesis that groups often benefit from racial heterogeneity. The extent to which racial diversity facilitates information exchange and problem solving certainly indicates advantages for heterogeneous groups, especially for complex decisions. But even interpersonal conflict—often mentioned as the principal negative result of diversity—may be useful when a group's primary goal is not boosting morale but rather good and thorough decision-making. Consider, for example, the jury, for which positive affect and group cohesion are less important than fact-finding ability and a willingness to consider the entire range of a community's viewpoints. In this setting, as in other contexts in which turnover is not a primary concern (or possibility), racial heterogeneity is likely to have positive effects on decision-making processes and outcomes.[56]

As Sommers emphasizes, the question of what makes an effective
deliberative process depends on the context—on the constraints
and goals of the particular institution. In the context of jury deliberation, he reports that one mock jury experiment provides preliminary support for the proposition that the cognitive processes
observed among individuals in racially heterogeneous groups differ from those found in homogeneous groups in ways that advance
the goals of the endeavor:

> In this experiment, racially diverse juries deliberated longer, consid-
> ered a wider range of information, and made fewer inaccurate state-
> ments when discussing the trial of a Black defendant than did all-
> White juries. Contrary to traditional conceptualizations of diversity,
> these effects were not attributable to the novel informational con-
> tributions of Black group members. Rather, White participants con-
> tributed more factual information to deliberations and made fewer
> errors discussing the case when on diverse versus all-White juries,
> suggesting that racial heterogeneity may have led to more thorough
> information processing during the trial. This study is noteworthy
> in that it provides the first evidence—albeit indirect and in a legal
> context—of a specific cognitive process by which a group's racial
> diversity may impact its individual members.[57]

Another promising avenue (and one that has received far less
attention, perhaps because it challenges cherished assumptions
about judicial neutrality) is the study of judicial decision making.[58]
For example, the legal scholar Cass Sunstein and his coauthors, in
a study of federal appellate-court decisions issued by three-judge
panels, concluded that a judge's ideological tendencies can be
predicted by the party of the appointing president. They found
that these tendencies led to dramatically different outcomes in
decision making, depending on whether or not the panel was
ideologically diverse. A judge's ideological tendency is likely to be
dampened if he or she is sitting with two judges of a different political party and amplified if he or she is sitting with two judges
from the same political party.[59]

In short, group dynamics are not a black box. There is a growing body of knowledge about group dynamics and how deliberation unfolds in a variety of collective contexts.[60] There is a growing
body of knowledge about organizational structure and its relation-

ship to norm creation, behavior guidance, group cohesion, group mobilization, and other similar group-wide emotional phenomena.[61] Institutions are uniquely placed to shape and guide moral intuitions. They can provide systematic feedback about what behaviors are acceptable or unacceptable.[62] They can communicate messages that educate the public and that influence both preconscious and conscious behavior.[63] In addition, they may build in not only time for reflection but mechanisms for including a range of perspectives and for encouraging the open and respectful interchange of ideas.

Left to their own devices, people are not very good at revisiting and correcting for their own misconceptions. Indeed, particularly when attitudes are deeply held, we are likely to protect our beliefs from contradictory or threatening information.[64] Moreover, the tendency to screen out contradictory evidence and to accept information only from "trusted" sources exacerbates group polarization. "Particularly with the sorts of symbolic, hot-button issues that are 'strongly connected to an individual's cultural identity'[65] the effect of additional information is often, perversely, to reinforce the chasm between opposing groups."[66] Institutions can be constructed to address these tendencies.

Institutional design and reform must be keyed to the considered aims and constraints of the institution in question and must build on what we know about the dynamics of decision making. The questions that require attention include these: what sorts of institutional arrangements will encourage the immediacy and connection that spur communal action, while building in the time and distance to be sure that we are taking the right sorts of action and that we can sustain it? What constitutes effective communication of a sort that addresses the concerns of the polity without stripping it of all relevant affect?[67] What arrangements will encourage empathy for others and respect for diverse viewpoints as well as the critical faculties that enable independent judgment? How should we structure political institutions that not only reflect but appraise, channel, and educate emotions, with an eye toward creating the conditions for a robust deliberative democracy? For those of us whose concern is with shaping institutions to promote just and deliberative processes and outcomes, these issues should be central to our inquiry.

NOTES

I am grateful to Jim Fleming for organizing and including me in this symposium, to George Marcus for his fine and provocative article, and to Kathy Abrams and Carol Sanger for enormously helpful comments on earlier drafts of this article.

1. George E. Marcus, "Reason, Passion, and Democratic Politics: Old Conceptions—New Understandings—New Possibilities," in this volume.

2. In her examination of the criteria for the role of affect in democratic deliberation, Sharon Krause distinguishes the "formal procedures of public deliberation as will-formation which generate coercively enforced law and policies" from the "more informal practices of deliberation as opinion-formation among citizens on issues of public importance." Sharon R. Krause, *Civil Passions: Moral Sentiment and Democratic Deliberation* (Princeton, NJ: Princeton University Press, 2008), 112.

3. Jeff Goodwin, James M. Jasper, and Francesca Polleta, "Emotional Dimensions of Social Movements," in *The Blackwell Companion to Social Movements*, ed. David A. Snow, Sarah A. Soule, and Hanspeter Kriesi (Malden, MA: Blackwell, 2004), 414–433.

4. Richard D. Lane et al., "The Study of Emotion from the Perspective of Cognitive Neuroscience," in *Cognitive Neuroscience of Emotion*, ed. Richard D. Lane and Lynn Nadel (Oxford: Oxford University Press, 2004), 6.

5. On the level of individual deliberation, for example, Antonio Damasio and other cognitive scientists have observed that subjects with impaired access to their emotions lose the ability to make decisions beneficial to their well-being or the welfare of others and sometimes lose the ability to make any decisions at all. Antonio R. Damasio, *Descartes' Error: Emotion, Reason, and the Human Brain* (New York: HarperCollins, 1994), 36, 193.

6. See Marcus, "Reason, Passion, and Democratic Politics," 139–145.

7. See, e.g., ibid. (discussion of identical circles beginning on 142).

8. Jerome Kagan, *What Is Emotion? History, Measures and Meanings* (New Haven, CT: Yale University Press, 2007), 25–26; Jack Pankseepp, *Affective Neuroscience: The Foundations of Human and Animal Emotions* (Oxford: Oxford University Press, 1998), 47–48; and Susan A. Bandes, "Victims, 'Closure,' and the Sociology of Emotion," *Law and Contemporary Problems* 72 (2009): 1, 6.

9. Marcus, "Reason, Passion, and Democratic Politics," 144.

10. See, e.g., Lane et al., "Study of Emotion from the Perspective of Cognitive Neuroscience," 3–10.

11. See, e.g., Marcus, "Reason, Passion, and Democratic Politics," 145.

12. Ibid., 143 (Figure 5.3).

13. Kagan, *What Is Emotion?*, 25–26 (citing Antonio Damasio, *Looking for Spinoza: Joy, Sorrow, and the Feeling Brain* [Orlando, FL: Harcourt, 2003], 51).

14. Ibid.

15. See my discussion of the Affect Heuristic in Susan Bandes, "Emotions, Values, and the Construction of Risk," *University of Pennsylvania Law Review* 156 (2008): 427, 428, and n.32.

16. Current research suggests that emotions may play a far smaller role in arriving at "[j]udgments that do not rely on memory-based information" and instead rely on "abstract and uninvolving stimulus materials, such as the word lists typically preferred by cognitive researchers." Emotions play a larger role in constructive judgment situations that require "active elaboration and transformation of the available stimulus information." Joseph P. Forgas and Rebekah East, "Affective Influences on Social Judgments and Decisions: Implicit and Explicit Processes," in *Social Judgments: Implicit and Explicit Moral Processes*, ed. Joseph P. Forgas et al. (Cambridge: Cambridge University Press, 2003), 204; see also William D. Casebeer and Patricia S. Churchland, "The Neural Mechanisms of Moral Cognition: A Multiple-Aspect Approach to Moral Judgment and Decision-Making," *Biology and Philosophy* 18 (2003):169, 188 ("Moral judgments tell us what we ought to think *so that* we know what to do. Isolating the doing from the knowing via an artificial experimental regimen can remove the directedness of moral cognition.").

17. Goodwin et al., "Emotional Dimensions of Social Movements," 12–13.

18. Bandes, "Emotions, Values, and the Construction of Risk," 427–439 (critiquing the bounded rationality model of decision making).

19. See also John A. Bargh and Tanya L. Chartrand, "The Unbearable Automaticity of Being," *American Psychologist* 54 (1999): 462 (arguing that nonconscious mental systems perform the lion's share of the work of making sense of the world and planning and engaging in courses of action).

20. If I am correct in my interpretation of Figure 5.9 and the accompanying discussion. Marcus, "Reason, Passion, and Democratic Politics," 159 (Figure 5.9).

21. The Milgram experiments, to take just one of Marcus's examples, may be interpreted as a lesson not only about blind obedience but also about the emotional conditions that encourage dehumanization, interfere with empathy and compassion, and create emotional distance from the object of pain. Susan A. Bandes, "Repellent Crimes and Rational Deliberation: Emotion and the Death Penalty," *Vermont Law Review* 33 (2009): 489, 513.

22. Marcus recognizes that emotion plays a role in both processes. Marcus, "Reason, Passion, and Democratic Politics," 144–145.

23. Anthony G. Greenwald, "Self-Knowledge and Self-Deception: Further Consideration," in *The Mythomanias: The Nature of Deception and Self-Deception*, ed. Michael S. Mylobodsky (Mahwah, NJ: Lawrence Erlbaum, 1997), 57; Susan A. Bandes, "Loyalty to One's Convictions: The Prosecutor and Tunnel Vision," *Howard Law Journal* 49 (2006): 475, 491–492.

24. Jonathan Haidt, "The Emotional Dog and Its Rational Tail: A Social Intuitionist Approach to Moral Judgment," *Psychological Review* 108 (2001): 814, 829.

25. Ibid., 820.

26. Ibid., 828.

27. For example Jeffrey Rachlinski, Chris Guthrie, and their coauthors have found that judges, like lay people, are influenced by unacknowledged intuitions. Rachlinksi, Guthrie, et al., "Blinking on the Bench: How Judges Decide Cases," *Cornell Law Review* 93 (2007): 1.

28. Dan Kahan and Donald Braman, "Cultural Cognition and Public Policy," *Yale Law and Policy Review* 24 (2006): 147, 147–148.

29. The report of the Financial Crisis Inquiry Commission on the causes of the current financial crisis splits along party lines in its assumptions about what aspects of human behavior caused the crisis—the greed and naïveté of individual first-time and unschooled investors or the greed, self-dealing, and conflicts of interest that beset financial industries and regulatory agencies. See http://cybercemetery.unt.edu/archive/fcic/2011031 0173538/http://www.fcic.gov/report.

30. I want to acknowledge and highlight the daunting definitional problems that arise in an interdisciplinary discussion of instincts, beliefs, attitudes, values, and ideologies. None of these terms has an accepted meaning across disciplines, and most are contested within disciplines as well. See Bertram Gawronski, "Attitudes Can Be Measured! But What Is an Attitude?" (editorial), *Social Cognition* 25 (2007): 573, 574; Bandes, "Emotions, Values, and the Construction of Risk," 424–427. But, whatever definitional scheme we choose, the basic point is the same. Sophisticated ideologies or worldviews about the role of government cannot operate free from assumptions about what motivates people and how people ought to act. But the interaction among intuition, attitude, and ideology is not unidirectional.

31. Bandes, "Emotions, Values, and the Construction of Risk," 432–433.

32. See, e.g., Marcus, "Reason, Passion, and Democratic Politics," 154–155.

33. Deborah Denno, "Crime and Consciousness: Science and Involuntary Acts," *Minnesota Law Review* 87 (2002): 269, 307.

34. Leonard Berkowitz, Sara Jaffee, Eunkyung Jo, and Bartholomeu T.

Troccoli, "On the Correction of Feeling-Induced Judgmental Biases," in *Feeling and Thinking: The Role of Affect in Social Cognition*, ed. Joseph P. Forgas (Cambridge: Cambridge University Press, 2000), 132–133.

35. Daniel Goleman, *Social Intelligence: The New Science of Human Relationships* (New York: Random House, 2006), 21.

36. See Jeffrey Rachlinski et al., "Does Unconscious Bias Affect Trial Judges?," http://papers.ssrn.com/sol3/papers.cfm?abstract_id=1374497 (measuring race and gender bias and finding that, once it is brought into consciousness, it can be ameliorated); Goleman, *Social Intelligence*, 300–301 (reporting on debiasing experiments); Samuel R. Sommers, "On Racial Diversity and Group Decision-Making: Identifying Multiple Effects of Racial Composition on Jury Deliberations," *Journal of Personality and Social Psychology* 90 (2006): 597 (discussing prompting effect of presence of racially diverse jurors on the deliberative dynamics of the jury); J. Correll et al., "Across the Thin Blue Line: Police Officers and Racial Bias in the Decision to Shoot," *Journal of Personality and Social Psychology* 92 (2007): 1006 (reporting on effectiveness of training on eliminating racially based aspect of police officers' split-second decisions to shoot). See also Susan A. Bandes, "Is It Immoral to Punish the Heedless and Clueless?," *Law and Philosophy* 29 (2010): 433, 440–442 (discussing the trainable nature of intuitions).

37. Krause, *Civil Passions*, 159.

38. Ibid., 163.

39. Ibid., 122.

40. Marcus notes this pejorative use with disapproval. Marcus, "Reason, Passion, and Democratic Politics," 166.

41. For an excellent discussion of these approaches, see Goodwin et al., "Emotional Dimensions of Social Movements," 2.

42. Kevin M. Carlsmith and John M. Darley, "Psychological Aspects of Retributive Justice," *Advances in Experimental Social Psychology* 40 (2008): 193; Jonathan Haidt and Fredrik Bjorklund, "Social Intuitionists Answer Six Questions about Moral Psychology," in *Moral Psychology*, ed. W. Sinnott-Armstrong (Cambridge, MA: MIT Press, 2008), 2:181 (arguing that moral judgment is a social process).

43. Joshua Cohen, "An Epistemic Conception of Democracy," *Ethics* 97 (1986): 1, 24.

44. Goodwin et al., "Emotional Dimensions of Social Movements," 16 (emotions permeate large-scale units of social organization such as states, political parties, movements, networks, and communities).

45. For classic works on how institutions communicate and enforce emotional norms, see Arlie Hochschild, *The Managed Heart: The Commercialization of Human Feeling* (Berkeley: University of California Press, 1985),

and Candace Clark, *Misery and Company: Sympathy in Everyday Life* (Chicago: University of Chicago Press, 1997).

46. Kathryn J. Lively and David R Heise, "Sociological Realms of Emotional Experience," *American Journal of Sociology* 109 (2004): 1109, 1125; Peggy Thoits, "The Sociology of Emotions," *Annual Review of Sociology* 15 (1989): 317.

47. Nicholas Tavuchis, *Mea Culpa: A Sociology of Apology and Reconciliation* (Stanford, CA: Stanford University Press, 1991), 99–100.

48. See, e.g., Sigal G. Barsade, "The Ripple Effect: Emotional Contagion and its Influence on Group Behavior," *Administrative Science Quarterly* 47 (2002): 644; Goleman, *Social Intelligence.*

49. See, e.g., Herbert Kohl, *Should We Burn Babar?: Essays on Children's Literature and the Power of Stories* (New York: New Press, 1995) (critiquing the myth that the Montgomery bus boycott began with a single, spontaneous act by an uneducated and politically naïve Rosa Parks and arguing that, instead, Parks's act was just one part of a deliberate and carefully planned strategy by a politically sophisticated group of civil rights activists).

50. See, e.g. "How Dominique Strauss-Kahn's Arrest Awoke a Dormant Anger in the Heart of France's Women," *The Guardian*, May 22, 2011, http://www.guardian.co.uk/world/2011/may/22/dominique-strauss-kahn-arrest-dormant-anger-france-women.

51. See generally introduction to Goodwin et al., "Emotional Dimensions of Social Movements" (discussing the emotions that lead to the origin, spread, and decline of social movements). The authors discuss, inter alia, "abeyance structures" through which "movements survive between periods of mass mobilization." Ibid., 21.

52. James Surowiecki, *The Wisdom of Crowds* (New York: Anchor Books, 2005).

53. Tina Rosenberg, *Join the Club: How Peer Pressure Can Transform the World* (New York: W.W. Norton, 2011), xix.

54. See generally Robert Goodin, "Democratic Deliberation Within," in *Debating Deliberative Democracy*, ed. James Fishkin and Peter Laslett (Malden, MA: Blackwell, 2003) (arguing for the importance of expanded empathy in democratic deliberation).

55. Sharon Krause suggests several such institutional reforms, including making schools and youth organizations more effective at developing the appropriate affective as well as intellectual faculties, encouraging national service programs, focusing on legal and institutional mechanisms that increase access to public deliberation and give voice to those who might otherwise be marginalized, and reforming juries. Krause, *Civil Passions*, 136–139.

56. Sommers, "On Racial Diversity and Group Decision-Making," 598.

57. Samuel R. Sommers, Lindsey S. Warp, and Corrine C. Mahoney, "Cognitive Effects of Racial Diversity: White Individuals' Information Processing in Heterogeneous Groups," *Journal of Experimental Social Psychology* 44 (2008): 1129, 1131 (discussing the results reported in Sommers, "On Racial Diversity and Group Decision-Making").

58. See notes 27 and 36 for reference to studies of the decision-making dynamics of individual judges.

59. Cass Sunstein et al., *Are Judges Political? An Empirical Analysis of the Federal Judiciary* (Washington, DC: Brookings Institution Press, 2006).

60. See generally *Emotion in Social Relations: Cultural, Group, and Interpersonal Processes*, ed. Brian Parkinson, Agneta Fischer, and Antony Manstead (New York: Psychology Press, 2005).

61. See generally Jonathan Turner and Jan E. Stets, *The Sociology of Emotions* (New York: Cambridge University Press, 2005).

62. Gerg Gigerenzer, *Gut Feelings: The Intelligence of the Unconscious* (London: Penguin Books, 2007), 157–158.

63. Ibid.

64. Ziva Kunda, "The Case for Motivated Reasoning," *Psychological Bulletin* 108 (1990): 480, 495.

65. Kahan and Braman, "Cultural Cognition and Public Policy," 154.

66. Susan Bandes, "The Heart Has Its Reasons: Examining the Strange Persistence of the American Death Penalty," *Studies in Law, Politics and Society* 42 (2008): 40.

67. See generally George Lakoff, *The Political Mind: Why You Can't Understand 21st-Century American Politics with an 18th-Century Brain* (New York: Viking, 2008); Drew Westen, *The Political Brain: The Role of Emotion in Deciding the Fate of the Nation* (New York: Public Affairs, 2007).

7

RELIABLE DEMOCRATIC HABITS AND EMOTIONS

CHESHIRE CALHOUN

As I understand George Marcus's project presented here as well as in *The Sentimental Citizen* and in *Affective Intelligence and Political Judgment,* coauthored with Russell Neuman and Michael McKuen, the central goal is to challenge the idea that the aims of democracy are best advanced by supporting and demanding higher levels of deliberation among the electorate.[1] The normative conception of citizenship that Marcus challenges requires of good citizens that they be knowledgeable, well versed on public-policy issues, capable of applying general principles to particular cases, and able to articulate for themselves and to others their reasons for taking the stands they do. In addition, Marcus aims to challenge a connected view of the role of emotion in democracy. On that view, while both political conflict and political solidarities may inevitably *cause* emotions, emotions ought to play no role in rational political judgment and action. As Kant said of inclinations, so the advocate of deliberative democracy might say of the emotions: "it must . . . be the universal wish of every rational being to be wholly free from them."[2] And, just as perfect political deliberators should wish to be free from the influence of emotion, so, too, they should wish to be free from the influence of partisan loyalties.

In Marcus's view, this normative conception of citizens as emotionless, nonpartisan deliberators is fundamentally misguided. It overestimates the role that conscious thought could possibly play in human life and underestimates the reason-subserving functions of "emotion systems." Rationality, he argues, does not depend on all of our judgments, choices, and actions being preceded by and based on conscious, reflective thought. It, instead, depends on our having in place serviceable habits of judgment, choice, and action, as well as a preconscious system that monitors how well those habits are working and that triggers—via anxiety—reflective thought only when those habits fail or risk failing us. Marcus argues that anxiety plays a critical role in human rationality by alerting us to when gathering more information and deliberating about what to do or think is warranted. What Marcus calls "enthusiasm" also plays a critical role in human rationality by providing the motivation for action. Thus, autonomous thought ultimately depends on our emotional capacity for anxiety, and autonomous action ultimately depends on our emotional capacity for enthusiasm.

What democracy needs, then, is not a citizenry that deliberates about every political choice. Democracy needs citizens who are neurologically designed to develop serviceable habits of political judgment and action—habits whose basis may not be articulable —and who are also neurologically designed to shift into conscious deliberation when reliance on habits seems risky. By adopting a dual-process model of human psychology, we need not pit reason against emotion or partisanship against deliberation.

There is much to admire in Marcus's view, particularly his attention to the much-ignored (by analytic philosophers at least) emotion of anxiety, his development of a conception of agency that does not require that only the privileged, educated classes be considered capable of autonomous thought and action, and his endeavor to overcome models of both reason and emotion that do not acknowledge the interconnections between the two.

That said, I want to raise some critical questions about how far Marcus's view in fact diverges from the Enlightenment opposition of reason to emotion and how far it *can* diverge from that view without giving deliberation a more central place in our conception of rational political actors. I then will briefly turn to the question of what a liberal democratic theory of emotions might look like.

The Enlightenment view of emotion might be thought of as composed of two basic features, one descriptive and one normative. Descriptively, emotion and rational thought are to be understood in terms of contrasting pairs of descriptors such as biased-unbiased, nonrepresentational-representational, noncognitive-cognitive, caused by external stimuli-responsive to reasons, physiologically based-cognitively based, motivating-motivationally inert, and so on. On the basis of some such contrast between emotion and reason, it is then possible to conclude that emotions are not the sorts of mental states that *ought* to be permitted to influence deliberation, judgment, and action and that it is a bad thing if they do.[3]

Marcus does not disagree with the first feature of the Enlightenment view. Emotions of anxiety, calm, enthusiasm, and depression differ from rational thought because they arise preconsciously and often do not make it to conscious awareness, whereas thought is always conscious. Enthusiasm and depression, for example, provide us with appraisals of the success or failure of habitual action "without any requirement of conscious intervention, so long as the current field in which action is undertaken is much like that which has gone before."[4] Emotions are nonrepresentational and nonsemantic, whereas conscious thought is both representational and semantic. Emotions are characterized by automaticity, whereas conscious thought is not. Emotions are linked to action-goals, whereas reflective thought is not.

In some respects, Marcus's contrast between emotion and reason is more extreme than anything one finds in the Enlightenment period. Descartes, for instance, thought that we can voluntarily (if indirectly) alter our emotional responses by representing the object of emotion in a different light; we can also deliberately retrain our natural emotional responses.[5] And Kant thought that the key moral emotion—respect for the moral law and for the dignity of persons—is made possible by our rational nature and makes possible genuinely moral motivation. He also thought that we could and ought to cultivate in ourselves compassionate feelings and our natural predisposition to sympathetic joy and sadness at others' states, since these feelings make it more likely that we will act on moral maxims.[6] This was his primary reason for condemning cruelty to animals.[7] These kinds of interplays between emotion and conscious thought are possible in part because Enlightenment thinkers assumed that our experiences of emotions are conscious experiences—we are aware of our emotions and can become aware of their causes; as a result, we can exercise control over whether and how we act on our emotions. Enlightenment thinkers also assumed that we have some control over our emotional dispositions themselves; we can train or retrain our emotional susceptibilities by altering how we think about the objects that cause our emotions, and this is something we can consciously set out to do with some hope of success.

Marcus appears to reject both the assumption that emotions are conscious and the assumption that we can consciously influence our emotional dispositions. The surveillance and disposition systems operate outside conscious thought, and the emotions they generate typically do so, as well. Moreover, Marcus appears to associate the emotions that motivate political action with preferences that are part of procedural memory to which we have no conscious access at all. So, for instance, he says that "just as we have no access to the precise details, let alone the execution of the sundry habits in daily life, we have no greater access—apart from after-the-fact observation and speculation—as to the fullness and range of our political habits."[8] And it is central to the view presented in his essay in this volume that "the fundamental relationship between cogitation (thinking) and affect (feeling) is temporal, not spatial," with affect always preceding.[9] So it looks as though our specific emotional susceptibilities will not be the sorts of things that we, as reflective conscious beings, could attempt to shape, both because our emotions themselves are typically not conscious and because the preferences and habits to which they are attached are not available to conscious awareness.

So why doesn't Marcus reach the Enlightenment conclusion that emotions should not influence deliberation, judgment, and action? The answer, I take it, has to do with the *status* of the *habits* that the disposition system monitors and on which the surveillance system can suspend action. Habitual skilled behavior, ranging from signing our names to investing trust in others or withholding it from them, is a product of preconscious, automatic mental processes governed by behavioral scripts that are stored in procedural memory. Although typically not accessible to conscious thought, those habits are nevertheless critical to a well-functioning being. When those habits govern higher-order skilled action—such as supporting a repertoire of causes, aligning oneself with a particular party, or going to the polls to vote—they constitute the sorts of habits that characterize rational beings. When those habits generally serve us well, the emotions of enthusiasm at successful enactment of those habits and depression when enactment is frustrated are rationally warranted. Those habits take on a different status under novel circumstances. Acting on them is not clearly rational, and the affect of anxiety, which interrupts action and triggers conscious reassessment, is rationally warranted.

In sum, for Enlightenment thinkers, reason gets connected to emotion via our capacity to rationally reflect on the causes of our emotions, as well as on our general emotional susceptibilities and our capacity to endorse those emotions, voluntarily cultivate new emotional susceptibilities, or choose to act on the dictates of reason, rather than emotional impulses. Reason thus gets, as Marcus says, "spatially" located above the emotions as their governor.[10] On Marcus's view, it is the effects of enthusiasm and anxiety themselves that do the governing by motivating us to stick with habits that it is rational for us to have and by triggering reflection on habits when the rationality of habitual action is challenged by new circumstances. So, despite Marcus's relegation of the emotions to preconscious, nonrepresentational states, he ends up with an even stronger endorsement of the role of emotion in the life of rational beings than was possible for Enlightenment thinkers. Emotions are in the driver's seat of human rationality.

This defense of the regulative function of enthusiasm and anxiety depends, however, on the rationality of the habits at issue. People acquire all sorts of irrational habits—from loading their diets with sugar to voting against candidates on the basis of their religion or race. Those habits can indeed, as Marcus claims, operate beneath the level of conscious awareness and may motivate action that conflicts with an individual's conscious beliefs. The many studies of gender and race bias in the assessment of credentials —a bias both races and both sexes exhibit regardless of conscious commitment to equality—is a good example of this. An enthusiasm supporting such habits hasn't much claim to importance in the life of rational beings. Marcus does acknowledge that enacting enthusiasm-supported habits in *novel* circumstances is rationally criticizable as blindly loyal and obstinate.[11] But even in nonnovel circumstances where our habits work quite well (as racist habits of perception work quite well to discriminate against minority racial candidates), those habits may be criticizable—not because they fail to serve the purpose they are designed for but because they are habits that rational individuals ought not to have in the first place.

People can also protect themselves from anxiety in all sorts of ways, thereby short-circuiting the regulative role of anxiety in provoking appropriate deliberation. Smokers protect themselves from anxiety that would trigger reflection about their habits by avoiding reading about lung cancer and heart disease. Racists protect themselves from anxiety about their habits of claiming race privilege in a racially diverse society by voting only for white candidates and living in racially segregated neighborhoods. If Marcus's view is that habits are acquired independent of conscious reflection and if novel external circumstances are the only possible triggers of anxiety, then it seems to me that his claim about the value of emotion in political life must be highly qualified. It might be qualified something like this: the fact that some (perhaps much) political action and judgment are matters of habit, supported by enthusiasm, *does not by itself* disqualify that action and that judgment from being rational. And the fact that some (perhaps most) political actors do not deliberate prior to judging and acting *does not by itself* disqualify those political actors from being rational. But these are very modest claims about the rationality of emotion, since it might turn out that most political habits are bad ones and that most people protect themselves against challenges to their habits of supporting injustice and inequality.

To get a stronger endorsement of enthusiasm and anxiety, we would need, first of all, to add some normative constraints on the kinds of habits rational political actors may have. Here is one such constraint: political habits are rational just so far as they can survive rational reflection, and enthusiasm is politically valuable just so far as it supports these kinds of habits. This, of course, is not too far from a Kantian view. Kant did not require that we deliberate prior to every action. He required that we act on maxims that could be universalized and thus that *could* survive rational reflection. Whether we do or do not run something like the universalizability test prior to action does not affect the status of the action. Nor did Kant require that our actions *not* be motivated by emotion

—indeed, human action must be motivated by emotion. What he required is that our motives be ones that reliably produce actions that conform to the moral law, as does the motivating feeling of respect.

One way, of course, to ensure that one's political habits can survive rational reflection is for those habits to be a product of rational reflection in the first place. In *Affective Intelligence and Political Judgment*, Marcus and his coauthors observe that "[c]itizens develop a comfortable set of standing decisions about political life —including their enduring views about the rewards of personal involvement, about the responsiveness and legitimacy of central political institutions and actors, and more specially about which political party is to be trusted with power."[12] One might reasonably think that, in general, the habits that support our higher-order skilled action are unlike procedural memory of how to write our names or raise a cup to our lips and more like the habits that James describes, such as habits of rising at a certain hour or beginning work tasks. Many of the latter habits were the results, at some point in time, of policy decisions, such as "early to bed, early to rise" or "make hay while the sun shines." Although voting in elections or partisan loyalty to candidates of a particular party might be described as habits, it is useful to distinguish habits that originate as a result of deliberation—call these commitments—and habits that originate in processes of habituation (of simply doing the same thing over and over again, because, say, it's required by law or by one's penmanship instructor). Commitments serve a function similar to habits by replacing the need for re-deliberation, an important function given that deliberation uses cognitive resources that ought not be expended in re-deliberations that are likely to reach exactly the same conclusion as one originally held. Among the kinds of commitments we make are normative commitments. One deliberates about which party's values one can endorse or about whether same-sex marriage should or should not be legally permitted.

I suppose one might "develop" political habits simply through unreflective habituation; and some unreflectively acquired habits —for example, of going to the polls, rather than using a mail-in ballot—may make no political difference. But the most reliable way to develop and check the serviceability of political habits that make a political difference is through some reflection on what habits one really wants to have as a good political actor in a liberal democracy.

How might Marcus address the further problem of political actors' protecting themselves against anxiety by choosing to insulate themselves from confrontation with the very circumstances that would cause them to reassess their political habits? This problem is particularly acute for Marcus, given that he rejects the view that good citizens *ought* to be seeking out information, reading position papers, listening to *Face the Nation*, and spending time in dialogue with the non-like-minded unless the novelty of their circumstances puts into question the serviceability of their political habits. In rejecting this deliberative view of citizenship, he is also rejecting the importance of citizens placing themselves in the very circumstances that might challenge their political habits, trigger anxiety, and initiate reflective reassessment. The problem is exacerbated by the view that anxiety is triggered only by novel circumstances, which puts agent deliberation entirely at the mercy of circumstantial factors. One alternative open to Marcus would be to allow for the possibility of our acquiring the capacity to *self-trigger* the surveillance system. Persons who have cultivated in themselves such liberal democratic dispositions as a passion for justice, aversion to prejudice and inequality, tolerance of difference, and commitment to principled action and judgment would, one would think, be the sort of persons who could self-trigger anxiety when their questionable political habits run up against, not novel circumstances, but their own virtuous democratic dispositions. Becoming knowledgeable about the preconscious processes that are highly likely to affect particular sorts of judgments for the worse could certainly be important to developing this capacity to self-trigger anxiety. As I mentioned earlier, multiple studies show that both men and women tend to devalue the credentials of people whose names are feminine or minority-raced regardless of the evaluator's views about gender and racial equality. Knowing this, one might reasonably cultivate self-distrust of and anxiety about one's automatic evaluations. In short, Marcus's endorsement of the value of anxiety to politics would be strengthened by incorporating part of the Enlightenment view, namely the idea that our emotional susceptibilities, including the susceptibility to

220   CHESHIRE CALHOUN

anxiety, are not brute facts about us but are open to cultivation
and redirection. I have been suggesting that it is important to pay attention not
just to the fact *that* enthusiasm and anxiety contribute to politics
but also to *what* we are enthusiastic or anxious about and *how* we
come to be enthusiastic or anxious in the ways we do. It seems to
me that the "what" and "how" questions must be central to any
theory about the role of emotions in democracy. I suspect that the
"what" and "how" questions end up beyond the scope of Marcus's
project because his main interest is in understanding the role of
emotions in *motivating political behavior*, not in sketching a *liberal
democratic theory of emotions*. If we take politics to center around the
formation of group solidarities, action to promote group causes
and candidates, and intergroup conflict, then, indeed, the emotions that support solidarity and political action (enthusiasm), as
well as the emotions that respond to intergroup conflict (hostility, anxiety), will be important ones to focus on. As Michael Walzer notes, "solidarity and hostility explain a great deal of political behavior."[13]

But, as I've been suggesting, this still leaves us with the question
of which emotions, felt toward what, comport with liberal democratic commitments. For linguistically competent, enculturated,
and norm-guided adults, most emotions are reason-sensitive attitudes (unlike, say, reflex startles and phobias). We may not be able
to bring about or terminate emotional responses *simply* by thinking differently, but we do take our emotions to be responsive to
and to be warranted by features of the world, particularly evaluative features.[14] We also assess the desirability or undesirability of
different emotional responses primarily in terms of the conceptions and evaluations that those emotions presuppose. A liberal
democratic theory of emotions would, most centrally, be an account of the emotions that are sensitive to persons' freedom and
equality and to the justice of demands, practices, institutions, and
distributions and that are appropriate responses to social-group
differences and differences in conceptions of the good. That is,
it would give us an account both of democracy-supporting emotional attitudes and of emotional attitudes that are fundamentally
at odds with liberal democratic values and liberal democratic conceptions of persons, social-group relations, value pluralism, and

justice. Secondarily, it would give us an account of the kinds of appeals to (or, more strongly, fomenting of) emotion both within solidarity groups and in public communication that are compatible with promoting the conceptions and values central to liberal democracy. It would also have something to say about the forms of emotionally expressive communication that do and do not comport well with democratic values, conceptions, and practices. The aim of such a theory of emotions would not be to explain behavior but to offer a normative account of democracy-supporting and democracy-undermining emotions.

Marcus observes that aversive reactions to political opponents include contempt, hatred, bitterness, disgust, loathing, and rage.[15] All of these aversive emotions, however, might be criticized from the perspective of liberal democratic values and conceptions. The attitude that most fundamentally reflects a liberal democratic conception of citizens as free and equal is respect—respect not in the sense of thinking well of individuals' particular values and enthusiasms but respect for the equal status of citizens in a liberal democracy, regardless of the merit or foolishness of their particular choices. Contempt, hatred, indifference, and disgust for others conceived as lesser beings whose life plans, devotion to causes and groups, and evaluative and conceptual commitments do not count or do not count for as much simply because they are lesser beings are incompatible with the fundamental conception of persons underlying liberal democracies.[16] This typically includes racial animus and animus against gays and lesbians.

Not all contempts, however, are equally antithetical to liberal democracy. What William Miller calls "downwards contempt"— the contempt of those high in social hierarchies for those beneath them—is more deeply antidemocratic than the "upwards contempt" of the socially low for the pretensions of superiority of the socially high; indeed, democratic egalitarian commitments tend to encourage upward contempt.[17] In general, contempt for what others do, say, and stand for is less antidemocratic than the contempt that degrades persons from equal moral and political status. But, even this less antidemocratic form of contempt may conflict with a toleration of pluralism. Liberal democracies are political systems designed to deal with the fact of difference not through repression of some but by fair accommodation of competing conceptions of

the good. Hatred and fear of difference, as manifested, for example, in xenophobia and promoted in the rhetorical construction
of some social groups as frightening or dangerous outsiders (to
"our" nation, religion, and so on), work against liberal democratic
aspirations to accommodate pluralism.

Perhaps equal in importance to the emotional attitude of respect are the passions for justice—resentment, indignation, outrage directed at wrongs and inequalities. A conception of persons
as free and equal is, in part, a conception of them as concerned
that the terms of social cooperation be fair and as emotionally responsive to failures to achieve fair terms. It is also to conceive of
ourselves and others as having the legitimate authority to make
claims on institutions and on fellow citizens to address wrongs.
The expression of injustice-sensitive anger, resentment, and indignation is thus a natural part of political criticism. As Karen Tracy
observes, "[c]entral to all notions of democracy are the rights of
citizens to express outrage and seek to bring about change if they
feel wrongs are being committed."[18] When justice-sensitive aversive emotions are connected to claims on others' behalf, those
emotions are also part of our repertoire of affiliative passions that
depend on our capacity to identify with others.[19] Behind hostility
to aggression against citizens of other nations, for example, "is a
mental picture of people like ourselves living quietly and peace-
fully in their own place, in their homes and homeland" who are
attacked without legitimate cause.[20]

Not all resentments, indignation, and outrage, of course, track
just entitlements. Some may track individuals' perception of what
their place in a social hierarchy conventionally entitles them to
and their fear of losing privileges or being required to accommodate others' claims. Given this, "reasonable hostility" needs to be
distinguished from hostilities that are not directed at injustices.[21]
Tracy develops a notion of "reasonable hostility" focused not on
the emotions themselves but on verbal criticisms in face-to-face
political discussions that imply disrespectful or undesirable things
about a person that the target perceives as insulting (e.g., that a
public official isn't committed to democratic values). Tracy's attempt to distinguish between reasonably and unreasonably hostile communication is, like the work on civil discourse that emphasizes the expression of mutual respect in political dialogue,

an effort to work out an account of which emotional attitudes, expressed in what ways, are and are not compatible with the spirit of democracy.[22]

Conceiving of fellow citizens in a liberal democracy as open to claims of justice and of political dialogue as aimed at the construction of just legal, economic, educational, and political institutions provides the warrant for maintaining a basic posture of hope. Individual hopes, however, will need to be adjusted in light of other's legitimate claims to having their passionate attachments taken into account. The hope that most supports democracy is not individual hope but what Valerie Braithwaite has called "collective hope." "Collective hope is a shared desire for a better society, articulated through a broad set of agreed-upon goals and principles, developed and elaborated through socially inclusive dialogue. Of particular importance in this process is being responsive to (listening to, seriously engaging with) private competing hopes in the community."[23] While hope, both individual and collective, supplies the motivation to continue challenging unjust social arrangements, bitterness and despair tend to signal individuals' inability to effectively participate in democratic processes.

In sum, a liberal democratic theory of emotions provides guidance about what emotions to cultivate or discourage and how to set the bounds of appropriate emotional expression in political communication. It also equips us to see that there might be something analogous to the public use of reason with respect to emotions. In political discourse, we invite others not just to share our views but also to share our emotions. Some emotions—including some enthusiasms, hostilities, and anxieties—ought not to be shared within a liberal democracy.

NOTES

1. George E. Marcus, *The Sentimental Citizen: Emotion in Democratic Politics* (University Park: Pennsylvania State University Press, 2002); George E. Marcus, W. Russell Neuman, and Michael MacKuen, *Affective Intelligence and Political Judgment* (Chicago: University of Chicago Press, 2000).

2. Immanuel Kant, *Groundwork of the Metaphysic of Morals*, trans H.J. Patton (New York: Harper Torchbook, 1964), 95–96.

3. This is in fact a caricature of Enlightenment descriptions of emotion.

4. George E. Marcus, "Reason, Passion, and Democratic Politics: Old Conceptions–New Understandings—New Possibilities," in this volume, 148.

5. René Descartes, *The Passions of the Soul*, arts. 45 and 50, in *The Philosophical Writings of Descartes*, trans. John Cottingham, Robert Stoothoff, and Dugald Murdoch (Cambridge: Cambridge University Press, 1985), 1:345, 348.

6. Immanuel Kant, *The Metaphysics of Morals*, trans. Mary Gregor (New York: Cambridge University Press, 1991), 250–251. For an overview of Kant's thinking about the role of emotions in morality see Allen W. Wood, *Kantian Ethics* (New York: Cambridge University Press, 2008), 34–41.

7. Kant, *The Metaphysics of Morals*, 238.

8. Marcus, "Reason, Passion, and Democratic Politics," 156.

9. Ibid., 139.

10. Ibid., 138.

11. Ibid., 160.

12. Marcus et al., *Affective Intelligence*, 133.

13. Michael Walzer, "Passion and Politics," *Philosophy and Social Criticism* 28 (2002): 617–633.

14. For a helpful explication of the sense in which carings are judgment-sensitive attitudes, see Richard Moran, "Frankfurt on Identification: Ambiguities of Activity in Mental Life," in *Contours of Agency*, ed. Sarah Buss and Lee Overton (Cambridge, MA: MIT Press, 2002), 189. Cheryl Hall develops a reason-sensitive account of political passions as "deep yearnings for values and activities perceived as good" in "Passion and Constraint: The Marginalization of Passion in Liberal Political Theory," *Philosophy and Social Criticism* 28 (2002): 727–748, 740.

15. Marcus, "Reason, Passion, and Democratic Politics," 151, 152.

16. For developments of the idea that contempt, indifference, and disgust are incompatible with liberal values, see, for example, Thomas E. Hill Jr., "Basic Respect and Cultural Diversity," in his *Respect, Pluralism, and Justice: Kantian Perspectives* (New York: Oxford University Press, 2000), 59; and Martha C. Nussbaum, *Hiding from Humanity: Disgust, Shame, and the Law* (New York: Oxford University Press, 2010).

17. William Ian Miller, "Upward Contempt," *Political Theory* 23 (1995): 476–499.

18. Karen Tracy, "Reasonable Hostility: Situation-Appropriate Face-Attack," *Journal of Politeness Research* 4 (2008): 169–191, 184.

19. Walzer, "Passion and Politics," 629.

20. Ibid.

21. Tracy's interest is in distinguishing verbal *acts* interpreted as ex-

pressing reasonable and unreasonable hostility. But, of course, hostile emotions might themselves be distinguished as reasonable or unreasonable.

22. See, for example, Amy Gutmann and Dennis Thompson, "Moral Conflict and Political Consensus," in *Liberalism and the Good*, ed. R. Bruce Douglass et al. (New York: Routledge, 1990), 134; Mark Kingwell, *A Civil Tongue: Justice, Dialogue and the Politics of Pluralism* (University Park: Pennsylvania State University Press, 1995); Cheshire Calhoun, "The Virtue of Civility," *Philosophy and Public Affairs* 29 (2000): 251–275.

23. Valerie Braithwaite, "The Hope Process and Social Inclusion," *Annals of the American Academy of Political and Social Science* 592 (March 2004): 128–151, 146.

8

DEMOCRACY AND THE
NONSOVEREIGN SELF

SHARON R. KRAUSE

George Marcus's illuminating chapter uses recent findings in neuroscience to put pressure on some of the foundational assumptions of both descriptive and normative democratic theory. In light of his challenges, we need to rethink not only the capabilities that we typically take for granted in democratic citizens but also the ideals to which we believe citizens should aspire. In particular, Marcus calls into question the capacities (and aspirations) for autonomous thought and action and for political judgment that is grounded in truth and guided by universal principles of right. Behind every conscious thought and action—and prior to every conscious political judgment—lie myriad preconscious neural processes. These processes deeply affect what we are capable of as citizens, and Marcus insists that they should also affect the normative standards that guide us in politics.

The essay is valuable on several fronts. First, it offers important empirical information about how the human brain works that is highly relevant to judgment and action and hence to the practices of democratic citizenship. In particular, it calls into question the ideal of the sovereign self that stands at the center of so much democratic theory, the autonomous individual whose identity and interests are transparent to herself and whose action is the self-initiated expression of her rational will. Second, it attempts to spell out the normative significance of its empirical findings and, specifically, to show how these findings should reshape our ideals of citizenship. Marcus is right to think that normative political theory can and should learn from the empirical sciences (both natural and social). Indeed, work that combines empirical and normative methods is currently emerging as an important new mode of political theory.[1] Third, Marcus fruitfully reminds us that deliberation is not the only thing that matters in democratic politics, however important it may be. Consequently, the deliberative ideal of citizenship ought not exhaust our standards of civic excellence. We should recognize the value of different forms of excellence among democratic citizens, which are suited to different kinds of political challenge, and we should acknowledge that these diverse virtues may sometimes stand in tension with one another.

For all these reasons, Marcus's essay is a welcome contribution to democratic theory, one that extends and enriches his influential prior work on affective intelligence. Nevertheless, the challenges it poses to our current thinking about democracy are deep. Indeed, they are deeper than Marcus himself acknowledges. Insofar as the theory of affective intelligence disrupts the ideal of the sovereign self, it raises important questions about the basis of political authority, the criteria for political legitimacy, the grounds of political responsibility, and the possibility of political change on behalf of justice. Marcus does not answer these questions; in fact, he hardly asks them. If we are to take affective intelligence seriously, as I think we should do, we will need to come to terms politically with the nonsovereign subject it entails, which means that we will need to articulate a vision of nonsovereign self-government. In what follows, I first raise some questions about Marcus's theory of affective intelligence, noting some inconsistencies in his account of how the different systems of neural processes are related to one another. I then consider Marcus's characterization of how the two systems figure in the activities of democratic citizens, showing that the particular model of citizenship he defends is likely to make trouble for justice. Finally, I raise some questions that go beyond the domain of citizenship to highlight deep problems of democratic self-governance that follow from the theory of affective intelligence. This final section of the chapter is less critical than exploratory; it means to open up questions for future research, questions that those of us who are convinced about the nonsovereignty of the self but committed to democratic politics must find ways to address.

1. TWO SYSTEMS OF NEURAL PROCESSING

Although the philosophical tradition has long regarded reason and passion as two very different phenomena, frequently at odds with one another, Marcus takes a different view. Drawing on recent findings in neuroscience, he shows the ways in which the mental activities traditionally associated with conscious judgment and decision making (i.e., reason) are in fact inextricably entwined with preconscious "sensory streams."[2] In particular, these preconscious neurological processes are required to generate the mental state of consciousness, including conscious reasoning or deliberation (139). The work that Marcus cites here provides fascinating insight into human mental functions. For instance, "[o]ur brains 'know' the gender of a newcomer four hundred milliseconds or more before we consciously observe the individual" (140). In fact, preconscious, visual processes involve "a vastly richer array of data about the external world than does consciousness," with "a ratio of 250,000 to 1" (142). As our brains process this vast amount of information, visual and otherwise, they automatically generate "affective appraisals" in response, a process that Marcus characterizes as "automaticity" (144). Although we "have no consciousness of these dynamics," they powerfully affect the conscious decisions we make (140).

Thus, we have "two, not one, mechanisms for knowing, judging, and action" (144). The familiar realm of conscious rationality is only part of the picture. Moreover, conscious rationality is, in many respects, a more cumbersome, less efficient system of neural processing than the preconscious, affective one. The "realm of the preconscious can obtain and act on its knowledge earlier and faster and is more deft in its capacity to execute precise movements" than are our conscious deliberative faculties (144). Marcus goes on to say that the two neural systems serve different functions. Preconscious mechanisms of appraisal and response, as embodied in what Marcus calls "the disposition system" (146), enable us to act quickly and aptly in familiar settings, where there is "a close match between past experience and present requirements" (144).

The disposition system generates decisions and actions unreflectively, largely as a matter of habit. Conscious reasoning, by contrast, is "a useful space" for assessing and responding to "novel or uncertain conditions" (145). It allows us to step out of our habitual responses and react reflectively and intentionally in ways that are better suited to the requirements at hand. Where the situational demands that we face are routine, the preconscious disposition system tends to direct our decisions and actions; when we confront unexpected challenges or uncertainties, the conscious, deliberative system kicks in. The mechanism that stimulates conscious deliberation to take hold is "the surveillance system." It is "a preconscious system" that rapidly identifies novelty and uncertainty in the situational environment (149). It signals these features to us by generating feelings of anxiety (150).

Marcus aims in the essay to "provide a unified account of how preconscious and conscious neural processes serve democratic politics" (145). Yet, the relationship between these two processes is ambiguous. On the one hand, Marcus clearly wants us to see the two systems as distinct. They are distinguished above all by the degree of awareness and intentionality they manifest: we are unaware of preconscious processes, and we exercise no intentions in conjunction with them, whereas we are always aware of our own deliberative reasoning, and we enact an authorial intentionality in this process that is absent from preconscious systems. Moreover, the two systems operate in different contexts, depending on whether the environment is routine or uncertain. On the other hand, however distinct the two systems are, Marcus insists that we "should not take these two states as mutually exclusive" (145). Deliberation itself relies on "numerous preconscious processes" in the sense that "even when we are in the deliberative mode, we are still influenced by affective states" (145). Moreover, the divide between conscious and preconscious states is permeable insofar as we can willingly move between them (164, 166).

If preconscious processes always permeate conscious deliberation, however, it is not clear that the two systems are as distinct as Marcus suggests. In particular, it seems doubtful that we could ever achieve the independence from the preconscious disposition system that Marcus himself sometimes associates with rational deliberation. "We are not limited by the preconscious mechanisms," he says at one point, for "we can also turn to and rely on our deliberative capacities via conscious mechanisms" (164). These deliberative capacities make possible "thoughtful consideration" that is "freed from the grip of our [preconscious] convictions" (159). Given all that he has said to establish that preconscious processes underlie our conscious mental activities, these claims are difficult to accept. At the very least, more work would need to be done analytically, and more empirical evidence provided, to show precisely which preconscious mechanisms can be transcended, under what circumstances, and how.

Ironically, even as Marcus means to dissolve traditional conceptions of rational autonomy, he falls back on them periodically. Alternatively, Marcus might pursue a fuller account of how affective, preconscious processes permeate deliberative reasoning, beyond simply stimulating it via the surveillance system. My own view of this is that, when we deliberate about what to do, our reflective considerations are motivated and guided by the concerns that constitute our considered convictions. These concerns have cognitive content, for they include principles of right and conceptions of the good. At the same time, they also have an affective valence in the sense that our moral principles and ethical conceptions are things we care about. We want to see them realized through our actions, and, consequently, deliberation about what to do is an affectively engaged enterprise even if it is not (and often should not be) highly charged emotionally.[3] Moreover, when deliberation is understood in this holistic way (i.e., in a way that fully integrates reflective and affective processes), it is better able to generate action than Marcus's own account allows. He regards deliberative reason as insufficient to generate action, in part because it has little affective content (136, 159). This assumption is another indication of the degree to which his model of deliberation recapitulates features of traditional thinking about reason and passion, features that Marcus ostensibly means to correct.

A related difficulty concerns the degree to which we can intentionally move between preconscious and conscious neural processes, as Marcus suggests we can do. Marcus indicates that, in addition to moving back and forth between consciousness and preconsciousness (164, 166), we can consciously intervene in preconscious routines to modify them (145). Yet, his depiction of the surveillance system allows for little intentionality in the movement from one mental state to the other. Itself a preconscious process, the surveillance system is what "activates deliberative processes" (150). Its purpose is "to preconsciously determine whether, at any given moment, executive function should remain within the preconscious realm (the default condition) or be shifted to conscious considerations" (153). This depiction seems to rule out conscious, intentional movement from preconscious to conscious systems. Likewise, the fact that "preconscious processes are hidden from us" (145) appears to rule out movement in the other direction, from a conscious, deliberative mental state to a preconscious one. To be the object of our intention, after all, the preconscious state would have to be an object of our conscious awareness, but this is something that preconscious mental processes by definition cannot be.

The effect of these ambiguities in Marcus's "two-systems" approach is to convey (however unintentionally) a portrait of human decision and action that fluctuates between being excessively mechanistic on the one hand and recapitulating the old ideal of deliberative autonomy on the other. What is needed is a clearer, more coherent account of human agency. To be sure, agency need not be equated with the traditional ideal of the sovereign subject. I take it as a virtue of Marcus's theory that it contests overly rationalist and voluntarist models of human agency, which locate agency narrowly in the exercise of autonomous reason and rational choice making. The sovereign subject as an individual who exercises rational control over decisions and actions is a chimera, however pervasive it may be in democratic theory today. The empirical evidence that Marcus brings to the table fruitfully dispels the myth of the sovereign subject. Yet, dispelling this myth is only half the battle. To sustain its significance for politics and morality, the theory of affective intelligence needs to show how a potent, nonmechanistic form of human agency is possible without the sovereign subject. I believe that this can be done; a nonsovereign model of human agency is in theory feasible and has been the subject of some interest in political theory recently.[4] Marcus himself has not yet accomplished this work, however. In particular, his theory needs a clearer account of how deliberation can involve preconscious processes without being strictly determined by them, both with respect to stimulating deliberation and with respect to the activity of deliberative reasoning itself. The theory of affective intelligence, if properly developed, could help to educate us to a new, nonsovereign yet potent understanding of human agency. That would be a major advance.

2. TWO MODELS OF CITIZENSHIP

Having laid out the two systems of neural processing, Marcus goes on to argue for a dualist ideal of democratic citizenship that tracks these two systems. Whereas the dominant views of democracy apply a singular set of standards for citizenship, emphasizing deliberative capacities in particular (166), Marcus recommends two separate sets of standards or ideals of excellence (159). The "dominant citizenship standards" emphasize the use of "deliberative faculties," reasoning as a conscious neural process, in political decision making and action (166). This singular standard is tied to the aspirations of a fully deliberative politics, aspirations that will prove to be a dead end because they presuppose a flawed conception of human nature (167). Theories of deliberative democracy neglect the role that preconscious neural processes play in decision and action, and they wrongly devalue the preconscious, affective disposition system that sustains unreflective loyalties, attachments, and identities. At least in certain contexts, the disposition system is more likely than deliberative reasoning to generate decisions that are apt and efficacious. We need two ideals of democratic citizenship, then, an ideal of the "partisan citizen" whose decisions and actions are driven by the preconscious disposition system and an ideal of the "deliberating citizen," who embodies conscious rationality (159). Each one has its own "contextual niche" (160). Specifically, "deliberation is apt in conditions of novelty," whereas partisanship is the better fit in conditions of familiarity (160). The best democratic citizens are both partisans and deliberators, adopting each orientation in turn as the circumstances require.

We have seen already that there is some ambiguity in Marcus's account as to whether or how citizens can intentionally move between preconscious and conscious neural processes, and this ambiguity carries over to the two forms of citizenship. Here I want to identify some further difficulties. Marcus is surely right to think that democratic citizenship requires multiple capacities and orientations and that different situational challenges call forth different combinations of these capacities and orientations. It is also true, as he emphasizes, that the various qualities required of us may sometimes conflict with one another. The kind of open-minded reasoning and thoughtful reflection characteristic of the deliberating citizen would be misplaced on the battlefield in the context of a legitimate war, for instance. That situation calls for steadfast courage, patriotic allegiance, and loyalty to one's comrades. And open-minded reasoning does not sit easily with patriotic allegiance. Yet, the specific combination of civic ideals that Marcus recommends is fraught with difficulties.

The first difficulty has to do with the viability of the deliberative ideal. Given what Marcus has said about the effects of "automaticity" on consciousness, it is striking to hear him conclude that "the foundational concepts of autonomy of thought, autonomy of action, knowledge, and moral judgment anchored in explicit consideration of and reliance on universal principles tell an important part of the story of the psychology of democracy" (164). In particular, they tell the part of the story that is captured by the ideal of the deliberating citizen. It is clear that he sees this part of the story as incomplete without an accompanying account of "the role of 'automaticity,' anchored in preconscious processes that enable and thereby empower citizens to grasp the essential features of the world they inhabit and to act" (164–165). Yet, Marcus insists here that the deliberative ideal is nevertheless important. The role of automaticity undermines autonomy of thought and action at a fundamental level, however, and in a comprehensive way, not in a way that is limited to particular situational contexts. On the theory of affective intelligence, preconscious processes always precede and continuously infuse conscious ones. The capacity for autonomy that Marcus associates here with the deliberating citizen is, on his own account, unavailable to us. Likewise, the "knowledge" of which Marcus speaks in this passage refers to "truth" as "access to the real state of the world," objective observation untainted by the subjective perspective of the individual observer and expressible in semantic terms (134). Elsewhere, however, he insists that our knowledge of the world always reflects preconscious sensory and somatosensory streams, as well as preconscious scripts that are

not semantic in their structure and that preclude the possibility
of unfettered access to the "real" state of the external world (141,
154). For the same reason, the possibility of political judgment
based exclusively on universal principles of right available strictly
through the machinations of conscious reasoning is highly doubtful. In short, the theory of affective intelligence does not simply
make the deliberative ideal of citizenship incomplete as a standard
of civic excellence; it renders this ideal impossible to achieve. Consequently, it is surprising and confusing that Marcus holds onto it
at all. His dual model of citizenship is troubled by his own ambivalence about the traditional deliberative ideal, for he simultane-
ously relies on and undermines this ideal.

There is also reason to worry about the impact on justice that
this two-track model of civic excellence is likely to have. The idea
that citizens should adopt the deliberative stance under conditions
of uncertainty (assuming that they can do so) and the partisan
stance where things are familiar invites unjust outcomes. After all,
cultural racism and sexism function precisely by normalizing prejudice and bigotry. They make unfair inequalities familiar and render our experience of sustaining these inequalities routine. Yet, on
Marcus's account, contexts that reflect normal, familiar, routine
patterns of interaction call for the unreflective, sometimes even
"obstinate" disposition that he associates with "the partisan citizen" (160). Citizens need the virtues of open-minded, thoughtful
reflectiveness (not to mention sensitivity to others) that constitute
the deliberative ideal, even in these familiar situations, if political
change in the direction of justice is ever to materialize. Notice,
too, that, if the deliberative stance is generated through the preconscious surveillance system only as a result of perceived uncertainty, then our ability to intentionally initiate social and political
change in opposition to the normalized routines of the status quo
will be seriously constrained, if not entirely ruled out.

Moreover, Marcus indicates that the ideal of the partisan citizen is appropriate to situations marked by "aversion," as well as
those characterized by familiarity (160). If we find ourselves "in a
state of heightened aversion while in uncertain conditions, then it
is quite appropriate to describe us as stubborn, blindly loyal, and
obstinate" (160). Previously, he had emphasized that uncertainty
stimulates anxiety (via the surveillance system), which automati-

cally generates a deliberative orientation. Here, uncertainty, albeit in combination with aversion, points in the opposite direction. Why? There is also significant slippage between descriptive and normative language in these passages. When Marcus says that "it is quite appropriate to describe us as stubborn, blindly loyal, and obstinate," the language suggests only that this would be an accurate description of our state. Yet, the thrust of his argument here is to defend what he calls "the normative suitability" of the dual model of citizenship (160). The "normative status of each citizenship orientation," he says, "depends on the accuracy of the affective appraisal" (160). Apparently, then, when we find ourselves (appropriately?) feeling aversion and uncertainty, we *should* be stubborn, blindly loyal, and obstinate. Political life is full of aversion and uncertainty, of course, especially in pluralistic democracies. We are constantly pressed to cooperate with others whom we dislike or mistrust and to make decisions together with them under conditions of uncertainty, even high risk. The entrenchment—and the normative justification and encouragement—of blind partisanship in such contexts are a potentially toxic prescription. Then, too, it is often when we feel the most threatened that we are most likely to indulge in injustice. At such times, we have the greatest need for the open-minded reflectiveness that the deliberative standpoint brings. As a democratic citizen, the white supremacist who is habitually averse to black people and hence inclined to discriminate against them should be obligated to act in a way that resists rather than blindly reflects his aversion, whatever he may in fact feel. This is not to say that deliberative reasoning (conceived holistically, in a way that integrates affective and cognitive operations) always yields normatively good results or leads to just outcomes. We can rationalize our way to all kinds of terrible things. Yet, if reflective deliberation cannot guarantee just outcomes, without it the possibilities for transforming entrenched patterns of prejudice and bigotry will be limited.

Marcus is absolutely right to think that democratic citizenship does and should take a variety of forms and answer to multiple standards of excellence. And both partisan loyalty and deliberative reflectiveness (when properly conceived) are valuable civic standards. The notion that the partisan and deliberative orientations are called into being automatically—and are justified normatively

—through preconscious processes that reflect nothing more than the psychological facts of aversion and anxiety is misguided, however. It may well be the case, descriptively speaking, that, when people feel aversion, they tend to adopt a more partisan mode and that, in familiar situations, people are less inclined to be reflective than when they face perceived uncertainty. Yet, if left unmitigated, both these tendencies are likely to generate or perpetuate a great deal of injustice. Our ideals of democratic citizenship—our standards of civic excellence—should direct our action toward justice, not away from it. For these reasons, then, the dual model of citizenship that Marcus defends is normatively insufficient, however descriptively astute it may be.

3. NONSOVEREIGN AGENCY AND THE POSSIBILITY OF DEMOCRACY

I want now to reflect briefly on some potentially fruitful but difficult challenges for democratic politics that Marcus's theory of affective intelligence poses, challenges that go beyond the issues surrounding democratic citizenship. As we have seen, Marcus's account contests the ideal of the sovereign subject by showing that autonomy of thought and action as traditionally conceived are untenable. All our conscious neural processes, the ones at issue in reflective deliberation and intentional choices, are preceded by and shot through with preconscious processes. The latter are outside our awareness and not easily subject to our control. Indeed, we have little access to the processes that shape our identities and behaviors (165). Our knowledge of ourselves is itself highly limited. Consequently, Marcus says, "Asking people what they are like may well elicit, even when honesty prevails, only a partial portrait. The missing elements reflect our inability to know what our preconscious inclinations hold" (165). Because so many of our choices are made preconsciously, "if we are asked to state our preferences, we often get them wrong" (155). We cannot ever really know ourselves because "much of what we 'know' is largely inaccessible to 'ourselves'" (157). Surely this overstates the case. While it is true that we can be self-deluded and that we are unaware of many sensory and somatosensory processes that transpire within us, most of us are not nearly as much in the dark about ourselves as Marcus suggests here. If we were, we would be constantly acting in ways that made no sense to us and that thwarted our desires, rather than satisfied them. We certainly do thwart our own desires sometimes, and we occasionally act in ways that we find baffling, but, for most (nonpathological) people, these experiences are the exception, rather than the rule. We can know ourselves because the experience of being a self, with familiar sets of interests and beliefs and familiar patterns of reasoning and desiring, is a common feature of human consciousness. Indeed, to be conscious at all (again, except in cases of pathology such as amnesia or mental illness) is to be conscious of being a particular person. And the consciousness of our own identity presupposes more self-knowledge than Marcus recognizes.

The lack of self-knowledge upon which Marcus insists gives rise to deep political problems. For one thing, it undermines the possibility of representative democracy. If I cannot know what my interests are, how can my political representatives be expected to know —and represent—them? And, if they are not representing my interests, how can their decisions be legitimate? Democratic legitimacy is generally thought to rest at least in part on the degree to which political decisions (or decision procedures) track the interests of citizens. If our interests are in principle unknowable, then it will be difficult to sustain political legitimacy and to distinguish legitimate decisions from illegitimate ones. Likewise, if we lack knowledge of ourselves, the whole basis of democratic political authority collapses. This authority rests on the will of the people, after all. The only political power that has authority over us, on the democratic view, is power that has been authorized by us, power that (however indirectly) reflects our wills. If our wills are hidden in the mists of preconscious neural processes and hence are constitutively unknowable, then democratic government will have no basis for its claim to authority. In addition, without self-knowledge and a coherent conception of individual agency, we cannot sustain personal responsibility—and, with it, the duties of democratic citizenship. Finally, the democratic ideal of self-government will need to be reconfigured. Absent knowledge of our own interests and wills and given that the real determinants of our behavior are processes that are beyond our conscious comprehension and control, we will be unable to avail ourselves of what we usually mean by self-government, defined as collective self-rule or shared control of decision and action. Thus, the disavowal of the sovereign subject that Marcus's theory of affective intelligence entails makes trouble for more than just the ideal of rational deliberation. It cuts to the heart of democratic self-government. It calls for fundamentally new ways of understanding not only the individual agency of the citizen but also the collective agency embodied in democratic authority. We need a nonsovereign conception of democratic self-rule that tracks the nonsovereignty of the individual subject.

The theory of affective intelligence thus has implications for democracy that run far deeper than Marcus acknowledges. To answer the challenges it poses, we need fuller accounts of individual and collective agency than the theory currently includes. I do not mean to suggest a return to the sovereign subject that Marcus so powerfully contests. What we need are nonsovereign models of agency. Such models would account for the pervasive interpenetration of affective and reflective processes, recognize the ways in which preconscious systems influence our conscious experience, and acknowledge that these processes are affected by prevailing relations of power (the latter is not something that Marcus takes up). At the same time, however, they would allow for a more coherent sense of self than what Marcus gives us here and a greater capacity for agency as action that is authentically one's own. All this is clearly beyond the scope of Marcus's essay and perhaps even beyond the scope of the larger research project that is the theory of affective intelligence. Still, it is work that will need to be done if the theory's great promise for democratic politics is to be redeemed.

NOTES

1. See, e.g., Brooke Ackerly, *Universal Human Rights in a World of Difference* (Cambridge: Cambridge University Press, 2008); Cristina Beltrán, *The Trouble with Unity: Latino Politics and the Creation of Identity* (Oxford: Oxford University Press, 2010); Michael Morrell, *Empathy and Democracy: Feeling, Thinking and Deliberation* (University Park: Pennsylvania State University Press, 2010); and Ian Shapiro, *The State of Democratic Theory* (Princeton, NJ: Princeton University Press, 2011).

2. George E. Marcus, "Reason, Passion, and Democratic Politics: Old

Conceptions—New Understandings—New Possibilities," in this volume, 139. Hereinafter I shall cite to Marcus's article by page number in the text.

3. This view is developed more fully in Sharon R. Krause, *Civil Passions: Moral Sentiment and Democratic Deliberation* (Princeton, NJ: Princeton University Press, 2008).

4. See, e.g., Linda Zerilli, *Feminism and the Abyss of Freedom* (Chicago: University of Chicago Press, 2005); Patchen Markell, "The Insufficiency of Non-domination," *Political Theory* 36 (2008): 9–36, and *Bound by Recognition* (Princeton, NJ: Princeton University Press, 2003); Jane Bennett, "The Agency of Assemblages and the North American Blackout," *Public Culture* 17 (2005): 445–465, and "The Force of Things: Steps Toward an Ecology of Matter," *Political Theory* 32 (2004): 347–372; Diana Coole, "Rethinking Agency: A Phenomenological Approach to Embodiment and Agentic Capacities," *Political Studies* 53 (2005): 124–142; and Sharon R. Krause, "Bodies in Action: Corporeal Agency and Democratic Politics," *Political Theory* 39 (2011): 299–324.

PART III

PASSION AND DISPASSION: PASSIONS AND EMOTIONS IN LEGAL INTERPRETATION

9

THE ANTI-EMPATHIC TURN

ROBIN WEST

Justice, according to a broad consensus of our greatest twentieth-century judges, requires a particular kind of moral judgment, and that moral judgment requires, among much else, empathy—the ability to understand not just the situation but also the perspective of litigants on warring sides of a lawsuit. In the 1920s, for example, Justice Benjamin Cardozo extolled the virtue and necessity of a broad-ranging empathy in his classic essay on the judicial craft, along with that of fidelity, reason, and wisdom.[1] In the 1970s, the great John Noonan, later a federal judge on the Ninth Circuit Court of Appeals, wrote an entire book on the topic, called *Persons and Masks of the Law*, in which he argued with considerable passion that good judging—even appellate judging—must be grounded in an empathic bond between judge and litigant and not solely on abstract rules that govern entities (and that Justice Cardozo lacked the capacity to develop such a bond).[2] Judge Richard Posner has recently opined that judging can't proceed without empathy—regardless of the pragmatic end the judge chooses to pursue.[3] Thus, while Posner has dropped his earlier steadfast insistence on efficiency as the goal of adjudication in favor of a more pragmatic utilitarianism, he has retained his insistence that the ability to understand the goals of others is of the essence of the art of judging. Justice Stephen Breyer noted at his confirmation hearings that, as a judge, he needs to be able to empathize broadly with all sorts of people who might be very different from anyone in his circle of family, friends, and acquaintances, and he found narrative literature—he mentioned *Jane Eyre* in particular —an invaluable source to help him in that effort.[4] The recently retired Justice John Paul Stevens also has urged that the ability to decide cases wisely and humanely depends in part—only in part, but nevertheless in substantial part—on just this empathic capacity.[5] This list could be vastly extended. It's fair to say, in fact, that, throughout most of the twentieth century, as well as much of the nineteenth, it would be hard to find an idea more basic or unchallenged, in the self-reflective writings of judges, or in legal scholarship, or in folk wisdom. One simply cannot judge another before walking in his shoes. Indeed, to suggest otherwise might be thought to be disqualifying.

It's particularly easy to see why empathic excellence has been such a familiar judicial ideal in a common-law system such as ours or, for that matter, in any system in which judges reason, at least much of the time, by way of analogy. A common-law judge, after all, reasoning in the way central to common-law adjudication, must decide if this case, litigant, or injury is like that one, in order to reach a decision in virtually every matter that comes before him. He must decide if this litigant in this tort case today behaved in a way like that one in yesterday's or if this contract clause, damage, or breach is like that one, if this transaction is like that one, if this defendant and that defendant are similarly situated. Likes, after all, must be treated alike. Formal justice, *stare decisis*, the rule of precedent, and virtually any conceivable understanding of the rule of law all require as much.[6] Is a malformed hand damaged by a botched operation that was itself induced by a promise that the hand could be made perfect really *like* a broken machine part that comes with a warranty? Is it *enough* like a broken machine that it would be appropriate to apply a damage rule from the law of contract designed for the latter to the former, rather than a damage rule taken from tort principles governing negligence?[7] Is the doctor's promise to make the hand whole enough like the manufacturer's promise that the machine will work that it makes sense to view both of these promises as *warranties*?[8] Is the loss of an opportunity to have an operation that might have but, more likely, would not have extended a life occasioned by a negligently faulty diagnosis enough *like* the loss of life suffered by negligent commission of surgery to justify a malpractice remedy for the loss of a slight chance at a substantially longer life?[9] Is this woman who has been denied a promotion, a jury of her peers, or a social security benefit because of gender enough like a man who has suffered a legal liability because of his race to warrant the application of constitutional principles intended to forbid state-based racial discrimination to discrimination based on gender?[10] Is sex really like race in that way; is sexism really like racism in that way? Is this couple that is not allowed to marry denied some fundamental right?[11] Is the right to marry really enough like the right to speech, assembly, privacy, and so forth to warrant an extension of principles first meant to govern the latter to the former? Is an unmarried individual's decision to take birth control really sufficiently *like* the decision of a married couple to do so to justify extending principles of familial privacy designed for the latter to the situation of the former?[12] And so on. To answer any of these questions, one must know a bit, often quite a bit, about machines, hands, the nature of promises, surgery, the art of diagnosis, the history of racism, the institution of marriage. And one must know, of course, quite a bit about the law of warranty, of contract, of negligence, of the Fourteenth Amendment, of what the Court held and did not hold in *Griswold*[13] or *Skinner*,[14] and so on. But one must also know something about feelings of loss: what does it *feel* like to lose the use of a hand or to lose even just a slight possibility of years of life? One must know something about pain: what might that injury feel like? How does it feel to be denied something that was promised? One must know something about desire, and need, and frustration: what is the basis of the need or desire to marry, to have one's intimate relations sanctified by the state, as well as by religious authority? How does it feel to be denied something important because of an "immutable characteristic"? One must likewise know something about the subjective feel of promising, and of warranting, and of diagnosing, and of discriminating. Analogous reasoning by definition seemingly requires empathic understanding, at least where it is people's utterly subjective situations, problems, fears, anxieties, suffering, opportunities, dreams, and foibles from which and to which one is analogizing. And, adjudication does proceed largely, albeit not entirely, by analogy. For that reason alone, some level of empathic ability, one might think, is a requisite of any judging in a common-law or case-method system that's worthy of the name. Excellent judging requires empathic excellence. Empathic understanding is, in some measure, an acquired skill, as well as, in part, a natural ability. Some people do it well, some not so well. Again, this has long been understood and has been long argued, particularly, although not exclusively, by some of our most admired judges and justices.

Somehow, however, this idea, viewed as so utterly mainstream in much of the past century's worth of writing about judging, has, in the first decade of the twenty-first century, become positively toxic, at least in the context of battles over confirmation to the Supreme Court. Through the course of those battles, we citizens are now very publicly being taught, by both senators and judicial nominees themselves, that empathic judging is not only not something to strive for in judging but something to avoid or even abhor. Empathy itself, we're told, is contrary to the rule of law. It is the precursor of impermissible activist judging. It runs the danger of sentimentalism. It is the very opposite of judicious behavior or outlook. Judges should be like umpires, so said our current Chief Justice, calling balls and strikes.[15] And umpires, obviously, need not and should not empathize with the need of a batter to improve his batting average so as to fatten his wallet, or of a pitcher to save his career by achieving a lower ERA, or of a small and overmatched child in a Little League contest to improve his self-esteem. Similarly, judges should not favor or hold out hope for the poor, the disadvantaged, or the oppressed; judges should apply the rule of law. What's good for the goose is likewise for the gander; the same law must apply to the international corporation and the impoverished individual. Empathy can't play a part. Judges, said Justice Sotomayor, need not be any more empathic than any other citizen, and the idea that they should, she reminded us all, was President Obama's notion, not hers.[16] Judges should apply the rule of law. Judges should be open-minded, Justice Kagan said, not to better understand every American who comes before them but to give every American a "fair shake."[17] Nobody's against a "fair shake." Empathy is not what's required, according to Kagan, Sotomayor, and Roberts, as well as the anti-empathy senators who quizzed them all, but, rather, objectivity and open-mindedness. If these confirmation battles are any guide, we have all collectively taken, we might say, an anti-empathic turn in our very crowded path of the law. What was once regarded as nonproblematically central to good judging is now regarded as antithetical to it. No one *challenged* this claimed antipathy between empathy and judicial excellence. How did that happen?

Maybe this particular turn in our thinking about law and judging is one of those things that is overdetermined. One hardly need search long and hard for explanations. Perhaps we have become a less empathic and less caring society, with less ability to perceive the situation of others. We've made ourselves unempathic, so there's no point in lauding empathy as a virtue or a skill or a capacity that grounds virtue, judicial or otherwise, if we're not very good at it anymore. Maybe we have become too polarized along lines of difference to notice the common humanity among us, or maybe we have all played too many video games or answered too many e-mails for empathy to have any purchase, as critics of cyberculture have long warned might happen, because we spend too many hours in front of boxes, rather than with human beings. There are other possibilities. In the constitutional context, the anti-empathy turn might be—indeed, it seems to be—a rhetorical arrow in a quiver that is squarely aimed at a cluster of cases embraced by two consecutive liberal activist Courts over the course of two decades: not at judicial activism in general but at *Roe*,[18] *Griswold*,[19] *Miranda*,[20] and a handful of other cases that famously aided pregnant women, criminal defendants, sexual libertines, and other outsider groups and did so with no clear text in the Constitution mandating that outcome. That's possible. Maybe, as a few commentators have argued, the target of the anti-empathy argument is not empathy per se but selective empathy: perhaps liberal and progressive judges have overempathized with pregnant women and underempathized with fetal life or the moral sensibilities of pro-life citizens or have overempathized with tort victims injured by faulty products and underempathized with the consumers who will pay the higher prices and possibly lose the benefit of the consumer surplus that might come from cheaper, albeit more dangerous, lawn mowers and kitchen appliances.[21] As argued somewhat obliquely by Herbert Wechsler in a classic law review article on the topic, maybe some of those progressive justices in the Warren Court years overempathized with those wanting to socialize with those of different races and underempathized with those preferring not to.[22] The critique of empathy-in-judging stemming from this line of complaint, then, is really a critique of selective empathy and the bias to which it leads. A collective sense among the empathy critics that there's no sensible way to engage in empathic judgment and at the same time guard against this selectivity might account for some of the impetus behind this turn.

There's one other possible explanation for the anti-empathic turn that appears prominently in the recent scholarly literature on this topic. As has been argued by a number of "emotion scholars" in law schools—and with particular force recently by Susan Bandes—the anti-empathy turn in our thinking about law might be proceeding apace on the basis of a sizable definitional mistake.[23] *Empathy* is not *sympathy*, Bandes and others (including Lynne Henderson in an early piece in the evolution of empathy literature)[24] remind us. Empathy tells us, perhaps, something about what others are feeling or at least gives us a hint of its feel. It is a source of information. Sympathy, by contrast, is the moral sentiment that aligns our interest with that of another in pain.[25] And, these scholars urge, if we keep the distinction firmly in mind, we can clear up a lot of the confusion that has prompted the anti-empathic turn. Empathy, just as the twentieth-century jurists argued, truly is necessary to adjudication and, as modern or postmodern skeptics might add, is always already present in any event. But, empathy simply gives the empathizer, including the judicial empathizer, access to a certain kind of knowledge—knowledge of the perspective of others. Empathy is not what motivates action. Sympathy is what motivates action. So, the overly sentimental judge who sympathizes with someone in pain—the tort victim, the downtrodden, the poorer of two litigants—may well be led astray by this unleashed moral emotion if, say, he is *inclined* to sympathize with those in the most immediate pain, or the most readily cognizable pain, or the pain with which he is most familiar, or the pain of those whose interests he politically favors. The judge must guard against all of these possibilities of bias and, accordingly, should reason, not feel, his way to the right conclusion. But, *empathy* is not the culprit, at least according to the empathy scholars. It's unleashed sympathy that is out of place. Empathy is what the judge needs in order to analogize sensibly. Sympathy is what he needs to keep *in check* if he is to apply the rule of law.

There may be some truth to all of these accounts and quite a bit to the last. It is, indeed, possible to empathize with someone's situation and not sympathize: "I understand what you're going through, but you get no sympathy from me." Bandes is right to insist on the distinction. In the remainder of this essay, however, I want to explore a different possible explanation for the anti-empathic turn in jurisprudence, albeit one that is compatible with Bandes's. The anti-empathy turn currently being expressed or implicitly endorsed by very high-ranking judges and justices in our understanding of judicial ideals, I will argue, is also a part of a larger shift in our paradigm of what good judging should be. That paradigm shift, I believe, is most clearly revealed not in the Supreme Court confirmation battles that spill over on the front pages of newspapers, but in the pages of law review articles and in the law school classroom. Its consequence, I will argue, is sharply felt, not only or even primarily in the Supreme Court's handling of the major social and constitutional issues of our time (which are better explained by political ideology) but, rather, in scholarly treatment of the common law of contract and tort—areas of law that have for a couple of centuries now formed the core of our understanding of the judicial craft. The anti-empathic turn, I want to argue, is a part of a "paradigm shift"—with apologies for the cliché—in our ideals of good judging, and it's the perhaps unintended consequences of that paradigm shift that I want to explore.

The paradigm shift I'll describe represents a culmination, or vindication, of Justice Holmes's audacious claim, in "The Path of the Law," near the beginning of the century just closed, that the common-law lawyer and the common-law judge of the future—that would be us, now—would be the masters of economics, statistics, and the slide rule, rather than the masters of Blackstone or black-letter law.[26] The new paradigm of good judging, Holmes predicted, would eventually depend heavily on quantitative sociological and economic tools of prognosis and prediction and would have much less need for either Blackstone or common-law precedent. In that regard, the new paradigm—which I'll sometimes call "scientific judging"—is forward looking: it looks to the consequences of decisions, rather than back to the governing law drawn from the past. Economics and sound policy fill the space once filled by engagement with past cases. There has been a transformation of that on which judges should rely in reaching their decisions, from rules laid down in the past to present understandings of future well-being, from precedent to social policy, from reliance on analogical reasoning based on past cases to economic or sociological reasoning based on welfare baselines. This shift is much noted, usually, although not always, with approval (particularly by the academic left but also by the libertarian right). Less noted, although most significant for these purposes, is this: the new paradigm has virtually no need for a judge who is capable of empathic engagement with litigants. In fact, it has little need for engagement with litigants of any sort, empathic or otherwise. Empathy is simply not a part of the paradigmatically modern judicial skill set. This, I will argue, should count as a significant cost.

I will not attempt to prove that this new paradigm has taken hold or even that it is clearly articulated in any single source (other than in Holmes's "Path of the Law"). Rather, in the remainder of this essay, I would like to closely explore just one piece of datum *exemplifying* this shift in our paradigm of good judging, by examining the evolution of the scholarly treatment of the "unconscionability" rule in contract law over the course of the past several decades. The unconscionability rule is generally understood to be, along with undue influence, constructive fraud, and requirements of good faith, one of a number of so-called policing doctrines (as in "policing the contract") that regulate the fairness of contracts. The fairly dramatic shift that has occurred in the past quarter-century in our understanding of policing doctrines in contract law in general and of the unconscionability doctrine in particular, I will contend, is emblematic of the larger shift in our paradigm of judging—a shift away not only from precedent but also from empathic regard for litigants and toward a concern with the welfare-enhancing consequences of decisions for future contractors. The social welfare that *ought to be* the primary concern of the judge, according to the scientific paradigm, is then defined in such a way that empathy for the class of those *other* persons—persons other than the litigant whose future welfare is being expanded or shrunk by the judge's decision—need not be employed. Rather, the welfare of those persons to which the judge should attend is defined by reference to observable, quantifiable behaviors that can be reckoned in fully nonempathic ways. There is no need to learn of their subjectivities through empathic understanding or otherwise. Empathy need not be in the toolkit.

In the first section, I contrast the traditional and more contemporary approach to the unconscionability doctrine, using the iconic case *Williams v. Walker-Thomas Furniture Company*,[27] as well as its scholarly treatment, as emblematic. In the second, I briefly explain how, in my view, this shift in the scholarly treatment of *Williams v. Walker-Thomas* (and related policing doctrines more generally) is reflective of and in some ways masks a larger shift in our guiding paradigm of adjudication—a shift away from a paradigm of moral judging to scientific judging. In the third and concluding section, I offer some suggestions as to why this new paradigm has taken such a hold on our legal imaginations and briefly criticize it, both specifically with respect to the unconscionability doctrine and more generally. I urge a return to a more classical understanding—one that rests quite explicitly on the centrality not only of precedent (Blackstone, common-law rules, and so on) but also of moral passions and moral emotions to the work of judging, of which empathy and sympathy both are sizable parts. Mostly, though, in this essay I just want to put in the record, so to speak, a piece of evidence for the claim that we have seemingly turned our back on a vision of moral judging that once embraced what Adam Smith dubbed the "moral sentiments" as essential to the work of judgment.[28]

1. THE TRANSFORMATION OF THE UNCONSCIONABILITY DOCTRINE

According to what I will call the "traditional understanding" of a number of contract-law doctrines familiar to virtually all first-year law students, the good judging in which good judges engage, when deciding cases governed by this sizable part of the law, requires a moral judgment *about* the distinctly moral quality of some sort of interaction between co-contracting litigants. These doctrines include the unconscionability doctrine itself[29] but also rules regarding the exercise of undue influence,[30] bad faith,[31] duress,[32] and constructive fraud[33] in contracting behavior likewise—themselves derived from two-hundred-year-old common-law principles, some of which are derived from rules of equity of even older vintage. Thus, the judge in these "policing" cases, by virtue of the governing *law*, must render a *moral* judgment about the *moral* quality of one party's contractual behavior vis-à-vis the other. He might have to decide, say, whether a contractor's negotiating behavior in the course of reaching an agreement was unconscionable, or whether one contractor exercised undue influence in the bargaining process over the other contractor, or whether one contractor's conduct constituted an unacceptable form of duress or exploited the duress of his co-contractor caused by other factors, or whether the contractor's behavior for any of these reasons or any other was an exercise of bad faith, or whether the contractor's seeming deceit constituted a form of constructive fraud—whether he failed to disclose something about the value of the subject matter of the contract that in all good conscience, given the circumstances, really should have been disclosed. The judge may have to decide whether the term or contract reached through any of these forms of morally dubious behavior was so unconscionably one-sided as to "shock the conscience."[34]

All of these legal "terms of art"—unconscionability, undue influence, bad faith—unlike what we are typically talking about when we invoke the phrase "terms of art," retain, in law, their quite ordinary and explicitly moral meaning, as understood by, well, everybody who's been raised well. Did the party's overbearing behavior in procuring a contract "shock the conscience"? Did it pass the "smell test"? Did it make you want to puke? Were the lopsided terms the parties eventually agreed to in themselves unconscionable? Did a loan contract bind the debtor to an interest rate that was obscenely usurious? Did a contract's lopsided terms—a sale of a plot of land for a hundredth or a thousandth of its market value or a loan with a 200 percent interest rate—violate various rules of equity, that venerated five(six-?)-hundred-year-old body of moral principles from which many of these "policing doctrines" are derived?[35] Did the defendant engage in "sharp practice" with someone who was obviously suffering from depression,[36] or from a manic mood disorder, or from a mental incapacity, someone who quite evidently could not protect his or her own interest, and was the stronger party's conduct in the face of all this just a little "too clever by half"? Did the stronger party exercise good faith throughout the negotiating process? Did one contractor take unfair advantage of the other's manifest need, or vulnerability, or age, or disability, or ignorance, or lack of education, or mental infirmity? Did one contractor deliberately attempt to cloud the co-contractor's common sense or assessment of his economic self-interest? Was the contract for any of these reasons just beyond the bounds of decency?

As has been pointed out by critics of these doctrines, the "traditional understanding" of these various principles—and they were ubiquitous throughout the nineteenth century's common law of contract[37] and a prominent part of at least the initial understanding of the Uniform Commercial Code's codification of sales law in the 1950s[38]—requires the judge to engage in a form of decision making that is both explicitly *moralistic*, with respect to the parties' behavior, and implicitly *paternalistic*, with respect both to the weaker party before him and to future parties that might be similarly situated. Let me take those in order. First, to decide whether a contract is unconscionable or whether a contractor's conduct was unduly influential in procuring it (and so forth), the judge must decide himself or must instruct the jury to resolve what are clearly questions of business ethics. "Unconscionable" and "undue influence" are and are understood to be moral standards, which are then made relevant to the legal issue by virtue of positive law. If the judge is to be true *to the law*, then he has to apply these moral standards (or instruct a jury to), and, if he is to apply these moral standards, he has to resort to the teachings of his moral sense or his moral conscience, and not only the teachings of precedent, of Blackstone, and of statutes. Whether or not a contract term is "unconscionable" depends upon what one decides of the applicability of that term of condemnation in the context of dealings between the two people, as judged by a test of conscience. Likewise, whether undue influence was brought to bear by one party upon the other or whether a party exercised bad faith, or engaged in constructive fraud, or exploited the other party's distress depends upon the moral quality of the relationship between the parties, as judged by somebody's conscience. If a judge decides it was, he should so hold, and, according to the law, he should then strike the contract or the offensive term. The "sharp dealer," the party

"too clever by half," will be deprived of the value of the contract
(although he might have recourse to some more limited remedy,
such as restitution, so as not to allow the weaker party to profit
from the entire ill-fated transaction), and the weaker party will be
relieved of the burden of performing an unconscionable contract, ·
and all of this will happen for straightforwardly moral reasons: the
contract, according to the judge who so held, is for some reason
immoral. Thus the "moralism" of these decisions.

Now, on the paternalism. One *effect* of striking the contract, in a
common-law system, is that some sort of rule of the case emerges
—or at least might emerge—from each decision in which the
judge writes an opinion and attempts to offer a holding. What that
rule *is* might be subject to debate or interpretation, but *that* a written judicial decision does sometimes produce such a holding, with
a range of possible meanings, really is not. The result of a decision
to strike a contract or term as unconscionable, unduly influenced,
procured through bad faith, or under duress, then, might be felt
not only by the parties immediately affected but by all "similarly
situated persons" who might enter a similar deal after the decision
is rendered and who might therefore be properly subject to the
holding that emerges from the decision. So, when a contract or
a contract term is struck as unconscionable, or a tactic as unduly
influential, or a clause as unenforceable because lacking in good
faith, then that contract, term, or tactic is unavailable to future
parties that might want to use such a term, tactic, or contract in
similar circumstances.

The now iconic facts of *Williams v. Walker-Thomas Furniture Company* (if not the case itself), decided in the 1960s, provides a serviceable example of both the moralism and the paternalism. The
cause at issue was the cross-collateral term in the installment sales
contract for consumer goods between the retail store and the indigent customer in that case, by which the buyer posted as "collateral" past products purchased from the store in exchange for
a sale of new goods paid for over time in installments such that
the buyer could lose all past purchased products if she defaulted
on a payment for the later-purchased goods. Judge Skelly Wright
famously decided, as a matter of law, that the trial judge had the
power to rule that "this cross-collateral term was unconscionable." Certainly, if the trial court had so ruled (the case was settled

instead), not only would the plaintiff *in that case*—Mrs. Williams herself—have been relieved of the obligation to go through with the contract (or pay damages) and the seller have been deprived of damages tied to breach of the unconscionable clause but also other buyers and sellers who might have *wanted to* include such a term would henceforth not have been able to do so. No future seller of consumer goods operating in low-income neighborhoods would include a cross-collateral loan term, once the word was out on the street, so to speak, that a judge would be likely to strike the term as unconscionable. The seller who is not able to include such a term would lose some real and expected income by virtue of that fact: such a seller might, after all, be making very risky loans to poor customers, a steady percentage of whom will in fact default. If a seller does not have access to this possible form of debt structuring for this class of consumers so as to maximize his recovery in the highly likely event of default and he wants to continue to do business in the neighborhood, he will obviously have to raise prices to cover the shortfall. If all such sellers in the neighborhood are similarly affected, what happens?

What happens, according now to legions of critics of this case, is that buyers, not sellers, bear the cost. Those buyers in poor neighborhoods who would prefer to buy cheaper consumer goods with onerous cross-collateral terms rather than higher-priced goods without those terms—perhaps because they predict that they will not default—are out of luck. They don't have such a package (low price plus cross-collateral loan terms) available to them. And, there may well be plenty of buyers who would prefer a deal with cheaper prices and onerous cross-collateral terms to a deal with higher prices but no onerous loan terms. But this option is taken off the table by virtue of Wright's decision. And that might happen quite a lot, if these policing doctrines are given free reign. Thus, poor consumers—one group the unconscionability doctrine is presumably designed to protect—lose out.

The decision, then, of a judge to simply strike a contract term such as the cross-collateral term that appeared in *Williams v. Walker-Thomas Furniture Company* as *unconscionable* is also *paternalistic* in two senses. The judge is, first of all, substituting his or her judgment for that of the weaker contracting party in the transaction itself, as determined at the time the party entered the contract. That party at that point in time viewed the contract in his or her own interest, even knowing (presumably) that there was a possibility he or she would default and lose the previously purchased goods. The buyer, knowing that possibility, assumed the risk of her own future default, and the court was in effect undoing that party's judgment that the risk was worth taking. The judge, in striking the term as unconscionable, essentially made the judgment that that assumption of risk was ill advised at the time it was undertaken, not just in retrospect after the risked event did indeed come to pass. But, second, and more important, it is paternalistic with respect to all those *future* parties that may be similarly situated to the parties involved in the initial litigation.

To return to the facts of *Williams v. Walker-Thomas*, if the trial judge were to find the term unconscionable, he would in effect be deciding that whether or not they want to, poor people should not purchase consumer goods under cross-collateral loan terms. (Wright did not himself make such a finding. He did, however, find that the trial judge had the power to make such a ruling, if the trial judge found the term morally repugnant, and remanded.)[39] Such a judgment would imply that buyers are better off paying higher prices without those terms or, if they are priced out of the market, forgoing the goods entirely, regardless of what they want. Not just Mrs. Williams, then, but all future consumers "in her shoes," should the trial judge so hold in Mrs. Williams's case, either will have to go without the stereo, television, or Mixmaster they would otherwise have been able to purchase or will have to pay higher prices. This entire class of purchasers, not just Mrs. Williams, will not be able to buy goods on these terms, essentially because some judge at some point decided that a term of this nature does not in fact serve their interest, even though *they* believe that it does. They cannot buy goods under contracts with such a term, even if they want to, because, in Wright's view, the term is unconscionable. Thus, the paternalism of the decision.

Williams v. Walker-Thomas Furniture Company was decided in the 1960s. What has happened to it in the meantime? Basically, the unconscionability doctrine across the board but also Skelly Wright's decision in *Williams v. Walker-Thomas* in particular have been the subject of a steady drumbeat of criticism over the past forty years, largely by scholars associated with the law and economics movement.[40] Their criticism, as well as the response to it, has largely focused on what the legal economists regard as the unwarranted paternalism central to both the unconscionability doctrine itself and *Williams v. Walker-Thomas* specifically. First, the critics argue, there can be nothing *morally* objectionable about a seller's conduct if both buyer and seller agree to terms and there are no adversely affected third parties: indeed, the resulting contract is *Pareto optimal.* Everybody consented. There can't *possibly* be grounds for moral complaint to a contract to which everybody affected by it consented.[41] So the paternalism can't be justified on moral grounds. But, furthermore, the judicial paternalism the doctrine effectuates can't be justified on welfare grounds, either; in fact, it will work against, not for, the interests of poor buyers as those interests are reflected in those buyers' choices. These buyers, like all buyers, have privileged access to their own preferences—no one knows their preferences better than do they themselves. Those preferences are revealed in their market choices, as are all buyers' preferences. Those choices and, therefore, those preferences and those buyers' individual and collective welfare are quite clear, relatively speaking: the buyers prefer low prices and cross-collateral terms, or they wouldn't opt for them. They'd find some other seller offering a different package, or they'd forgo the purchase altogether. Their welfare, like everyone's welfare, is increased by satisfaction of their preferences, which are, in turn, revealed through their market choices. Therefore, to remove this market choice by judicial fiat simply reduces their welfare.

So, although it is natural to "feel badly" for Mrs. Williams herself, as one contemporary commentator puts it[42]—to sympathize with her, in effect—that sentiment is actually at odds with the interests, welfare, and desires of Mrs. Williams herself at the time of purchase and with others in Mrs. Williams's circumstances. That "feeling" we might have or that a judge might have for Mrs. Williams or for someone in her position turns out to be a bad guide to the judicial decision that might aim to improve her well-being. Thus, the moralism the judge deploys with respect to the litigants before him, particularly those parts of it motivated by simple sympathy for the plight of a poor and uneducated buyer trying to deal with a sophisticated retailer, leads directly to a form of paternalism—in the form of the rule the court articulates—that decreases rather than increases the welfare of the class of people toward whom the decision is directed. In brief, it's counterproductive.

That's the guts of the attack on this doctrine, and it has been made repeatedly and in various forms over the past forty years since *Williams v. Walker-Thomas* was decided. It has even become, in a sense, conventional wisdom that what Skelly Wright did in *Williams* with all the best motives in the world was in fact bad for poor people. If you want to help poor and uneducated buyers, for heaven's sake, hold them to their contracts. Judge Wright did the contrary, and the result was nothing but a loss of consumer surplus that otherwise would have been enjoyed by the very people he was trying to help.

That is where things stood in the scholarly literature on *Williams*, until about the mid-2000s. Since that time, however, a "behavioral" rather than "classical" economic analysis of both *Williams* and the unconscionability doctrine has emerged, with a strikingly different conclusion. In an exceptionally lucid article titled "A Traditional and Behavioral Law and Economics Analysis of *Williams v. Walker-Thomas Furniture Company*," Professor Russell Korobkin of UCLA law school *also* decries Skelly Wright's reasoning in *Williams v. Walker-Thomas*—and the reasoning he suggests the trial court below employed—but nevertheless ultimately defends the decision's outcome on economic grounds. Sometimes, Korobkin explains, according to the behavioral, as opposed to the classical, legal economist, judicial paternalism of the sort deployed in *Williams v. Walker-Thomas* might be justified, and more often than the classical legal economist is inclined to believe. When it is, though, it is justified *not* on the moralistic and paternalistic grounds that individuals just don't know what is good for them and that it's wrong for market actors to take advantage of people who are so deluded. Rather, limited judicial paternalism might be occasionally justified on the grounds that sometimes individuals are not very good at figuring out the probabilities that they'll get what they decide "is good for them" from the various choices in front of them, given certain constraints on their abilities to reason about their options. Paternalism is justified, in other words, not on the grounds that "people are idiots" (as Duncan Kennedy artfully put the point in his classic defense of judicial paternalism from the mid-1980s)[43] but, rather, on the grounds that individuals—even smart and educated nonidiotic individuals—are often not particularly *rational*. We all suffer from a host of disabling defects in our ability to make rational judgments, all of which cause many of us, maybe even most of us, to misfire when choosing among the various options with which markets present us. Free markets, it turns out, given irrational market actors, don't so reliably maximize human welfare, even in seemingly *Pareto optimal* transactions to which all parties consent. So, *if* it can be clearly shown that a litigant and the class of which the litigant is representative in a contract-policing case suffers from some such defective decisional heuristic, then it's sensible for the court to adjust the contract accordingly.

And, in the *Williams* case itself, it's quite possible that Mrs. Williams was suffering the effects of at least four such defective decisional heuristics, as Professor Korobkin goes on to show in his article. Her decision was likely "selective," meaning that she failed to consider all attributes of the product she was buying (she focused on the stereo, rather than the payment clause); noncompensatory (meaning that she likely failed to compare and trade off the utility of various attributes of the product against each other —the payment clause actually reduces the expected utility of the stereo in ways she did not appreciate); her assessment of the probability that she might default was likely and unduly discounted by virtue of her "overconfidence" or "optimism bias," making her incapable of accurately understanding the limits to her own power to ward off bad future outcomes; and she likely underestimated the risk of bad outcomes because of her unwarranted reliance on an "availability heuristic," meaning that she unduly relied on the low incidence of default among her friends and neighbors, when assessing her own potential risks, simply because those were the comparators available to her. Given the likely presence of all four of these defective decisional heuristics, her decision making was likely unsound because it was irrational and thus could not be relied on to ensure that the clause would be in the contract only if efficient (if it truly benefited sellers more than it hurt buyers, as reflected in the price). Because of her defective decision making, a court then might be justified in intervening—*not* so as to frustrate the welfare-maximizing efficiency-directed goals of contract law and markets, as the critics of unconscionability have charged, but, rather, to promote them.[44] This is paternalistic, Korobkin

concludes, but it is a limited and warranted paternalism: it takes
the parties' goals as given but then nudges the parties in the direction they would have decided in light of those goals if they'd been
behaving rationally.[45]

Thus, behavioral economists such as Korobkin, like the classical
economists he criticizes, urge courts to decide cases such as *Williams* by reference to the incentives the rule creates for similarly
situated parties in the future, rather than by reference to the men-
dacity of the parties' conduct or the outrageousness of the terms
they strike. The behavioral economist, however, is more skeptical
about the rationality of *all* individuals' reasoning when entering
contracts. If the decisions made by contractors or potential contractors and particularly by consumers are systematically distorted
by various psychological tendencies that inhibit full rationality
when they are seeking to translate their preferences into market
choices, then there is a narrow opening for warranted paternalism. This limited paternalism, however, has nothing to do with
and should not be motivated by a "shock to the conscience"; it has
nothing to do with moral revulsion over the unconscionability of
a term, or bargaining tactics that are "too clever by half," or sharp
dealing or shadowy bargaining. Rather, it should be motivated by
a decision to compensate, in the direction of efficiency and social
wealth, for widely shared near-universal design defects, so to speak,
in our capacity to reason about risks and potential benefits. Turns
out we're not very good at it. Where our contract choices show
that, a court might be warranted in undoing them.

The differences between classical and behavioral law and economics are important, but, nevertheless, their commonalities are
more so, and at any rate it is their shared distance from the traditional understanding of the unconscionability doctrine that
I want to highlight. So let me directly address those differences,
beginning with the economic understanding, and then turning to
the traditional. First, as Seana Shiffrin has cleanly argued, law and
economics scholars of the unconscionability doctrine have largely
ignored that doctrine's moralism.[46] Second, legal economists urge
judges in these cases to focus not on the litigants' behavior but
on the incentives the rules that will emerge from these cases will
create for future litigants. Third, and related to the second point,
both focus overwhelmingly on the terms of the contracts that are

challenged, rather than on the interaction of the parties before them. Fourth, and most important, while the behavioral economist sees more irrationality in our choices and thus more scope for a doctrine such as unconscionability, both the behavioral and the classical economist see efficiency or net social welfare as the goal that should guide the judge in these cases, rather than any judgment about or even concern for either the well-being of the parties before him or the morality of their conduct. Both see the role of the judge as being the third party who can facilitate contractual relations by enforcing contracts against later-regretful parties and who will thereby set proper incentives that will efficiently increase social net welfare. The way to do that is to enunciate rules that steer the parties and all future contractors toward wealth-maximizing behavior—typically, although not always, by holding parties to the terms of their original bargain. Departures from that premise should be articulated in rules that compensate for systematic irrational behavior caused by decisional heuristics that cloud understanding of risk and benefit. The transformed unconscionability doctrine more or less holds as much.

Now contrast that with the traditional understanding of the doctrine. The judge in an unconscionability case might indeed "feel badly" for Mrs. Williams or someone in her position—it's only human nature to do so, as Korobkin points out.[47] She's poor and uneducated, was dealing with a sophisticated retailer, and signed a contract with a ridiculously burdensome loan term in order to secure the credit to purchase consumer goods that she didn't particularly need. Likewise, such a judge might be appalled by the immoral behavior of the seller. On the traditional model, those feelings—feeling badly for the weaker party, feeling appalled by the conduct of the stronger—not only guide the judge's decision but are virtually fully determinative. The decision the judge makes, on the traditional understanding, is a decision about the parties' behavior, and it is both informed and motivated by moral feelings of empathy, sympathy, and disgust. But those *feelings*, according to the legal economists, are not what the judge should attend to. He should put them aside. Indeed, the judge in such a case should not focus on the litigants *at all*. He should put *them* aside. Rather, the judge's decision, according to legal economists—and on both sides of the paternalism debate—should be guided exclusively by concern for the incentives for future conduct that result from the rule his decision will create for the class of people "similarly situated" to the litigants. The judge's role in these cases is *not* to judge the immorality of the conduct of the particular litigants that come before him, as judged by a test of conscience. Rather, it is to put forward a rule that is as efficient as possible or that leads to the greatest net social welfare as understood in classical economic terms for the type of contracts of which the particular is an instance. This basic premise—that the judge's role is to specify a rule for future conduct that will incentivize wealth-maximizing behavior—is shared by economics-minded commentators on both sides of these cases. That shared methodological premise is at the heart of the new paradigm, and that shared premise, quite simply, is a commitment to scientific rather than moral judging.

2. BRAVE NEW JUDICIAL WORLD
THAT HAS SUCH PEOPLE IN'T

Against these criticisms of the unconscionability doctrine and the transformation of that doctrine to which those criticisms have led, scholars outside the law and economics movement—notably, Duncan Kennedy,[48] Anthony Kronman,[49] and, more recently, Seanna Shiffrin[50]—have defended either the doctrine's moralism or its strong paternalism as warranted. Often, of course, buyers in contracts such as these do not know the terms they're accepting and therefore may not have made an informed decision regarding the purchase. Sometimes, however, they do know, as might have Mrs. Williams; the Walker-Thomas Furniture store was well known to the residents of its Washington, DC, neighborhood, as were its lending practices.[51] Even with full knowledge, Kennedy, Kronman, and Shiffrin have all argued, albeit for different reasons, moralistic or paternalistic intervention here might be justified. Shiffrin justifies intervention on the grounds that judges—who are also of course themselves moral actors—have no business coming to the aid of immoral business practices, while Kennedy argues that buyers often do not know their own best interest and that courts should help them promote that true interest when they have the opportunity to do so. Kronman argues, on more deontological grounds, that the lack of knowledge, lack of integrity, or lack of good judgment on the part of weaker parties sometimes justifies the attendant loss of some level of individual autonomy. Buyers, after all, are besotted by a consumerist culture that encourages sellers to construct consumer desire and then consumer demand for products that have no connection to either need or pleasure. And consumers fall for it, again and again and again. Consumers might fully understand the consequences of default but underestimate, and badly, the chance that they will default, not because of hard-wired decisional defects in rationality but because they have been overinfluenced by advertisers who encourage identification of viewers with successful and healthy avatars. Similarly, consumers might fully understand what they want and don't want but not understand at all the precariousness of their own finances. Or, perhaps they simply want too many things. They shouldn't be buying television sets and stereos using bedroom furnishings as collateral when they are on a severely limited budget and have eight children to feed, clothe, and house. They are making bad choices, and those bad choices are adversely affecting not only them but their children and other dependents as well.

I generally side with the defenders of Judge Skelly Wright, *Williams v. Walker-Thomas Furniture Company*, paternalism, moralism, and the unconscionability doctrine all. Consumer sovereignty in these circumstances sometimes is not worth the pain it brings. That judgment is well reflected in the hundreds of public-law constraints on private contracting, from minimum-wage and maximum-hour laws to child labor laws, limits on the alienability of body parts, safety and health regulations that constrain free contracting for employment, lemon laws that limit our ability to buy cheap and defective automobiles free of the cost of limited warranties, nondisclaimable warranties of habitability, and so on. There should be nothing alarming about common-law doctrines that charge judges with the work of making the same sorts of judgments on a case-by-case basis through a limited number of doctrines in the course of common-law reasoning.

Here, though, I don't want to focus on that debate. Rather, I want to note some interrelated features of the traditional understanding of the unconscionability doctrine that I believe are also emblematic of the traditional paradigm of judicial reasoning and that are almost routinely overlooked in these debates by both

critics and defenders of judicial paternalism. Those features are
jettisoned by the new paradigm of scientific judging, on which the
modern version of the unconscionability doctrine now rests.
The first is the doctrine's moralism. As Shiffrin suggests in her
exhaustive philosophical reconstruction of the unconscionability
doctrine, this doctrine, developed in equity courts, was motivated
by moralistic revulsion at the contracting behavior of stronger parties, not simply on paternalism per se.[52] It didn't have as much to
do with consumers' bad choices as it had to do with sellers' bad
behavior. Courts didn't want to lend their hand to immoral business practices.[53] The early-nineteenth-century cases in particular,
more directly influenced by the equitable maxims from which the
policing doctrines themselves flowed, were quite explicit about
this. The judge's decision that a contract term was "unconscionable" was grounded *not* in a desire to lay down a rule that would
take a market option off the table for future parties but, rather,
in a moral reaction to the specific conduct and circumstances of
the parties before him. The twentieth-century *Williams v. Walker-
Thomas Furniture Store* was not much different in that regard. The
offending term in *Williams* might, Judge Wright held, be found
by the trial court to be "unconscionable," but *not* because Wright
believed that, from that moment forthwith, buyers should never
again be permitted to enter contracts with cross-collateral loan
terms, even if they want to, either because "people are idiots" or
because they suffer from impaired rationality. Rather, the trial
court below should be empowered to strike the term if the judge
found a cluster of factors that pertained to the particular case to
be, simply, unconscionable: that the buyer was indigent, which the
seller in that case knew; that the buyer had eight children, which
the seller knew; that, on the buyer's limited monthly income, the
buyer could not possibly make the requisite payments for the stereo she was seeking to purchase, which the seller either knew or
should have known; that the buyer had only a small balance out-
standing on the prior purchased items when she entered the offensive contract, which the seller knew; and that the buyer at the
time of default had long since paid considerably *more* than the purchase price of those prior purchased items, which, of course, the
seller knew. On such a record, Wright held, the trial judge below
would be within his power to strike the term.[54] All of these factors,

about these people and their interaction with each other, are what might collectively "shock the conscience."

Second, the unconscionability doctrine, on the traditional model, rests on a particularism that is not only not reducible to the rule that might follow from these cases but that is actually in considerable tension with it. This attribute of traditional judicial reasoning is completely elided in the contemporary intra-economic debate over the purported paternalism at the heart of the unconscionability doctrine. The judge deciding whether a contract or a term is unconscionable is concerned with the specific situation of the parties before him and the morality of their interaction, viewed against the backdrop of the commercial setting and informed by the dictates of conscience. The decision that a term or entire contract is unconscionable, on the traditional model, is about what these people did, read against a backdrop of what they should have done and what others in their industry, as well as the judge himself, thinks about what they did. It is not about a class of future contractors, or a generic type of term, or a form of contract, and how some potential future class of contractors might be incentivized. It is about whether this contractor's past behavior did or did not conform to norms of decency. For the holding of a case about unconscionability to affect market transactions in the future, whether or not "paternalistically," it has to be cast in general terms. However, the moral emotion, as well as the judicial reasoning, that actually prompts a judge to strike a contract term consists largely of a reaction to particular past behavior. The generality of the paternalistic rule that is the target of the contemporary critics of unconscionability is at odds with the particularity of the situation that on the traditional model is the object of the judge's inquiry.

Thus, it is inaccurate to say that Skelly Wright held in *Williams v. Walker-Thomas* that cross-collateral terms in consumer contracts are unenforceable because they are unconscionable or even that such terms in contracts with poor people are unenforceable. The trial judge below was repulsed by the reprehensible conduct of the particular seller in the case before him and said so. He also said that he didn't think he had the power to strike the contract.[55] Skelly Wright, on appeal, held that unconscionability is a constraint on common-law contracts cases that arise in the District of Columbia and was so even before the passage of the Uniform Commercial

Code, so that, contrary to what the trial judge believed about the state of the law, he did have the power to refuse to enforce the contract if he found it to be unconscionable.[56] The case was then settled. However, the finding of unconscionability that might have been forthcoming had there been a retrial and had the judge followed Wright's lead would have followed from the trial judge's response to the particular circumstances, behavior, weaknesses, and needs of the parties.

Of course, had there been such a finding and had the trial court written an opinion saying as much, then that decision in turn might have constrained future market behavior. Or, it might not have. The trial court might have found the terms unconscionable *only* in these precise circumstances: eight kids, the price of the collateral goods less than the amounts already paid, nonessential item, and so forth. But the breadth of any rule the court might have articulated would have been *inversely* related to the strength of the finding of unconscionability, not correlated with it. So, if the trial judge had ultimately found that the seller's callous disregard of the specific circumstances besetting the plaintiff rendered that seller's behavior unconscionable, then the rule generated would have been quite specific, covering only circumstances in which sellers behaved just as had the Walker-Thomas Furniture Store salesman, and with buyers situated just as was Mrs. Williams. If, on the other hand, the judge had found that the cross-collateral clause itself was unconscionable, regardless of the circumstances or behavior of either party, then the rule, as well as its paternalistic impact, might have been overbroad, because it would have been well beyond the circumstances that gave rise to the moral revulsion that prompted it.

Third and most important, *both* the backward-looking, particularistic, and moralistic ground of an unconscionability decision *and* the forward-looking paternalistic rule that might follow from it on the traditional model should be informed by the judge's moral sense—and, hence, in part, by moral emotions and moral sentiments, including both empathy and sympathy. The judge might or might not be morally repulsed by the parties' behavior. He won't know, however, whether or not the behavior is morally objectionable unless he can empathize with both parties to the transaction and then register a stronger sympathetic response to either one or the other. That's just the nature of the beast. If the commercial behavior of this retailer was shocking to the conscience, it was so because of the unreasonably exploitative nature of the seller's tactics and the overexposure of the buyer to excessive and unreasonable risk, as well as excessive and unreasonable costs of default. One cannot reach a judgment on either prong of this without exercising one's moral sense and thus employing one's moral emotions. The background moral norms of the industry play a role, but not an exhaustive one. Whether the seller's behavior was reprehensible or not depends upon the judge's moral sense, and the exercise of that moral sense depends on his employment of his capacity for empathic regard for both litigants. That empathic regard, in turn, facilitates his sympathetic engagement with the buyer's struggles and the market imperatives of the seller's business, and then with whether or not the seller treated the buyer decently in light of those struggles and imperatives. This is the basis of his decision.

These traditional structural features of the judge's role are highly visible within the contours of the unconscionability doctrine: again, unconscionability law has its historical roots in "equity," which was for several centuries a separate body of procedures and institutions, governed not by legal rules but by principles, themselves squarely premised on moral truths and *not* particularly generative of legal precedent and holdings. Nevertheless, the three structural features of the traditional understanding of the unconscionability doctrine that I've noted—the moralism, the backward-looking particularism, and the role of moral sentiments such as sympathy and empathy—were not peculiar to that doctrine and not at all peculiar to either policing doctrines or those policing doctrines that stem from equity. Rather, they were part of the traditional paradigm of good judging in common-law cases quite generally. The judge in common-law cases across the board was expected to understand the situation of the litigants before him or her and to make a judgment about their situation against the backdrop of preexisting norms, many of which—not just a few —were quite explicitly moral in content. Some came from industry standards, some from the community's positive morality, and some were simply universal moral standards outright. So: a defendant did or did not act "reasonably" when it neglected to insulate an electrical wire along a bridge on which children played.

Whether other bridge owners did so is relevant to the resolution of that issue, as should be the expense of the insulation and the probability of an electrical injury. But neither exhausts the inquiry. The judge must decide (or instruct a jury to do so) whether or not the failure to insulate the wire or to place a warning sign was reasonable, not solely whether or not other bridge makers thought it was reasonable. Similarly, a judge must decide whether a plaintiff did or did not "accept a risk" of injury when he foolishly boarded an obviously defectively designed motorcycle; whether a seller did or did not "unduly influence" a buyer with overbearing sales tactics; whether a buyer was or wasn't under duress when she foolishly agreed to a contract in an abortion clinic that relinquished too many of her rights against potential malpractice; whether a commercial dealer did or did not act in "good faith" when he reduced the quantity delivered under an outputs contract to zero; whether the price on which the parties agreed for a piece of land was or wasn't unconscionably low or the interest rate unconscionably high. These moralistic norms of conduct—the negligence standard itself, the acceptance-of-risk doctrine, undue influence, good-faith constraints on output contracts, duress rules, and, of course, the unconscionability doctrine—*permeated* the common law; indeed, moralistic norms well outnumbered the nonmoralistic norms in tort law. When Holmes railed against moral categories, words, and turns of phrase in the "Path of the Law," urging for the sake of clarity that we purge moral terms such as "duty," "recklessness," "intent," and so on from consciousness as well as the law reports by "washing the law in cynical acid"[57]—thereby flushing them out of the legal system—he was not attacking a straw person or a vague idea. Moral norms constituted the content of much of the common law. Unconscionability was one area in which they did so explicitly. It was certainly not the only such area. The common law was moralistic, through and through.

And, second, not just in unconscionability cases, not just in the policing doctrines, and certainly not just in equity cases but in *all* common-law cases, according to the traditional paradigm of good judging, the breadth of a rule generated by a decision's holding was a function of the importance of distinguishing particular facts. On the traditional understanding, a judge does not enunciate *rules* at all. Rather, he enunciates *holdings*. There is a difference. The holding of a case is subject to a particular kind of interpretation and can change over time. It has this open-ended, always-subject-to-interpretation quality, in fact, precisely because it is *not* a rule and doesn't operate as one. Its content is subject to argument. It is narrow when understood as contingent upon a sizable number of the case's distinguishing facts and broad if contingent on only a few. It can be both at once, to different readers. It can be narrow one day and broad the next. Neither lawyer is in bad faith or misrepresenting a thing when one argues "for" a narrow holding of a case decided yesterday and another argues "for" a broad holding of the same case. Which it is depends not upon anything embedded in the case itself but upon the use to which the holding is later put, the art of the lawyer or judge using the case, and the circumstances of the new case in which the holding is invoked as authority. All of this is what is distinctive about the skill of reading and using cases in legal and judicial argument; all of this also distinguishes the judicial work of articulating holdings from the legislative or administrative art of issuing rules. The ability to read and use case law by extracting holdings from a past case in such a way as to render the case authoritative for a present case is at least a part of the distinctive skill of good lawyering. It is not as large a part of the lawyer's professional life as Langdell believed it to be, for sure. Law schools may well do contemporary law students a major disservice by focusing so exclusively on this work, this skill, or this art, particularly in the first year of law school. Surely, students should learn much else besides, including the rule-making arts of legislation and the dispute-resolving functions of arbitration and mediation. But, nevertheless, the work of extracting the holding of a case by determining the breadth or narrowness of that holding by reference to the relevant facts so as to apply it meaningfully to another "set of facts" is unquestionably a major part of a lawyer and judge's education, as well it should be.

Third, doing this well depends upon use of capacities for both empathy and sympathy—what philosophers used to call the moral sense. As discussed earlier, the bare work of analogy depends upon empathic ability. But, more particularly, application of the relevant substantive law does so as well. To decide that a contract is unconscionable requires empathic engagement with the situation of both parties and a dollop of situation sense as well. To decide

that it was unreasonable not to insulate the wire on the bridge, or
that it was so clearly not unreasonable as not to permit a jury even
to consider the question, or that it was undue influence on the
part of a medical professional to convince a young woman to sign
a contract relinquishing legal rights in an abortion clinic, or that
a usurious interest rate was agreed to only under duress, requires
empathetic engagement with both parties' perspectives. To decide
to come to the *aid* of one or the other of the parties and relieve
the distress or compensate for the injury or release someone from
the obligation to perform a contract or pay damages requires sympathy. One is inclined to help someone in such a situation if one
has first empathized with that party and that party's adversary and
then finds the party's situation sympathetic. At least on the traditional understanding of good judging, the judge must embrace,
not shy away from, his capacity for empathetic and sympathetic engagement with the parties before him.

So, the contemporary understanding of at least the unconscionability doctrine—forward looking, anti-empathic, and focused
on future parties and general rules—is at odds not only with the
traditional understanding of that doctrine but with the traditional
paradigm of good judging. Is this just an anomaly? Maybe the unconscionability doctrine, as currently understood by legal economists, is simply a poor fit with adjudicative method. The other
possibility, though, is that the revised understanding of the unconscionability doctrine evidences the prevalence or at least the
power of a new or emerging paradigm of judging with which the
revised understanding is fully compatible. If so, then the structural
features noted earlier regarding the ways in which judges should
reason in unconscionability cases are true across the board: they
hold for judging, period, not just for judging unconscionability
doctrines. If so, then it is the new paradigm of *judging*, not just a
new understanding of the unconscionability doctrine, that is explicitly and emphatically antimoralistic, forward rather than backward looking, abstract rather than particularist, and reliant upon
social science and empirical method rather than upon empathic
regard followed by sympathy for guidance. Is this right? Do anti-
moralism, nonparticularism, and a turn toward a social-scientific
regard for the decisional life of law's subjects (and away from
ethical judgment informed by empathic regard for the subjective

well-being of litigants) characterize our new paradigm of judging? Is scientific judging, rather than empathic judging, the new paradigm, the ideal toward which our judges are being urged to aim? Quite possibly. Beginning with Holmes's pithy declarations on the topic,[58] continuing through a good bit of legal realist writing, and now in a wide swath of contemporary law and economics scholarship, twentieth-century legal scholars have urged, in opposition to traditional understandings of the goals of adjudication, that net social welfare, particularly as created through voluntarist transactions, should be the goal that judges pursue when deciding common-law cases of tort and contract, rather than the vindication of moral principle or the protection of parties from their own worst instincts or from the actions of private actors who would take advantage of them.[59] The consequence of this has been, in part —but only in part—to tilt common-law adjudication toward libertarian outcomes—toward, rather than against, Herbert Spencer's social statics, in ironic point of fact.[60] Another and somewhat less noted consequence of our journey down this particular Holmesian path of the law has been a redefinition of basic common-law concepts and categories away from their natural language and moral or moralistic meanings and toward an amalgam of the purely positivistically legal and the social-scientific. Thus, "unconscionability" is redefined to mean the exploitation of a decisional heuristic that tilts buyers toward irrationality in markets.[61] Likewise, and much earlier in the century, "contract" was being redefined to mean a "promise that either an event will come to pass or its equivalent value in dollars will be paid," rather than an exchange of promises carrying with them a moral obligation of their performance.[62] "Negligence" has come to mean "conduct with regard to which the expected damage it might cause times its probability exceeds the cost of prevention,"[63] rather than that which a prudent and reasonable person should avoid, and "duty" means the absence of immunity from the obligation to act. "Tort law" is a catch-all word for liability that should be imposed if and only if transaction costs have rendered impossible a voluntary transaction between an actor and victim, with its content determined by the hypothetical contracts those parties would have entered into if they could have, rather than by any conception of what a healthy life with sensibly conscribed duties of care for others should entail.[64] Likewise, a contractual promise that is breached entails a duty to pay damages only if the expected payoff of the promise is higher than the promisor's expected cost of performance, and not otherwise—and so on.[65] All of this is just as Holmes hoped for in "The Path of the Law," and all of it has more or less come to pass; the common law has been bathed in cynical acid, albeit with no guarantee that the bath has brought us the added clarity he hoped would be the happy result. One murkier result of that bath, whether or not it is one he championed, is that, as in the unconscionability cases, judicial outcomes in a wide range of cases—torts cases that turn on definitions of negligence or contributory negligence, efficient breaches of contract, outputs contracts, duty or lack of duty—do not turn on the judge's sense of the moral quality of the interaction between the litigants. Rather, such cases turn on the judge's understanding of how the incentives he creates through the rules he fashions might impact the welfare of others, as ascertained through a quasi-scientific study of their choices, hypothetical, implied, or otherwise.

Likewise, for a wide range of cases, scholars increasingly urge that common-law judges should focus less on the litigants and more on the future transactions or dealings that the rules they articulate will affect. Law and economics scholars, in particular, quite routinely urge that judging should be neither backward looking nor particularistic. But the view is by no means limited to law and economics theorists. Most mainstream legal scholars—including liberal, progressive, and critical legal scholars—concur that adjudication should be forward looking and general and not limited to the particulars of the facts before it. Adjudication *should be*, in short, legislative in form and outlook. Given their indeterminacy, precedent and past cases in general provide little guidance in any event. Courts should seek to maximize welfare. Their work is no different from the legislator's; it's simply housed in a different building.

This consensus that adjudication should be forward looking and general, rather than backward looking and particularistic, has its origin of course in realist reforms and jurisprudence: the true motive and meaning of a court's decision, according to Holmes and his legions of twentieth-century followers, is "social policy." The judge should act as a quasi-legislator within the interstices of rules laid down. The common law is simply an incomplete codification; the judge's work is to complete it. On this basic realist point, left-leaning critical scholars are in complete accord with libertarian-leaning legal economists: that the judge acts as a quasi-legislator is simply a reiteration of the lack of any substantive difference between law and politics. There are, of course, political differences between these groups of scholars, and the differences show up in the scholarship: Kennedy and Kronman, for example, embrace paternalism in both the legislative and the adjudicative spheres on political and moral grounds, while Epstein and Posner resist it in both. But they are all as one on the nature of judging. The judge's job is to maximize net social welfare. They differ only over their conceptions of in what that welfare might consist. They don't differ on the judge's role in creating it.

And, last, the new paradigm of judging has no need for the exercise of judicial moral sentiment or the faculties of sympathy and empathy at the core of that human capacity. Empathy, in fact, is basically the collateral damage in this ideological war between traditional and scientific paradigms of adjudication. Neither empathy nor sympathy is required by the new model for *any* of the judicial tasks for which it was seemingly central in the old model. The judge on the new model is less concerned with precedent, so there is no need to engage in the sort of empathetic imaginings that Bandes and others have characterized as essential to analogical reasoning. Nor need the judge exercise whatever moral sense (or sentiment) is required to appreciate and apply moralistic legal categories. Once the law is washed in cynical acid, the judge has no need for those moral sentiments that might register engagement with the moralistic categories that have been washed away. The judge need not empathically walk in litigants' shoes before judging them: his decision should attend, rather, to the incentives or disincentives for future conduct that his decision might create, with the goal of maximizing future net social welfare. When doing so, he might have to acknowledge, at least if he attends to the teachings of behavioral economics, the need for limits on consumer voluntarism in unfettered markets and might accordingly be inclined to enunciate rules to that effect. He will then have to decide whether a group of buyers or market actors might be susceptible to a decisional heuristic that will pervert the rationality of their choices on

various markets. If so, legal rules that will restrain those markets
might come into play: limits on the waivability of warranties, the
unconscionability doctrine itself, tort-based limits on contractual
agreements, and so forth. But the target of this paternalistic intervention is decidedly *not* human suffering but, rather, human irrationality, and the goal of it is not relief from suffering or immoral
or unethical business behavior but, rather, correction of irrational
choice. The determination, then, of whether or not there is such a
failing of rational choice requires deference to social-scientific expertise on the behavior of actors in markets, not empathic engagement with litigants. Whether or not the judge ought to respond
and how, once a finding of such irrationality has been made, depends on the judge's view of the relation between the ideals of
rationality and his understanding of the importance of individual
choice, even assuming perverse irrationalities. Should he favor
the former—call it welfare, ideally and rationally construed—he
might intervene into market choices, rejiggering in line with what
a perfect choice would have yielded. If he favors the latter—call it
liberty—he might let the perverse or irrational market choice lie.
Either way, though, the decision is not informed by empathy and
most decidedly not motivated by either disgust with immoral business behavior or by a sympathetic identification with the plight of
litigants, poor or otherwise, who might be seeking relief from the
suffering occasioned by their own ill-conceived choices.

3. THE ROOTS, APPEAL AND LIMITS OF SCIENTIFIC JUDGING

A full history of the emergent paradigm of scientific judging is
obviously beyond the scope of this discussion, but it's worth identifying just three of the "signposts along the road"[66] originating
in either law or sister disciplines. The first was a development in
American legal theory; the second comes out of economics and
the third, political theory.

First, legal theory. In the first three decades of the past century,
"legal realists" famously rebelled against the then traditional paradigm of moralistic judging, as well as the "brooding omnipresence in the sky" that informed it, by which they meant the common law in general and Langdellian pretenses of the common
law's autonomy and "completeness" in particular. That "brooding

omnipresence," it's now easy to see in retrospect, came with some profoundly conservative biases: biases toward capital and against labor, for stronger contracting parties and against weaker ones, and for business and industry and against their victims, whether on the job, in dangerous workplaces, or off, in rural fields and urban streets alike. Realists railed against the identification of the nineteenth-century common law with both an immutable natural law and constitutional law that favored individual rights of property and contract over collective interests, all with a moralistic overlay. And they found plenty of allies in the progressive politics of their era, from labor organizers to some state court judges, a somewhat progressive Congress, FDR's White House, the American Pragmatist movement in the academy, and, eventually, of course, a majority of the Supreme Court. The existing common law, the realists argued, was not perfect, not complete, and, most important, not in line with the needs of the people. Judges of the common law and Justices of the Supreme Court, with Oliver W. Holmes Jr. leading the charge in both fora, were broadly encouraged to find a way to turn away from common-law precedent as a guide to both adjudication and constitutional interpretation.

If the common law is not only unduly protective of capital but also incomplete and at best an indeterminate guide for decision making in any event, then what? To what *should* courts, judges, and lawyers turn when filling the interstitial gaps in the law, if not from general principles drawn from prior cases? First Holmes and then the realists had an imperfect answer to that question, but they did have an answer: judges should turn to the then-nascent social sciences. The lawyer and judge of the future, again, would be the man of the slide rule and economics, not the man of Blackstone, precedent, and the past. Science should guide the judge's inquiry into the content of social welfare, and social welfare should guide his inquiry into the content of the law. Science should be the method and welfare the goal.

And what are the teachings of the sciences on the question of social welfare? How do we ascertain welfare? The second signpost, I believe, came from one influential answer to that question that emerged from midcentury economics. Central to midcentury economics was the claim, which eventually became an article of faith, that actors cannot intersubjectively compare the subjective utilities of other persons.[67] The gulf between our minds is just not bridge-able. We cannot know whether a pinprick hurts someone else more than a broken leg from a fall,[68] to paraphrase a twentieth-century version of this claim; we cannot know whether pushpin is more or less pleasurable, welfare enhancing, or worthy, than poetry, to borrow from Jeremy Bentham's formulation of a related skepticism.[69] We are all too different to make such comparisons by generalizing from our own experience, and the difficulties in grasping the hedonic pleasures and pains of others block our ability to make such comparisons directly. The consequence of a firm belief in this severe limitation on our abilities, for purposes of any political activity that aims to increase welfare, is profound. One person, whether judge or legislator, with the power to distribute goods or services or resources who aims to do so in a welfare-enhancing way cannot truly *know* whether one person's enjoyment of a dollar—or sufferance of the infliction of a kick in the shins—is "comparable" to, lesser than, or greater than that of another. We can't truly know that a rich man's enjoyment of a marginal dollar is less than a poor man's or that the kick in the shins hurts less than the broken bone or more than the pinprick. Therefore, the simple quantitative or additive function that Bentham envisioned when he imagined utility metrics as a pathway to welfare maximization is just dysfunctional. They don't work. We can't *know* overall welfare by adding utiles, where utiles are tied to subjective pleasure, because we can't compare them across persons. The empathic knowledge of the subjectivity of others—the knowledge that the loss of a dollar by a rich person actually is less painful than the loss of a dollar by a poor person or that the loss of collateral is so painful to a buyer as not to be worth the loss of the consumer surplus that might be enjoyed, should a clause requiring that loss be allowed—is just not up to the task of generating enough information to actually answer questions of total welfare that in turn require that sort of interpersonal comparative knowledge. And this is empathic knowledge that any potential sympathizer who aims to increase welfare will need, whether the sympathizer be Adam Smith or Karl Marx. We can't empathize our way to the knowledge that Bentham's utility calculus demands.

    If we want to maximize social welfare, then, as Holmesian realists proclaimed, whether through adjudication or through legislation, the best and only *window*, so to speak, into the subjective individual utility functions of others and, therefore, into their subjective well-being is revealed preferences, as demonstrated by choices in open markets. In part, and as commonly understood, the inclination of contemporary utilitarians, welfare economists, and others to rely on revealed preferences as a window into subjective welfare—and, in turn, to rely on fulfilled market choices as a vehicle for maximizing the satiation of those preferences—is because, absent infirmity, the individual himself has come to be regarded, for familiar antipaternalist or Millian reasons, as the best judge of his own interest. But not exclusively. Reliance on preference as a window into well-being and on fulfillment of choices that reflects preference as the best vehicle for maximizing that well-being is *also* the natural consequence of the assumption that came to be widely held among economists at midcentury, to wit, that the individual is just as *incapable* of knowing the subjective utility of others as he is *omniscient* regarding his own. He knows his own well-being perfectly or at least better than others do, for Millian or liberal reasons. As important, though, he knows the well-being, pleasures, and pains of others *not at all*—he can't know or compare their subjective utility with that of others. Put the Millian and economic claims together and they yield this sum: the individual can't be wrong about his own utility functions, and he can't be right about the subjective pains and pleasures of others. The individual's preferences are best revealed through his choices, and his choices are fully discoverable through the empirical methods of the social sciences.

If we take seriously the inability to intersubjectively compare utilities, then it directly follows that *empathy* is both *inadequate* to the task of learning enough of the subjective well-being of another so as to increase social welfare—we can't intersubjectively compare the subjectivity of others—and *unnecessary*. Revealed preferences are what we need to know; indeed, they're all we need know, and, furthermore, all we can know. The contemporary ubiquity of this claim—the claim that we are incapable of intersubjective utility judgments, that we just don't know whether someone is more hurt by a broken knee than a forgone candy bar, given the irreducible differences between us and the difficulty of penetrating the mind of another—is, thus, the second "signpost along the way." With the acceptance of the claim that one moral agent cannot possibly inter-subjectively compare utilities, I believe, came a degradation of the acceptability of moral judging that required empathic and sympathetic engagement with the well-being of others—an engagement with others that requires precisely the intersubjective comparisons of those others' mental states that the economic hypothesis warns are impossible. Moral judging then took another hit.

The third signpost along the path from moral to scientific judging was the rise, two-thirds of the way through the twentieth century, of a theory of liberalism steadfastly committed to state neutrality regarding questions concerning the nature or content of the good life, in both political theory and jurisprudence, that coincided in time with a turn toward robust libertarianism in the country's politics. Both counsel deference to an individual's assessment of his own welfare, and both then counsel likewise deference to either markets or democracy on questions regarding the content of the social welfare to which courts should attend. If we synthesize all of this—the forward-looking jurisprudence of the realists, economists' skepticism regarding our ability to understand empathically the pains or pleasures of others, and liberals' disdain for public morality and the rise of liberal and libertarian theories of the state committed to neutrality on questions of the good in the 1970s through to the present—the increasing dominance of scientific judging and the demise of moral judging, I believe, are hardly surprising.

There are, finally, additional emotional or, indeed, sentimental reasons, I believe, for the appeal of scientific adjudication to contemporary scholars. Let me point to two. First, legal scholars and judges now fear the erratic results suggested by untethered empathic adjudication more than we did in the past, partly because we now, in contrast to then, broadly assume a radical indeterminacy in preexisting law. Radical legal indeterminacy is no longer the view of outliers; it is, rather, a widely shared conventional wisdom. Obviously, scientific judging, in part, appeals simply because it speaks to the craving for certainty in the face of a presumed indeterminacy that underscores a good bit of both law and legal writing. If indeterminate law can't provide certainty—and many judges and lawyers and likely most scholars are convinced it can't —then scientific ideals might.

In larger part, though, I believe, the continuing appeal of scientific adjudication as an ideal of judging stems, at least in legal scholarship, from the blurring of legislation and adjudication, as well as of administration and adjudication. The claim that there is no difference in the goals of administration, legislation, and adjudication is now widely shared not only among law and economics scholars but also by critical legal scholars and, to a lesser degree, mainstream legal scholars as well. Both Richard Posner and Duncan Kennedy have argued, in very different contexts, of course, that judges are in effect quasi-legislators and should reason as such. For Kennedy, our resistance to this idea stems from a residual false consciousness that accords fetishistic validity to democratically obtained ends, and, for Posner, it stems from an old-fashioned, pre-pragmatic, pre-Holmesian faith in the wealth-enhancing virtues as well as the coherence of nineteenth-century common law.[70] For most legal thinkers today, the judge is a quasi-legislator. The ideal of good adjudication, then, should not be notably different from the ideal of good legislation.

So, where does empathy fit into the skill set, so to speak, of the ideal legislator? For many political theorists today and for many scholars of legislation in the legal academy, it ranks low. Both public-choice theorists and their critics value social-scientific expertise—not empathy—as that which should guide legislation and administration.[71] On this view, which I am not commending, legislators should be committed to improving the welfare of all, but the tie that binds them to that common good is electoral accountability, not moral sentiment. If the electoral system is working properly, legislators can make legislative decisions on the basis of their own self-interest, and the value of those decisions, in effect, will trickle down to those to whom the legislator is electorally responsive. So, if adjudication is truly *no different* in goal from legislation—law is politics, and judges no less than legislatures aim and should aim for social welfare, as Holmes and his followers all said—then there is no reason on Earth that their methods should differ. Judges, too, then, should use the slide rule, rather than the heart, to ascertain social welfare and then should rule accordingly.

Finally, what's to lose, as we move from moral to scientific ideals of adjudication? I think we lose two things of consequence. First, we lose the moral interpretation of many of our common-law concepts that have been given articulation in moral adjudication over the past century and a half. We lose, for example, the idea of a contract as a promise, rather than a prediction of the occurrence of either an event or a damage payoff. We lose the idea of a tort as a harm occasioned by individual recklessness or negligence and borne by relatively innocent individuals who therefore deserve recompense, rather than the terms of a hypothetical contract between strangers who can't make deals in the face of transaction costs. We lose the idea of the "policing doctrines," such as the unconscionability and undue influence rules, as distinctively moral limits on market behavior, rather than as rules that attempt to capture and correct for heuristic defects in rationality, and we lose the last thread of a connection between our current legal doctrine in these common-law areas and the abandoned moral principles at least sometimes employed by the equity courts of the past.

Second, and I believe of greater consequence (these judicially created common-law moral rules are of limited scope, no matter how they are defined), or at least what I've tried to stress here, we lose the distinctive adjudicative arts. We lose, for example, the idea of the difference—and the idea that there is a difference— between a holding and a rule. More broadly, we lose the idea of the common law and of the judicial opinion as a repository for wisdom that can flexibly mutate to meet changing facts but that emerges from particularistic decision making. Of course, we gain, as well: we gain, perhaps, more finely tuned rules, a better sense of when market transactions are driven by irrationality, and, at least if judicial decision making is effective, we gain a more rational marketplace. In that rational utopia, judicial empathy has no place, but it is not needed; we will all do just fine on our own deciding what pleases us.

No matter how we regard it, though, it is clear that judicial empathy has no role to play in scientific judging. Thus my conclusion: the demise of judicial empathy is best regarded as a piece of the collateral damage in the movement from traditional, moralistic, and particularistic reasoning to forward-looking scientific adjudication. Empathy is as irrelevant to the new paradigm of judging as it was central to the old. It can only do mischief. No wonder, then, that Justices Sotomayor and Kagan, no less than the Chief Justice, have so little to say in its favor.

NOTES

1. "The spirit of the age, as it is revealed to each of us, is too often only the spirit of the group in which the accidents of birth or education or occupation or fellowship have given us a place. No effort or revolution of the mind will overthrow utterly and at all times the empire of these subconscious loyalties. . . . The training of the judge, if coupled with what is styled the judicial temperament, will help in some degree to emancipate him from the suggestive power of individual dislikes and prepossessions. *It will help to broaden the group to which his subconscious loyalties are due.*" Benjamin N. Cardozo, *The Nature of the Judicial Process* (New Haven, CT: Yale University Press, 1921), 181–182 (emphasis added).

2. John Noonan, Preface, *Persons and Masks of the Law* (Berkeley: University of California Press, 2002), ix.

3. "Another cousin of intuition and another major factor in judicial decisions in the open area is 'good judgment,' an elusive faculty best understood as a compound of empathy, modesty, maturity, a sense of proportion, balance, a recognition of human limitations, sanity, prudence, a sense of reality, and common sense." Richard A. Posner, *How Judges Think* (Cambridge, MA: Harvard University Press, 2008), 117.

4. "I read something that moved me a lot not very long ago. I was reading something by Chesterton, and he was talking about one of the Brontës, Emily Brontë, I think, or *Jane Eyre* that she wrote. He said if you want to know what that is like, you go and look out at the city, he said—I think he was looking at London—and he said, you know, you see all those houses now, even at the end of the 19th century, and they look all as if they are the same. And you think all those people are out there, going to work, and they are all the same. But, he says, what Emily Brontë tells you is they are not the same. Each one of those persons and each one of those houses and each one of those families is different, and they each have a story to tell. Each of those stories involves something about human passion. Each of those stories involves a man, a woman, children, families, work, lives. And you get that sense out of the book. So sometimes, I have found literature very helpful as a way out of the tower." Testimony of Stephen G. Breyer, U.S. Congress, Senate, Committee on the Judiciary, *Nomination of Stephen G. Breyer to Be an Associate Justice of the Supreme Court of the United States*, 13 July 1994, 103rd Congress, 2nd sess. (Washington, DC: Government Printing Office, 1995).

5. Stevens is often lauded as having been our most empathetic Supreme Court justice, particularly given the narrowness and privilege of his background. See, e.g., Martha Nussbaum, *Poetic Justice: The Literary Imagination and Public Life* (Boston: Beacon Press, 1995), 99–104.

282 ROBIN WEST

6. The literature on analogical reasoning in common law systems is vast. For general discussions, see Cass Sunstein, "On Analogical Reasoning," *Harvard Law Review* 106 (1993): 741–791; Frederick Schauer, "*Formalism*," *Yale Law Journal* 97 (1988): 509–548; Anthony Kronman, "Precedent and Tradition," *Yale Law Journal* 99 (1990): 1029–1068.

7. *Hawkins v. McGee*, 146 A. 641 (N.H. 1929).

8. Ibid., 643.

9. For clear elucidations of the "loss of chance" doctrine in tort law, see *Matsuyama v. Birnbaum*, 890 N.E.2d 819 (Mass. 2008), and *Herskovits v. Group Health Coop. of Puget Sound*, 664 P.2d 474, 477 (Wash. 1983).

10. In the 1970s, the Supreme Court loosely analogized sex distinctions in state and federal law to other insidious forms of discrimination, eventually concluding in a handful of cases that sexual distinctions in law should be subjected to "intermediate scrutiny" and finding a number of state and federal laws or regulations unconstitutional under the test. See, e.g., *Reed v. Reed*, 404 U.S. 71 (1971) (preference in state law given to male estate administrators ruled unconstitutional); *Frontiero v. Richardson*, 411 U.S. 677 (1973) (military benefit automatically given to widows but not widowers, on presumption that widows but not widowers are "dependents," ruled unconstitutional); *Craig v. Boren*, 429 U.S. 190 (1976) (state statutes that precluded the sale of low-alcohol beer to boys under the age of twenty-one and girls under the age of eighteen ruled unconstitutional).

11. *Perry v. Schwarzenegger*, 704 F.Supp.2d 921 (N.D. Cal. 2010).

12. *Eisenstadt v. Baird*, 405 U.S. 438 (1972).

13. *Griswold v. Connecticut*, 381 U.S. 479 (1965).

14. *Skinner v. Oklahoma*, 316 U.S. 535 (1942).

15. See "Text of John Roberts Opening Statement," last modified 12 September 2005, *USAToday.com*. Statement of John G. Roberts, Jr., U.S. Congress, Senate, Committee on the Judiciary, *Confirmation Hearing on the Nomination of John G. Roberts, Jr., to Be Chief Justice of the United States*, 12–15 September 2005, 109th Congress 1st sess., (Washington, DC: Government Printing Office, 2005), 55.

16. See Ari Shapiro, "Sotomayor Differs with Obama on 'Empathy' Issue," last modified 14 July 2009, *NPR.org*. Testimony of Sonia Sotomayor, U.S. Congress, Senate, Committee on the Judiciary, *Confirmation Hearing on the Nomination of Hon. Sonia Sotomayor to Be an Associate Justice of the Supreme Court of the United States*, 13–16 July 2009, 111th Congress, 1st sess. (Washington, DC: Government Printing Office, 2010), 120–1211, 134–135.

17. Carrie Johnson, "Kagan Vows Restraint if Confirmed to Supreme Court," *NPR.org*.

18. *Roe v. Wade*, 410 U.S. 113 (1973).

19. *Griswold*, 381 U.S. 479 (1965).

20. *Miranda v. Arizona*, 384 U.S. 436 (1966).

21. John Hasnas, "The Unseen Deserve Empathy Too," *Wall Street Journal*, May 29, 2009, at A15.

22. Herbert Wechsler, "Toward Neutral Principles of Constitutional Law," *Harvard Law Review* 73 (1959): 1–35, 34.

23. Susan Bandes, "Empathetic Judging and the Rule of Law," *Cardozo Law Review De Novo* 2009 (2009): 133–148, and "Empathy, Narrative, and Victim Impact Statements," *University of Chicago Law Review* 63 (1996): 361–412.

24. Lynne Henderson, "Legality and Empathy," *Michigan Law Review* 85 (1987): 1574–1654.

25. The classic statement of this account of empathy comes from Adam Smith. Adam Smith, *The Theory of Moral Sentiments* (Boston: Wells and Lilly, 1817), 1–23.

26. "For the rational study of the law the black-letter man may be the man of the present, but the man of the future is the man of statistics and the master of economics." O. W. Holmes Jr., "The Path of the Law," *Harvard Law Review* 10 (1897): 457–478, 469.

27. *Williams v. Walker-Thomas Furniture Co.*, 350 F.2d 445 (C.A.D.C. 1965).

28. Smith, *The Theory of Moral Sentiments*, 4 (defining the moral sentiments of his examination as "our fellow-feeling with any passion whatsoever," that is, sympathetic feelings both pleasant and painful).

29. See *Williams*, 350 F.2d 445, regarding the viability of the unconscionability doctrine prior to the passage of the Uniform Commercial Code in the District of Columbia and Uniform Commercial Code § 2-302 for the Code's unconscionability rule. The Court explained the doctrine in now familiar procedural and substantive terms:

> Unconscionability has generally been recognized to include an absence of meaningful choice on the part of one of the parties together with contract terms which are unreasonably favorable to the other party. . . . In many cases the meaningfulness of the choice is negated by a gross inequality of bargaining power. . . . The manner in which the contract was entered is also relevant to this consideration. Did each party to the contract, considering his obvious education or lack of it, have a reasonable opportunity to understand the terms of the contract, or were the important terms hidden in a maze of fine print and minimized by deceptive sales practices? Ordinarily, one who signs an agreement without full knowledge of its terms might be held to assume the risk that he has entered a one-sided bargain. But when a party of little bargaining power, and hence little real choice, signs a commercially unreasonable contract with little

or no knowledge of its terms, it is hardly likely that his consent, or even an objective manifestation of his consent, was ever given to all the terms. In such a case the usual rule that the terms of the agreement are not to be questioned should be abandoned and the court should consider whether the terms of the contract are so unfair that enforcement should be withheld.

Williams, 350 F.2d at 449–450. See also *Armendariz v. Foundation Health Psychcare Services, Inc.*, 6 P.3d 669 (Cal. 2000), for the summary of California's unconscionability doctrine in the context of a mandatory arbitration clause in an employment contract, and *Brower v. Gateway 2000 Inc.*, 676 N.Y.S.2d 569 (1998), for summary and application of unconscionability doctrine as codified in the Uniform Commercial Code § 2-302.

30. Undue influence is a defense to the enforcement of a contract where a stronger party has acted upon a weaker party's infirmities in extracting agreement to an unfair contract. The infirmities may arise from a status differential—ward and guardian, teacher and student, professional and client, or even husband and wife—or from temporary conditions impeding upon the weaker party's will that do not rise to the level of contractual incapacity, such as extreme distress over a pending termination of a job or the emotional distress of needing to procure an abortion. See, e.g., *Odorizzi v. Bloomfield School District*, 54 Cal. Rptr. 533 (Cal. Ct. App. 1966) (agreement to resign after being threatened with being exposed by employer/school district as a homosexual was obtained under undue influence, and Plaintiff is not bound by it). See also *Broemmer v. Abortion Services of Phoenix, Ltd.*, 840 P.2d 1013 (Ariz. 1992) (invalidating an arbitration provision in a medical *clinic's* admittance form because of patient's emotional distress, stating that an adhesion contract will not be enforced unless "they are conscionable and within the reasonable expectations of the parties. This is a well-established principle of contract law; today we merely apply it to the undisputed facts of the case before us.").

31. Uniform Commercial Code §1-201 b (20) ("'Good faith' . . . means honesty in fact and the observance of reasonable commercial standards of fair dealing.").

32. *Odorizzi*, 54 Cal.Rptr. at 533.

33. Constructive fraud might exist in the absence of an actual intent to deceive when a party fails to disclose material facts regarding the value of a transaction, in circumstances in which the co-contractor is incapable of discovering those facts. A good discussion can be found in *Strong v. Jackson*, 781 N.E.2d 770, 772 (Ind. Ct. App. 2003).

34. See *Woolums v. Horsley*, 20 S.W. 781 (Ky. Ct. App. 1892).

35. See discussion of the equitable origin of the unconscionability doctrine in Howard O. Hunter, *Modern Law of Contracts* (Eagan, MN: Thomson

Reuters, 1999), §19:39, and S. M. Waddams, "Unconscionability in Contracts," *The Modern Law Review* 39 (1976): 369–393.

36. *Williams*, 350 F.2d at 448 (quoting the lower court opinion, which condemned the "sharp practice and irresponsible business dealings" of Walker-Thomas but held that the contract was enforceable).

37. For a classic history of the communitarian role of these doctrines in the first half of the nineteenth century particularly, see Morton Horwitz, *The Transformation of American Law, 1870–1960: The Crisis of Legal Orthodoxy* (New York: Oxford University Press, 1992).

38. See Uniform Commercial Code §§1-201 (b) (20) ("good faith" means honesty in fact), 2-302 (courts may strike unconscionable contract terms), 2-314 (unless modified or excluded, all goods have an implied warranty of merchantability), 2-315 (when a seller knows of a buyer's particular purpose for a good, there is an implied warranty of fitness for that particular purpose unless the warranty excludes or modifies the expectation).

39. *Williams*, 350 F.2d at 448.

40. The two most influential critics, one from the political right and one from the political left, were Richard Epstein and Arthur Leff. See, e.g., Richard A. Epstein, "Unconscionability: A Critical Reappraisal," *Journal of Law and Economics* 18 (1975): 293–316; Arthur Leff, "Thomist Unconscionability," *Canadian Business Law Journal* 4 (1979): 424–428; Arthur Leff, "Unconscionability and the Code—The Emperor's New Clause," *University of Pennsylvania Law Review* 115 (1967): 485–559, 487.

41. For a full argument to this affect, see Richard Posner, *The Economics of Justice* (Cambridge, MA: Harvard University Press, 1983), 88–115 (discussing the ethical value of consent).

42. Russell B. Korobkin, "A 'Traditional' and 'Behavioral' Law-and-Economics Analysis of *Williams v. Walker-Thomas Furniture Company*," *Hawaii Law Review* 26 (2004): 441–468, 448.

43. Duncan Kennedy, "Distributive and Paternalist Motives in Contract and Tort Law, with Special Reference to Compulsory Terms and Unequal Bargaining Power," *Maryland Law Review* 41 (1982): 563–658, 633.

44. Korobkin, "A 'Traditional' and 'Behavioral' Law-and-Economics Analysis of *Williams v. Walker-Thomas Furniture Company*," 458–462.

45. For a full argument (outside contract law and instead in the world of regulation) on the role of minimal, or "libertarian paternalism," see Richard Thaler and Cass Sunstein, *Nudge: Improving Decisions about Health, Wealth, and Happiness* (New Haven, CT: Yale University Press, 2008).

46. Seana Valentine Shiffrin, "Paternalism, Unconscionability Doctrine, and Accommodation," *Philosophy and Public Affairs* 29 (2000): 205–250, 229–30 ("Although judicial opinions reflect a range of concerns, sometimes including pure concern for the position of the disadvantaged

party, a dominant concern of judges is self-regarding: it is to avoid facilitating the actions of an exploiter rather than to act to protect the disadvantaged party. A survey I conducted of many leading unconscionability cases reveals that in nearly every successful claim the court focused on the conduct of the stronger party, not on the weakness or needs of the weaker party.").

47. Korobkin, "A 'Traditional' and 'Behavioral' Law-and-Economics Analysis of *Williams v. Walker-Thomas Furniture Company*," 448.

48. Kennedy, "Distributive and Paternalist Motives in Contract and Tort Law," 633.

49. Anthony T. Kronman, "Paternalism and the Law of Contracts," *Yale Law Journal* 92 (1983): 763–798.

50. Shiffrin, "Paternalism, Unconscionability Doctrine, and Accommodation."

51. Korobkin, "A 'Traditional' and 'Behavioral' Law-and-Economics Analysis of *Williams v. Walker-Thomas Furniture Company*," 454.

52. Shiffrin, "Paternalism, Unconscionability Doctrine, and Accommodation," 223–224.

53. Ibid., 221.

54. *Williams*, 350 F.2d at 448.

55. *Williams v. Walker-Thomas*, 198 A.2d 914, 915 (D.C. App. 1964) ("A review of the legislation in the District of Columbia affecting retail sales and the pertinent decisions of the highest court in this jurisdiction disclose, however, no ground upon which this court can declare the contracts in question contrary to public policy.").

56. Judge Wright cited both Supreme Court doctrine and the Uniform Commercial Code as authorities. *Williams*, 350 F.2d at 448 ("We do not agree that the court lacked the power to refuse enforcement to contracts found to be unconscionable. . . . [T]he notion that an unconscionable bargain should not be given full enforcement is by no means novel.").

57. Holmes, "The Path of the Law," 461.

58. "I think that the judges themselves have failed adequately to recognize their duty of weighing considerations of social advantage. The duty is inevitable, and the result of the often proclaimed judicial aversion to deal with such considerations is simply to leave the very ground and foundation of judgments inarticulate, and often unconscious, as I have said." Ibid., 488. "You see how the vague circumference of the notion of duty shrinks and at the same time grows more precise when we wash it with cynical acid and expel everything except the object of our study, the operations of the law." Ibid., 469.

59. Epstein, "Unconscionability: A Critical Reappraisal," and "Surro-

gacy: The Case for Full Contractual Enforcement," *Virginia Law Review* 81 (1995): 2305–2342; Posner, *The Economics of Justice.*

60. See *Lochner v. New York*, 198 U.S. 45, 75 (1905) (Holmes, J., dissenting) (stating, famously, that the Constitution "does not enact Mr. Herbert Spencer's Social Statics").

61. Korobkin, "A 'Traditional' and 'Behavioral' Law-and-Economics Analysis of *Williams v. Walker-Thomas Furniture Company*," 462.

62. Holmes, "The Path of the Law," 462 ("If you commit a contract, you are liable to pay a compensatory sum unless the promised event comes to pass, and that is all the difference.").

63. *United States v. Carroll Towing Co.*, 159 F.2d 169, 173 (2nd Cir. 1947) ("Possibly it serves to bring this notion into relief to state it in algebraic terms: if the probability be called P; the injury, L; and the burden, B; liability depends upon whether B is less than L multiplied by P: i.e., whether B is less than PL.").

64. R. H. Coase, "The Problem of Social Cost," *Journal of Law & Economics* 3 (1960): 1–44.

65. Richard Posner explains the theory of efficient breach as follows: A better argument is that a penalty clause may discourage efficient as well as inefficient breaches of contract. Suppose a breach would cost the promisee $12,000 in actual damages but would yield the promisor $20,000 in additional profits. Then there would be a net social gain from breach. After being fully compensated for his loss the promisee would be no worse off than if the contract had been performed, while the promisor would be better off by $8,000. But now suppose the contract contains a penalty clause under which the promisor if he breaks his promise must pay the promisee $25,000. The promisor will be discouraged from breaking the contract, since $25,000, the penalty, is greater than $20,000, the profits of the breach; and a transaction that would have increased value will be forgone.
Lake River Corp. v. Carborundum Co., 769 F.2d 1284, 1289 (7th Cir. 1985).

66. With thanks to then-Judge Cardozo for this lovely phrase, which he used in a classic common-law case to guide the courts toward recognition of a promissory estoppel doctrine. See *Allegheny College v. National Chautauqua County Bank of Jamestown*, 159 N.E. 173, 175 (N.Y. 1927).

67. Lionel Robbins, *An Essay on the Nature and Significance of Economic Science* (London: Macmillan, 1945), 139–140.

68. Mark Kelman, "Choice and Utility," *Wisconsin Law Review* 1979 (1979): 769–797, 779.

69. Jeremy Bentham, *The Rationale of Reward* (London: John and H. L.

Hunt, 1825), 206 ("Prejudice apart, the game of push-pin is of equal value with the arts and sciences of music and poetry.").

70. Compare Richard A. Posner, *Law, Pragmatism, and Democracy* (Cambridge, MA: Harvard University Press, 2005), 57–62, with Kennedy, "Distributive and Paternalist Motives in Contract and Tort Law," 623.

71. For a critical overview, see Mark G. Kelman, "On Democracy-Bashing: A Skeptical Look at the Theoretical and 'Empirical' Practice of the Public Choice Movement," *Virginia Law Review* 74 (1988): 199–274.

10

SYSTEMS AND FEELINGS

KEN I. KERSCH

Robin West's "The Anti-Empathic Turn"[1] is an unusually provocative and important reflection. Its central claim is that, in deciding cases, today's judges are increasingly pressed—educated/trained/inclined—to think of themselves not as doing justice between the parties before them but, rather, as resolving the dispute to produce rules that fit as neatly as possible into a broader regulatory system. As such, judging (once a moral exercise, centered on the parties to the lawsuit, who were truly *seen*) is now largely an occasion for the engineering and maintenance of a larger and impersonal administrative and regulatory system (in which the parties —once complicated, individualized human beings—are now mere illustrations/cases in point/vehicles that simply *prompt*). West laments this development and (implicitly, if not expressly) calls for a return to the increasingly lost tradition of moral, party-centered, "empathetic" judging.

In this brief comment, I agree with West's central claim regarding a regime change in the nature of the judicial role. But I question her account of the decline of "empathy"—including her illustrative use of Judge J. Skelly Wright's canonical opinion in *Williams v. Walker-Thomas Furniture Co.*[2] I argue that the changes she acutely observes are so deeply implicated in the nature of the modern social welfare state that, even if it were possible to reverse them and revive an earlier "lifeworld" (which is doubtful), to do so would be extremely radical (not to mention, potentially, highly reactionary).[3]

1. WHAT ARE WE TALKING ABOUT WHEN
WE TALK ABOUT EMPATHY?

West is very good about surveying the array of actual and possible criticisms of the use of the term "empathy" in recent scholarship and political debate concerning its proper role in law and judging. But, despite the fact that she anticipates some of my own objections and attempts to meet them, I remain unpersuaded by her arguments and continue to hold those objections nevertheless.

First, I don't understand what the term "empathy" really means in this discussion. It needs to be clarified. At one point, West defines it as "the ability to understand not just the situation but also the perspective of litigants on warring sides of a lawsuit."[4] She adds that "[o]ne simply cannot judge another before walking in his shoes. Indeed, to suggest otherwise might be thought to be disqualifying" for a judge.[5] Indeed, in law, the lingua franca of analogical reasoning "by definition seemingly requires empathetic understanding."[6] If by empathy West simply means the capacity of the judge to have a rich understanding of the nature of the situation of both litigants—imagination as a route to full information[7]—then I don't think anyone (including those she would take to be partisans of "anti-empathic" judging) is opposed to it. If empathy means a rich ability to inhabit the situation, no one, even today, is against it. Who would deny that better judges understand more, not less? In light of this, might West be better off claiming that, today, judges are either (1) less interested in understanding the full facts surrounding the legal disputes they are charged with resolving, including the "personal" facts speaking to the "state of mind" of a party, which often remain legally relevant, or (2) less perceptive in apprehending those facts? Put otherwise, might she be better off framing the question as involving a reduced level of curiosity or insight among contemporary judges?

West cites the recent public/political debates in which the model of the empathetic judge took a major beating—including the attack on President Obama for indicating during his campaign a desire to appoint empathic judges to the bench, the attack on one of his Supreme Court nominees, Sonia Sotomayor, on the grounds (in light of earlier statements she had made) that she might herself be one of those empathetic judges, and Chief Justice

John Roberts's insistence in the opening statement of his confirmation hearing that it is the job of the judge to act as a dispassionate umpire calling balls and strikes. The charge in these political dust-ups was that empathy in judging is contrary to the rule of law. West raises the possibility that the attack on empathy in judging by conservatives—although phrased in general terms—may have been, in reality, a critique of selective empathy. As she writes, "the target of the anti-empathy argument is not empathy per se but selective empathy" by progressives/liberals. Actually, at least so far as this political sparring is concerned, it seems to me that this is precisely right. In contemporary political discourse, empathy almost always means liberal empathy. Although West's focus is largely on questions of private law (like the contract dispute in *Williams v. Walker-Thomas*), in constitutional law, the empathizing judge invariably feels the need for welfare rights, abortion rights, and gay rights and is particularly solicitous of the rights of political and religious dissenters, criminal defendants, and so on—the entire panoply of policy positions that identifies a contemporary judge as "liberal."[8] As such, an empathizing Court is a liberal Court.[9] And a conservative Court is heartless. It seems clear to me that contemporary conservatives are attacking selective liberal empathy—something that is apparent not only in these political conflicts, but in politicized "empathy" scholarship in the legal academy.[10]

There is, incidentally, no better case of the term "empathy" being used as a synonym for liberalism (as conservatives understand perfectly) than West's exemplar of the empathetic judge, Judge J. Skelly Wright.

2. J. SKELLY WRIGHT: SCIENTIST

Judge Wright was a southerner from New Orleans who grew up poor and who struggled economically during the Great Depression.[11] As the first district judge to place a school board under an injunction ordering a desegregation plan and, in turn, the first district judge to draw up his own desegregation plan in the face of inaction by a board, Wright was a pioneer in wielding judicial power aggressively to advance social reform.[12] He was also a staunch defender of Warren Court activism.[13]

Wright certainly described the process of judging in a way that one suspects West would celebrate. "Courts," Wright wrote in a prominent article in the *Cornell Law Review*, "are concerned with the flesh and blood of an actual case. This tends to modify, perhaps to lengthen, everyone's view. It also provides an extremely salutary proving ground for all abstractions; it is conducive, in a phrase of Holmes, to thinking things, not words, and thus to the evolution of a principle by a process that tests as it creates."[14] Thomas Grey has described Wright as a judge "with a stronger than usual sense of substance over form."[15] Michael Bernick described him as a judge with "the ability to pierce through formalisms, and the innumerable complexities and subtleties, to see the essential truths within."[16] Arthur Miller described Wright as harboring "an abiding sense of injustice" and as "adher[ing] to a personal conception of justice." In conversations with Miller, Wright described his judicial philosophy simply: "I try to do what's right."[17]

Wright defended this approach and distinguished it from the more abstracted "scholarly tradition" of the legal process school that challenged the Warren Court and its methods. His chief target was Alexander Bickel, the author of *The Supreme Court and the Idea of Progress*, who, Wright argued, in insisting upon the reasoned and value-neutral application of abstract rules and principles, was instructing judges to be "insensitive to the legitimate claims of the powerless" and to rule in ways that advanced the interests of the wealthy and powerful.[18] Bickel's charge was, in effect, that the Warren Court had pursued empathy instead of following (pursuant to its duties) the dictates of reason.[19] Wright emphasized in particular the "fatally unrealistic" nature of the "neutral principles" approach to constitutional adjudication of Bickel and his compatriot Herbert Wechsler, which insisted that the Court hew strictly to the dictates of abstract principle—which Wright argued was impossible. Bickel then added that, if those dictates could not be followed in their purest form, the Court should simply decline to decide the case. Wright characterized this approach as "damned-if-you-do, damned-if-you-don't." It would result, Wright argued, in a situation in which "the rest of us would be left to our own devices in exercising our constitutional rights and liberties."[20]

But, although he himself would strenuously deny the charge,[21] Wright was no less concerned with forging and maintaining the broader regulatory system than the types of judges West criticizes.

His bottom line, however, was not efficiency but egalitarianism. For Wright, the job of courts was to be aggressive enforcers of community ideals. A passionate defender down the line of the Warren Court's egalitarian activism, he insisted that "Today, the most important of those ideals is political equality" and trumpeted that Court's advancement of "the egalitarian ideal."[22]

West takes Wright's opinion in *Williams v. Walker-Thomas* as the quintessence of a judge doing case-specific, party-centered justice. But, actually, his focus in that opinion is on framing Mrs. Williams as a representative of her economic status and education level— that is, in fitting her into the system that he is concerned with and trying to reform. West misses this.[23] Wright himself believed in systems regulation. Tellingly, in contrasting the activism of the pre–New Deal conservative Court to that of the Warren Court, Wright himself wrote: "The Nine Old Men were trying to halt a revolution in the role of *government as a social instrument,* while the Warren Court is obviously furthering that effort."[24] In contrasting Wright with law and economics school judging, for example, we have not a case of individualized justice versus a regulatory system but a case of dueling systems—one focused on efficiency, the other on egalitarianism. Of course, one can argue that, as a social value, efficiency is unfeeling and coldblooded, and egalitarianism is warm and empathetic. Is this what West really means when she says we are "a less empathic and less caring society"? But if West's argument is that—a lament for the lost egalitarian judge—I think we'd do better to shift the focus off judging as a process and onto the broader topic of empathy and political philosophy, acknowledging that both types of systems-regarding judging are simply instruments to achieving different systemic ends.

In fairness, I think there is more to West's argument than this. Unlike many other treatments of the topic, West's does a good job of not falling unreflectively into liberal/left clichés. In her critique of the new model of judging she is criticizing, West expressly notes that, while the nature of the approach she is condemning is perhaps most apparent in the paradigmatic law and economics judge, the same inclination is inherent in progressive/liberal legal realism, which conceptualizes law as a form of public policy and emphasizes its integral/constitutive relationship to the emergent modern administrative state.[25] In making this point—despite the fact that she thinks that Wright's ruling in *Williams v. Walker-Thomas* is an exception to this trend on the liberal/realist side, rather than yet another illustration of it—I think she is absolutely right.

Is Wright—who celebrated "government as a social instrument" and the role of judges as its helpmate—really that different from West's *bête noire*, the judge as "master of economics, statistics, and the slide rule, rather than the master of Blackstone or black-letter law?"[26] Not if we look to one of Wright's progenitors, Herbert Croly, who strikingly re-imaged the symbol of justice under a progressive state:

> Instead of having her eyes blindfolded, she would wear perched upon her nose a most searching and forbidding pair of spectacles, ones which combined the vision of a microscope, a telescope, and a photographic camera. Instead of holding scales in her hand, she might perhaps be figured as possessing a much more homely and serviceable set of tools. She would have a hoe with which to cultivate the social garden, a watering pot with which to refresh it, a barometer with which to measure the pressure of the social air, and the indispensible typewriter and filing cabinet with which to record the behavior of society.[27]

The paradigm shift within law to a focus on systems, as opposed to individuals, is of enormous significance. Historically, it is a major progressive—not conservative—accomplishment, a process that has been brilliantly detailed by the intellectual historian Thomas Haskell. What we are really talking about, I'm afraid—since West has mixed in this concept of "the decline of empathy"—is the invention of the modern social sciences and the proposition that they would be of use to an activist, problem-solving, modern regulatory state that, of necessity, treats people less as individuals and more as aggregates. It is this that bumped off common-law legalism and Blackstone.[28] To say that this paradigm change was the death knell of empathy, of course, is to get things almost precisely backwards. Populists and progressives intended to create a state that cared. But the modern state's method was to be scientific, and individualism of the sort that West ostensibly wants to reclaim—as prior to the advent of civil libertarianism and the fictions that the progressive state found necessary to sustain its ongoing anti-individualist strains—clearly got in the way.[29]

There are important ways in which this paradigm shift involved the sometimes ruthless suspension of empathy in service of the system—for ostensibly progressive ends. I illustrate this at length in my book *Constructing Civil Liberties*. In my chapter detailing the ways in which the traditional common law (and constitutional law) of labor was dismantled to make space for labor unions in the modern, progressive, interest-group liberal state, I demonstrate the nature of this anti-empathetic turn in service of the weak, powerless, and excluded (the progenitors of Ms. Williams).[30] I use the Supreme Court's neglected Norris LaGuardia Act decisions as one of my primary illustrations. *Senn v. Tile Layer's Union* is a case in point well worth downing as an antidote to misunderstanding *Williams v. Walker-Thomas* as a supposed paradigmatic instance of judicial empathy.[31]

The *Senn* case involved the legality of picketing, which destroyed the company of a (very) small businessman. Paul Senn ran his Milwaukee tile-laying company mostly out of his home, did a significant amount of the work with his own hands (though he employed a handful of journeymen and helpers, depending on the amount of work available), and barely made enough money to support his wife and four children—all the more difficult during the depths of the Great Depression. His business was initially not unionized. It became a target of the Milwaukee's Tile Layer's Union, whose objective was to fully unionize the city's tile-laying industry. Notably, the objective of unionizing Senn came from outside the company; it was not sought by his employees, who were by all accounts happy with the way things were. But a union-based order required that all individuals in the industry be folded into the ordering collectivities of the system so that the unionized businesses were not undercut in the tile-laying market: to sustain the system, wages, hours, working conditions, and so forth had be standardized.

Remarkably, however, this was not a case of a company resisting unionization. Senn agreed to unionize his small company and to follow all the benchmark standards of the system. The snag, though, was that that system required the hermetic separation of "labor" from "management" for systemic regulatory purposes. The Tile Layer's Union demanded that Senn totally refrain from doing any more of the tile-laying work with his own hands; that is, that he re-adjust the nature of the work he did personally so as to become unambiguously "management" and not "labor." This, Senn insisted, he simply could not afford to do. The union then set upon him to drive him out of business, with picketing and other forms of direct action that sought to tar his business with the label "unfair to labor." Traditionally, Senn would have had common-law protections against this type of injury to his business. But the Norris LaGuardia Act was aimed at eliminating those protections to promote unionization. In a bone-chilling piece of systems analysis, Justice Louis Brandeis dismissed the notion that empathy for Senn's plight was in any way relevant to the Court's decision: the modern world needed to be organized according to collectivities, and, as the world was remade anew, Senn's suffering was simply a bump in the road.

One can find empathy in abundance—with a heavy focus on the parties to the case itself, however—in the dissents by Justices Pierce Butler, Willis Van Devanter, James McReynolds, and George Sutherland—tribunes of the legal order whose demise West (unwittingly?) seems, in her chapter, to lament. How, I wonder, does this case and those like it (many of which I discuss in *Constructing Civil Liberties*) relate to the supposed imperative of empathy in judging of which many seem to be so fond? Should this case be paired with *Williams v. Walker-Thomas*? I think the dissents in *Senn* —with their moralism and paternalism—are actually a better case of what West purports to be describing (with her patent nostalgia for the "Blackstonian" common-law legal order) than Wright's opinion, which I see as very much in the Brandeisian tradition.

It should go without saying, of course, that no one was more influential in effectuating the "shift away from a paradigm of moral judging to scientific judging" than Louis D. Brandeis. Should he be the villain in West's story? Or does he get a pass because his ultimate objectives were egalitarian?

Of course, as the story moved on from progressivism to liberalism, things developed further. Let me propose another villain in the move away from the Blackstonian common-law model celebrated by West—the public-law litigation movement, including Charles Hamilton Houston, Thurgood Marshall, the NAACP Inc. Fund (which Wright knew well and supported), and, more generally, the entire public-law litigation movement, as brilliantly anatomatized in a famous *Harvard Law Review* article by Abram Chayes.[32]

The whole point of this form of litigation, as Chayes lucidly explained, is to abstract from the parties to the lawsuits themselves and to draft them into service as vehicles for leveraging the courts to initiate significant, system-wide changes in public policy.

3. The Traditional Judge

This raises for me a basic question: who is this creature that West is yearning for here, the traditional empathetic judge? Were nineteenth-century American judges, in their focus on the specific cases and application of traditional common-law legal categories, really more understanding and/or empathetic? Were they more in touch with their "viscera," emotions, and feelings than modern judges?[33] If, as West pleads, "one must also know something about feelings of loss: what does it *feel* like to lose the use of a hand or to lose even just a slight possibility of years of life?"[34] to be a good judge in cases like *Hawkins v. McGee*, then are the pre–New Deal judges paragons of such feelings? If not, were they at least more willing—unlike modern judges—to bring whatever feelings they had to the table as an integral part of the process of deciding cases? If so, is this necessarily a good thing? Are Blackstone and black-letter law synonymous with "empathy"? I don't see this at all.

Who is this profoundly moral, imaginative, listening judge without paradigm, sensitive only to the individualized case and the people before him in all the richness of their humanity? When did he sit? He is (as Max Weber described the model and ideal) a *kadi* —a wise man under a tree (though Martin Shapiro details how even the actual *kadis* didn't really fit the picture).[35] He is Solomon.

4. The System Is the Empathy: The New Deal

Let me nominate a Solomon for our time, albeit a fictional one, depicted on film. William Wellman's remarkable (pre-Code) *Wild Boys of the Road* (1933) culminates in a courtroom scene in which an initially nonempathetic judge—with the National Recovery Administration's Blue Eagle emblem looking down over his shoulder —pulls back from the brink of a hard, law-like decision and rules in a case-specific, compassionate, human way.[36] The film is not just set during the Great Depression. It is all about the economic collapse and the enormous human cost it entailed. The movie's heroes are two mischievous but warmhearted small-town teenage boys whose parents lose their jobs to the economic cataclysm. Not wanting to be a burden to their families, which can no longer support them, the boys, in a cross-country odyssey, join an army of others in hitting the rails, hopping freights looking for work. They soon meet a girl of about their age—dressed as a boy—in a boxcar, and she becomes their boon companion. Along the way, life is hard, but the three are strong: they face down railyard bulls, inhabit squatter camps (and, briefly, a Chicago brothel, while bedding down temporarily with the girl's prostitute aunt)—until, inevitably, they are driven out by police (in one scene—but certainly not all—the police are portrayed as empathetic to the teenagers' plight: "How do you think I feel?" snaps one. "I have kids at home myself."). But the police turn on the fire hoses nonetheless, and the trio is forced to move on yet again. Along the way, one of them (Tommy) loses his leg to a freight train and must hobble about on a makeshift crutch (Tommy's life is saved by a doctor who is willing to treat him for free, after the kids rouse the doctor at his home late at night; he amputates Tommy's leg, not in a hospital but—without anesthesia, outside, by the light of a bonfire—in a squatter's camp).

The film's youthful protagonists end up living with hundreds of others in a New York City shantytown and set out to look for work. Remarkably, the other boy, Eddie, finds a job as an elevator operator. There's a catch, though. He must buy an alpaca coat to work the job, and he needs to do so immediately. Desperate, Eddie hits the streets to panhandle. The girl (Sally) tap-dances on the sidewalks of Manhattan for coins. And then, in what finally seems like his big break, two men offer to give Eddie more than the amount he needs if he will go across the street to a movie theatre cashier, hand her a note, and bring them the box she will give him (the men tell the credulous Eddie that the cashier is a relative of theirs, with whom they can't be seen). Of course, the note demands the cashbox, the teller screams, and Eddie—on the cusp of at long last finding work—is arrested.

This is how he comes before a judge, in a New York City juvenile court. The apparently stern judge seems to regard Eddie and his friends as petty criminals. He asks for some basic facts: what are your names? Who are your parents? Where do you live? They tell him nothing. If they are going to be that way, the judge lectures them sternly, the law gives him no choice but to lock them up. "Tell me the whole story," the judge pleads. "Let me be your friend. I want to help you."

Sure you do, Eddie says, with dripping skepticism. But soon he breaks down, launching into a bitter, heartbreaking lament about riding the rails and homelessness, and the spreading joblessness, and his despair, and the despair of others across the country, before dissolving in tears. The camera then pans up to the wall behind the judge as Eddie weeps: we see the Blue Eagle emblem, bold and proud, with its inscribed motto— "We Do Our Part." The judge has clearly been affected (after this scene, he goes into his chambers and gazes at an autographed photo on his desk reading "To Dad" from his own teenage son, whose image, we learn, was weighing on his heart and mind during this moving courtroom moment with Eddie). "I'm going to do my part. Now I want you to do yours," the judge tells Eddie. "I know that things are going to get better soon," he tells them, in an apparent allusion to the New Deal. "We'll find a spot for you. You'll all be given a chance." He promises to get all three of them jobs and to help them to eventually reunite with their families.

The liberal judge in this case is clearly the picture of empathy —which the courtroom scene underlines. But, ultimately, the boys will be saved by the system itself. They will be integrated into it through the programs of the New Deal. All—government officials, businesses (proudly displaying the Blue Eagle logo), and ordinary people—will commit to doing their part to support the new system against the old common-law order. It is the system itself that is compassionate and empathetic. In the modern world, this is how things are done.

5. CONCLUSION

Wild Boys of the Road, a moving film, is ultimately hopeful—a paean to the promise of the emerging social welfare state. But it, of course, elides some of the more tragic elements of building systems and the perhaps paradoxical movement away from treating people as individuals in service of a more secure, more equal, future.[37] Cases like *Senn* are needed to give us a fuller picture. This modern state was forged in a hail of economic, political, and moral crises: depressions, wars, social movements for group equality. Its aims may have been, in part, compassionate. But it involved systems-building in service of those aims, with all of the focus on statistics and aggregates the construction of any elaborate regulatory system entails. Its reimagination of the nature of the judicial process was an important part of that process.

The old Blackstonian common-law order that West looks back upon wistfully was hardly empathetic, nor were its judges more in touch with their emotions or those of the parties appearing before them.[38] As the legal modernists who sought to replace it with more progressive, policy-focused understandings recognized, the concerns for power and equality had to be embedded as animating features of the activist modern administrative state. Far from entailing a movement from formalism to an open, experimental pragmatism (at least in any simple sense), it involved a displacement of one set of value-laden legal formalisms by others.[39] In many respects a product of the Great Depression itself, Wright— in fact, not much older than the suffering teenage protagonists whose plight was portrayed in *Wild Boys of the Road*—was thoroughly convinced that, in decisions in cases like *Williams v. Walker-Thomas*, he was moving beyond ideology, aggregates, and systems toward ruling simply on an individualized, case-specific basis—to doing, as he explained, "what's right." Naturally, many law professors sharing Wright's substantive political views and outlook, looking back on his career, see it exactly the same way.

But Wright's words about using government—and law—as a "social instrument" betray his misapprehension of the nature of his own endeavors. With hindsight, we should be able to see this nature a lot more clearly. If Wright appears more empathetic, it is because the substantive and systematic political ideology in whose crucible his views were forged and of which he is a paradigmatic judicial exemplar is, as a system, with its own (sometimes rigid, even blinding) categories and formalisms, more empathetic. It is not because Wright heard each case on its own, unique terms, understanding it richly and fully, intellectually, and emotionally, as a prelude to doing "what's right," like some latter-day *kadi* or Solomon—or as wise, Blackstonian common-law judges once did in some dimly imagined—but possibly retrievable?—days of old.

NOTES

Douglas Hassett, BC '11, provided research assistance and helpful conversation. Dustin Sebell provided additional research assistance.

1. Robin West, "The Anti-Empathic Turn," in this volume.
2. Williams v. Walker-Thomas Furniture Co., 350 F. 2d 445 (D.C. Cir. 1965).
3. Robert C. Post, "Defending the Lifeworld: Substantive Due Process in the Taft Court Era," *Boston University Law Review* 78 (1998): 1489–1545.
4. West, "The Anti-Empathic Turn," 243.
5. Ibid., 244.
6. Ibid., 245.
7. See Susan A. Bandes, "Empathetic Judging and the Rule of Law," *Cardozo Law Review De Novo* (2009): 133–148; Susan A. Bandes, "Empathy, Narrative, and Victim Impact Statements," *University of Chicago Law Review* 63 (1996): 361–412.
8. See Jeffrey A. Segal and Harold J. Spaeth, *The Supreme Court and the Attitudinal Model Revisited* (New York: Cambridge University Press, 2002).
9. See, e.g., Morton J. Horwitz, *The Warren Court and the Pursuit of Justice* (New York: Hill and Wang, 1999).
10. See, e.g., Lynne N. Henderson, "Legality and Empathy," *Michigan Law Review* 85 (1986–1987): 1574–1653.
11. John Minor Wisdom, "J. Skelly Wright," *Loyola Law Review* 32 (1986): 303–310.
12. See J. W. Peltason, *Fifty-Eight Lonely Men: Southern Federal Judges and School Desegregation* (Urbana: University of Illinois Press, 1971), 221–243; Michael S. Bernick, "The Unusual Odyssey of J. Skelly Wright," *Hastings Constitutional Law Quarterly* 7 (1979–1980): 971–999.
13. Wisdom, "J. Skelly Wright," *passim.* See also Arthur S. Miller, *A 'Capacity for Outrage': The Judicial Odyssey of J. Skelly Wright* (Westport, CT: Greenwood Press, 1984) (foreword by William J. Brennan).
14. J. Skelly Wright, "The Role of the Supreme Court in a Democratic Society—Judicial Activism or Restraint?" *Cornell Law Review* (1968): 1–28, 13. The process Wright describes here is a good articulation of philosophical pragmatism, in which principles are defined only through their application to fully apprehended real-world facts. See John Dewey, *The Quest for Certainty: A Study of the Relation of Knowledge and Action* (New York: Minton, Balch, 1929); John Dewey, *Experience and Nature* (London: Allen and Unwin, 1929). This raises the question of the degree to which pragmatism can be defined (or misapprehended) as a form of empathy in a way that is distinguishable from more categorical, deductive forms of philosophical

inquiry into the nature and application of principles. See also J. Skelly Wright, "Professor Bickel, the Scholarly Tradition, and the Supreme Court," *Harvard Law Review* 84 (1971): 769–805. I would note that Holmes himself, though often characterized as a pragmatist, is hardly known for his empathy—though, interestingly, liberals once misperceived him as a supreme empathizer. See, e.g., Catherine Drinker Bowen, *Yankee from Olympus: Justice Holmes and His Family* (Boston: Little, Brown, 1955). See Albert W. Alschuler, *Law without Values: The Life, Work, and Legacy of Justice Holmes* (Chicago: University of Chicago Press, 2002).

15. Thomas C. Grey, "J. Skelly Wright," *Hastings Constitutional Law Quarterly* 7 (1979–1980): 873–877, 874.

16. Bernick, "The Unusual Odyssey of J. Skelly Wright," 999.

17. Miller, *Capacity for Outrage*, 3–4, 7.

18. Wright, "Professor Bickel, the Scholarly Tradition, and the Supreme Court," 769–805.

19. Ibid., 772.

20. Ibid., 777, 778, 782. Herbert Wechsler, "Toward Neutral Principles of Constitutional Law," *Harvard Law Review* 73 (1959): 1.

21. See Wright, "Professor Bickel, the Scholarly Tradition, and the Supreme Court," 789–795.

22. Wright, "The Role of the Supreme Court in a Democratic Society," 23.

23. See Muriel Morisey Spence, "Teaching *Williams v. Walker-Thomas Furniture Co.*," *Temple Political and Civil Rights Law Review* 3 (1993–1994): 89–105.

24. Wright, "The Role of the Supreme Court in a Democratic Society," 2.

25. Holmes, "The Path of the Law," *Harvard Law Review* 10 (1897): 457.

26. West, "The Anti-Empathic Turn," 249.

27. Herbert Croly, *Progressive Democracy* (New York: Macmillan, 1914), 369.

28. Thomas L. Haskell, *The Emergence of Professional Social Science: The American Social Science Association and the Nineteenth Century Crisis of Authority* (Urbana: University of Illinois Press, 1977).

29. This is a central theme of my book *Constructing Civil Liberties: Discontinuities in the Development of American Constitutional Law* (New York: Cambridge University Press, 2004).

30. Ibid., 134–234.

31. *Senn v. Tile Layer's Union*, 301 U.S. 468 (1937).

32. Abram Chayes, "The Role of the Judge in Public Law Litigation," *Harvard Law Review* 89 (1976): 1281.

33. See Carol Sanger, "The Role and Reality of Emotions in Law,"

William and Mary Journal of Women and the Law 8 (2001–2002): 107–113. There seems to be no absence of "viscera" in either the opinions of judges of an earlier era, or of contemporary conservative judges, if the expression of disgust is any measure of the presence of emotion in judging. See, e.g., *Reynolds v. United States*, 98 U.S. 145 (1878); *Bowers v. Hardwick*, 478 U.S. 186 (1986). Justice Scalia, for one, seems very much in touch with his inner moralist. See generally Martha C. Nussbaum, *From Disgust to Humanity: Sexual Orientation and Constitutional Law* (New York: Oxford University Press, 2010); William Ian Miller, *The Anatomy of Disgust* (Cambridge, MA: Harvard University Press, 1997). See also Barrington Moore Jr., *Moral Purity and Persecution in History* (Princeton, NJ: Princeton University Press, 2000).

34. West, "The Anti-Empathic Turn," 245.

35. Max Weber, *Economy and Society* (New York: Bedminster Press, 1968); Martin Shapiro, *Courts: A Comparative and Political Analysis* (Chicago: University of Chicago Press, 1986).

36. *Wild Boys of the Road* (d. William A. Wellman) (1933).

37. It might be useful in this regard to consider what John Stuart Mill —negatively reflecting on his father and Jeremy Bentham (of course a great enemy of the common law and a clear proponent of the modern state)—referred to as the "dissolving influence of analysis." Mill, *Autobiography* (New York: Columbia University Press, 1924) (chapter titled "A Crisis in My Mental History"). This is very much about the role of feelings in imagination and understanding, something Mill tells us he neglected in his commitment to liberal reform to the point of total mental collapse—a profound mental depression.

38. See Stephen Skowronek, *Building the New American State: The Expansion of National Administrative Capacities, 1877–1920* (Cambridge: Cambridge University Press, 1982); Karen Orren, *Belated Feudalism: Labor, the Law, and Liberal Development in the United States* (Cambridge: Cambridge University Press, 1991); Victoria Hattam, *Labor Visions and State Power: The Origins of Business Unionism in the United States* (Princeton, NJ: Princeton University Press, 1993).

39. Kersch, *Constructing Civil Liberties*.

11

ANTI-EMPATHY AND DISPASSIONATENESS IN ADJUDICATION

BENJAMIN C. ZIPURSKY

1. Introduction

Robin West's depiction of the anti-empathic turn in adjudication[1] is credible, detailed, and depressing. Most striking is the contrast she draws between the pervasive historical acceptance of the importance of empathy in a great judge and the prevalence of an anti-empathic jurisprudence today. I agree with West on several of her important claims: that this shift has occurred and that it is unfortunate that it has occurred; that Judge Skelly Wright's decision in *Williams v. Walker-Thomas Furniture Co.*[2] is defensible and commendable; that empathy has an important epistemic role in adjudication; and that moral principles underlie the common law and that a scientistic turn has moved us away from these principles. Nevertheless, there are several junctures at which I disagree with Professor West's rich and provocative essay, and so I shall begin by setting forth two of my disagreements. The latter part of this commentary highlights two especially valuable contributions of Professor West's article, aiming to push them further than West has done. In her eagerness to defend the role of empathy in adjudication, Professor West has embraced a sort of rationalism that purports to show why empathy is critical to legal reasoning. While the first part of this response raises questions about whether empathy is as critical to legal reasoning as she asserts, the latter part suggests that empathy may sometimes be significant in adjudication in legitimate and important ways that should not necessarily count as part of legal reasoning itself.

2. The Role of Empathy in Legal Interpretation

West appears to depend upon two different arguments for the epistemological claim that empathy is necessary in adjudication. One is that analogical reasoning requires empathy, and a second is that traditional common-law reasoning is rooted in particularistic, backward-looking reasoning from moral principles and that reasoning of this type requires the utilization of moral sense, which, in turn, requires empathy.

Let's start with analogy. West argues that judges must answer questions about whether there is sufficient similarity between two distinct things in order to engage in analogical reasoning, which is in turn required to answer legal questions like: "Is the doctor's promise to make the hand whole enough like the manufacturer's promise that the machine will work that it makes sense to view both of these promises as *warranties*?"[3] In order to do so, she writes,

> one must also know something about feelings of loss: what does it *feel* like to lose the use of a hand or to lose even just a slight possibility of years of life? One must know something about pain: what might that injury feel like? How does it feel to be denied something that was promised? One must know something about desire, and need, and frustration: what is the basis of the need or desire to marry, to have one's intimate relations sanctified by the state as well as by religious authority? How does it feel to be denied something important because of an "immutable characteristic"? One must know something about the subjective feel of promising, and of warranting, and of diagnosing, and of discriminating.[4]

She then concludes: "Analogous reasoning by definition seemingly requires empathic understanding, at least where it is people's utterly subjective situations, problems, fears, anxieties, suffering, opportunities, dreams, and foibles from which and to which one is analogizing."[5]

There are two problems with this argument. First, part of what reasoning by analogy involves is selecting commonalities between two superficially different kinds of things. For better or worse, the commonalities selected are typically objective features. Moreover, the grounds for deeming the commonalities sufficiently similar to warrant the same legal treatment typically involve a principle that engages the diverse scenario in similar ways. It is simply not clear why it is relevant to know what it would feel like to have a damaged hand in ascertaining its similarity to a defective machine.

The second problem is greater than the first, for perhaps Professor West simply chose an unfortunate example. Even if we assume that it is important to be able to reflect on what it feels like to have a damaged hand, it is not clear why empathy is required for that. Each judge will likely have had some body part damaged. One can hear the plaintiff's arguments and refer to one's own experiences. One need not feel the plaintiff's pain in order to know what it feels like. Part of why we want judges to be experienced people is that we want them to be able to refer to their own subjective states in order to form an idea of what the plaintiff is describing. Empathizing involves experiencing, in a vicarious manner, what others experience. Being able to grasp intellectually the features of another's experience by using one's own as a basis is quite a different thing.

A more general version of this second problem is that excellence in empathic powers is more important for *discovering* attributes of the fact patterns than it is for *grasping or understanding* the facts or attributes alleged. Unlike, for example, therapists or counselors or friends or perhaps lawyers, judges—especially at the appellate level—need not discover the facts but must rather appreciate the facts as they have already been articulated and perhaps demonstrated. Now, of course, it is *possible* for persons to be so lacking in empathic abilities that they are literally incapable of even understanding or grasping attributes that lawyers or lower courts have alleged—they are unable to get their minds around the way another person might feel—and, in this sense, perhaps it is true that empathy is essential in adjudication. But the absence of empathy at this level is almost a psychological deficit or disorder, and there is no reason to believe that judges who are praised for not yielding to empathy are people with a deficit like this.

The second argument is developed by reference to *Williams* and unconscionability doctrine:

> [*B*]*oth* the backward-looking, particularistic, and moralistic ground of the unconscionability decision *and* the forward-looking paternalistic rule that might follow from it on the traditional model should be informed by the judge's moral sense—and, hence, in part, by moral emotions and moral sentiments, including both empathy and sympathy. The judge might or might not be morally repulsed by the parties' behavior. He won't know, however, whether or not the behavior is morally objectionable unless he can empathize with both parties to the transaction and then register a stronger sympathetic response to either one or the other. That's just the nature of the beast. If the commercial behavior of this retailer was shocking to the conscience, it was so because of the unreasonably exploitative nature of the seller's tactics and the overexposure of the buyer to excessive and unreasonable risk, as well as excessive and unreasonable costs of default.[6]

There are two ways to interpret this passage: narrowly and broadly. On the narrow reading, we might understand Professor West to be making the point that the concept of unconscionability in the law has a moral-emotional nature to it, such that a person cannot discern its absence or presence without exercising something in the nature of moral-emotional faculty. The broad reading starts from a proposition concerning the nature of a faculty of moral judgment; a faculty of moral judgment simply is a moral sense, and moral emotions, including empathy, are an integral part of that.

The narrower view is plausible, but it has two problems. The first is that it appears to beg the question before Wright—whether the unconscionability doctrine is part of the common law and whether it should be—rather than whether (assuming that it is) there is unconscionability in this particular case. It is the metaquestion that troubles the economists, not the first-order factual question. Assuming that human beings have the power to "sense" an attribute of moral repulsiveness with a certain degree of accuracy, the question is whether that moral repulsiveness meter should be used to strike contracts. It is not at all obvious to me that one needs the meter to make that judgment call. The larger problem is that unconscionability is, on its face, morally subjectivistic, and most legal concepts and moral concepts are not like this at all.

The difficulty with West's broader view is that it is simply highly contentious as a matter of moral epistemology. It is one thing to say that one's understanding of a particular set of interactions requires grasping the facts in all their complexity and that doing so requires maturity of judgment and a well-honed sensibility, including a variety of emotional sensitivities. It is quite another to depict moral judgment as a special power whose deliverances have a kind of subjective feel like moral repulsion. The latter is far too narrow a view of how moral judgments fit into patterns of justification and explanation, how they are expressed, and how they are developed. I do not think Professor West means to embrace a form of moral intuitionism that posits a moral emotional power, but the form of the argument she puts forward suggests that sort of view.

3. The Rejection of Moral Reasoning and the Rise of the Scientistic Role

West makes no bones about her dislike of the Holmesian world of legal thinking that we have watched unfold over the past century. She blames Holmes and his scientistic disciples for the anti-empathic turn.

> Beginning with Holmes's pithy declarations on the topic, continuing through a good bit of legal realist writing, and now in a wide swath of contemporary law and economics scholarship, twentieth-century legal scholars have urged, in opposition to traditional understandings of the goals of adjudication, that net social welfare, particularly as created through voluntarist transactions, should be the goal that judges should pursue when deciding common-law cases of tort and contract, rather than the vindication of moral principle or the protection of parties from their own worst instincts or from the actions of private actors who would take advantage of them. . . . [A] somewhat less noted consequence of our journey down this particular Holmesian path of the law has been a redefinition of basic common-law concepts and categories away from their natural language and moral or moralistic meanings and toward an amalgam of the purely positivistically legal and the social-scientific.[7]

As to this point, I bring Professor West happy news from the world of tort theory; we are all over this issue. The past twenty-five years of common-law theory in general and tort theory in particular have been, if nothing else, a sustained attack on the reductive instrumentalism of Holmes and his followers—both the high-end followers in the law and economics movement in legal academia and the lower-end followers in the American Law Institute and the treatise writers. My co-author John Goldberg and I have taken Judge Cardozo as the champion of a progressive and pragmatic conception of adjudication that is nevertheless backward looking and takes moral concepts and the common law seriously.

And, yet, for reasons that should now be evident, it is not clear that the Holmesians brought about the anti-empathic turn in quite the way Professor West describes; there is a competing account of how the anti-empathic turn came about. A standard riff of defenders of empathy and emotion in adjudication is to distinguish true empathy-contribution cases from those in which the affective contribution of emotion is entirely noncognitive—feeling bad for the powerless litigant and therefore siding with the little-guy plaintiff in a civil case against a rich company or feeling bad for the criminal defendant against the mighty government. In these cases, the judge as a human being is motivated or drawn to jump to one litigant's side of the issue because the judge feels bad for that litigant or because the judge *feels for that litigant.* But, argues West, following Bandes,[8] Henderson,[9] and many others, empathy can contribute in other ways to the justifiability of a decision: it can make a cognitive contribution, not simply an affective one.

Nevertheless, candor requires that we say much more about the role that sympathy and empathy have played in American legal history over the past fifty years. And I think Professor West's account of the reasons for the anti-empathic turn are incomplete without a more fulsome review of what occurred. Judges like Skelly Wright during the 1960s and 1970s were progressives who felt the pain of the litigants. Just because it is philosophically cogent to understand empathic responses as connected to an awareness of reasons that generate justifications of a sort whose soundness can be demonstrated in nonaffective terms, it does not follow that these judges did not sometimes decide as they did because of sympathy for one side or the other. It strikes me as simply unrealistic to deny that Justice Brennan and Justice Marshall and Justice Blackmun were, in part, political actors who sometimes aligned themselves with one side of a dispute because of a desire to help the weaker party.

Conversely, it seems to me important to admit that the judges on the other side often took their position because they were not so moved or because they were countermoved by other forces. Part of the anti-empathic backlash is plainly political, not simply jurisprudential. The view is that the Warren and Burger Courts' great expansions of constitutional rights were partly a feeling-based modification of the law; the powerless gained some power relative to the powerful because some of the decision makers in place were motivated by sympathy for the weak and disempowered as they faced off against the stronger and more established. My own view is that there is some truth in this characterization of what happened. Moreover, there are indeed institutional and constitutional concerns about those changes that merit serious consideration.

Perhaps this understates the concern. There is probably some truth in the charge that power was overused because of judges' faith in their own righteousness and the moral superiority of their judgments and opinions. Even assuming that this is true, however, the anti-empathic turn is a serious overreaction to a mindset that may have been, on some occasions, overly influenced by the judicial desire to make change in people's lives. To put it differently, progressives must face up to the consequences of their own confidence in the capacity of courts to realize progressive agendas through compassion-enhanced adjudication of constitutional rights. This agenda and its partial success are part of the reason for the anti-empathic turn. Moreover, in common-law areas, nationally prominent courts like the United States Court of Appeals for the District of Columbia and the California Supreme Court followed the United States Supreme Court's lead in taking an aggressive role in reshaping the law so that it better realized a progressive vision that takes seriously the needs and well-being of the weak, not just the strong.

Ironically, many of these inspiring progressive judges were themselves in the grip of the same Holmesian realism and forward-looking view as are today's law and economists. In other words, Holmesian realism about law was behind the trajectory of the law and legal scholarship in the 1960s and 1970s, *including its progressive aspect.* If this is what generated the anti-empathic turn, then West's claim that Holmesian thinking is the cause of the anti-empathic turn is correct, but not for (or not only for) the reasons she says.

4. ANTI-EMPATHY AND DISPASSIONATENESS

The name of Professor West's chapter—"The Anti-Empathic Turn" —is notable in two respects. One is that it belongs to a genre of academic titles, like Richard Rorty's "The Linguistic Turn,"[10] that signal a presentation of a piece of intellectual history and thereby help us to gain perspective. Another, which is both more important and more obvious, is the use of the neologism "anti-empathic." To my knowledge, Professor West has coined it. My visceral reaction to the phrase is roughly what it would be to the phrase "anti-children" or "pro-garbage." It is not actually oxymoronic or self-contradictory, but it is nearly anomalous to talk about an anti-empathy principle in adjudication. And that is plainly Professor West's point.

Of course, this is her word, not the word of those whom she is criticizing, and so perhaps she is exaggerating. I doubt it. What her phrase suggests is a risk that is surely worth confronting directly. The risk is that, even if the critique of 1960s progressive adjudication was in some ways justifiable, the countermovement is extremely dangerous. We have seen that, in constitutional theory, for example, while it is plausible that the Warren Court was too untethered from history, strict originalism is a startling and untenable overreaction. So, too, in the normative theory of adjudication more generally, including on the question of empathy. It is one thing to express skepticism of the view that adjudication of legal questions requires exercise of a moral sense and that empathy is the key to moral judgment and that moral judgment is the key to legal judgment. It is a wholly different thing to insist that judges expunge empathy from the set of capacities they use to engage in legal reasoning and in deciding cases.

Part of what President Obama saw in then-Judge Sotomayor was a normal person who was comfortable in her own skin and comfortable in human affairs, especially legal affairs. There was no vow on her part not to act as a person with a variety of intellectual capacities in judgment, including an awareness of what it is like to be in someone else's shoes. Unfortunately, by choosing the word "empathy," the president called to mind the critique of progressive activism, which I believe was not what he meant.

If all that were meant by the critique of his mention of empathy was a warning that freewheeling egalitarian justice-seeking faces some institutional competence concerns, that would be one thing. But the anti-empathy movement we see from the likes of Justice Scalia and once saw from Chief Justice Rehnquist has a different cast from this. It expresses a reverence for a certain sort of dispassionateness, a sort of studied and artificial resistance to aspects of judgment that display sensitivity to how people feel. This actually distorts the processes of legal judgment and moral judgment. The worry that a fact-finder cannot judge unconscionability without some exercise of empathic capacities is itself a reason for not having an unconscionability doctrine, on this sort of view. While I have my doubts about empathy as a moral sense and about the role of empathy in analogical reasoning, that is no reason to take an anti-empathic turn in legal or moral thinking. A powerful argument in favor of empathy is that an anti-empathic principle is artificial, destructive, and distortive as a practical maxim of adjudication.

5. MORE ROOM FOR EMPATHY AND COMPASSION

Finally, Professor West is absolutely right to raise questions about the institutional setting within which various sorts of reasoning are used, and her discussion of *Williams* from an institutional point of view is deeply insightful and illuminating. It is critical that Wright was asking the question of whether, *if* the trial judge found that the terms were unconscionable, the court could have declined to permit the plaintiff to enforce its alleged legal right. It is also important that this was not a claim for money damages but a claim to have a writ of replevin issued and actually to have things taken out of the defendant's home.[11] The question was, in part, whether powers akin to equitable powers and akin to powers used in granting injunctive relief are ones that the court could decline to exercise because of the sense that it was lending its power to the plaintiff's overreaching. That is a far narrower question than is typically attributed to *Williams*, and it is plainly a far less radical decision when understood this way.[12]

More important, courts have historically permitted and required a kind of discretion when allowing judicial power to be used to do things to people, rather than when it is simply a question of entering an award for money damages; indeed, an emotionally wide-gauged sense of equity is supposed to enter into decisions about injunctive relief. Although replevin is not generally subject to equitable defenses,[13] the question of how to conceptualize the role of unconscionability in an action for replevin and the relevance of overreaching are far more nuanced than that which the economists have brought to bear on *Williams.*

I would like to end on a larger note, however, and one that may seem to be somewhat self-contradictory. Empathy scholars—myself included—have tended to embrace a sort of rationalism: while it may be institutionally objectionable for sympathetic feelings toward a litigant's situation to have an impact on the judge, it is not objectionable for empathy as an epistemic power to enter the analysis—it is essential.[14] It seems to me now that this view concedes too much, in two different respects. First, there are situations in which an appropriate feeling for one of the litigants—for his or her hardship—may and perhaps should have an impact upon the judge's decision. This is true in various equitable cases, as I have mentioned. But it is true in a wide range of other cases where judges are specially empowered to play this sort of role; mercy in sentencing is a good example. Again, there are institutional reasons why we segment these decisions in different ways.

Even in high-level appellate adjudication where unreviewable interpretive decisions are made, it is hardly clear that the feelings of sympathy or empathy should have no role. The distinction between a feeling on the one hand and a source of knowledge on the other does not exhaust the possibilities. Often, emotional feelings that arise when a judge confronts a fact pattern or argument can have an impact of a quite different sort; they can lead the judge to feel that the right answer *must be* on a certain side, and this can lead him or her to dig deeper and think harder in the legal analysis. Compassion and empathy can be motivating forces. To put it differently, a passion for justice can motivate judges to make legal progress and moral progress. An empathic recognition of feelings of deprivation, injury, or oppression can lead to such a passion. If a judge is honest and faithful to the law, the desire to reach a certain result will not inevitably lead to that result. But, without empathy and compassion, we are far less likely to see a passion for justice. And, without a passion for justice, we are less likely to attain authentic interpretations of the law.

NOTES

1. Robin West, "The Anti-Empathic Turn," in this volume.
2. *Williams v. Walker-Thomas Furniture Co.*, 350 F.2d 445 (D.C. Cir. 1965).
3. West, "The Anti-Empathic Turn," 244 (emphasis in original).
4. Ibid., 245 (emphasis in original).
5. Ibid.
6. Ibid., 266–267 (emphasis in original).
7. Ibid. 271.
8. Susan Bandes, "Empathic Judging and the Rule of Law," *Cardozo Law Review De Novo* (2009): 133–148.
9. Lynne Henderson, "Legality and Empathy," *Michigan Law Review* 85 (1987): 1574–1654.
10. *The Linguistic Turn*, ed. Richard M. Rorty (Chicago: University of Chicago Press, 1992).
11. *Williams*, 350 F.2d at 447 ("[A]ppellee sought to replevy all the items purchased since December, 1957. The Court of General Sessions granted judgment for appellee. The District of Columbia Court of Appeals affirmed, and we granted appellants' motion for leave to appeal to this court.").
12. It should be recognized that Judge Skelly Wright himself used both weaker language emphasizing the permissibility of a lower court's decision not to enforce the contract ("[w]e do not agree that the court lacked the power to refuse enforcement to contracts found to be unconscionable," ibid., 448) and stronger language tending to suggest the lack of a valid contract ("we hold that where the element of unconscionability is present at the time a contract is made, the contract should not be enforced," ibid., 449). While the former suggests a narrower framework for thinking about the significance of the case, the latter suggests the broader one that has typically been followed in the literature interpreting the case.
13. Edward Yorio, *Contract Enforcement: Specific Performance and Injunctions* (New York: Aspen Law and Business,1989), 306.
14. Benjamin C. Zipursky, "*DeShaney* and the Jurisprudence of Compassion," *New York University Law Review* 65 (1990): 1101–1147.

12

EQUITY OVER EMPATHY

BERNADETTE MEYLER

In "The Anti-Empathic Turn,"[1] Robin West inquires what accounts for the contemporary aversion to judicial empathy, an aversion represented not only by the political right's response when President Obama extolled empathy but also by his own Supreme Court appointees' avoidance of the term.[2] West's conclusion connects the shift away from empathy to the rise of a scientific model of judging. Under this new paradigm, social science replaces moral judgment, calculation of future utility supplants backward-looking assessments of circumstances, rules overshadow particularism, and judging becomes assimilated to legislation.

Many features of this explanation are intuitively appealing and are borne out by examination of recent judicial rhetoric and practice. Nevertheless, I contend here that the set of dichotomies West propounds too readily conflates empathy with moral judgment and proper judicial reasoning with an assessment of actual, rather than hypothetical, factual scenarios. Furthermore, the binary pairs of empathy/scientism and particularism/rules do not always line up with each other in judicial practice. As a result, West's generalizations about the effects of the anti-empathic turn on actual judicial approaches do not adhere across the board and, most notably, contrast with the realities of constitutional decision making under the Roberts Court, which has frequently prioritized the more particularized, "as-applied" form of decision making over "facial" constitutionally based challenges, without even paying lip service to empathy. By instead disaggregating empathy from equity and focusing on the latter rather than the former, one can recover a form of judicial reasoning that captures many of the virtues of moral judgment while insisting upon a less stark distinction between judging and legislating and between assessments of the past and the future. At least certain versions of the practice of equity can also furnish a check against one of the downsides of empathy—excessive identification with the individual who has suffered, rather than comprehension of his or her plight.

From early in her piece, West associates empathy with the common law, asserting that "[i]t's particularly easy to see why empathic excellence has been such a familiar judicial ideal in a common-law system such as ours or, for that matter, in any system in which judges reason, at least much of the time, by way of analogy."[3] The primary legal example she addresses, that of unconscionability in contract law, likewise arises from a common-law context. At the same time, however, as West acknowledges, much of the family of contract-law doctrines to which unconscionability belongs—which also includes "undue influence, bad faith, duress, and constructive fraud"—"derive[s] from rules of equity."[4] To the extent that common law and equity were merged pursuant to the 1938 Federal Rules of Civil Procedure—a development advocated for and anticipated by David Dudley Field's partial procedural code in the nineteenth century—the distinction between the two today may be pragmatically irrelevant.[5] Nevertheless, the echoes of equity call up the deep-seated jurisprudential differences that this mode of adjudication long maintained with the common law. Within sixteenth- and seventeenth-century England, the jurisprudence of equity claimed to remedy the rigors of the common law, which was itself perceived as precisely the kind of rigid and rule-bound system that West eschews. Recalling the roots of equity allows the excavation of a particularized and ethically situated jurisprudence somewhat distinct from the emotionally based one of empathy, although certainly not diametrically opposed to it.

West's concentration on the common law also leads to a generalization that elides important recent developments in constitutional decision making. As she claims, "Most mainstream legal scholars—including liberal, progressive, and critical legal scholars —concur that adjudication should be forward looking and general and not limited to the particulars of the facts before it. Adjudication *should be*, in short, legislative in form and outlook."[6] This statement, while arguably perfectly applicable to contemporary decision making in common-law areas, conflicts to some extent with the Supreme Court's embrace under Chief Justice Roberts of what David Franklin has recently called "the traditional model of constitutional adjudication."[7] The traditional model suggests that "as-applied" challenges, where the Court considers the constitutionality of a statute or administrative action with respect to the parties and facts before it, constitute the prototype of constitutional adjudication and that "facial" challenges, where a law or section thereof is simply struck down, represent the exception.[8] In a number of recent cases involving areas like voting rights and abortion, the Roberts Court has expressed a distinct preference for this traditional model by deferring invalidation of legislative provisions to as-applied challenges that might possibly arise at a later date.[9]

On the basis of the argument of "The Anti-Empathic Turn," this seems like a development West should applaud, despite its association with a Supreme Court presided over by John Roberts, the very person who analogized judges to umpires at his confirmation hearing, a comparison that has come to represent the opposite of the empathic position. Indeed, one of the principal reasons for prioritizing as-applied over facial challenges pertains to a distinction between the judicial and the legislative roles. Although, as Gillian Metzger has observed, the various justices' rationales for their stances on facial and as-applied challenges differ widely,[10] the Court's recent statements about the subject suggest a coherent view concerning the respective forms of empirical analysis in which a court and a legislature should engage and, furthermore, the guise that the results of those empirical analyses should take within the text of a statute. Furthermore, this vision correlates with what West deems appropriate for adjudication as opposed to legislation, largely involving the assessment of empirical situations that have already transpired.

The principal areas that have been affected by the disfavor into which facial challenges have fallen are abortion and voting rights.[11] In the 2007 partial-birth abortion case, *Gonzales v. Carhart*,[12] Justice Anthony Kennedy's opinion for the Court continually emphasized that it was rejecting the "broad, facial attack" brought against

Congress's enactment. Likewise, in two voting rights cases decided the following year, *Washington State Grange v. Washington State Republican Party*[13] and *Crawford v. Marion County Election Bd.*,[14] the Court again insisted that facial challenges would be viewed skeptically. Rejecting the facial challenge to the law at issue in *Washington State Grange* because the statute possessed a "plainly legitimate sweep," Justice Thomas's majority opinion placed weight upon the fact that "[r]espondents object[ed]" to the law "not in the context of an actual election, but in a facial challenge."[15] Partly because the consequences of the legislation had not been established through the analysis of a concrete election event, the facts necessary for determining the potential unconstitutionality of certain applications of the law were not available for judicial perusal. As-applied challenges could, like facial ones, be brought pre-enforcement. Nevertheless, as Caitlin Borgmann has argued, the preference that the Roberts Court has expressed for as-applied challenges appears to map onto the demand for a showing of actual harm.[16]

The consequences of this approach are demonstrated most tangibly by Justice Kennedy's opinion for the Court in *Carhart*. The Court's prior cases had urged that, when the states or the federal government acted to legislatively restrict the availability of abortion, the resulting statutes were obliged to provide exceptions to the general rule for cases in which the health of a woman might be endangered by the absence of an abortion or the prohibition of a particular method of procuring one. As Justice Ginsburg explained the earlier decisions in her dissenting opinion in *Carhart*, "In keeping with this comprehension of the right to reproductive choice, the Court has consistently required that laws regulating abortion, at any stage of pregnancy and in all cases, safeguard a woman's health."[17] Although the law at issue in *Carhart*, the Partial-Birth Abortion Act of 2003, permitted an exception from criminal sanction for doctors performing an abortion "necessary to save the life of a mother," it did not contain a more comprehensive provision covering situations in which the health of the mother might be endangered short of a threat to her life. According to Justice Kennedy's opinion, this absence was insufficient to invalidate the statute on a facial challenge.

In justifying this conclusion, Justice Kennedy relied heavily upon a particular conception of legislative evaluation of empirical evidence and judicial assessment of necessity in specific cases. As he contended, citing to the opinions of experts on both sides of the question, "[t]here is documented medical disagreement whether the Act's prohibition would ever impose significant health risks on women."[18] The conclusion from this disagreement should, he argued, be to avoid facially invalidating a statute on the basis of a legislature's discretionary judgment about the empirical evidence. A different form of evidence might, however, arise in a particular case, which would render this specific situation amenable to judicial intervention. As Justice Kennedy maintained:

> In these circumstances the proper means to consider exceptions is by as-applied challenge. . . . This is the proper manner to protect the health of the woman if it can be shown that in discrete and well-defined instances a particular condition has or is likely to occur in which the procedure prohibited by the Act must be used. In an as-applied challenge the nature of the medical risk can be better quantified and balanced than in a facial attack.[19]

In other words, legislatures should be free to disregard some evidence of burdens falling upon a particular subset of individuals who will be affected by a statute, and courts may only subsequently provide individualized exceptions or redress for specific plaintiffs or groups thereof.

This approach represents a substantial alteration to the "undue burden" test derived from the Joint Opinion in *Planned Parenthood of Southeastern Pennsylvania v. Casey.*[20] Whereas *Casey* had evaluated the terms of the statute at issue itself in assessing whether it imposed an undue burden on the woman's right to choose in various instances, *Carhart* indicates that a burden will be considered undue in the context of a facial challenge only when the concrete existence of that burden has been empirically established in particular cases. Similarly, under Justice Stevens's lead opinion in *Crawford*, a burden upon potential voters will not be viewed sufficiently severe to justify facial invalidation of a statute without substantial empirical evidence that would allow the Court "to quantify . . . the magnitude of the burden on [the] narrow class of voters or the portion of the burden imposed on them that is fully justified."[21]

Rather than assessing the existence of a burden from the structure of a statute or its requirements, the Court is, thus, moving toward evaluating such burdens on a case-by-case basis, in accordance with as-applied challenges. This tendency signals a shift in the respective fact-finding roles of the judiciary and the legislature. Under this new framework, statutes must reflect a best legislative judgment about the advisability of a particular policy scheme. They need not, however, anticipate the potential for their provisions to weigh particularly heavily on the rights of certain groups or individuals. If the statute does wind up burdening rights in this manner, the Court will assess the resulting burdens in specific instances, as they arise. The notion that such case-by-case adjudication may lead to too little, too late, seems to have fallen out of view.

In each of these instances, the Roberts Court appears to adopt West's advice and to distinguish between the kinds of factors judges, as opposed to legislators, should take into account. These opinions might concur in her view that the circumstances of each individual case should dictate the outcome of adjudication and that evaluation of the wisdom of general policies should remain in legislative hands. At the same time, however, the cases speak the language of science, not empathy. Justice Kennedy resorts to individualized determination only upon deeming medical science inconclusive in its general pronouncements. Under this logic, empathy may not assist in revealing the necessity of a medical procedure; instead, expert assessment will demonstrate its importance in a particular instance. Individualized adjudication is here divorced from any necessary connection with empathy and instead simply associated with a different form of scientific evaluation.

This example not only demonstrates the ascendancy, at least in constitutional law, of something like what West otherwise extols removed from its empathic frame but also stands in contrast with another tradition of particularized decision making—that of equity. The jurisprudence of equity, while also emphasizing the potential discrepancy between general rules and individual cases, does not limit itself to retrospective evaluation of specific factual scenarios but instead encourages those creating and applying laws to imagine the instances of their application. Furthermore, while one kind of equitable decision crafts an exception to the generality of the law, another form purports to realize the law's own intention, which can be fully expressed only through its implementation in the individual case. These two features of equity permit it to negotiate between the general and the particular, rather than remaining stuck in the dichotomy between the backward-looking focus of adjudication and the prospective orientation of legislation.

As Kathy Eden persuasively argued in *Poetic and Legal Fiction in the Aristotelian Tradition*, equity linked law with fiction for Aristotle and those writing in his wake. A comment of Justice Breyer's that West herself quotes seems to place him within this tradition. As Breyer remarked at his confirmation hearings, alluding to G. K. Chesterton's evaluation of the Brontë sisters, literature may provide a way to differentiate among the stories of those who could, from an external perspective, appear identical.[22] Similarly, for Aristotle, Eden writes, "[F]iction like equity renders the individuality of experience more demonstrable and therefore more knowable."[23] Rather than disclosing the actuality of individual experience as a memoir might, fiction instead allows the reader to hypothesize specific circumstances that might distinguish one subject's life from that of another. For Breyer, such an imaginative exercise feeds back into judicial practice; as he claimed, "I have found literature very helpful as a way out of the tower,"[24] a tower that elite courts share with academia.

While the deployment of the imaginative exercises fiction supplies might simply seem useful practice for confronting the specific realities of cases brought before a judge, the tradition of equity suggests that hypothesizing particular applications of general legal principles may also assist in adjudicating justly. Within Aristotle's writings, equity or *epieikeia* furnished a means for correcting the errors caused by the application of law's general rule to the specific case. This modification was justified not simply as an alteration of the law with respect to the individual instance but, rather, as an elaboration of the legislator's intention. Because the legislator could not or would not envision each potential scenario in which the rule he created might be implemented, a judge was required to consider the fit between the particular circumstances and the putative reasons for the law. As Eden writes:

> [E]quity accommodates each individual case, negotiating between the universality of the law and the randomness of particular circumstance (*ta genomena*). In this way, Aristotle maintains, equity is not superior to absolute justice, "but only to the error (*hamartēma*) of

absolute justice due to its absolute statement" (*Nicomachean Ethics*, 5.10.6). The error inherent in the law, moreover, belongs originally to the legislator, who, like all agents, acted with or without intention, either failing to notice a particular set of circumstances, or deliberately overlooking them in the interests of framing a universal statement applicable to most cases. . . . Consequently, when the law is either silent or inappropriate before a particular case, the preservers of the law must interpret the intentions of the lawgiver by inferring what he would have legislated in view of the present situation.[25]

Although the role of the judge remains quite distinct from that of the legislator under this account, their fields of inquiry overlap. The legislator aims at constructing a general rule but in doing so necessarily overlooks certain instances of its application. The judge, or "preserver" of the law, then attempts to reconstruct the intention of the legislator and to apply this intention to an unforeseen or unforeseeable set of circumstances. Under this vision of equity, the judge fulfills or realizes the intention of the law instead of simply modifying the rule because injustice will result from its implementation.

This strand of thought about equity reemerged in the Anglo-American tradition with Christopher St. German's dialogue *Doctor and Student* and Edward Hake's *Epieikeia*.[26] Whereas St. German's treatise emanated from an ecclesiastical tradition of equity, Hake's partook more of Renaissance humanism.[27] Already, in St. German's 1532 work, a certain ambiguity characterized equity, according to which, in Dennis Klinck's words, "equity is sometimes outside the law, located in a separate place, so to speak, while sometimes it is intrinsic to the law."[28] When located outside the law or, at least, the common law, equity was most prominently associated with the Court of Chancery.[29] One example St. German furnishes illuminates how the procedures available in Chancery could remedy unjust outcomes of the common law. Early English common law was notoriously stringent about written documentation, requiring sealed writs for the commencement of civil actions and mandating that a release from a sealed obligation be as formal as the original document.[30] On some occasions, this latter practice might, as St. German observes, lead an individual who had already discharged his debt but failed to obtain a written acquittance to be forced to pay again.[31] In this case, the wronged person's only recourse would take him out of the common-law courts to the Court of Chancery, where he could avail himself of the remedy of a subpoena, through which the parties could be compelled to testify about the continued existence or lack thereof of the debt.[32] As St. German wrote, extending the same principle to unnamed similar instances, "he is without remedye at the common lawe: yet he maye be holpen *in equity* by a sub pena/ & so he may in many other cases where conscience servyth for hym."[33] The Chancellor's conscience and inquiry into the consciences of the parties in a fashion not permissible under common law here allows for modification of the stringency of common-law rules.

This passage from St. German uncovers a potential problem with West's assimilation of the traditions of equity and the common law, an assimilation that occurs in several passages of her piece. Most notably, after acknowledging that the contractual doctrine of unconscionability "has its historical roots in 'equity,' which was for several centuries a separate body of procedures and institutions," West insists that "the moralism, the backward-looking particularism, and the role of moral sentiments such as sympathy and empathy" were "part of the traditional paradigm of good judging in common-law cases quite generally."[34] As the opposition St. German presents between the common-law's rigidity and equity's accommodations demonstrates, however, sympathy, empathy, and even particularism were conspicuously absent from certain areas of the common law, at least in the sixteenth century. The rise of the modern conception of contract itself has sometimes been explained as the outcome of jurisdictional competition between the courts of equity and of common law in the early seventeenth century, which forced the common law to adopt legal fictions that would enable it to mimic some of the flexibility of equity.[35] This and other moments of intersection between equity and common law should not obscure the historical differences between the traditions, historical differences highlighting the contrast between equity's capacity for particularism and the common law's adherence to rules.

At the same time, however, the ambiguous character of equity meant that it constituted a part of, rather than simply an escape from, the common law. Hake's subsequent intervention insists more emphatically than St. German's on equity as a component of law itself and, in particular, of the common law. As the character

Hake responds to his interlocutors' initial expositions of the nature of equity, "I conceive it somewhat cleere that if the lawe we speake of be a good lawe and well grounded, then the *Equity* that must be used to the correction of the generalitye thereof cannot be said to be the *Equitye* of the judge, but of the lawe."[36] Hake then adduces Aristotle in support of his argument, interpreting Aristotle to say "that *Equity* which seemeth to be owte of the lawe or besides the lawe, because it is not to be seene in the wordes of the lawe (but yet within the lawe as beinge within the meaninge of the law), is by the judge or expositor of the lawe to be applyed to the same law."[37] The division of Hake's dialogue further insists upon the inseparability of law and equity, treating first "Equity in General," then "The Equity of the Common Lawes of England"—a section that comprehends both case law and statutes—and only finally, and rather briefly, "The Equity of the Highe Courte of Chancery." As this organization suggests, Hake's contention that equity derives from the laws themselves leads him to spend the entirety of the second part of his work explaining precisely how ordinary law can be reconciled with equity.

Even before reaching this section, however, Hake furnishes an example that illuminates the approach to equity as itself a component of law.[38] He explains that a "particuler custom" in derogation of the general custom of the common law exists in the Isle of Man; according to this unwritten principle, any individual who steals a chicken must receive the death penalty. Hake then hypothesizes that an impoverished inhabitant purloined a small amount of chicken from a traveling fowl salesperson. He resolves the question of whether the perpetrator should be hanged "according to the generality of this particuler custome" by first extrapolating the intent or reason of the law and then applying this intention to the specific circumstances. The reason is to be discerned not by examining the actual origins of the law but, instead, by extrapolating from local conditions why it was probably developed; the reason is that "by the which by all likelihood the custome had his commencement." Rather than examining the stated intent of those who first instituted the custom, Hake deduces the intention or "reason" of the law from the circumstances of its creation. Because of the extreme scarcity of livestock on the island, the owners of such livestock would suffer greatly if deprived of their food source.

The same would not be true for the traveling poulterer. Hence, Hake concludes, in this case the perpetrator should not die, because "touchinge the custome, howsoever hee be within the generality thereof, yet he is cleerely . . . without the meaninge thereof."

Two imaginative leaps occur in this example. First, Hake determines the reason for the law itself by examining statements about how highly meat is valued on the Isle of Man and reports that it remains scarce. From a contemporary perspective, we might say that he examines the policy rationale behind the law. Although engaging in judicial reasoning here, he does not limit himself to the particulars of a specific case but, rather, diagnoses the general principle underpinning the particular custom. Second, he envisions an instance in which the law could be applied in a manner contrary to the reasons for its creation. One could interpret his example as an actual instance that had already occurred, but he does not definitively present it as a precedent, instead speaking of it as a "case or example." In this hypothetical episode, equity suggests that the literal language of the law should not be applied. Furthermore, this equitable interpretation stems not from outside the law but from the dictates of the law itself.

Another example that Hake employs relies less on the reason or intent of the particular law and more on the notion that the law of nature underlies all law, which must be presumed not to contradict that overarching principle. Hake lays out the backdrop of a law specifying that any man who refuses to return goods delivered to him to their rightful owner will have to pay treble damages, then presents a case in which a sane man gives his sword to a friend and wishes to reclaim it after having gone mad. Under those circumstances, the one in possession of the sword should not have to forfeit any money "for that to putte a sworde into a madde mannes handes is to give occasion of murder, which were againste the law of God, for to committe murder and to geve occasion of murder is all one and equally forbidden by the lawe of God and againste the lawe of Nature."[39] If, in the context of the particular custom from the Isle of Man, Hake was able to discern a disparity between the intent of the law and its application in a potential instance, here a certain implementation of the general legal rule would controvert the law of nature.

From this vantage point, we might return to West's dichotomy between legislative and judicial reasoning. Even within the tradition of equity, the most particularized form of Anglo-American adjudication, judges mediated between legislative and judicial forms of thought and imagined, as well as assessed, evidence. Furthermore, the line between carving out exceptions and creating rules is itself permeable. Hake describes the temporal unfolding of the process whereby particularized exceptions themselves become general rules, connecting the individual case with general principles. Although the exceptions found implicit within common-law rules themselves become rule-like, they were initially generated out of an equitable mode of judicial reasoning upon the particulars of certain real or imagined circumstances:

> [A]lbeit that length of tyme hath nowe so brought to passe as that theise and all other the like exceptions which in the beginning were *tacitae* and hidden (as to the visible aspect of the lawe) are nowe become expressed even as the lawes themselves are, so as a man may saie of them that they are themselves become grounds or maxims as well as the principall grounds whereof they are exceptions, yet (no doubt) at the first theise secondary grownds were none other than silent exceptions from the generality of the lawe, and were from tyme to tyme applied unto particularities as the *Equity* of the same lawe did require.[40]

If judges first discover exceptions to the generality of the law within particular cases, these judicial exceptions may themselves become evident only when formalized into grounds or maxims. On the one hand, the meaning and reason of the law must be read to entail exceptions; on the other hand, those exceptions themselves become rules when judicially articulated over a period of time.

Empathy itself appears in a different light within this jurisprudence of equity. Although the passions play a role, the form of empathy involved partakes more of the judgments about and feelings for a fictional character—someone along the lines of *Jane Eyre*'s protagonist—than empathy for a friend. Rather than entailing fellow feeling for the specific identity of the one confronting the court, this kind of empathy involves the capacity to envision story lines that the general frameworks of the law have excluded, whether inadvertently or not. Instead of prioritizing the person before the court, whose identity or affiliations might furnish extraneous reasons for empathy or the lack thereof, this approach focuses on the applicability of the law to particular scenarios, narratives that courts have always been capable of conceiving.

The interplay between common law and equity over the course of Anglo-American legal history demonstrates that the tradition of the common law itself partook of generality, as well as particularity. To the extent that West's objections to a more scientific jurisprudence rest on its deviation from hindsight-based, particularistic reasoning, this development is nothing new. Furthermore, as a number of the Roberts Court's recent decisions demonstrate, an insistence on science can assume a variety of forms, including a requirement that empirical proof be displayed in particular instances. Focusing more on equity and less on empathy might, however, allow for a different kind of critique of the metaphor of the judge as umpire, one that would acknowledge the importance of the various kinds of legal imagining that have characterized our jurisprudential tradition and have enhanced our efforts to seek justice within the law.

NOTES

1. Robin West, "The Anti-Empathic Turn," in this volume.
2. Ibid., 246–247.
3. Ibid., 244.
4. Ibid., 251–252. Jody Kraus has separated some of the historically common law from the historically equitable components of American contract law:

American contract doctrines originating in the English common law courts include the doctrines of offer and acceptance, consideration (including the illegality and immorality doctrines), capacity, duress, warranties and conditions, impossibility, fraud-in-the-execution, expectation damages, foreseeability, and avoidability, as well as the plain meaning rule and the parol evidence rule. Along with these historically legal contract doctrines, American contract law also absorbed and developed doctrines originally developed in Chancery "to mitigate the rigours of the Common law." Such doctrines include fraud-in-the-inducement and intentional misrepresentation, negligent and innocent misrepresentation, fraudulent nondisclosure, unilateral and mutual mistake, specific performance and other injunctive relief, expanded versions of the common law doctrines of capacity and duress, and illegal and immoral consideration. American contract law also adopted equitable doctrines specifically designed to vitiate clear common law rules: the penalty doctrine, the forfeiture doctrine, the equitable exceptions to the parol evidence rule, and the part-performance exception to the Statute of Frauds. Jody Kraus, "Contract Design and the Structure of Contractual Intent," *New York University Law Review* 84 (2009): 1023, 1042–1043. The doctrine of unconscionability itself arose in England out of defenses available in the Court of Chancery, which adjudicated according to the principles of equity. See Daniel Klerman, "Jurisdictional Competition and the Evolution of the Common Law," *University of Chicago Law Review* 74 (2007): 1179, 1191.

5. See generally Stephen H. Subrin, "How Equity Conquered Common Law: The Federal Rules of Civil Procedure in Historical Perspective," *University of Pennsylvania Law Review* 135 (1987): 909 (treating the federal merger of law and equity and discussing the extent to which it shifted the emphasis of adjudication towards equity and away from the common law); Stephen H. Subrin, "David Dudley Field and the Field Code: A Historical Analysis of an Earlier Procedural Vision," *Law and History Review* 6 (1988): 311 (explaining the ways in which the Federal Rules did and did not track the vision embodied in Field's earlier code).

6. West, "The Anti-Empathic Turn," 272.

7. David Franklin, "Looking through Both Ends of the Telescope: Facial Challenges and the Roberts Court," *Hastings Constitutional Law Quarterly* 36 (2009): 689, 694.

8. Ibid., 694–695 (describing the "traditional model").

9. The campaign finance case *Citizens United v. FEC*, 130 S. Ct. 876 (2010), has furnished a much-discussed exception to this trend. See Michael Halberstam, "The Myth of 'Conquered Provinces': Probing the Extent of the VRA's Encroachment on State and Local Autonomy," *Hastings Law Journal* 62 (2011): 923, 943 ("In *Citizens United*, the Court went out of its way to strike down congressional limits on corporate and union expenditures on political campaigns in a case that could easily have been treated as an applied challenge to the McCain-Feingold Act.").

10. Gillian E. Metzger, "Facial and As-Applied Challenges under the Roberts Court," *Fordham Urban Law Journal* 36 (2009): 773, 774 ("[T]he Court has made little effort to describe the contours of as-applied litigation and has justified its preference for as-applied claims on diverse grounds that yield different implications for the types of such claims litigants can bring.").

11. See B. Jessie Hill, "A Radically Immodest Judicial Modesty: The End of Facial Challenges to Abortion Regulations and the Future of the Health Exception in the Roberts Era," *Case Western Reserve Law Review* 59

(2009): 997, 998 ("[T]he Supreme Court has turned away facial challenges or otherwise expressed a preference for making decisions on an as-applied basis in a number of cases since Chief Justice Roberts joined the body. Examples range across a wide spectrum of subject matter, including voting rights cases, an Americans with Disabilities Act case, and—somewhat more surprisingly, given the Supreme Court's traditional solicitude for facial challenges in these contexts—First Amendment and abortion cases."); ibid. at 1014 (contending that, despite Chief Justice Roberts's claims of judicial modesty, the outcome of prioritizing as-applied challenges in the abortion context instead "require[s] judges to remain embroiled in the abortion controversy and decide issues arguably well beyond their competency").

12. 550 U.S. 124 (2007).
13. 552 U.S. 442 (2008).
14. 553 U.S. 181 (2008).
15. *Washington State Grange*, 552 U.S. at 449.
16. See Caitlin E. Borgmann, "Holding Legislatures Constitutionally Accountable through Facial Challenges," *Hastings Constitutional Law Quarterly* 36 (2009): 563, 589 ("[I]f the Roberts Court's hostility to facial challenges is genuine, it is worth considering what might be fueling that hostility. At least two principles may drive the Court's rejection of facial invalidations: (1) a belief that complete invalidation is a drastic remedy that should not be granted absent a showing of actual harm, and (2) a belief in the importance of concrete facts in adjudication.").
17. *Carhart*, 550 U.S. at 172 (Ginsburg, J. dissenting) (citations omitted).
18. Ibid., 162.
19. Ibid., 167.
20. 505 U.S. 883 (1992).
21. *Crawford*, 553 U.S. at 201.
22. See West, "The Anti-Empathic Turn," 281 n. 4.
23. Kathy Eden, *Poetic and Legal Fiction in the Aristotelian Tradition* (Princeton, NJ: Princeton University Press, 1986), 54.
24. West, "The Anti-Empathic Turn," 281 n. 4.
25. Eden, *Poetic and Legal Fiction*, 43–44.
26. As Darien Shanske has written, "Aristotle's account of equity has been received into the legal tradition many times and this reception is ongoing today." Darien Shanske, "Four Theses: Preliminary to an Appeal to Equity," *Stanford Law Review* 57 (2005): 2053, 2054. More specifically, "Writers like Christopher St. German (whose *Doctor and Student* came out in 1532) and Edward Hake move right from their reading of Aristotle to their application of his teaching to the contemporary legal situation." Ibid., 2064.

27. See D.E.C. Yale, *Introduction*, in Edward Hake, *Epieikeia: A Dialogue on Equity in Three Parts*, ed. D. E. C. Yale (New Haven, CT: Yale University Press, 1953), xvi.

28. Dennis R. Klinck, *Conscience, Equity, and the Court of Chancery in Early Modern England* (Burlington, VT: Ashgate, 2010), 46.

29. See John H. Langbein, Renée Lettow Lerner, and Bruce P. Smith, *History of the Common Law: The Development of Anglo-American Legal Institutions* (Waltham, MA: Wolters Kluwer, 2009), 317–320 (discussing Chancery and the other early courts of equity).

30. Ibid., 86–105 (describing the writ system); ibid., 322 (explaining that "Seal also defeated a plea of discharge, such as a claim that the debtor had already paid the debt, unless that discharge was appropriately evidenced—by a sealed release, physical cancellation (destruction) of the obligation, or the creditor's confession of satisfaction on the court record. Under the so-called equal dignity rule, seal was required to defeat seal.").

31. *St. German's Doctor and Student*, ed. T. F. T. Plucknett and J. L. Barton (London: Selden Society, 1974), 77–79.

32. See Langbein et al., *History of the Common Law*, 282–83.

33. Plucknett and Barton, *St. German's Doctor and Student*, 79.

34. West, "The Anti-Empathic Turn," 267.

35. As J. H. Baker writes of the sixteenth and early seventeenth centuries, "Intervention by the Chancery was no slight factor in influencing the common-law judges to recognise and nurture new or better remedies." J. H. Baker, *An Introduction to English Legal History* (New York: Oxford University Press, 2002), 327. Dan Klerman explores the role of the interplay between Chancery and common law courts in the development of contract law over a longer historical trajectory in "Jurisdictional Competition and the Evolution of the Common Law."

36. Hake, *Epieikeia*, 11.

37. Ibid., 15.

38. The example is discussed in ibid., 19–20.

39. Ibid., 18–19.

40. Ibid., 50.

INDEX

Abrams, Kathy, 48–49

Aeschylus, 167

Affective intelligence, theory of: application of neuroscience to democratic politics, 145–154; conditions of familiarity versus conditions of novelty, 158, 160; consciousness as a space for "error correction," 145; distinction between partisan citizen and deliberating citizen, 159–161; the disposition system, 146–149; dual-model character of, 144, 158–159, 162–165; implications of for the possibility of democracy, 226–228; implications of for nonsovereign models of agency and self-government, 227–228, 231, 236–238; reassessment of normative standards for democracy in light of, 154–165; re-imagining democracy on the basis of, 165–168; the surveillance system, 149–154; two routes to judgment and action, 157–165; two systems of knowledge, 154–157

Anscombe, G. E. M., 84

Anti-empathic turn in judging: claim that it is implicated in nature of modern social welfare state, 289; competing account of as backlash against Warren and Burger Courts' expansion of constitutional rights, 309–310, 311–312; distinction between empathy and sympathy and, 248–249; explanations for, 247–251; as expressing a reverence for dispassionateness, 311–312; modern view that empathic judging is contrary

to the rule of law, 246–247, 291; paradigm shift from empathic to scientific judging, 249–251, 280; paradigm shift within law from focus on individuals to a focus on systems, 293–297; selective liberal empathy and, 247–248, 291; traditional view that judging required empathy, 243–246; transformation of unconscionability doctrine as exemplifying, 250–251; Warren Court egalitarian activism and, 291–293. *See also* Empathy in judging; Scientific judging; Unconscionability doctrine

Anxiety: capacity of citizens to self-trigger, 219; role of in human rationality, 213; as triggering reflection when habits fail, 213; value of to politics, 210

Aquinas, St. Thomas, 109

Arendt, Hannah, 134, 163, 195

Aristotle: on capacity to rule, 135; on equity, 321, 324; on moral judgments, 161; on vengeful anger, 78, 79, 82, 83, 84, 89, 90, 93–102, 104–109

Bandes, Susan, 59, 248–249, 273, 309

Barber, Benjamin, 129

Basic moral values: claim that are sentiments, 7; claim that do not arise through reasoning, 10; differ across cultures, 10; as historical artifacts, 11; implication that some moral disputes are not rationally resolvable, 14–16; as not explained by biological

Basic moral values (*continued*)
  evolution, 10; reasons for differences
  of, 11–13
Baumeister, Roy, 144
Beck, Glenn, 196
Bentham, Jeremy, 276
Berlin, Isaiah, 29, 158
Bernick, Michael, 292
Bickel, Alexander, 292
Blackmun, Harry (Justice), 309
Blackstone, William, 248, 251–253, 275,
  294, 297
Borgmann, Caitlin, 318
Braithwaite, Valerie, 223
Brandeis, Louis (Justice), 296
Breyer, Stephen (Justice), 243, 321
Burger Court, 310
Burke, Edmund, 136, 161, 163
Butler, Joseph (Bishop), 79, 84, 91
Butler, Pierce (Justice), 296

Cacciatore, Joanne, 57–58, 62
Cardozo, Benjamin (Justice), 243, 309
Chayes, Abram, 296–297
Chesterton, G. K., 321
Citizens: conception of as deliberating,
  159–161; conception of as partisan,
  159–161. *See also* Dual model of
  citizenship
Consciousness. *See* Affective intelligence, theory of; Dual model of neural processing; Reason and emotions
Constructive sentimentalism claim:
  legal and political implications of,
  13–16, 39; and self- versus other-
  directed manifestations of disapproval, 8–9, 26–27; sympathy and
  empathy in, 9–10; that does not
  imply moral relativism, 20, 26, 29,
  31; that implies moral relativism, 16;
  that moral judgments are emotions
  of disapproval and approval, 8–10;
  that moral judgments are susceptible
  to irrelevant emotions, 13–14; that
  moral judgments contain emotions,
  6–7; that some moral disputes are

not rationally resolvable, 14–16.
  See also Sentimentalism
Crawford v. Marion County Election Bd.,
  318
Croly, Herbert, 294

Damasio, Antonio, 193
D'Arms, Justin, 100, 105, 106
Deliberation: does not operate free
  from emotion or intuition, 196–200;
  group versus individual, 190, 200–
  205; and institutional design, 200–
  205; judicial decision making bodies
  and, 204–205; peer pressure and,
  203; problems with focusing on the
  autonomous individual in, 200–202;
  relationship between heterogeneity of decision making body and,
  203–204; "wisdom of crowds" and,
  202–203
Democracy: application of neuroscience to understanding, 139–145,
  145–154; assessment of electorate's
  competence, 129–133; contrast
  between pre-modern and post-
  Enlightenment presumptions concerning, 135–139; defenses of, 130–
  131; empirical premises underlying
  normative standards for, 133–139;
  importance of focus on deliberation
  in conceptions of, 130–131; need
  for nonsovereign conception of,
  227–228, 231, 236–238; reassessing
  normative standards for in light
  of theory of affective intelligence,
  154–165; re-imagining of on basis
  of theory of affective intelligence,
  165–168; as resting on conflicting
  principles, 127–129; and taxonomy
  of mental states of reason, emotion,
  and interest, 135–139; understanding of reason and emotion in
  normative standards for, 131–133;
  use of imagination in, 161–165;
  variants of, 128–129. *See also* Affective
  intelligence, theory of; Emotions,